Remembering Utopia:
The Culture of Everyday Life in Socialist Yugoslavia

Remembering Utopia:
The Culture of Everyday Life in Socialist Yugoslavia

edited by
Breda Luthar and Maruša Pušnik

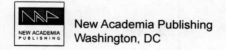
New Academia Publishing
Washington, DC

New Academia Publishing, 2010

Printed in the United States of America

Library of Congress Control Number: 2010923698
ISBN 978-0-9844062-3-4 paperback (alk. paper)

New Academia Publishing, LLC
P.O. Box 27420
Washington, DC 20038-7420
www.newacademia.com - info@newacademia.com

Contents

Illustrations

Acknowledgments

In preparing this book we have been helped in different ways by many people. Special thanks go to our dear friend and mentor, Hanno Hardt, who encouraged us to prepare this volume and kindly edited the contributions. He provided invaluable advice and insightful comments. We would also like to thank Slavko Splichal for his generosity, intellectual inspiration, and financial support for this volume. Without the wonderfully organized Andreja Trdina, research assistant in the Media and Communication Studies department at the Faculty of Social Sciences, who helped us with the technical aspects of the final draft, this volume would not see the light of day. We are extremely grateful to Ulf Brunnbauer, University of Regensburg, Dejan Djokić, Goldsmiths College, University of London, and to an anonymous reviewer for some particularly perceptive suggestions and ideas. Many thanks also to our friends at the Faculty of Social Sciences, University of Ljubljana (Vida Zei, Tanja Oblak Črnič, Dejan Jontes, and many others), who have been important and supportive individuals during this long journey. They have made our life in a »transitional academic institution« less frustrating and academic work less lonely and more meaningful. We have missed too many deadlines and are very grateful to all contributors for their stoic patience. We would also like to express our profound gratitude to all informants for sharing their memories and life-stories, which have made our book a good blend of scholarship and compelling narrative. We also wish to thank various institutions and individuals for permission to reproduce copyright material. Contributors and editors have made every effort to trace copyright holders, and the editors are prepared to make the

necessary arrangements with anyone, who has been unintention-
ally overlooked. We owe great thanks to the publisher, New Academia Publishing and especially to Anna Lawton, who endorsed
our project and believed in us despite failed deadlines to keep this
book project on track. Last, but not least, we would like to thank
our families for their understanding and love and for the most precious and constant intellectual, emotional and moral support.

Breda Luthar
Maruša Pušnik
Ljubljana, November 2009

Introduction

The Lure of Utopia
Socialist Everyday Spaces

Breda Luthar and Maruša Pušnik

The contributors to this book have analyzed various everyday cultural practices in socialist Yugoslavia, including negotiations by its subjects with the state, and appropriations of power. The chapters are linked by a common interest in mundane and ordinary aspects of life under socialism and in the ways in which state power was exercised and negotiated at the level of personal experience and everyday life. Popular culture, in the form of any officially sanctioned aesthetics of mass spectacle or everyday cultural practice (e.g., national festivals and their popular reception, daily television viewing, youth cultures or Eurovision pop song contests, tourism, fashion, sporting practices and body control, or shopping and smuggling) is at the heart of the analysis: how does society understand and represent itself and how is it constructed through representation and gaze? The focus of our interest is on both, the material practices of everyday life, and the discourses that frame them.

This volume includes articles from history, sociology, cultural studies, media studies and studies of visual and consumer cultures. The case-study essays suggest how individuals supported, reinforced or resisted and challenged the political system, and how they appropriated material culture to cope with the conditions of daily life. Some contributions, ranging from the immediate post-war utopian age in the late 1940s to the collapse of Yugoslavia in the late 1980s, emphasize institutional constraints, while others focus on the capacity of individual agency to negotiate structural constraints. Popular culture is taken seriously with an acknowledgment of the necessarily political nature of the "popular."

To paraphrase Michael Billig, this is a book on "banal socialism."[1] Indeed, we contend that socialism cannot be understood without considering its "banality" and without revealing the extraordinary in the apparent naturalness of ordinary life.

Although Yugoslavia collapsed less than 20 years ago, traces of its cultural and material life rapidly disappear in the past. But the more the lived, internal memories of socialist Yugoslavia are lost from year to year, the more they are maintained by some exterior signs – "sites of memory" or *lieux de mémoire*[2] – spaces with a residual sense of a specific socialist Yugoslav continuity. These sites of memory may function as the border stones of the socialist age; they are moments of history "plucked out of the flow of history, then returned to it – no longer quite alive but not yet entirely dead, like shells left on the shore when the sea of living memory has receded."[3] When analyzing the past we should bear in mind that we are dealing with worlds realized and manifested only in the memories of people, in various archival sources, or in other material traces/artifacts. Today socialist Yugoslavia still lives in two kinds of memories (if we borrow Maurice Halbwachs' analytical model): in the inner, internal, personal or autobiographical memory of people and in the exterior, borrowed, social or historical memory.[4] Both memories of Yugoslavia are addressed by this book.

The everyday and the ordinary are at the center of relationships of economic, political, symbolic and communicative powers in socialist Yugoslavia with different authors uncovering the complex memories and memory sites of various aspects of the ordinary, unremarkable, and taken-for-granted daily practices during the time of socialism. Theoretically speaking, they address connections between the agency of individuals, the role of political power in orchestrating daily life across a dispersed set of practices, and forms of non-conformity. Consequently, this volume offers a diverse range of materials on the everydayness of socialism and socialist modernity. The shared orientation of diverse contributions becomes more obvious when contrasted with what is too often absent from the dominant discourse regarding the era of socialism. Traditionally missing in many histories of socialism are precisely those cultural and social accounts of the textures of life with narratives of the experiences and practices of ordinary people. Instead, the majority of work on (Yugoslav) socialism is focused on institutional aspects of socialism within the fields of political science or history.

This volume avoids interpretations of "real" life under socialism, which stress the study of social structures and rely mostly on political and institutional histories, but scrutinizes ordinary, everyday life in socialism while moving away from institutional history, extraordinary events and canonic personalities. We agree with Nick Couldry, who argues that if we are serious about studying culture, we cannot avoid listening to the individual voice.[5] We also avoid the simplified, so-called totalitarian paradigm that rests on the "dichotomous picture" of the totalitarian socialist Yugoslavia, where state and society, official ideology and everyday practice are sharply distinguished as two opposite entities.[6] This volume offers at least a glimpse at the heterogeneities and conflicts within a normative socialist culture and gives some insight into the relation between official culture and its internalization or subversion by individuals. Contributions in this volume focus on different aspects of everyday practices (sports, television viewing, holidays and tourism, or shopping) or on the official and unofficial discourse of everyday life (women's magazines on cooking and housekeeping, official politics on tourism, physical exercise and body control, or canonization of heroic personalities in staged spectacles).

Yet, popular culture, although a part of everyday life, is not necessarily representative of the popular experience of ordinary people, nor can the experience of culture be reduced to its most visible meanings. However, the discourse reveals at least partially the intertextual context of everyday life in Yugoslav socialism, or the "lived culture," as Raymond Williams would argue.[7] Ideally two domains of socialist culture – a whole way of life and the forms of signification (films, magazines, newspapers, books, or laws) that circulate in a society – are studied together. The background for studying everyday practices and popular representations is provided by the study of power and resistance that cut through everyday life and social practices and that should be studied at several levels: the disciplinary power of the state and para-state institutions, gender and class relations, ethnic differentiation, and finally, power relations in the relationship of the peripheral, "communist" East and the central, "civilized" West.

Furthermore, aside from political reasons for the persistence of a "totalitarian paradigm" as the articulation of cold war values in studies of socialism, there is also a gender aspect to the lack of studies about socialist everyday life. Everyday life is, on one hand, linked to the daily rituals of private life, mostly within the domestic sphere and traditionally controlled by women, such as cooking or shopping, which are typically associated with women as a gendered skill. On the other hand, there is the masculine version of the everyday in public spaces (work, sporting events, or popular cultural events).[8] Studies of socialism involving macro structures or spectacular aspects of socialism have excluded particularly accounts of the everyday lives of women and the feminine version of everyday. The latter was regarded as a sphere of reproduction and maintenance, or as a feminine space to be subjugated to the pursuit of a higher purpose or the heroic.[9]

To approach socialism from the vantage point of everyday life and through a micro-history of the ordinary means attempting to grasp the everyday without relegating it to institutional codes or to private perceptions of individuals and to recognize the social in the individual. Or, according to micro-historians, we should be able "to see a world in a grain of sand."[10] The entanglement of the institutional/social and the individual is at the centre of our work; the study of everyday cultures and experiences or memories always makes some connections to the general social system and its discursive apparatus while implying a different understanding of how power works in society.

Remembering Socialist Yugoslavia: A Brief Historical Background

Among many models of the socialist system none was "typical" according to Katherine Verdery. Each had its specific internal structure while sharing certain features with some but not all other socialist countries.[11] Here is a brief summary for readers not entirely familiar with the distinct Yugoslav version of socialism, including some of the milestones in its post-war history from 1945 to its breakup in 1991.

Yugoslavia (called the Kingdom of Serbs, Croats and Slovenes in 1918, and named Kingdom of Yugoslavia in 1929) was a multi-ethnic state, underdeveloped economically and in terms of democratic traditions. Cultural and economic differences between the Catholic northwest (which had belonged to the Habsburg Empire before WWI) and the Muslim and Orthodox south were significant with Serbia in a contested political position of dominance in the country. Yugoslavia was reconstituted during WWII (November 29, 1943) by the partisan resistance movement dominated by communists on a liberated territory in occupied Bosnia. In January, 1946, the new constitution officially established six socialist republics and two autonomous provinces and designated Belgrade as the federal capital. On this basis federal authorities in the multi-ethnic and multi-national state – with its three official languages, Serbo-Croatian, Slovenian and Macedonian, – succeeded for a long time to suppress any form of nationalism. From its beginning Yugoslavia was built on the political concept of "brotherhood and unity," which became its guiding principle and national motto; it was an idea which should have prevented ethnic tensions and the dominance of any single ethnic group. The slogan had its roots in the partisan movement during WWII, but emanated originally from a gymnastics movement (Sokol) at the beginning of the 20th century.

Contrary to other eastern European countries, Yugoslavia was never liberated or occupied by the Soviet army. The Communist Party as a leading organizing force in the resistance movement during WWII had provided moral or cultural leadership and was perceived as a national liberator. Consequently, "Yugoslavness" had its strongest roots in the pan-Yugoslav partisan resistance movement and in a paternalistic father figure, Tito. The consensus regarding egalitarian state socialism and cultural leadership of the communists/liberators after WWII had important consequences for Yugoslav socialism and its distinctiveness in Eastern Europe. After the war, during a period of reconstruction, the Yugoslav federation was built and reproduced on a discourse of victory introducing a Soviet-type administrative socialism with its cult of physical work, collectivism, anti-capitalism, and a five-year economic plan. The aim was to build a socialist country with the aid of massive voluntary work. Sovietization was based on state intervention regarding the economic and social life of society, and as part of a messianic project of creating a new Soviet civilization while implementing a Soviet socialist strategy of modernization. This utopianism was actually a part of the sovietization of Eastern Europe, which "involved the transplantation of institutions and methods developed in the USSR into the very different environments provided by the states of Eastern Europe after 1945."[12] At that time, for instance, most of the Yugoslav countryside received electricity, private property was nationalized (although the process of nationalization lasted almost 20 years), private entrepreneurship was reduced, and heavy industry was promoted at the expense of producing consumer goods.[13] In the 1950s Yugoslavia represented the fastest growing economy in the world, partly because of its low starting point.

Until 1948 Yugoslavia had maintained a close relationship with the Soviet Union. However, Yugoslav communists emerged from WWII as liberators, as the engine of the resistance movement, with a history of an independent and authentic revolution. Accordingly, they were self-confident and conducted an independent foreign policy in the Balkans that challenged Soviet interests, including absolute control of the Soviet Union over the Balkan peninsula. In 1948, amidst tense relations between Tito and Stalin, the Soviet Union demanded a dominant position in Eastern Europe while Yugoslavia tried to keep its political independence and hegemony in the Balkans. Stalin accused Tito and Yugoslavia of nationalism, of departing from Marxism-Leninism and of exhibiting an anti-Soviet attitude. Consequently, Yugoslav communists were expelled from the Communist Information Bureau (Cominform/Informbiro), which had been founded in September 1947 as the official forum of the international communist movements.

Following Tito's break with Stalin and the withdrawal of Yugoslavia from the Eastern bloc – provoked largely by the power stand-off between the two communist leaders and their parties – Yugoslavia's communist leadership opened up to the West, which granted Yugoslavia economic support in the many years to follow, and looked for alternative models of socialism.[14] In the 1950s the economy was partially liberalized, and Yugoslavia began to introduce a certain level of democratic labor practices – called workers' self-management – "a form of conceptional syncretism leaning towards a fusion of Marxist, Proudhonist, Blanquist, and other mutually often antagonistic socialist ideas."[15] It adopted an independent form of "self-management socialism," informally called Titoism in the West. According to Avgust Lešnik, the peculiarity of Yugoslavia's post- or neo-Stalinism rested in its transition from a totalitarian to an authoritarian system.[16] Yugoslavia pursued a policy of neutrality during the cold war and became one of the founding members of the non-aligned movement in 1961 under Tito's leadership.

If the late 1940s and 1950s are characterized as a period of administrative state-socialism, the 1960s introduced a more liberal, open and decentralized political system. Many observers have noticed that Yugoslavs at that time had far greater liberties than citizens of the Soviet Union and other Warsaw Pact states.[17] According to Sabrina P. Ramet, due to political and economic instabilities in the country during the early 1960s, the first liberal voices within the communist leadership appeared and advocated greater decentralization.[18] Compared to other Eastern European countries, Yugoslavia had developed much more open relations with the capitalist world regarding civil liberties, including the mobility of its citizens, and economic and cultural exchanges with the West. At the beginning of the 1950s borders to the West had been partially opened for Yugoslav citizens, and by 1967 all visas were abolished; Yugoslavia became the first socialist country to open its borders to all foreign visitors and to abolish visa requirements for its own citizens (see chapters by Luthar, Taylor and Duda below). Consequently, open borders since the 1960s and the relative ease of travel to the West for ordinary citizens along with regular cultural and economic exchanges with the Western world, including Western credit, were distinct characteristics of Yugoslav socialism. In times of economic prosperity, there was a strong consensus among Yugoslavs that "the best system in the world" was neither a totalitarian communist nor an exploitative capitalist one. Criticism of its anomalies, however, was ever present, and the gap between the formal, official version of reality and people's own experience was considerable.[19]

However, the multicultural idea of "brotherhood and unity" was fragile; with rising economic difficulties the precarious national equilibrium accomplished through putting institutional restraints on Serbia's power came to an end.[20] Ethnic tensions escalated for the first time in the 1970s, resulting in protests, known as the

Croatian Spring of 1971 in Zagreb, when large numbers of Croats demanded greater civil liberties and greater Croatian autonomy and protested against Serbia's hegemony in Yugoslavia. In 1974 a new constitution was ratified granting more rights and independence to the individual republics and provinces and thereby to local national elites. Moreover, the individual republics also obtained the right to unilaterally secede from Yugoslavia. While these reforms satisfied most of the republics, the Serbian elite resented the new constitution since it effectively reduced Serbian hegemony and influence in Yugoslavia. When Josip Broz Tito died in 1980, the event symbolically represented a harbinger of the Yugoslav break-up; the post-Tito era[21] was a new period in Yugoslav history with economic problems escalating into uncontrollable agony, featuring a hyperinflation rate of more than 200 percent.[22] By 1980 foreign debt accounted to more than 40 percent of inflowing foreign currency. Ethnic tensions grew, and the legacy of the 1974 constitution sharpened the conflict of interest and the rise of nationalism all over Yugoslavia (e.g., Slovenia and Croatia demanded the decentralization of the federation, the Albanian majority in Kosovo demanded the status of a republic, Serbia sought absolute domination over Yugoslavia, while the nationalist communist politician, Slobodan Milošević, rose to power in Serbia). The pervasive nationalization of public and private life involved the marginalization of any alternative political discourse involving the "nullification of complex identities by the terrible categorical simplicity of ascribed nationality," according to Roger Brubaker.[23]

During the 1980s Yugoslav citizens had to cope with economic crises, growing unemployment rates and shortages of some everyday consumer goods (e.g., coffee, fuel, detergents). The economic system totally collapsed and some regions, like Slovenia or Croatia with the highest per capita GDP in the country (Macedonia, Kosovo and Montenegro had the lowest), refused to drain their budgets for subsidies to other regions.[24] Two opposing concepts of political and economic development clashed. National sentiments slowly started to overwhelm federal politics and fortified ethnic nationalisms. There was no return to socialist Yugoslavia, and in 1990 the first democratic multi-party elections were held in all socialist republics of Yugoslavia, first in Slovenia and Croatia (April) and finally in

Serbia (December). Nationalist parties won in almost all of the federal republics, claiming ownership over their ethnic territory. The newly elected nationalist governments could not see any common interest; Slovenia and Croatia were oriented toward greater autonomy and demanded a loose confederation of six republics with the right to self-determination, while Serbia favored Yugoslav centralism and, therefore, Serb hegemony. Everywhere political authority had been reconfigured along national lines. Before the break-up of Yugoslavia, which officially started in June 1991 with the Yugoslav wars, the approximate population of the country had been near 23 million people with multiple, scattered identities, various collective heritages, plural memories and diverse cultural traditions.

The Operational Logic of Everyday Culture: Everyday and Power

Research about socialism/communism typically tends to draw attention to official aspects of power and dissent and to state politics rather than to negotiations of state power within the sphere of ordinary life. Emphasis is given to an officially promoted high culture or to officially sanctioned high cultural alternatives, rather than to mainstream or transgressive popular cultural practices.[25] These histories tend to presuppose a powerful state and a party with its official ideology on one side, and repressed, manipulated or collaborating citizens on the other side. This notion of power is partly a consequence of the positivistic, epistemological and methodological background of the research. Yet it is also clearly a political statement, which marginalizes certain voices and discourses by using a certain form and source material at the exclusion of others.[26] Socialism/Communism is considered as totalitarian regime, whose exercise of power is based exclusively on coercion and force, physically invoked without a more consensual or diffuse system of power. At an epistemological level this is false, even for more repressive regimes in Eastern Europe; hence we argue here that in the case of Yugoslav socialism, which operated with significant popular consent for the moral leadership of communists, the internalization of dominant norms of social subjectivity had to be taken into account. We believe that it is important to concentrate on power and manipulation, but also on resistance and consensus, on generality but also on particularity, on the discursive apparatus but also on experience.

Thus, this volume relies on an understanding of power as a dispersed network of disciplinary productions open to multiform resistance at the level of everyday culture. Socialist everyday life had been continually under scrutiny to ensure the effective governance of social subjects; we are interested in those forms of governance that sought to regulate everyday life, drawing on the insight that the functioning of power is not confined to official institutions and articulated ideological narratives, or parliament, political parties, or to the Communist Party. Rather, power works as a pervasive network, which weaves itself into the most ordinary utterances, into the forms of common sense and everyday practices.[27] To limit the study of power to its official manifestations and to limit the study of resistance to its official political opposition (e.g., dissidents), obscures the way power operates at the level of everyday and the ways it had been imprinted on routine activities, personal relations and popular consciousness. In fact, power and tactical resistance are fully encountered at the level of everyday culture and ordinary life. The shift of our analytical focus to everyday life thus rests on an understanding of power as a matter of joint consent and coercion and socialist ideology as a lived, habitual social practice. Because, according to Pierre Bourdieu, "subjects do not, strictly speaking, know what they are doing that what they do has more meaning than they know."[28]

It is particularly important to understand the consensual rather than the coercive nature of power working at the level of everyday life, especially in the case of Yugoslav socialism. Yugoslavia modified Soviet-type socialism; it introduced a certain degree of labor democracy within an authoritarian one-party system, opened its borders to the West for its citizens and enabled prosperity and consumer culture unlike any other Eastern Europe country with the decentralization of production and Western credit. Therefore, the key question to be addressed by studies of different aspects of everyday life in socialism is how cultural leadership and consensus regarding socialist ideology were established, secured, and reproduced but also negotiated and questioned at the level of habitual everyday practices.[29] Differently expressed, an analysis of power in socialism/communism should move away from its legitimate forms in central locations to the working of power at the margins, in its local forms, where it becomes dispersed throughout social institutions and practices. It would be a mistake to reduce power to its intentional position of working from above and people's behavior to performance of fake complicity.[30] The latter is not to be understood as duplicity, or as a false, official face which people were supposedly forced to show in public life for official performances of loyalty, but as a hegemony that united individuals by consent rather than by coercion with power working at the level of subjectivity. Ulf Brunnbauer argues correctly that the notion of "duplicity," used by Kligman, presupposes that the real world of autonomous action was in the private sphere, the space of authenticity, while the fake world was the world of public complicity.[31]

The readings in this volume clearly suggest, that there was another dimension of power relations also to be taken into account besides the working of state power at the level of an ordinary life. Symbolically, Yugoslavia was the result of a Western gaze imposing its hegemony on the non-Western periphery. The otherness of socialist Yugoslavia was defined in terms of its peripheral position and backwardness and in terms of the particularity of its socialist ideology/values. There was a constant sense of secondariness in Yugoslav identity. Yugoslavia existed symbolically under Western eyes, and its citizens depended on Western Europe's evaluation of Yugoslavia and on non-European nations to shape the image of their country abroad and their own cultural identities (see Vuletić's chapter on the Eurovision song contest and the uneasiness of Yugoslav competitors "performing Yugoslavia" before a Western gaze). The construction of an imaginary Orient within the geography of Europe helped give coherence to the ideas of the West and provided a mirror for Europe to see its own supremacy.[32]

Thus, this book also attempts to de-Westernize, or better, to de-colonize the discourse on Central/Eastern Europe as Europe's periphery or its Orient. In Andreas Huyssen's words this would mean joining the postcolonial critique of Western history as fundamentally implicated by an imperialist, nationalist and racist Western modernity.[33] Moreover, since the history reconstructed and recorded here is also the history experienced by most of the contributors, the book represents a valuable historical context for understanding our contemporary cultural identities, or to say it with Pierre Nora: "We seek not our origins but a way of figuring out what we are from what we are no longer."[34]

Since society cannot be reduced to a single coherent model, we argue that the everyday cannot be analyzed by investigating only the official discourse, which typically takes on an ideational form, and exclude views that may expose a more amorphous experience. Any analysis of the official discourse and structures, institutions and official politics should be supplemented with research on ordinary everyday tactics and practices, hidden aspects of experience and modes of operation not in the service of the hegemony. Thus, the study of official discourses and normative institutions should be complemented by a study of innumerable other practices that remain "minor," as Michel de Certeau suggests.[35] Practices are to be understood as acts that afford the opportunity to evade official strategies of power like contestations of official strategies in socialism; for instance, double celebrations on state holidays, such as May 25 (The Day of Youth and Tito's birthday) or November 29 (The Day of the Republic). Two types of celebrations existed side by side – exclusive official ceremonies/spectacles emphasizing formality, reified symbolism, hierarchy and authoritarian aesthetics of mass rituals, and inclusive unofficial celebrations/carnivals with picnics, rock concerts, drinking on the verge of drunken orgies, dancing, and socializing with a language of its own.[36]

The everyday is situated somewhere in the gap between the individual and his/her tactics. By focusing on the microanalysis of everyday we wish to stress the agency of individuals in their daily lives and different forms of non-conformity as well as the impossibility of reducing society to a neatly coherent model, only too frequently addressed as such in totalitarian paradigms of analyses of socialism. However, at the same time, we offer an insight into how structural and institutional constraints have framed socialist subjectivity and ordinary culture in socialism. If it is true that the grid of discipline is becoming clearer and more extensive in modernity, as argued by Michel Foucault,[37] it is all the more urgent to discover how an entire society resists being reduced to it, how everyday practices conform to or manipulate the mechanisms of discipline in order to evade them and finally, what kind of practices, as argued by de Certeau, "form the counterpart, on the consumer's (or dominee's) side, of the mute processes that organize the establishment of socioeconomic order."[38]

De Certeau's ambitions are very similar to Foucault's goal to discover and analyze the multitude of tactics articulated in the details of everyday life. However, his approach is different in that it brings "to light the clandestine forms taken by the dispersed, tactical, and make-shift creativity of groups or individuals already caught in the nets of 'discipline'."[39] De Certeau distinguishes between two types of social action: tactics and strategies. Strategy is an intended action; it is the manipulation of power relationships that postulates a place of its own and is best represented by the regulatory strategies of official power. Strategy is thus a function of place that can serve as the basis for generating relations with an exterior, distinct form (competitors or objects). Tactics, on the other hand, are a calculus, which cannot count on a spatial or institutional localization, or on a border to the other as a visible totality. Stanley Cohen and Laurie Taylor argue that fights against reality for ordinary people are rarely frontal assaults, but more often interludes or temporary breaks.[40] Tactical actions are short term and situational. The space of tactics is the space of the other and, therefore, a practice of the weak (in the case of socialism, smuggling, the grey economy, or evading work in the workplace).[41] These multiform and fragmentary procedures compose the network of anti-discipline. The tactics of consumption, or the ingenious ways in which the weak make use of the strong, is an approach to everyday life when one cannot shape its variables. This set of undomesticated practices, which are hardly subversive but have a symbolic value, lend a political dimension to everyday practices.

De Certeau insists on the difference between the production of the image and the secondary production, which is taking place with the utilization of that image[42] and which should be understood as production, although this form of production-consumption is hidden, because it takes place in fields already occupied and defined by large systems of production (media institutions, urbanism, law). In short, production is considered as consumption (of public space,

media images, material commodities, official representations) manifested in the way products imposed by the dominant order are
used by consumers. An analysis of the operational logic of culture
should be approached by the study of cultural representations (media narratives, fashion, official documents) as well as by the study
of what one does with these representations (the modes of behavior).[43] The key question in the study of everyday is, therefore, how
products, imposed by a dominant order (laws, rules, norms, space,
images) are used? What kind of production is taking place with
that consumption? Everyday practices/tactics should show us how
partial strategic control can be and how people's use of a dominant
social order (rituals, representations, laws) can deflect its power.

Along with the analysis of production/consumption, in de Certeau's sense, we should keep in mind how social structures, institutions and discourses as a domain of power, shaped and determined
the everyday, which is always a product of history. We should thus
navigate between these poles, from the generality of social institutions and the power of structures to the particularity of everyday
life and the resistance to structural constraints to critically scruti-
nize the operational logic of culture in socialism. Research on everyday is not limited to the description of countless everyday practices and particularities, but should discover how the institutional
and structural is articulated at the level of everyday and ordinary
life, and how the "supraindividual" is always included specifically
at the level of individual experience. Everyday life studies should
thus focus on everyday practices and subjective experience while
bearing in mind the institutional frames of the cultural life.[44] In the
daily life of Yugoslavs the polytheism of scattered practices/tactics
served as a space of confirmation of the status quo and as a space of
resistance to the status quo.

Although the study of everyday considers culture in relation
to issues of power and resistance, not all contributions to this
volume deal explicitly with power and not every manifestation of
power or tactical resistance is as significant as any other one, nor
specific for socialism. Another focus of this volume is the ordinary
culture of a period: specific structures of feeling of socialism, a
particular way of life, and forms of subjectivity produced by the
socialist modernization process. Raymond Williams suggests that

the most difficult thing to grasp in studying any past period is this felt sense of the quality of life at a particular place and time: a sense of the ways in which particular practices combine into a way of thinking and living.[45] Williams' "structure of feeling" is the culture of a period: "It is the particular living result of all the elements in the general organization. It is never learned in a formal sense."[46] Structure of feeling suggests a relatively consistent communal way of looking at the world and sharing a number of referent points, which are the base for everyday action and discourse. The structure of feeling of a period is grounded in the everyday, the rigid and habitual, in the mundane details of the ordinary life and in the gray zone of semi-official practices. It does not refer just to public ideals and official ways of life and their social character, but also to their omissions and transgressions. The sphere of micro-everyday practices represents a fertile ground for observing the meeting point of structure and agency. The structure of feeling of Yugoslav socialism in the contributions below here is accessed either through memories or through the material, documentary culture. We also believe that we can gain a better grasp of the past structures of feeling by using a broader spectrum of voices.[47]

Personal memories can help us understand individual or collective experiences and the operative logic of everyday culture in socialist Yugoslavia after WWII. However, along with oral history accounts and personal memory, some essays in this volume are also concerned with a variety of cultural forms, which may be engaged in acts of remembering. Once socialism as an ideological and social project and its everydayness have gone and many carriers of its structure of feeling have perished, the nearest we can get to the structure of feeling of this particular period is through the material, documentary culture. Practically this means investigating the sites of memory as the remains of a socialist memorial consciousness – archival sources, historiographical accounts, memorials and monuments, state regulations, media representations, visual or material culture, preserved rituals, ceremonies, habitualized practices or fashion conventions and distinctions of that period, or private diaries and family photos. In short, *Zeitgeist*, the actual sense of living, or the deep community of that period may be recovered and demythified through various memorial traces remaining of the socialist world.[48] In addition, a plurality of methods (from fieldwork, in-depth interviews, textual and visual analyses to comparative historical methods) are employed in this volume to reveal how the socialist ideology was translated into everyday experience and how everyday life was bent and shaped by socialist ideology. However, everyday culture and practices are not a purposeful political critique of a social system by organized action, nor are they necessarily a counter-hegemonic subversion of a dominant social order and a form of symbolic defiance. They are not inherently one thing or another, instead, there is a perpetual negotiation between their roles as forms of subjection, reproduction of order and resistance. Therefore, we should always historicize them at any particular moment as a site of constant negotiation and changing political meanings.

commodities

Forms of Remembering Yugoslavia: Nostalgia and Revisionism Reconsidered

Memories and sites of memory are indispensable for reconstructing the socialist network of small daily practices that governed everyday life in Yugoslavia. In their collective or individual form they testify to remembering or recollecting Yugoslav socialism as a meaning-making cultural activity, which grants meanings to past practices. Questions regarding the socialist past nowadays are a constant ingredient of public debates all over Eastern Central Europe. The legacy of communism stirs up ambivalent feelings, deep emotions, affection or hatred among the residents of these states and plays a significant role in the structuring of their present cultural identities. Also in countries of the former Yugoslavia we witness a kind of struggle with the socialist past; there appear to be two major official treatments or forms of remembering Yugoslav socialism in the broader public discourse, in popular culture and in the professional, academic discourse. Either a nostalgic cultural relationship to Yugoslavia is structuring the process of remembering, or politically motivated historical revisionism, or a redefinition of the Yugoslav past is shaping collective and individual memories of people. As analytical concepts both lack explanatory power to elucidate what Yugoslavia and socialism were about and both are used more for an ideological consolidation of the present situation than for a thorough analysis of the past.

Nowadays numerous popular cultural artifacts and media representations – from movies, music, posters, advertisements, and t-shirts to cups decorated with Yugoslav themes – the popularity of a dot-yu internet domain, and even a basketball league with teams from across the former Yugoslavia are treated by many academic texts as a form of nostalgia. The latter has supposedly spread across the former Yugoslavia simply as a way of longing for the socialist past. But such interpretations are too narrow to encompass people's present relations to the past and usually ignore the more complex aspects of these cultural phenomena. What is entirely overlooked in this supposedly critical academic discourse is the commodification of the past of Yugoslavia, socialism, and especially of Tito, which has spread through different popular, promotional discourses, and which actually only invent, create and foster Yugo-nostalgia. Edgerton warns that such popular historical forms commodify the past itself. They are less committed to rendering a factually accurate depiction than to animating the past for millions by accentuating those matters, which are most relevant and engaging to contemporary audiences.[49]

Consequently, Yugo-nostalgia should rather be treated as a cultural product of a specific economic context of post-socialist societies that has spread across the Balkans than as a growing nostalgic yearning for the Yugoslav past and an intrinsic characteristic of people's relation to the past, like most contemporary cultural theorists would define it. Such simplified and romanticized interpretations of nostalgia are too easily dismissed as people's sentimental and melancholic relation to Yugoslavia and might overlook a more complex relationship of capitalist societies to their socialist past. It is important to bear in mind that Yugo-nostalgia is also an institutionalized form of commodified styles or sets of practices involved in complex processes of remembering and forgetting. Marita Sturken warns that a tourist relationship to history is more and more characteristic of contemporary societies[50] and thus we can argue that Yugo-nostalgia is embodied in various Yugo texts and objects; it represents a kind of "kitschification" of memory and the past. Nowadays memory is more and more produced at the intersection of media and consumerism. While it is true that nostalgia is centrally concerned with loss and involves yearning for what is not attainable, to define the appearance of Yugo-nostalgia solely in this way, however, means ignoring a whole way of understanding how the past may actively engage with the present and future. Michael Pickering and Emily Keightley suggest that we need to reconfigure the concept of nostalgia or move beyond it, since the concept itself lacks a degree of explainability.[51]

First, Yugo-nostalgia should be reconsidered as a form of selective remembering, or as a strategy of dealing with the past by creating continuity where discontinuity should be. After the demise of Yugoslavia in 1991 the real Yugoslav socialist environment had disappeared. The flow of Yugoslavia's multicultural socialist history was severely interrupted by the emergence of new ethno-national states and a capitalist regime. Second, Yugo-nostalgia should not be treated simply as a people's intrinsic wish or yearning for a return to socialist Yugoslavia, because pining for a lost past has its roots in the specific socio-political-economic conditions of the region, such as the struggle with the legacy of wars in the 1990s, or economic hardship and political corruption during the transformation to a multiparty political system and a capitalist consumer oriented economy. Similarly, Dominic Boyer notices in the case of East Germany "that ostalgie is a symptom but it is, in my opinion, neither the symptom of eastern longing for a return to the GDR, nor for the jouissance of authoritarian rule, as it is most often interpreted."[52] Yugo-nostalgia should thus be reconsidered as a manifestation of the second stage towards post-socialist normalization, following the first phase, which, according to Boyer, is the criminalization of the communist regime and distancing from it.[53] Third, Yugo-nostalgia should be reconsidered also in the conceptual realm of the spatial imaginary. The reality of living in small, unknown countries creates feelings of longing for a large and well-known country, such as Yugoslavia. Yugo-nostalgia is not just sentimentality for the socialist past, as commonly argued by romantic cultural theorists, but constitutes a broader concept; that is, a yearning for a vast territory, and for security and safety offered by the vastness of Central or Middle Europe. Renato Rosaldo speaks of an imperialist nostalgia, which means a yearning for more stable and ontologically secure worlds while mourning for what one has destroyed.[54]

Yugo-nostalgia, therefore, is the projection of a utopian past into the future of post-socialist societies that have emerged from Yugoslavia. What is called Yugo-nostalgia is a broader transference of utopia – the ideal social arrangement, well-being and prosperity, order and safety – into the everyday realities and uncertainties of the present living conditions. The romanticization and idealization of the past overlooks that a desire to return to the Yugoslav socialist past grows with unstable or risky conditions in post-socialist societies; the latter struggle with global economic and cultural flows while positioned between the socialist legacy and a sudden confrontation with the neo-liberal capitalist economy. These cultures of risk are full of uncertainty and insecurity, as defined in Ulrich Beck's sense,[55] and create fertile grounds for such a relation to the past. Andreas Huyssen believes that we turn to memory for comfort and safety,[56] and Yugo-nostalgia may offer comfort through a utopian vision of safety, justice and reassurance, borrowed from the fantasies of past socialist worlds.

Moreover, the turbulent downfall of Yugoslavia and the disintegration of the socialist system in 1991 brought about the implementation of democratic political structures and a market economy as well as the need for changes in the politics of interpreting recent history. Today the writing of history about Yugoslav socialism is under severe pressures of revisionism, which – as the opposite of nostalgia – leans towards the denigration of this past. Numerous public debates – from political to historiographic discussions about the contemporary political relationship to Yugoslavia – have been focused primarily on the redefinition and moral assessment of socialist society and its regime. There appears to be a very powerful, politically motivated need to redefine the role and the meaning of a common Yugoslav socialist past according to present conditions.

In general, these politically motivated historical narratives about the Yugoslav past are based on a selective treatment and interpretation, which either underestimates the whole era and reduces its importance in recent history or reinterprets the experience of the socialist period solely through two perspectives. The first one reduces the Yugoslav experience to aggressiveness and to the dictatorship of the Communist Party. Missing from such accounts is a broader interpretation of the recent past that would contextualize the socio-cultural components and people's experiences with oppressions as well as the pleasures of socialism. The second one redefines the shared experience of Yugoslavia's antifascist past. Socialist Yugoslavia built its commonality on the Second World War experience, on the National Liberation Front and the partisan movement; together they became the central signifiers of being Yugoslav. Nowadays the partisan movement is usually equated with the communist revolution mainly featuring its totalitarian aspects. Most of these historiographic studies rely mainly on investigations of political repression and censorship, poverty, rapidly growing nationalisms in the 1990s, the cult of Tito, and his role and that of party officials in imprisonments and carnage.

Former Yugoslav societies are facing political instrumentalization of the past, which is an attempt to build an ideological consensus of how to perceive the Yugoslav past. Remembering and forgetting are imposed in the present political climate since selective remembering is one of the most important mechanisms of surveyance among contemporary power structures. They result in shaping people's memories because social memory is always the selected presence of the past. Halbwachs maintains that individual recollections always rely on the frameworks of social memory: "This is why society tends to erase from its memory all that might separate individuals, or that might distance groups from each other. It is also why society, in each period, rearranges its recollections in such a way as to adjust them to the variable conditions of its equilibrium."[57] The history of Yugoslav socialism, therefore, does not end where the existing official historiographic interpretations stop. According to Hayden White, historiography is much more about telling stories inspired by contemporary perspectives than about recapturing and conveying any kind of objective truth about the past.[58] Thus, we should be extremely mindful of such contemporary truth-making discourse regarding socialism, which appears in public and in academic fields, filled with reinterpretations of the past, which aim to affirm political and cultural alliances in former Yugoslav societies and help divide the public politically and culturally.

Such revised histories and forms of remembering are, in the first place, a function of producing delimited nation states and their politics. The invention of the past, in Eric Hobsbawm's terms, propels the processes of intense national homogenization, while specific versions of history can be mobilized to support a specific image of a national identity or a particular political regime.[59] With the fall of Yugoslavia in 1991 the old common Yugoslav signifiers were suddenly unsuitable for representing new emerging nationhoods. New national knowledge and distinct national histories had to be constructed for intensely nationalizing these societies, which needed to move away from the Yugoslav experience and the idea of brotherhood and unity. References to a totalitarian communist past and to the uniqueness of their own national experiences became more than convenient. Katherine Verdery warns about such partial descriptions of the socialist past and argues that the main themes regarding socialism and the transition literature are connected to civil society, marketization, privatization and nationalism.[60] Once these reinterpretations of the past firmly enter public consciousness and collective memory they come to pass for reality and start restructuring present identities. Such historical revisionism introduces the historiography of oblivion. Tessa Morris-Suzuki warns that the purpose of this kind of historiography is not simply to revise understandings of the past, but to obliterate the memory of certain events from public consciousness.[61]

However, nowadays both, historical revisionism and nostalgia, promote a new politics of truth which rearranges past events either to justify the current situation and to legitimize certain political actions or to romanticize the past and to replace present conditions with escapism or curiosity: did socialism provide more or fewer opportunities for a better life? In any case, the politically and culturally produced amnesia of Yugoslavia's socialist past cannot be ignored. These representations of the Yugoslav past, which also relate to some typical myths of socialist East Central Europe, push the collective memory of these societies through significant changes. In the case of Yugoslavia we might argue that its history is not what is revealed, but rather what remains hidden.

Outline of the Book

This book offers a selection from a plethora of everyday life spaces developed and acquired by socialist Yugoslavia. Numerous microhistories, narratives, interviews, statements, images, texts, objects and relics accumulated by the contributors to this volume become the glue of a grand narrative about a specific period in recent history that has stigmatized the twentieth century, the Balkan and the broader Central European region and with it effected current anxieties, priorities and values in these regions.

The first part of the book deals with frameworks of remembering Yugoslavia and Tito; how Yugoslavia has been inscribed in people's memories, and how people identified with Yugoslavia and Tito through various means provided by the state and applied to people's daily lives. Here questions are posed about the representation and appropriation of the political and cultural life of Yugoslav socialism in people's daily routines. In *First and Last Emperor: Representations of the President, Bodies of the Youth*, Bojana Videkanic takes an interest in the image of the president, Josip Broz Tito, and why he was at the centre of all symbolic practices in Yugoslavia to become the central signifier of Yugoslavness. She addresses the political, cultural and visual spectacle created in socialist Yugoslavia known as The Day of Youth, on May 25 which celebrated Tito's birthday and the life and work of Yugoslavia's youth. Videkanic analyzes visual representations related to The Day of Youth and Tito to understand the massive enthusiasm for this holiday. The Yugoslav youth became a signifier of the healthy nation and one capable of taking ownership of its future. Its youthful bodies and their physical/symbolic power were used to uphold the president's power. Borrowing from several paradigms, including an alternative socialist modernity, specificities of the socialist dictatorial system, and the father figure embodied in Tito, her chapter offers a framework for understanding why Yugoslavia's post-socialist societies recently constructed an ambivalent and rather problematic relationship to them.

Danka Ninković Slavnić's chapter, *Celebrating Yugoslavia: The Visual Representation of State Holidays* further builds on visual images of Yugoslavia by analyzing visual representations of two central Yugoslav holidays, The Day of Youth and The Day of the Republic, in two major daily newspapers, Slovenia's *Delo* and Serbia's *Politika*, between 1974 and 1990. Photographic representations of state holidays helped anchor the dominant ideology of socialist Yugoslavia. As powerful symbolic propagandistic means these photos predominantly showed the beauty of Yugoslavia, promoted a hegemonic gaze focused only on an idealized normality but omitted problems and weaknesses. The coverage created a common, mental frame of reference and feelings of unity among nationally, economically and religiously diverse parts of the country. Ninković Slavnić concludes that the state was an ideological construction, while visual materials engaged in the construction of a socialist state were also involved in its collapse through the erosion of a common symbolic field.

In the chapter, *Officers without an Army: Memories of Socialism and Everyday Strategies in Post-Socialist Slovenia* Tanja Petrović deals with how people's memories shape their present living conditions in a specific society. The author concentrates on former officers of the Yugoslav People's Army, who are predominantly of Serbian origins, who had served on the territory of Slovenia and who have continued living there after 1991. She asks how their memories are affected by the present post-socialist Slovenian context, which has been unfavorable to them, and how their present values, beliefs, actions and roles in the Slovenian society are shaped by their forms of remembering. A negative image of these officers is maintained mainly by the Slovenian political discourse, which seeks to sustain and reproduce the myth of Slovenia's struggle for independence. Petrović shows that their feelings of exclusion and obsolescence are a product of a radical loss of context and the ideological network of socialism in which they enjoyed high social status and retained their self-esteem.

The second part of the book provides a survey of how the structure and apparatus of a socialist ideology were appropriated at the level of popular culture of Yugoslavia. The predominance of this chapter lies on music culture. Dean Vuletić in his chapter, *European Sounds, Yugoslav Visions: Performing Yugoslavia at the Eurovision Song Contest*, follows the Yugoslav debates regarding Yugoslavia's participation and selection of contestants and discusses the reasons for their lack of success, thereby offering insights into Yugoslavia's troubling political and cultural identity and its exclusion from the economic and cultural core of Europe. The Eurovision song contest, which began in 1956, had a special significance in the cultural life of Yugoslavia, which – due to its nonaligned status – was the only Slavic and Eastern European country to take part in it during the Cold War. Participation should have confirmed Yugoslavia's membership in the cultural sphere of Western Europe. However, it was not easy to successfully imitate Western pop and Western culture, in general. Inquiries by Yugoslav cultural elites regarding Yugoslavia's relative marginality and its lack of success at the Eurovision contests reflected wider debates over cultural and political identities of Yugoslavia, its semi-oriental position, its "backwardness" and its ambivalent relationship to the West. Vuletić reflects on the hegemonic relations involved in the organization of the Eurovision song contest and the cultural hegemony of the Western group of contestants, and more generally, provides evidence of the hegemonic position of Western Europe in relation to the European periphery (a group of Mediterranean contestants, such as Israel, Turkey, Greece, or Cyprus). Vuletić's analysis is an example of how the gaze of the West was constitutive of Yugoslavia's ambivalent subjectivity as Europe's semi-orient.

Radina Vučetić in her chapter, *Džuboks (Jukebox) – The First Rock'n'roll Magazine in Socialist Yugoslavia* investigates rock music by analyzing the magazine, *Džuboks*, which, in May, 1966 featured the Rolling Stones on its cover and brought rock'n'roll to Yugoslavia on a large scale. She focuses on the early period of the publication and offers examples of how rock music and the magazine played an important role in bringing the spirit of the West to Yugoslav socialist society in the 1960s. Vučetić establishes what these new rock'n'roll idols meant for a socialist youth and how they changed their everyday life by structuring their musical tastes, their ways of dressing, behaving, or listening to music charts on radio and by introducing entertainment, such as partying in disco clubs, or visiting rock concerts. Moreover, for Vučetić the rock'n'roll magazine in socialist Yugoslavia was a political phenomenon, because it was also a powerful force that began announcing social and political changes in the country.

Gregor Tomc's chapter, *A Tale of Two Subcultures: A Comparative Analysis of Hippie and Punk Subcultures in Slovenia* assesses the subcultural life of Yugoslavia. He analyzes and compares two distinct Slovenian rock subcultures, hippies of the 1960s and punks of the late 1970s and their appropriation by the socialist world. Yugoslavia lagged behind western industrial societies regarding youth subcultures, which were politically not part of the everyday life scene until the 1980s. After presenting socialist politics of the popular culture scene, Tomc compares both subcultures in socialist Slovenia with their Western counterparts. The former were a product of the socialist internalization of a subcultural Western style, rearranged for socialist circumstances. Tomc concludes that individual hippies or punks in Slovenia produced subcultural worlds that were as authentic as those which originally inspired them.

Martin Pogačar's chapter, *Yugoslav Past in Film and Music: Yugoslav Interfilmic Referentiality*, offers an account of how popular culture (cinema, television and popular music) and its personality system were used as complementary historical and symbolic sources for a common collectivity, and how popular culture mediated a shared Yugoslav experience. According to Pogačar, popular culture assisted in creating a Yugoslav imaginary that hosted narratives and common identifiers, which (ideally) facilitated the creation of a transnational community. Pogačar investigates two paradigmatic popular texts with a cult status in former Yugoslavia, a television series, *Reckless Youth* (1975) and a feature film, *You only love once* (1981), both connected by the appearance of the same personalities and a shared musical soundtrack. His "Yugoslav interfilmic referentiality" describes the intertextual entanglement of different domains of popular culture, which symbolically contributed to the creation of the "Yuniverse." Popular culture shaped the field of common cultural experiences and reemerges through forgotten or dismissed cinematic traces of the Yugoslav past. Today, referentiality contributes to the nostalgic discourse, which is closely related to identity-quests, while filmic representations allow for recovering the structure of feeling of the depicted era. Pogačar argues that contemporary television series and film figure as narratives of an unfulfilled striving for a more just social order and a better future.

The third part of the book addresses issues of different leisure spaces and practices in socialist Yugoslavia. Leisure is usually seen as the opposite of work and as a category against which work is commonly defined. Work is believed to have been the most important part of socialism and a significant determinant of a socialist identity, which shaped people's lives. This section emphasizes that time away from work was important ingredient of socialism. Moreover, the contributors to this section show how free, unreserved time at one's own disposal was ideologically influenced and, on the other hand, rearranged for the socialist purposes. Maruša Pušnik in her chapter, *Flirting with Television in Socialism: Proletarian Morality and the Lust for Abundance*, contextualizes the penetration of television technology in socialist homes between the late 1950s and the early 1970s to disclose how television constructed specific frames of mind among people, and how they possessed, used and perceived television. Pušnik addresses the beginnings of television in socialist Slovenia through people's memories to discover how television was reinvented for the purposes of a socialist ideology and how its images of the Western world affected people's daily routines. The chapter describes meaning and ambivalence of television uses for a work-oriented socialist society. The individuals' search for pleasures and the celebration of Western life-styles clashed with the modesty, resignation and humbleness of a proletarian morality. Television technology was a linkage between the new consumer culture and modernization processes and the reproduction of the existing socialist ordering of the world.

Gregor Starc's chapter, *Sportsmen of Yugoslavia, Unite: Workers' Sport between Leisure and Work*, analyzes sporting practices in Yugoslavia from a socialist perspective of work and leisure. The author explores personal narratives and texts about sporting practices, that is, Yugoslav labor union inspired sports and physical exercises in factories, the socialist understanding of competition and spectatorship, mass sporting events, as well as socialist scientific interventions that legitimized the relations between physical culture and work. Sporting practices as leisure were characterized by ambivalent feelings, since leisure was considered idleness, the worst enemy of socialist work, and a sign of an exploitative mode of western capitalist production. However, inspired by communist ideals, people and the propagating authorities translated leisure and sports into physical culture, an original socialist practice, which made sports and leisure constitutive parts of the production process. Sporting practices were used as means of active regeneration, which consequently increased production, and physical culture became a central tool of education and entertainment among Yugoslav citizens.

Modernization brought to Yugoslavia by socialism was closely linked to modern mass leisure, including also international tourism, as addressed in Karin Taylor's and Igor Duda's chapters. Tourism reached Yugoslavia in the 1960s and significantly changed life in resort towns and villages along the Adriatic coast, accelerating economic and cultural modernization and the rise of a consumer culture. Igor Duda begins his chapter, *Adriatic for All: Summer Holidays in Croatia*, with an analysis of the developing tourist industry in Yugoslavia, and mass tourism in Croatia from the 1940s to the late 1970s based on official statistics, archives, travel guidebooks and personal narratives. Tourism becomes a symbol of well-being. Duda describes the official tourist policy and the ideology of domestic "social" tourism. He traces the shift from collective tourism, organized by labor unions, to individual, commercial tourism and the rise of tourism as popular culture. Karin Taylor's chapter, *"SOBE": Privatizing Tourism on the Workers' Riviera*, looks at the development of private tourist accommodations in two Adriatic resorts and how tourism was one of the important factors of social transformation that had also included industrialization, urbanization, or gender emancipation. Taylor offers testimonies of people who provided private tourist accommodations, to domestic and foreign tourists in coastal towns and suggests how the expansion of urban leisure-time activities and contacts with Western European tourists shaped consumer ethos and changed expectations and social practices in the resorts.

Consumption is the focus of the fourth section of this volume. Breda Luthar writes in *Shame, Desire and Longing for the West: A Case Study of Consumption* about social experience of a culture of shortages and different practices of acquiring goods in the 1950s and 1960s Yugoslavia; they included shopping trips to Italy, when the border between a capitalist Italy and a socialist Yugoslavia opened gradually. Over time, seasonal shopping trips to Italy became regular social events and developed in the 1970s into a mass shopping frenzy. Luthar focuses on the formal properties of the cultural and communicative practices of "going shopping to Italy" by drawing on the personal memories of former shoppers, whose strongest individual memory of life in state socialism had been the lack of desired goods and the culture of shortages. She explores the symbolic meaning of goods, traumatic border-crossings, experiences of facing customs officers, communicative tactics of shoppers/smugglers, and gender divisions, as well as ethnic and class differentiation involved in shopping expeditions. Memories of scarcity, desires, and the symbolic meaning of goods, mingle with recollections of foreignness and inadequacy when faced with the West in Italian Trieste.

In their chapter, *Cooking in Socialist Slovenia: Housewives on the Road from a Bright Future to an Idyllic Past,* Blanka Tivadar and Andreja Vezovnik analyze the discourse on cooking, food preparation and housekeeping in a popular women's magazine, *Naša žena* (Our Woman), published since 1941 and promoting the official view of the woman's role in society and official gender politics after 1945. The authors explore the genre of cooking and housekeeping, advice columns, the transformation of their content and rhetorical strategies from the end of the 1940s to 1990. Their textual analysis reveals the main ideological mechanisms behind the articles. Socialism saw the woman as an indispensable caretaker of the nation, and the widely read women's magazine advised women to embrace traditional gender roles. Political engagement was seen as the transfer of a moral life from home into the public arena. For at least twenty years the magazine spread the ideology of time-saving convenience to assist a growing food industry by connecting time-saving convenience with the socialist work ideology; in the 1980s, however, the former was slowly replaced by the duty to enjoy leisure time while healthy eating was no longer a civic duty. Tivadar and Vezovnik suggest that advise in *Naša žena* shifted from the end of the 1970s when the magazine advised women on "how to cook socialism" to how to build a nation state and prepare for living in a risk society in the 1980s. Neither discourse (authoritarian with explicit instructions and playful, gentle and covert tips) left much room for freedom.

Djurdja Bartlett in her case study, *Žuži Jelinek: The Incredible Adventures of a Socialist Chanel,* analyzes the life of Žuži Jelinek, a fashion designer, local celebrity, and owner of the most appreciated post-war private fashion salon in the Croatian capital, Zagreb. Private fashion salons of the 1950s were supposed to add some sophistication to the image of socialist fashion. Bartlett explores the role of fashion, the smart dress and conventional good taste in socialism. In Yugoslavia, the aestheticization of everyday life was approved at least to a certain degree; however, the quality and style of domestic ready-to-wear clothing was plagued by a lack of professional knowledge, and the new industry proved unable to produce smart, good-quality dresses. Seamstresses and private fashion salons were substitutes and supplements for an underdeveloped clothing industry. In a rapidly urbanizing Zagreb, private fashion salons preserved their fashion rituals and retained their pre-war cultural capital and expertise. Bartlett describes how fashion salons helped the process of civilization and modernization for a new, unsophisticated elite and how new civilizing rituals were cultivated through the medium of minimalist smart dresses. Classicist and minimalist fashion, promoted by Jelinek, without transgression, performed two different symbolical roles – opposition to Stalinism and access to the much craved modernity. Bartlett argues that in the 1950s the official discourse borrowed aesthetic categories from petit-bourgeois "good taste" and conventional elegance with boundaries between appropriateness and inappropriateness clearly marked. Socialist good taste was the merger of a proletarian style and petit bourgeois good taste.

This volume ends with *A Face in the Market: Photography, Memory, and Nostalgia*, a photo essay by Hanno Hardt, which features the Ljubljana market in the 1980s Yugoslavia. These photographs – taken between 1984 and 1989 – of buyers and vendors from all parts of Yugoslavia offer yet another encounter with the multicultural and multiethnic nature of Yugoslavia, and become a reminder of the lost possibilities of socialism and multicultural diversity.

Notes

[1] Michael Billig, *Banal Nationalism* (London: Sage, 1995).

[2] Pierre Nora, "General Introduction: Between Memory and History," in *Realms of Memory: The Construction of the French Past*, ed. Pierre Nora (New York: Columbia University Press, 1996), 1.

[3] Pierre Nora, ibid., 1996, 7.

[4] Maurice Halbwachs, *On Collective Memory* (Chicago: The University of Chicago Press, 1992).

[5] Nick Couldry, *Inside Culture* (London: Sage, 2000), 52.

⁶ Ulf Brunnbauer, "Alltag und Ideologie im Sozialismus – eine Dialektische Beziehung," *BOI* 23/2005 (2005): 13. See also Susan E. Reid and David Crowley, eds., *Style and Socialism. Modernity and Material Culture in Post-War Eastern Europe* (Oxford: Berg, 2000).

⁷ See Raymond Williams on three levels of culture: lived culture of a particular place and time, recorded culture, and the culture of the selective tradition. Raymond Williams, *The Long Revolution* (London: The Hogarth Press, 1992/1961), 49.

⁸ See Ben Highmore, "Introduction: Questioning Everyday Life," in *The Everyday Life Reader*, ed. Ben Highmore (London: Routledge, 2002), 1–36.

⁹ See Mike Featherstone, *Undoing Culture* (London: Sage, 1995), 54–71.

¹⁰ David A. Bell, "Total History and Microhistory: The French and Italian Paradigms," in *A Companion to Western Historical Thought,* ed. Lloyd Kramer and Sarah Maza (Oxford: Blackwell, 2002), 265.

¹¹ Katherine Verdery, *What Was Socialism and What Comes Next* (Princeton: Princeton University Press, 1996), 11.

¹² Arfon E. Rees, "Introduction: The Sovietization of Eastern Europe," in *The Sovietization of Eastern Europe: New Perspectives on the Postwar Period,* ed. Balazs Apor, Peter Apor and Arfon E. Rees (Washington: New Academia Publishing, 2008), 1.

¹³ On the nationalization of the economy see Jože Prinčič, "Podržavljanje gospodarstva," in *Slovenska novejša zgodovina,* ed. Neven Borak et al. (Ljubljana: Mladinska knjiga, 2005), 873–8.

¹⁴ Oto Luthar, ed., *The Land Between. A History of Slovenia* (Frankfurt am Main: Peter Lang, 2008), 459.

¹⁵ Oto Luthar, ibid., 2008, 459.

¹⁶ Avgust Lešnik, "Informbirojevski spor leta 1948," *Časopis za zgodovino in narodopisje* 69, 2 (1998): 287.

¹⁷ Neil Barnett, *Tito* (London: Haus Publishing, 2006), 14.

¹⁸ Sabrina P. Ramet, *Nationalism and Federalism in Yugoslavia, 1962–1991* (Bloomington: Indiana University Press, 1992), 84–5.

¹⁹ See Sharon Zukin, *Beyond Marx and Tito: Theory and Practice of Yugoslav Socialism* (London, New York: Cambridge University Press, 1975).

²⁰ Roger Brubaker, *Nationalism Reframed. Nationhood and the National Question in the New Europe* (Cambridge: Cambridge University Press, 1996), 70.

²¹ John Borneman, *Death of the Father: An Anthropology of the End in Political Authority* (Oxford: Berghahn Books, 2003), 165–7.

²² For detailed information on the inflation rate in the 1980s see *Statistički godišnjak Jugoslavije 1991* (*Statistical Yearbook of Yugoslavia 1991*).

[23] Roger Brubaker, ibid., 1996, 20.

[24] One of the sources of ethnic tensions resided in a policy, which demanded that more developed regions (particularly Slovenia and Croatia) finance the development of underdeveloped regions with complete disregard for the market situation. This had led to a series of misguided projects and dramatic loss of funds.

[25] Socialist Yugoslavia has rarely been studied from the perspective of an ordinary life; however, there are a number of studies of everyday life in socialist Eastern European countries. See for example Sheila Fitzpatrick, *Everyday Stalinism: ordinary life in Russia in the 1930's* (Oxford: Oxford University Press, 2000), Daniela Koleva, *Biografija i normalnost* (Sofia: Lik, 2002). Others include Susan E. Reid and David Crowley, eds., *Style and Socialism. Modernity and Material Culture in Post-War Eastern Europe* (Oxford: Berg, 2000), Juka Gronow, *Caviar with Champagne. Common Luxury and the Ideals of the Good Life in Stalinist Russia* (Oxford: Berg, 2003), and Judd Stitziel, *Fashioning Socialism: Clothing, Politics and Consumer Culture in East Germany* (Oxford: Berg, 2005).

[26] See also Michael Pickering, *History, Experience and Cultural Studies* (New York: St. Martin's Press, 1997).

[27] See Michel Foucault, "The Subject and Power," in *Art after Modernism: Rethinking Representation*, ed. Brian Wallis (New York: The New Museum of Contemporary Art, 1999), 430.

[28] Pierre Bourdieu, *Outline of a Theory of Practice* (Cambridge: Cambridge University Press, 1977), 79.

[29] On internalization and habitualization of socialist ideology and on the Bulgarian case of colonization of everyday see also Ulf Brunnbauer, ibid., 2005, 11.

[30] Gail Kligman, *The Politics of Duplicity. Controlling Reproduction in Ceausescu's Romania* (Berkeley, London: University of California Press, 1998).

[31] Ulf Brunnbauer, ibid., 2005, 11.

[32] David Morley and Kevin Robins, *Spaces of Identity* (London: Routledge, 1995), 136–7.

[33] Andreas Huyssen, *Present Pasts: Urban Palimpsests and the Politics of Memory* (Stanford: Stanford University Press, 2003), 5.

[34] Pierre Nora, ibid., 1996, 13.

[35] Michel de Certeau, *The Practice of Everyday Life* (Berkeley: University of California Press, 1988), 48.

[36] On the topics of the medieval pagan carnival as the unofficial folk celebration and resistance to the power hierarchy, which separated the official Christian Church from folk culture, see Mikhail Bahtin, *Rabelais and His World* (Bloomington: Indiana University Press, 1984).

[37] Michel Foucault, *Vednost-oblast- subjekt* (Ljubljana: Krt, 1991).

[38] Michel de Certeau, "Introduction to the Practice of Everyday Life," in *The Everyday Life Reader*, ed. Ben Highmore (London: Routledge, 2002), 66.

[39] Michel de Certeau, ibid., 2002, 66.

[40] Stanley Cohen and Laurie Taylor, *Escape Attempts. The Theory and Practice of Resistance to Everyday Life* (London: Routledge, 1992).

[41] See also Ian Buchanan, *Michel de Certeau. Cultural Theorist* (London: Sage, 2000), 87.

[42] Michel de Certeau, ibid., 1988.

[43] De Certeau's focus in his research is not on subjects but on the operational logic of culture. See Ian Buchanan, ibid., 2000, 93.

[44] Highmore argues that if everyday life studies are interested in everyday life at its most vivid and intense, they will need travelling to those places where everyday life is at its most liminal. Particularly interesting for the studies of everyday are those moments when everyday life breaks down and is interrupted. Ethnography, for instance, should deal with extremes rather than with cultural norms. See Ben Highmore, ibid., 2002, 19.

[45] Raymond Williams, ibid., 1992/1961, 47. Annales historians coined the term *mentalités*, which was widely used in cultural history in the 1950s and 1960s. This is an imprecise term, which covered everything from religiosity to traditional popular culture, but it was essentially and at its best, a history of cultural assumptions of a period. Mentality, according to Vovelle, is the conceptualized expression of a concrete practice and is written in the field of ideology, although ideology is only one level or viewpoint of the field of mentality. Although mentality is never closely operationalized by the historians of mentalities, it could be understood, to a certain degree, as a synonym for structures of feeling or collective imaginaries revealed by the analysis of a relationship between the objective circumstances of people's lives and the ways they live them, how they talk and think about them when they remember them. See Michel Vovelle, *Ideologies and Mentalities* (Chicago: University of Chicago Press, 1990). Another possible synonym would be Bourdieu's notion of a habitus as an "acquired system of generative schemes objectively adjusted to the particular conditions in which it is constituted." Habitus emanates from collective and communicative memory. See Pierre Bourdieu, ibid., 1977, 87.

[46] Raymond Williams, ibid., 1992/1961, 48.

[47] See Erica Carter and Ken Hirschhkop, "Cultural Memory: Introduction," *A Journal of Culture, Theory, Politics* 30 (1996–97): vii. See also Michel-Rolph Trouillot, *Silencing the Past: Power and the Production of History* (Boston: Beacon Press, 1995).

[48] On deep community see "The Analysis of Culture" in Raymond Williams, ibid., 1992/1961.

[49] Gary R. Edgerton, "Television as Historian: A Different Kind of History Altogether," in *Television Histories: Shaping Collective Memory in the Media Age*, ed. Gary R. Edgerton and Peter C. Rollins (Lexington: University Press of Kentucky, 2001), 4.

[50] Marita Sturken, "Tourists of History: Souvenirs, Architecture, and the Kitschification of Memory," in *Technologies of Memory in the Arts*, ed. Liedeke Plate and Anneke Smelik (New York: Palgrave/MacMillan, 2009).

[51] Michael Pickering and Emily Keightley, "The Modalities of Nostalgia," *Current Sociology* 54, 6 (2006): 920.

[52] Dominic Boyer, "Ostalgie and the Politics of the Future in Eastern Germany," *Public Culture* 18, 2 (2006): 361–4.

[53] Dominic Boyer, ibid., 2006, 361–81.

[54] Renato Rosaldo, *Culture and Truth: The Remaking of Social Analysis* (London: Routledge, 1993).

[55] Ulrich Beck, *Risk Society: Towards a New Modernity* (London: Sage, 1992).

[56] Andreas Huyssen, ibid., 2003, 25.

[57] Maurice Halbwachs, ibid., 1992, 182–3.

[58] Hayden White, *Tropics of Discourse: Essays in Cultural Criticism* (Baltimore: John Hopkins University Press, 1985).

[59] Eric Hobsbawm, "Introduction: Inventing Traditions," in *The Invention of Tradition*, ed. Eric Hobsbawm and Terence Ranger (Cambridge: Cambridge University Press, 1993), 2.

[60] Katherine Verdery, ibid., 1996, 11–2.

[61] Tessa Morris-Suzuki, *The Past within Us: Media, Memory, History* (London: Verso, 2005), 8.

Part II

Remembering Tito and Yugoslavia Before and After the Fall

2

First and Last Emperor
Representations of the President, Bodies of the Youth

Bojana Videkanic

Is It Nostalgia or Something Else?

I remember very vaguely, when I was three years old, and on the way with my mother to visit my grandmother. My mother decided to take the streetcar, a twenty minute ride that wove through most of Sarajevo's mid and downtown. It was a busy day, rush hour, and the streetcar was filled with people returning from work. At one point, as we passed by a large office building, for no apparent reason I shouted "there he is mom, there he is!" Half confused half embarrassed my mother asked me "who is there?" I shouted back "Tito!" Naturally, everyone on the streetcar had heard me and laughed. Unknowingly I had recreated a curious and rather bizarre scene of ideological identification which has caused me, even as a toddler, to recognize and embody the notion of the president as the ultimate symbol of power. The complicated, often bewildering environment of socialist Yugoslavia provided fertile ground for the creation of various representational discourses which served to establish multifaceted relationships among the state, its citizenry and finally its president. In short these representational discourses served as particular body politics in which the leader and the citizens entered a variety of public unions, or contracts, that enabled the symbol of the leader and his power to proliferate through the bodies of the citizens, in this case youth.

My first encounter with the representational apparatuses in socialism serves to illustrate the potency of those apparatuses in building an effective body politics. President Tito's visual representations therefore emphasize three important points. First, they point to the symbolic and actual space which President Tito's body and his image occupied in the public and private realms in the former Yugoslavia. The "omni-presence" of president's image/body, its symbolic existence and its interaction with the bodies of citizens is interesting precisely because of the kind of power it had and still has in the minds and memory (collective and individual) of those who were born and lived in the region during the 20th and into the 21st centuries. Secondly, the visual representations address the polarity and the complexity of Tito's political power in Yugoslavia, being both dictatorial/ totalitarian and friendly at the same time. Anthropologist and historian Maja Brkljacic relying on Peter Brown states:

> We might thus argue that by picturing Tito as a *patronus* and an *amicus* and by building an intimate relationship between him and his protégées (Yugoslavs), a very "rich combination of power and intimacy" was established which helped, in my view, to keep him close to the masses without at the same time undermining or threatening his position of unquestioned power: one was supposed to believe him not on the grounds of fear but love.[1]

Thus, Tito's actual body (and representations of,) traversed a very fine line between close proximity and balanced distance in order to keep itself present in the public consiciousness. Finally, my childhood encounter with the president's image also shows that the relationships between youth and president were structured around admiration, adoration, and strange symbolic exchange that could be characterized as secular religiousity.

These complex networks of meaning and exchange between president and citizens, youth especially, will be more closely examined vis-a-vis a particular event and the visual apparatuses related to it. The so-called The Day of Youth was celebrated on May 25, and was officially sanctioned as Tito's birthday, but later adopted as a national holliday of all the youth.[2] Each year a couple of months prior to May 25 the whole country started preparations for the event. Posters, postal stamps, radio and TV shows were circulated to announce the day. A special design contest was held for the best designs of the "štafeta" or the *relay baton*. Schools, factories, athletic clubs and other institutions all sent out their young candidates to carry the baton across the land. In the week prior to The Day of Youth the streets were lined with people trying to show their appreciation for the president. They carried flowers, signs and cheered as the baton was carried along. Tito's name was revered and celebrated wherever there was a public gathering. Children stood in their best uniforms with red caps and blue scarfs singing and dancing. Sporting events were held during the festivities to show young bodies in action. Farmers, miners and workers all came in their best uniforms to show the symbols of their particular trade in solidarity with the youth. And finally when May 25th came along all of these multifaceted, multisensory events concluded with the president receiving The Day of Youth baton staged in the capital of the former Yugoslavia. I remeber as a child watching TV images of these final celebrations taking place at the stadium in Belgrade. They were colorful, dramatic, large and most importantly full of life as children and young adults created various shapes with their bodies, paraded with guns, and danced. It all seemed larger than life, I remember the slogans "we are all Tito" and the cheering that would insue each time someone would utter it as if taking part in the Christian eucharist.

This was an ultimate ritualized event in which specific kinds of powers were transferred from person to person, from territory to territory and from the nation to the president. Like in the medieval contact with the relic the citizens were able to, if only for a moment, touch the body of the leader embodied in the relay baton. Visual representations that captured these events show the moments in which the body of the president became a universal signifier of power. These were also the moments when bodies of the citizens partook of that power through their participation in carrying the relay baton. Once reenacted in front of a live audience, signifying visual practices of The Day of Youth were then further carried into the mass media where the body of the leader was expanded and took on new symbolizations becoming fully mobilized to subsume all other representations of the State (flags, coats of arms, money etc.).

An event such as The Day of Youth provided a ritual, symbolic network through which Yugoslavian society renewed its commitments to shared ideological mechanisms. The cohesiveness

Final celebrations for president Tito's birthday and The Day of Youth, Stadium JNA, Belgrade, Serbia, c. 1980s.

of social networks was created through ritualized process of the public spectacle. Referring to Durkheim, Amitai Etzioni argues that rituals such as public holidays, recreate important social bonds which would be lost if the society was left to its many centrifugal, individualistic activities of everyday life.[3] He states:

> Rituals provide one major mechanism for the recreation of society, one in which the members of a society worship shared objects and in which they share experiences that help form and sustain deep emotional bonds among the members.[4]

However, in the case of Yugoslavia, the public spectacle was expanded both temporally and geographically to include months of preparations through local baton relays, school events and similar micro spectacles. Apart from creating coherent social contract among citizens, such ritualization of everyday life and culture in socialism also needs to be understood as existing in a complex matrix of relationships in which the body of the leader and the body of the people interacted. The Day of Youth was one among several public spectacles that were used to enable power transfers and create unity through and with the body of Josip Broz Tito. In his work on Tito's relationship to power and totalitarian systems, Ugo Vlaisavljevic argues that the complexities of rule in totalitarian systems need to be looked at in relationship to the leader and in the entire political and social matrix thus:

> The leader, in fact, does not manage his position or the logic of the system under his rule: in this sense he could not have known what to do. The *political form or matrix* itself, which is essentially labeled with his name, is not his product, it is something the leader finds himself in.[5]

Therefore, there can be no power without the existence of a social constellation or network of relationships, which would make the continuation and proliferation of such power possible. The leader has to be embodied through the citizenry and The Day of Youth provided an opportunity for such an act of embodiment to take place. I argue that this and other similar spectacles served to create a sense of unity among the peoples of Yugoslavia, but more importantly initiate the youth into the body of the state. Thus, the following may be understood as an effort to register and reexamine the potential impact of representational practices on the body politics, and the ways in which this was negotiated and mobilized in the specific environment of socialist Yugoslavia. Coming to terms with these notions also stems from the personal need to reposition myself as a specific cultural hybrid, born and raised in socialist modernity, intellectually reared in capitalist postmodernity, and resident in a contemporary context often ignorant of the lessons from the socialist past.

Socialist Modernities

Conceptualizing The Day of Youth and numerous events which took place around it needs to be conducted in a twofold way. First, this event and the larger cultural or socio/political relations in socialist Yugoslavia need to be seen as a part and parcel of a socialist modernity, one that is altogether idiosyncratic. Secondly, the event also functions, as mentioned within a representational body politics which as Ugo Vasilijevic, argues with Claude Lefort, is based on "a strong regime of imaginary" and "an adequate economy of embodiment."[6] The confluence of external forces personified in Western politics towards communist Eastern Europe, and internal forces of politics of ritualization, created a powerful socialist everyday in which the symbolic, the imaginary, and the Real coexisted side by side consequently creating a hybrid modernity. The Day of Youth is emblematic of this because it embodied all the elements of the socialist life: the presence of the leader, the secular rituals, and most importantly country's greatest asset it's youth. In its later versions, the celebration became a mixture of socialist parades and Westernized media events with youth performing ostentatious dance routines, rock concerts, and multi media presentations. The hybridization of The Day of Youth consequently made it look like an entertainment show and less like a political propaganda.

"To think in terms of 'alternative modernities' is to admit that modernity is inescapable."[7] Dilip Parameshwar Gaonkar in the introduction to his book *Alternative Modernities* acknowledges the importance of the notion of modernity in the West, but also in the rest of the world. However, this acknowledgment, he argues, needs to encompass the particularity and the hybridity of this idea as it took root outside of the traditional Western historical, intellectual and geopolitical context. Such an alternative idea of modernity needs to be conceptualized by looking at the permeable border of the Western Modernity and its influence upon those who are not considered to be a central part of Western narratives and yet who were strongly influenced by them. Gaonkar calls this approach to understanding modernity *a cultural modernity*, a concept that is capable of acknowledging that each culture/society adopted and adapted to various modernist paradigms in different, and often quite unexpected ways. He posits that the unfolding of modernity takes place under specific circumstances and through a specific set of parameters.[8] Where the process of modernization (of creating industrialized, legal and economic modern structures,) needs to be separated from the modernist cultural development which often took specific forms – one of which can be seen in the example of Yugoslavian socialist/totalitarian culture.[9] Therefore, there can be no *one* singular modernity but rather modernities that are hybrid and quite idiosyncratic. Instead of accepting the overarching universalism or the *jargon* of modernity, the Yugoslavian case as with many others around the world, is seen as a particularity, or a localization of concepts that modernity has imposed. It is within such a set of precepts that I want to situate the specificity of Yugoslavian socialist modernity with its own cultural and socio-political matrix. While it can be argued that socialist Yugoslavia belonged to both Eastern (Eastern Block) and Western Europe, its relationships with both were complicated by the fact that it navigated this space of *in-between* by neither entirely accepting the Communist narratives of the Eastern Block nor the capitalist "alternatives" preferred by the West. Representational practices which were created and maintained through events like The Day of Youth are a part and parcel of this implicated negotiation of space and time between East and the West and between two economic and political polarities.

Lastly, the notion of alternative modernities may also provide a basis for constructing a response to the current surge of amnesiac histories which choose to create artificial breaks with the perceived "dark pasts" and conveniently circumvent the legacies which those pasts affirmated.[10] So history and memory are conflated or confused and the sites of memory, as Pierre Nora argues, become "swept away by history."[11] Contemporary late modern idioms tend to contextualize the recent past in polar opposites (as the radical difference between East and West,) or by representing modernity as one uniform movement. Because of such conceptions the communist past is swept aside as finished, or as ultimately evil and unimportant. However, what Yugoslavian modernity does show us is that the cultural, symbolic, or representational affiliations constructed in the time of communism have structured public consciousness and influenced the ways in which citizens have identified themselves. Ramifications of such structuring of public consciousness still persist even though in a transformed rather than overt way.

Wrestling with Representation

The power or capacity of the visual sign to convey meanings is only "virtual" or potential until those meanings have been realized, at the other end of the meaning chain, the cultural practices of looking and interpretation, the subjective capacities of the viewer to make images signify.[12]

Thus the truth of the lure of the spectator's gaze lies in the system of representation.[13]

In order to understand the significance of The Day of Youth as a symbolic representational mechanism that served to build national identity and extend president's body into the consciousness of the people, we need to locate and acknowledge that no visual representation can exist outside of cultural practice which gives that representation its meaning. There is no production of meaning or what Stuart Hall calls the existence of the *meaning-system* without participation of the viewer who gives that representation its proper place within the social order. Therefore, representation needs to be seen, first and foremost, as a *discursive* practice that ultimately functions within the larger socio/political realm through which our subjectivities are constructed in relationship to and through the work of normative structuring. Consequently, The Day of Youth functioned not only as a conscious reminder of state's and president's power but as a subconscious system of representation. Parades, floats, displays of bodies, parachute landings, whole stadium singing songs, youthful exuberance and powerful speeches were only some of the elements of the spectacle which overwhelmed spectators through the senses. All of these nurtured an environment in which an individual organically became a part of the socialist whole both through active participation (youth who carried the batons and participated in mass floats,) and by seeing everything as part of live and TV audiences.

Subconscious power of visual representation is embedded in its very functioning making spectacles capable of impacting viewers outside of the strictly discursive frame of reference. This we could call the *affective* work of visual representation. The affective stems from the immediate physical impact of the visual "even when its precise meaning remains, as it were, vague, suspended-numinous."[14] Lawrence Grossberg describes affect in terms of its possibility to create social connections. He posits that affect is *a-signifying* and varied in its forms and structures.[15] Affect may be described as *intensity* which forms a series of maps which navigate person's non-linguistic relationship to the world. More importantly affect is related to what Grossberg calls "the feeling of life" which means that affect is socially transmitted or translated so that we are capable of picking-up on it.[16] The Day of Youth as a public spectacle functioned both discursively and affectively. Apart from the obvious cultural and political meanings imbedded in youthful floats each participant who was part of the parades also affectively embodied the stories or ideologies played out. Unlike actors who play a part, these youths became the ideology through their bodies transforming The Day of Youth into a secular ritual. These ritual events point to the importance of signification in social spaces and speak to the impact of an affective life in the creation of relationships with ideological apparatuses. Consequently, when we all sat in front of our TV screens, stood on the street corners, or sat at the stadiums, we were all part of the affective functioning of the socialist system. We were all taken by the "feeling of life" and the identity it provided for us.

In his work on representation and representational practices, Louis Marin discusses public spectacles such as parades, military marches, and processions. He argues that all such events, secular or religious, are ritual in nature and operate through a "structure of repetition."[17] The element of repetition and sequencing of time, unfolding in specific order point to the "symbolic structure" which is organized in terms of liturgy and formal order.[18] Furthermore, Marin argues that these events operate as narrative embodiment of the system of values existing in a given community or society. What this means is that apart from the importance of representation in constituting and reinscribing meanings within the public realm, those who participate in such events (viewers and participants alike,) affectively reenact the narrative of the social order through their bodies just like the faithful who for example in Catholic processions reenact the stations of the cross and in so doing actually relive them. Such investments in the social require more than just intellectual acceptance of the act being performed, but need to include emotional as well as bodily identification on part of the participants. So for example a usual Day of Youth celebration at the stadium would have several thematic components each of which celebrated different achievements of youth in socialist Yugoslavia. Participants created enormous flowers, flags, words and machineries with their bodies. The body became a common property, a conductor of powerful ideologies and as Foucault argues the body became "the property of society, the object of collective and useful appropriation."[19]

Representational practices related to The Day of Youth may also be understood as both reliving the past and restructuring the present. This was an occasion when the youth were conscripted into the corpus of the nation. Numerous manifestations were structured around a specific sequence of events all pointing towards President Tito as the ultimate father figure. The affective nature of the father figure was inscribed in his body through his calculated gestures, texture of his voice and carefully chosen clothes.[20] Finally, the affect created through his body was then transmitted to the youth who were participating in singing and dancing for the president. The youth were in a way actively rebuilding the body of the president through their own bodies. Lastly, these visual devices and structures denote that signifying practices cannot exit without those who engage with them either through creating or participating.

Final celebrations for president Tito's birthday and The Day of Youth, Stadium JNA, Belgrade, Serbia, c. 1980s. The inscription SKOJ, shaped by the bodies of young gymnasts on the stadium, reads *Savez komunističke omladine Jugoslavije* (*Association of the Communist Youth of Yugoslavia*).

The Young Body/Old Body

> Yugoslavian youth is the pride of our peoples. From the end of the War, as during it, and until today, the youth has invested a lot of work so that our country could get out of the backwardness in which it was. And not only backwardness but also destruction brought upon on us by occupation forces... The nation, which has such youth, is truly fortunate (Tito in his speech to Yugoslavian Youth at the occasion of the 1979 Day of Youth.)

President Tito's emphasis on the importance of youth in the life of the nation stems from every nation's need to continue its social, political, cultural and, of course, national systems through progeny. Moreover, the body, especially a young body serves as a perfect metaphor for the nation in terms of physical fitness and aesthetic "appeal." When it comes to totalitarian systems such as the one in the former socialist Yugoslavia from 1945 to 1991, images and actual bodies of youth served as embodiment of a healthy, vibrant, and virile nation like the communist system itself. In her book *Photography and Propaganda* Milanka Todic writes that the "the photographs of mass parades and Tito's birthday celebrations … constitute the true allegory of communism."[21] She states that such visual representations were used to lead the gaze of the viewers towards bodies of youth perceived as ultimate sites of the new individual who has completely traversed the old bourgeois system and entered an age of socialist reconstruction.

The emphasis on the role of Yugoslavian youth in the country's "destiny" started relatively early. During World War Two in all of the republics of the former Yugoslavia, high school and university students played an important role in the anti-fascist movement. A large number of young people were also involved in many battles fought by *partisans* against German occupying forces. In the years following the war, Tito and those around him emphasized the importance of the role the Yugoslavian youth had played in the country's life. Many were involved in the voluntary youth brigades organized to rebuild the basic infrastructure and industry. President Tito's speeches and those given by the apparatchiks were filled with references to the importance of the youth movement and its impact on the country's economy, politics, and security. Another idea often emphasized was related to the catchall slogan "bratstvo i jedinstvo" or "brotherhood and unity." The role of youth was seen as crucial in terms of establishing good relations between different nationalities coexisting in Yugoslavia at the time. Yugoslavia's peculiar economic and political system as well as its relations with the West and the East created an idiosyncratic version of socialism that had to carefully manoeuvre in internal and external politics.

Yugoslavian socialist culture was negotiated through an intricate body politics that paired the symbol of the president (the father figure) with other symbols – workers, farmers, industry and development, and, of course, the youth. In 1957 President Tito renamed May 25 as The Day of Youth; this transfer enabled him to engage the potent symbol of youth and wed it to his own benevolent/paternal representations. The Day of Youth became a televised, highly embedded media event which brought Tito's image and the images of thousands of youths into the homes of every Yugoslavian citizen. It has been suggested that over the course of its forty year history there were some 20 000 relay batons carried across Yugoslavia.[22] Each year every republic would elect its own representative to carry the baton fashioned in numerous designs. People who carried it had to be deserving youths either through their public service work, and intellectual or athletic achievements. Photographs, news reports, books and TV shows reproduced the event for those unable to see it firsthand. However, other spectacles were created for live audiences across the nation and these included, for example, welcoming committees, where relays traveled from city to city and stopped in major centers. Historian Ivan Colovic locates two kinds of relay batons: primary ones and local batons.[23] Primary batons were carried through the whole country and finally presented to the president, while local batons were carried regionally and presented to local city officials.[24] People would line the streets to see the relay. Some cities organized concerts and other cultural events in honor of the relay (read: Tito). Every primary and many secondary schools had its "day of the Youth baton" events when the students together with teachers and administrators would celebrate the passing of the relay. The largest and most extravagant spectacle took place at the stadium in Belgrade (then the capital of Yugoslavia) where the relay baton concluded its journey and was personally turned over to Tito by a member of the Yugoslavian youth. Thus, The Day of Youth was not just one event in the capital, but it represented months of preparations which included carrying the baton across the country, mass celebrations in larger urban centers, and the culmination at the Yugoslav National Army Stadium in Belgrade. Ivan Colovic argues that the relay passage created a symbolic network through which all parts of Yugoslavia were joined.[25] This network constructed through the bodies of young people and interconnected across the nation, also symbolically recreated the president's body. While carrying the youth batons, citizens symbolically outlined an image of Tito, carved it into the land itself, and into the geography of each region. The landscape of the country became the landscape of Tito's body transforming the entire nation into his physical presence.

The images from the period tell us that The Day of Youth occasions were also the spectacles of the body. The potent corporeal presence of the leader was merged with the representations of youthful and strong bodies. This is what Ugo Vlaisavljevic calls the phenomenon of embodying the entire society in Tito or "in the figure of the leader."[26] Through translation of the leader's aging body into the bodies of young people Tito's symbolic transformation from a mere mortal to an immortal was complete. In his now classic study of the representation of King Louis XIV, Louis Marin suggests two important functions of royal representation. First, representation serves to substitute the physical presence of the king. He writes that "as the place of representation then, there is a thing or a person

Tito receiving his relay baton at the Stadium of JNA, Belgrade, Serbia, c. 1960s.

absent in time or space, and a substitution operates with a double of this other in its place."[27] Representation of the king serves to reassert his presence. The image of the president, the pomp associated with the Youth baton and the relay-related rites served to reposit Tito's power and presence even in his absence. According to Marin often the substitute, the representation which serves to reinstate leader's power, is more potent than the actual physical body. In Tito's case this observation holds greater currency because it is precisely through his *absent* presence, through the multiplication of his images and inscription of his body, and through young bodies creating mass floats, filling television screens, audio addresses and other symbolic representations, that his power was kept alive. When the baton was carried from republic to republic, and when it was welcomed by legions of young elementary and high schools students, Tito was present. In anticipation of the solemn event, each school would gather students in the schoolyard, dressed in their best clothes usually blue or black skirts/pants and a white shirt topped off by a red scarf and a blue cap. Before the Youth baton would enter the school yard, children would sing, dance, recite poems and recreate important historical events such as World War II battles. Although unaware of, and absent from these events, Tito was present through the reenactment of these commemorative staged spectacles in his honor.

The second function of representation according to Marin is to intensify the presence of the absent leader. He writes that "to 'represent,' then, is to show, to intensify, to duplicate a presence."[28] Representation extends the power through repeated regimes of duplication. During The Day of Youth activities in Yugoslavia, the presence of the leader was intensified, his power, both political and moral, heightened through the sheer multiplication of images. Among photographs from the period are numerous images of the leader emblazoned on flags, portraits, paintings and banners. Tito's bold, upright paradigmatic pose, the enormous scale of the images and their public presence in the central locations made his *absent presence* more pronounced. Thus, everyone acted as if in his presence with words and actions weighted carefully so that the president would be proud of his youth.

Photograph of the welcoming festivities for Tito's relay baton, c. 1980s.

The first effect of the representational framework and the first power of representation are the effect and power of presence instead absence and death; the second effect and second power are the effect of subject, that is, the power of institution, authorization, and legitimization as resulting from the functioning of the framework reflected upon itself. If, then, representation in general had indeed a double power – that of rendering anew and imaginarily present, not to say living, the absent and the dead and that of constituting its own legitimate and authorized subject by exhibiting qualifications, justifications, and titles of the present and living to being – in other words if representation reproduces not only de facto but also de jure the conditions that make its reproduction possible, then we understand that it is in the interests of power to appropriate for it for itself. Representation and power share the same nature.[29]

Finally, Marin argues that representation needs to enter into institutional relations to be fully realized. In other words, there needs to be a public and an institutional validation of representation of the king (leader) to attain legitimacy and consistency in the public realm. Accordingly, constitution of citizens' subjecthood has to be obtained not only by inserting representation into everyday culture, but via mechanisms of structural support found in legal, economic, and political organizations. By this I mean institutions which legitimate the president's status (parliament, courts, government institutions,) and those which create cultural and socio/political meanings (national television stations or national theater houses, or educational institutions.) A proliferation of the leader's representations would be virtually impossible without large apparatuses that reach great numbers of people. In Yugoslavia, such agencies of legitimation have always participated as the secondary network of meaning so that, for example, The Day of Youth manifestations were always closely followed in the media, publicized in hospitals, factories and schools with posters and announcements, and the national postal service issuing stamps with the image of the president and the Youth baton design for that year. Consequently, as Marin argues, the power and the ways in which it proliferates in society go hand in hand with the ways in which visual representation proliferates, one cannot go without the other (as we are often reminded in various recent global and local political races).

The First and Last Emperor

If Reagan stood on every pedestal presented, and draped himself in every flag in sight, the entire series of national icons would converge towards him. He would be catapulted out of their already elevated plane to an even higher one: he would be the substance of the substance of unity, the essence of the essence of subjectivity. He would be what made mother's milk wet. All he had to do was remain in perpetual motion, circulating from one hallowed site to another, not just arrogating to him their life-giving powers by raising them to a higher power.[30]

Tito's Yugoslavia is an excellent example of the symbiotic relationship between the leader and the people. Other communist countries had similar events such as Spartakiads, May 1st parades and October Revolution celebrations. The Day of Youth belongs to such mass events and represents "the" power spectacle in which all national symbols, Tito's body being the most important one, coalesced to form a representation of the state as active, youthful, strong, and prosperous. This utopian vision of the present and the future was furthered by the exuberance of mass exercises, mobile floats, parachute landings, electronic displays, and elaborate dance choreographies reenacted in the stadium with the leader in attendance. These curios and highly ideological displays of power and prowess were created as sites of remembrance of the past. The past was re-lived first through the participants and then through those who watched either at home or in attendance at the event. But it was primarily the youth who were remembering corporeally, by reenacting history which symbolically passed through their bodies as they created mass floats representing Tito's name, Yugoslavian flags, peace symbols, or Communist Party insignia Milanka Todic writes that "the mass spectacles of the body formed key cultural models of behavior according to which the whole apparatus of the new social community functioned."[31] Therefore, such mass spectacles may be understood as didactic models through which young people were educated about their past and more importantly were shown what the communist future holds for them. Again the young body was shaped, not only for remembrance of the past, but through the vision of what Yugoslavia could become, for creation of the new future. Tito's speeches during these events always carried a twofold message: one that reminded the participants and viewers of future past/future perfect struggles the country had endured, and of future hardships and successes. This didactic linking of the past and the future through young bodies was meant to represent the continuation of the communist revolution. In numerous books written about The Day of Youth the notion of continuing with what was accomplished in the past through struggles led by Tito was constantly stressed. Borisav Dzuvegovic, a sociologist writing about The Day of Youth in 1974 states:

> The Day of Youth is a day which needs to be constantly linked to struggles and successes, life and work goals, hopes and dreams of the young generations, as well as revolutionary spirit and activities inspired by the great revolutionary himself, signifying thusly the complete continuity of our revolution. (*author's translation*)[32]

Furthermore, a very interesting and seemingly paradoxical relationship was formed between the leader and the youth. In the course of his public appearances Tito always appeared both distant and very close. In photographs taken at various events, he is usually seen surrounded by people; however, there is always a space between his own body and the bodies of those around him. He is never in close contact with people; keeping his distance yet smiling, being friendly, yet always separate from the masses. Tito's presence was felt everywhere, there are still stories of friends of friends who have seen him, but in reality not many had close access to him. Maja Brkljacic argues that this close, yet distant relationship between Tito and the citizens of Yugoslavia recalls the traditional Christian relationship between believers and their patron saints.[33]

Thus, the deliberate and well-calculated space between Tito and the Yugoslavian people was meant to create a particular mode of representational address in which the president would be immortalized by being in an anachronical space. In such a space Tito's body did not exist in real time, it was present but was not in the same realm as the rest of the citizenry. In a way his physical presence was sanctified and transformed into an image. Louis Marin argues that "the king is only truly king, that is, monarch, in images."[34] Consequently, he can only "exist" as an iconic sign, even when he literally walks among his people. The body becomes detached from its physicality (becomes pure image, pure symbol,) and is able to enter different kinds of significations. When theorist Brian Massumi discusses representation of the former president Ronald Reagan, he argues that the presidential image creates the basis for national unity.[35] The image becomes the substance which multiplies its subsumed symbols such as body, family or flag. However, by subsuming them, it is also reproducing them into infinity of possible signifiers.[36] The president's body/image, unlike other elements in the multiplication of signifiers, wants to become the Signifier, the One, the Sap of the national unity, or the "wetness" of the nation/mother's milk, as Massumi argues.[37] The president's image becomes everything and nothing – capable of subsuming or entering any and all symbolizations, any and all spheres of life. In a way, it can be attached to everything and at the same time keep its separate nature. When analyzing the spectacle of The Day of Youth and President Tito's comportment and interaction with people, we can begin to understand how a body is no longer just a body but an ultimate presence which is revered as a religious icon. Thus, totalitarian, communist reality was unable to function without the divine presence, without the patron saint, or a transcendent father who is the ultimate benevolent eye watching over his people, present at all times. Yugoslavian youth was always in his presence, always supposed to behave as if he was watching them, always at their best. And as they carried the Youth baton (the president's body) they were also carrying the icon of the godfather.

Massumi also emphasizes the importance of the "body without image" in the proliferation, sanctification, and ubiquity of president's body/image. This notion is based on the idea of the "body without organs" in the work of Deleuze and Guattari.[38] The body without image is a state in which certain aspects of the body (vocal and visual according to Massumi) become detached from the flesh itself. These aspects, he argues, "take a life of their own, entering self-propagating apparatuses of social circulation that exceed the individual (orally transmitted memory, portraits, statues, written history, documentary film and video, archives, birthplace museums, coinage and stamps)."[39] The body looses a static, unified image. The image becomes capable of taking over many different guises and subsuming many different symbols. The physical body transcends its primary meaning and is capable of taking on new meanings. Such workings of the body are imbedded in, and carried by, social dynamics and apparatuses. Accordingly, the youth baton is a perfect example of the body without organs. Tito's body sanctified, mediated, and transformed into a pure image, is attached to the physical, phallic object which is then carried or given life to by young Spartan bodies. It flows in the intermediate space between live bodies and the symbolic phallus. Just like Reagan in the 1980's

ŠTAFETA MLADOSTI 1983.

Štafetu mladosti 1983. godine prvi je poneo mladi radnik MARIN MATEŠIĆ iz Zadra. Noseći štafetu duž cele zemlje, mladi Jugoslavije su manifestovali svoju ljubav odanost tekovinama revolucije i rešenost da čuvaju i naslave putem kojem nas je poveo Josip Broz Tito. Na završnoj manifestaciji proslave Dana mladosti, 25 maja, štafetu je predao MIODRAG MRDAK, pomorski oficir iz Bara.

Autor štafete: NEGOVAN NEMES

Photograph of a version of Tito's relay baton, designer: Negovan Nemes, wood 1983. (Photograph courtesy of Muzeji Hrvatskoga Zagorja.)

United States, Tito's representations were the wetness of mother's (nation's) milk. And it is precisely because of his ability to symbolically transfer his power onto others, to become everything and anything for the whole country that Tito's power became omnipresent. This could be qualified as an act of transubstantiation, or an act through which the image of a leader's body becomes his reality. [40] Massumi argues that the power of Reagan's image was in its continuous slippage, that is, in its continuous proliferation and multiplication. Similarly, President Tito's representation was so successful because it was in continuous (literal) movement and its grafting onto the bodies of the Yugoslavian youth.

The End of an Era

Even after Tito's death in 1980, The Day of Youth celebrations continued. They were held as if nothing had happened, as if the president was still alive. The relay baton was carried from hand to hand, from province to province to its final spectacle in Belgrade. The cultic power of Tito's representation persisted and remained unabated until 1987 when the very notion of The Day of Youth was questioned. Every year before the celebrations commenced, there was a nation-wide open competition for The Day of Youth poster. In 1987 the Slovenian avant-garde art collective NSK (Neue Sloweniche Kunst) submitted its proposal for the poster. From thousands of posters their design was accepted and announced the winner. Very shortly after the poster had been chosen and was published in the national press, it was discovered that the design was based on the painting *The Third Reich* (1936) by a German painter Richard Klein. Embarrassed officials quickly pulled the poster from public display. The irony was that government officials were attracted to the work that harkened back to the Nazi past, a past that in the collective consciousness of Yugoslavia stood for the ideology of archenemy given Yugoslavia's World War Two struggle against German occupation. This incident ignited the questioning of the celebrations of The Day of Youth and the kind of ideologies it espoused, ideologies of unquestioned collectivity, totalitarianism and oppression. What NSK ultimately wanted to bring to public attention were similarities between Nazi and communist regimes thus commenting on all oppressive regimes making them equally problematic. The fact that Yugoslav officials chose Nazi poster proved NSK's point and created an unprecedented, unintentional internal critique of the communist system. The 1987 scandal also brought to the surface the problematic and complex relationship between representations of power and socialist ideologies and marked the last year of The Day of Youth. Exactly forty years after the first relay baton was carried from Tito's birthplace in Kumrovec, Croatia, the event was discontinued. Five years later Yugoslavia will begin its cannibalization proving that it was the power of the leader, his symbolic and actual corporeal presence in everyday socialism that held the country together.

Notes

[1] Maja Brkljacic, "A Case of a Very Difficult Transition: The Ritual of the Funeral of Josip Broz Tito," *Limen: Journal For Theory and Practice of Liminal Phenomena,* no. 1 (2001), http://limen.mi2.hr/limen1-2001/maja_brkljacic.html.

[2] The history of The Day of Youth and the relay baton started very early. The first recorded baton was carried in 1945. The event was initiated by youth from Kragujevac (a region in Serbia, ex-Yugoslavia.) This was often recorded in the official communist history texts as a self-organizing movement to thank Tito for his work on the building of the Yugoslavian nation. Borisav Djuverovic, one of the official historians/sociologists of the baton, wrote a book on the history of the Youth baton in which he states that the youth of Yugoslavia planned to start with the event of the baton as early as 1944–45 while the country was still in war with Germany. However, according to him, the country was soon liberated and the baton was now freely passed through the country. Less than ten years later Tito himself has requested that the so-called Tito's Baton be renamed Youth baton and that the day of his birth be changed into The Day of Youth. In his address on the occasion of his birthday in 1957 he praised youth for their efforts and stated that his wish is that his birthday be the day, which would celebrate youth achievements in the war and their constant struggle for the good of the country.

[3] Amitai Etzioni, "Toward a Theory of Public Ritual," *Sociological Theory* Vol. 18, no. 1 (2000): 41.

[4] Amitai Etzioni, ibid., 2000, 41.

[5] Ugo Vlaisavljevic, "Titov Najveci Dar: Prazno Mjesto Moci," in *Vlas-TITO Iskustvo: Past and Present,* ed. Radonja Leposavic (Beograd: Samizdat B92, 2001), 81.

[6] Ugo Vlaisavljevic, ibid., 2001, 93.

[7] Dilip Parameshwar Gaonkar, "On Alternative Modernities," in *Alternative Modernities*, ed. Dilip Parameshwar Gaonkar (Durham & London: Duke University Press, 2001), 1.

[8] Here Gaonkar refers to Charles Taylor who in his text *Two Theories of Modernity* talks about two ways of characterizing modernization in a cultural sense. His argument stems from reading two discourses of modernity cultural and acultural. Acultural view of modernity reads modernity as a unified, monolithic "culture-neutral" process, while cultural discourse views modernity as a process of cultural developments, which are highly specific, localized, and which could be contrasted to other cultures of modernity including their predecessors (Charles Taylor, "Two Theories of Modernity," in *Alternative Modernities*, ed. Dilip Parameshwar Gaonkar (Durham & London: Duke University Press, 2001), 172–3.

[9] By Yugoslavian culture I refer to the multiple meaning making processes from popular forms of music and entertainment, to avant-garde cultural productions. However, here I also include "official" cultural products and projects sponsored by the state one of which of course is The Day of Youth. Such projects (including military marches, parades and general public holidays,) were always imbued with ideological constructs focusing on Tito and his role and importance in the socialist struggle, as well as the larger notion of the country as an entity, which needs to be constantly defended and kept alive. The usual language of such constructs always reminded citizenry of the history of their country, Tito's heroic role in organizing that history, and the future, which is ahead.

[10] The often reverberated idiom of "the dark communist past" was used especially in the early 1990's during the immediate post-communist era. Politicians, as well as, other public figures would initiate this idiom quite often in order to distinguish themselves from what was perceived as an evil period in the history of post-communist nations. Unlike other communist countries of Eastern Europe, in Yugoslavia this term became a political/ideological weapon that served to assert specific nationalistic discourses which were often brought up as a way of discerning between the seeming freedom which nationalism now provided and the totalitarian system that closed off any possibility of having national identity asserted. Unfortunately, this kind of approach created an amnesiac view of history through which the fifty years spent in communism were truly left in the dark without ever really coming to terms with the legacies that that period has left.

[11] Pierre Nora, "Between Memory and History: Les Lieux De Memoire," *Representations. Special Issue: Memory and Counter-Memory* no. 26 (1989): 8.

[12] Stuart Hall, "Introduction: Looking and Subjectivity," in *Visual Culture: The Reader*, ed. Jessica Evans and Stuart Hall (London, Thousand Oaks, New Delhi: SAGE Publications in association with Open University, 1999): 310.

[13] Louis Marin, *On Representation*, trans. Catherine Porter (Stanford: Stanford University Press, 2001), 15.

[14] Stuart Hall, ibid., 1999, 311.

[15] Lawrence Grossberg, *We Gotta Get Out of This Place: Popular Conservatism and Postmodern Culture* (London & New York: Routledge, 1993), 80.

[16] Lawrence Grossberg, ibid., 1993, 80.

[17] Louis Marin, ibid., 2001, 41.

[18] Louis Marin, ibid., 2001, 41.

[19] Michel Foucault, *Discipline and Punish: The Birth of Prison. 2nd Edition* (New York: Vintage Books, 1995), 109.

[20] One of the most intriguing and probably most interesting aspects of President Tito's life was his penchant for the so-called "good life". He was known for his good taste in clothes, and all the photographic documents of his life and work were carefully staged to show his taste and elegance. Indeed he was known as a "bon vivant" both during his presidency and after his death. Such a conscious usage of clothes and gestures to create an aura of authenticity and elegance proves that Tito understood very well what the impact of appearance has on political life.

[21] Milanka Todic, *Photography and Propaganda 1945–1958* (Banja Luka: JU Knjizevna zadruga, 2005), 51.

[22] Ivan Colovic, "On Models and Batons," in *VlasTITO Iskustvo: Past and Present*, ed. Radonja Leposavic, trans. Vladimir Brasanac (Beograd: Samizdat B92, 2005), 153.

[23] Ivan Colovic, ibid., 2005, 153.

[24] Ivan Colovic, ibid., 2005, 153.

[25] Ivan Colovic, ibid., 2005, 154.

[26] Ugo Vlaisavljevic, "Tito's Greatest Gift: The Vacant Seat of Power," in *VlasTITO Iskustvo: Past and Present*, ed. Radonja Leposavic, trans. Vladimir Brasanac (Beograd: Samizdat B92, 2005), 80.

[27] Louis Marin, *Portrait of the King* (Minneapolis: University of Minnesota Press, 1988), 5.

[28] Louis Marin, ibid., 1988, 5.

[29] Louis Marin, ibid., 1988, 6.

[30] Dean Kenneth and Brian Massumi, *First and Last Emperors: The Absolute State and the Body of the Despot* (Brooklyn, NY: Autonomedia, 1992), 93.

[31] Milanka Todic, ibid., 2005, 127.

[32] Borislav Dzuverovic, *25 Maj – Dan Mladosti* (Beograd: Popularna

Biblioteka, 1974), 7.

[33] Maja Brkljacic, ibid., 2001.

[34] Louis Marin, ibid., 1988, 8.

[35] Dean Kenneth and Brian Massumi, ibid., 1992, 90.

[36] Massumi argues that the unity always leaves excess that cannot be contained by it – or "remainder of the spirit." The remainder constantly seeks something else to absorb it. So out of the constant play between unity and its own excess, more and more signifiers are born and the space of the nation is overtaken by its own remainder.

[37] Because of the inherent play of the excess within the relationship of the signifiers and the unity, president's body is always found lacking, always found caught in-between, in a slippage. The spiraling process of unification through the body of the president is always-already caught in the game of lack and want. It is "trapped in a dialectic of immanence and transcendence that can have no synthesis" (Dean Kenneth and Brian Massumi, ibid., 1992, 95.) President's body trapped in this process becomes fragmented, divided and always in the process of disappearance. At the end, only an image is left, an image that is videotaped or digitalized, copied into an infinite number of copies and send off/ projected for the millions of other bodies which become its surrogates. Massumi furthers his argument of the unity and the presidential body by adding that unity always stands in addition to, or "alongside" the "multiplicity it unifies" (ibid., 101.) He states that because this unity cannot fully subsume all the elements it plays with, there has to be something else that can actually include everything – al of the elements, all of the signifiers. Such a mechanism, Massumi writes: "Subtending and surrounding the body and body image of the national unifier and the bodies and images they bring together, there is another kind of body that has no image – that can never have one because it is only ever in-between. There is a body without an image that inhabits the gaps" (ibid., 108.) The space of the body without an image is a void. Reagan's body became imageless in order to perform its role of that sap. His body became projected through the mass media; he became a non-human in order to be projected to the body of the state, to those anonymous millions of bodies of his citizens who absorbed the residues, excesses of his image, of the "national sap." Presidential body therefore, became infinitized and it still hovers through different apparatuses. The very fluidity of it guaranties its proper functioning.

[38] Body without organs is a term which Deleuze and Guattari use to describe the idea of any kind of organized structure. They argue that the social and non-social functions in and around an individual happen in terms of flows. The body without organs is the structure that organizes

and controls these flows. It has the ability to be everything and nothing to subsume all flows and because of that it can bring forth structures and direct flows. Under the term flow they understand any flow (words, urine, thoughts, blood etc.) The body of the leader or the body without an image wants to become this organizing structure through which all flows need to pass. As such it can become everything to everyone, become the element of national unity but at the same time a structure that controls it (Gilles Deleuze and Felix Guattari, *Anti-Oedipus: Capitalism and Schizophrenia* (Minneapolis: University of Minnesota Press, 1983), 40.)

[39] Dean Kenneth and Brian Massumi, ibid., 1992, 138.

[40] Louis Marin, ibid., 1988, 8.

3

Celebrating Yugoslavia
The Visual Representation of State Holidays

Danka Ninković Slavnić

Introduction

Mentioning Yugoslavia usually brings to mind memories, associations, and images among its contemporaries that are connected with state holidays. The latter were periods when the basic values of the country were propagated strongly and unambiguously. But how were highly abstract ideas and concepts, which are difficult to imagine (such as, worker self-management, brotherhood and unity, or socialism), visibly represented? Which themes and motifs were used to make the principles and ideology of Yugoslav society tangible and more familiar to ordinary people? How were state holidays, and thus the country, represented?

Some answers may emerge from the study of visual representations of two holidays in two major newspapers, *Delo* (Slovenia) and *Politika* (Serbia). These daily newspapers from two republics were selected to observe differences of media constructions of the holidays. Both had been established as major daily newspapers, and their editorial policies were in harmony with the republics' political mainstream. This analysis uses a constructionist approach to representation, which suggests that meaning is constructed by the social subjects, using representational systems – concepts and signs.

According to this approach, we must not confuse the *material* world, where things and people exist, and the *symbolic* practices and processes through which representation, meaning and language operate. Constructivists do not deny the existence of material world. However, it is not material world which conveys meaning: it is language system or whatever system we are using to represent our concepts. It is social actors who use the conceptual systems of their culture and the linguistic and other representational systems to construct meaning, to make the world meaningful and to communicate about that world meaningfully to others.[1]

Consequently, this approach suggests that without meaning in the object, in this case, Yugoslavia, the object may have different meanings to different people (for example, in different republics, or to different generations of people). Also, meaning is not fixed; it is changing, which is important for an explanation of changes in the representation during the period under investigation. Another important premise is the understanding of ideology as inseparably woven into every kind of representation. The concept of ideology used in the analysis is Antonio Gramsci's idea of hegemony:

> At base, hegemony is all about ideology. But it is ideology writ large: the idea of an all-encompassing dominant ideology whose scope extends throughout all social, cultural and economic spheres of society. The concept of hegemony is linked with the complex set of claims about what could be a coherent viewpoint on the world.[2]

People accept this point of view as common sense and natural, because a dominant group uses persuasion (not just brute force) to reach consent and projects as normal its own way of seeing the world. Hegemony is not gained forever, and other groups or classes may become potential agents of change.

> Unlike the fixed grip over society implied by "domination", "hegemony" is won in to-and-fro of negotiation between competing social, political and ideological forces through which power is contest, shifted or reformed. Representation is key site in such struggle, since the power of definition is major source of hegemony.[3]

Therefore, the mass media are places where values and norms are reinforced and where the dominant ideology is reproduced but also challenged. And this is accomplished through all kinds of messages. This analysis focuses on the ideological work in press photography, which is typically seen as inherently objective and truthful.

This belief has grown up with the medium and it is still routinely in play whenever we open a book or magazine or newspaper. The historian Beaumont Newhall put it most succinctly when he argued that "the photograph has special values as evidence or proof." We believe it because we believe our eyes.[4]

But visual reporting is neither neutral nor free from cultural and historical circumstances. Furthermore, it carries the marks of society, its dominant ideology, and its professional discourse. Although existential realism and the use of the camera (as an impartial machine) position photographs in a specific, privileged relation to reality, it is very important to remember that "photographs are never 'evidence' of history; they are themselves historical," according to John Tagg.[5]

This study addresses the visual representation of holidays as a site where dominant social values, changes in times of difficulties, and media policy reveal themselves. It will identify the elements of visual propaganda, topics and strategies found appropriate by these two newspapers for representing the country. It is through visual representations that social relations, values and ideas become visible. By choosing dominant subjects, photographs privilege some themes and influence our perception of community. The analysis spans four years between 1974 (the year of the last SFRY constitution) and 1990 (the last year of the state's existence) and consisted of a critical reading of three issues of each newspaper, before, during and after a holiday. This chronological approach exposes variations in the meaning of these holidays and their importance during the period of a weakening and collapsing federal state. It also depicts changes in the visual representation of these holidays as part of ideological shifts, showing which motifs were marginalized, disappeared, or replaced by others, while the state was headed toward its end.

State Holidays

State holidays in Yugoslavia were more than just a series of free days. They were strongly woven into the life of ordinary people and are not forgotten, even though the country collapsed more than 15 years ago. In a way, these holidays outlived their own country, they are still present in media reports and are recognized by different social groups in their own ways.[6] Like any state holidays, these ones, too, were the expression of social values and norms. Based on the celebration of an important historical event, they use memories about heroic deeds and the achievements of extraordinary people to reinforce a socialist ideology, retain tradition, and inspire the community. To reveal the media treatment of their underlying values, two holidays, The Day of Youth (on Tito's birthday) and The Day of the Republic, are included in this study.

Considering the number of participants and its effect on memory, The Day of Youth was the largest and most impressive holiday among all of them, with every third citizen participating in the celebration during its 43-year existence. "In the seventies, The Day of Youth was a spectacle connected with other numerous activities at schools, on streets and besides sacrament of the president, this holiday also had the spirit of a spring holiday."[7] The celebration of Tito's birthday (May 25) started in 1945, when young people and workers' representatives from different parts of Yugoslavia carried nine relay batons to Zagreb, where they handed them to President Tito. Twelve years later this holiday became The Day of Youth, as suggested by Tito: "Although this day is celebrated as my birthday, I think we should give it another name: the day of our youth, the day of sports, a young generation and its further intellectual and physical progress."[8] Several relay batons became a symbol of devotion to the leader and his deeds – *Štafeta mladosti* (the Youth Baton Relay). The first one set off from Kumrovec, Tito's birthplace and was started every year from another place, commemorating dates, places and events in the history of the Yugoslav people. The route of the Youth Baton Relay passes through numerous towns across Yugoslavia, symbolically connecting people of different nationalities from all republics and provinces. It was the most spectacular promotion of the idea of brotherhood and unity. Because of its participatory and joyful nature, the event had a great potential for socializing new generations in the spirit of the dominant ideology. Its success was measured by the fact that many young people chose this date to become members of the Communist Party. The culmination of The Day of Youth was the hand-over of the baton relay to Tito by a young boy or girl in a Belgrade stadium. The central celebration was a spectacle – *slet*, a rally of thousands of young people, who demonstrated their gymnastic dexterity. In a flawless performance, they created different symbols and motifs with their bodies. Their performance was broadcast nationwide to an audience larger than at the time of the Olympic Games. The celebrations of The Day of Youth went through two different phases – before and after Tito's death. The latter period was marked by doubts about the concept and its significance under new circumstances. Seven years after his death, The Day of Youth became the first Yugoslav holiday to cease to exist.

The Day of the Republic ranked at the top of the state holidays and marked the birth of the Federal Republic of Yugoslavia, considered to be the most important event for the future of the post-war country. AVNOJ (the Anti-Fascist Council for the Liberation of Yugoslavia) and Josip Broz Tito had decided on November 29, 1943, that postwar Yugoslavia would not be a kingdom, but a federation of six equal republics. The Day of the Republic was the commemorative celebration of their historical and political decision, honoring achievements of the partisans' fight, and glorifying the basic principle of Yugoslavia's economic and political system. The state used the occasion to reward individuals and collectives for their achievements. It was one of three two-day holidays (along with New Year and May Day) in Yugoslavia. At primary schools, first graders were inducted into the Pioneers. The ceremony, which included oaths, were organized in schools or public squares. Employees usually combined the holiday with weekends for short trips or visits of relatives in the country. The latter marked the event by preparing food for the winter, followed by a feast. While The Day of Youth was a spectacle for the whole country, the Day of the Republic took on an atmosphere of local, family rituals. How much this holiday was accepted by common people may be seen by the number of weddings on that day. During Yugoslavia's heydays that date was booked for months in advance across the country.[9] With the disintegration of

Yugoslavia, the holiday vanished sooner or later. In Slovenia it happened after independence and the passage of a new law regulating holidays in November 1991, while in Serbia it remained in effect until 2002.

Delo & Politika

Delo and *Politika* are daily newspapers with long traditions – *Politika* was the first daily newspaper in the Balkans (published since 1904) and *Delo* was established in 1959 by a merger of two newspapers, *Ljudska pravica* (The People's Right) and *Slovenski porocevalec* (The Slovenian Reporter). At first glance, they seem to be similar newspapers. Both were printed in the Berliner format with the written text their dominant component. During 1974 to 1990 *Delo* was transforming (as announced in the header) from *Glasilo socialistične zveze delovnega ljudstva Slovenije* (The Voice of Socialist Alliance of the Working People of Slovenia) to *Samostojen časnik za samostojno Slovenijo* (The Independent Newspaper for an Independent Slovenia). In the period of socialism the header included the well-known socialist slogan, *Proletarci vseh dežel, združite se* (Proletarians of the World, Unite!). During that phase of its history, red ink (emblematic for the communist ideology) was used on its front page to emphasize the importance of certain events. On those occasions, the regular blue logo was exchanged for a red one, and the main text on the front page was boxed in the same color, making it immediately obvious that certain events were considered special, important, and historic. For example, the Tenth Congress of the Communist Union of Yugoslavia, holiday issues, and supplements for the Day of the Republic Day used red ink this way.

Although *Delo* and *Politika* were similar types of daily newspapers, their front pages differed significantly. *Delo* featured a very diverse and difficult to scan front page with many short news items and reports (usually more than ten), and two or three photographs, often news photographs among them. On the other side, the *Politika* front page carried two or three main stories, and short news items at the bottom of the page. This layout suggested very strongly the main topics of the day. With just one photograph (across two of five columns) and overloaded with plain text, this kind of front page did not grab the reader's attention. Both newspapers used the same tactics to emphasize the importance of an event. Part of the front page was dedicated to it, and published photographs were increased in size (by a column) and numbers. State holidays were treated in this fashion until the mid-1980s.

An overall impression suggests that photojournalism in *Politika* lagged behind *Delo's* efforts. Photographs in *Politika* were ancillary to texts and usually part of a report. Photographic objects were mostly taken with a normal lens and from an eye-level. This approach to visual reporting tends to make photographers invisible. By concealing a person behind the camera, it suggests to readers that they are in the presence of objective, undistorted pictures of reality. Photography is treated as a testimony (based on the belief that the camera cannot lie), with the underlying assumption that photography is the result of technical performances of the camera, and not a deliberate visual statement by a photojournalist. Names of photographers (or photo agencies) were rarely published. It was more the exception than the rule. The masthead did not contain information on any sub-editor or photo editor. The choice of the word – *"snimio"* (recorded by) in front of photographer's name also indicates the prevailing attitude in *Politika* that a photograph is taken, not made. *Delo*, on the other hand, published the name of a photographer or agency (Reuters, UPI, Tanjug) and the masthead (except in 1974) named the editor of photography, Joco Žnidaršič. This may suggest that despite their subordination to text, photographs in *Delo* were recognized as inevitable participants in media representations and in the construction of reality.

Photographs in regular editions of *Delo* were slightly, but not significantly, better positioned than in *Politika*, but a clear distinction was made by supplements in *Delo* (*Sobotna priloga* and *Slavnostna priloga*). Their visual narratives were an independent form. Pictures and words were treated as two different, but equally important ways of communication for a modern individual. The selected photographs were based on more aesthetic criteria, had no strict connection to the text, and were sometimes juxtaposed to the printed word in ways, which showed the possibility for new metaphorical interpretations. The supplements were a kind of display case for the achievements of photographers. *Sedam dana* was *Politika's* color supplement (6 of its 12 pages were printed in

full color). This technical advantage was used to show the beauty
and power of color photography. It was the only place for regularly
published photo pages. The creative potential of this supplement
was limited to a choice of topics. Visual reporting in *Sedam dana* was
generally restricted to TV productions and occasionally to political
and social events of utmost importance.

Visual Representation in 1974

Celebration of The Day of Youth was the front-page topic in the
analyzed newspapers. Both published photographs of the same
moment – the delivery of the baton to Tito.

That precise moment was repeated in the Yugoslav press for
years and became a recognizable image and part of people's collective memory. The connection between this holiday and the federal
president, Tito, is obvious at first sight – his pictures dominate the
visual coverage.

All photographs of the central celebration, published in *Delo*, included Tito. He was the one for whom the Relay baton was meant,
he received greetings, and even the picture of *slet* featured him in

On the photograph, published in *Delo*, a young worker is delivering the
baton to Tito at the celebration of The Day of Youth. The photo is titled,
Slovesen trenutek (*A solemn moment*).

the foreground, watching the performance (Tanjug). These visual clues, and especially the last one, indicate that the mass choreography was designed for his eyes. He was the main spectator, and the central celebration is meant to be a message for him.

Politika displays two photographs of Tito directly related to the holiday. He is, however, as the leading Yugoslav politician, present in visual reports about other events, and it is difficult to distinct between the holiday representation and other images of him. Numerous picture of Tito (with foreign politicians; when he was named president for life; or in the context of the Tenth Congress of the Communist Party) are evident signs that political life in the country was closely associated with one person. Not mere evidence of an existing concentration of power in one person, photographs were part of a hegemonic interpretation of event as a "normal" and "natural consequence" of his deeds and character. Beside Tito, however, ordinary people had a prominent place on the pages of *Politika*. The baton passed through hundreds of hands of relay runners and visited many places in the country. Citizens who gathered to see and welcome it are pictured in photographs from Obrenovac, Belgrade and on a color photo page from Piran (D. Urosević in *Sedam dana*). They are repetitive images: a proud young carrier showered with warm greetings from citizens on streets or squares. The happening is represented as a participatory event, strongly connected with the life of a community, and supported and produced by that community. Pictures of approval are a well-known motif in different kinds of political propaganda. They show the legitimacy of an idea. Here these pictures are used to visually construct consensus (the audience as "everybody") and reinforce beliefs in the dominant value, embodied in state symbols and the *"štafeta"*. The choice of people, whose pictures are possibly to be seen on the pages of newspapers, reveals the approach of the media to a wider social environment. "It is likely that the people in the photograph will have been chosen for their – in Barthes's expression – 'canonic generality'; that is to say, each individual represents his or her own 'type,' each individual stands for a class of individuals."[10]

The individual standing for a young socialist worker (in both newspapers) was a man chosen to hand over the Relay baton to Tito, Vojko Mahnič. He represents the type of a hard worker in a factory, a member of the Communist Party, active in the local community, willing to learn more, who started from scratch, but became appreciated at work and respected by his colleagues. His pictures were published in prominent places, usually reserved for famous people, like in the *Portret tedna* section (the weekly portrait section in *Delo*) and on the front page of the color supplement (in *Politika*). *Politika* was motivated to give publicity to individuals like him as "the best young communist worker." They are identified by headshots or pictures in their work environment, accompanied by texts, which describe their personal and professional values. These adolescents are shown as successful and as a good example for their generation.

> More then any other textual system, the photograph presents itself as "an offer you can't refuse". The characteristics of the photographic apparatus position the subject in such a way that the object photographed serves to conceal the textuality of the photograph itself – substituting passive receptivity for active (critical) reading.[11]

The fact that individuals, whose pictures are seen in newspapers, represent social ideas and values (in this case the values of the working class and socialist society) may go unnoticed.

Delo and *Politika* published three-day editions for the Day of the Republic. A significant difference between them was *Delo's Slavnostna Priloga,* while the rest of the issues focused on similar subjects and treated them alike. Front-page reports about the holiday included a visual coverage of Tito's activities. He was shown at the opening of a memorial center in his birthplace, Kumrovec. *Delo* also featured him laying the cornerstone of a nuclear plant in Krško (photographer, Joco Žnidaršič). The nuclear plant had been labeled as a project of extreme significance, which was underscored by the choice of the individual who symbolically laid its foundation. These pictures assumed people's confidence in Tito. By showing him (the man who also laid foundation for the country), readers were assured of the importance of this new object, the first of its kind in the country. The construction of new buildings was proof of economic and overall progress and operated as its metaphor.

The consequence of a decentralized media system meant that each newspaper reported about any achievements in its own republic, with the exception of those accomplishments considered being the most important ones. Pictures of new objects were accompanied in *Politika* by photographs of existing companies, which achieved good results. One example of a successful factory was chosen from each republic to convince readers that all republics were economically strong.

Different awards and medals were presented for the Day of the Republic. Therefore, both newspapers used headshots of winners of the AVNOJ award (the most important one, given for the contribution to the development of society) in an effort to present these individuals to the public. A group of individuals who did not receive any formal recognition was also presented in the journalistic discourse of *Politika* as ordinary people with an extraordinary devotion to their country, which made them worthy of being subjects of a report. Visual messages about the holiday were omnipresent. They also found their place in advertising sections, which indicates the strong connection between the official ideology and economics. Newspaper advertising during the socialist period was mostly for domestic companies. If it had any visual element in its composition it was either a drawing or a photograph of products (e.g., Gorenje refrigerators, Zastava cars, RIZ televisions, book covers from large publishers). Usually, individuals were not depicted and any kind of context was omitted. In the holiday issue *Delo* had two pages of advertisements specially designed for the occasion. A picture of a partisan monument and the message, *29 November Dan republike,* occupied the center of the page, surrounded by advertisements of Slovenian enterprises. *Politika* also featured appropriate holiday advertisements. They were mainly congratulatory messages in an already existing layout. Beobanka, however, introduced an especially designed advertisement; the numeral 29 was printed in the colors of the flag with the red star in the middle.

These examples are curiosities, because they merge political propaganda with commercial advertising. They address people as citizens in the first place. Instead of promoting products, they declare loyalty to the socialist system of Yugoslavia.

A picture, published in *Politika*, is an example how Beobanka's (Beogradska banka) advertisement appropriated the national holiday, 29 November.

Official symbols were accompanied by some less formal, but equally familiar ones: the Yugoslav spirit of brotherhood and unity was represented in both newspapers by a group dressed in the folk costumes of different nations; the color photograph of the Federal Parliament building as a symbol of the federal state (surrounded by fireworks, which added a festive atmosphere to the image) was published in *Sedam dana* (photographer, Dobrivoje Urošević). "Every photographic image is a sign, above all, of someone's investment in the sending of a message. Every photographic message is characterized by a tendentious rhetoric," Allan Sekula points out.[12] These photographs are visual propaganda, based on well-known symbols, messages about success, and people's loyalty to values of a socialistic Yugoslavia.

Delo's supplement, *Slavnostna Priloga*, stands out from the rest of the newspapers. It has a specific layout and a vertical panorama photograph is used across the page. Their connection with any written accounts is remote (except interviews, of course). Free from the daily routine, photographs are used to offer another, different look at subjects. They are creative expressions with a strong interest in composition and rhythm (photographers include Joco Žnidaršič, Tihomir Pinter, Egon Kase, Janez Zrnec, Leon Dolinšek, Milan

Orozen Adamič and Sveto Bušič). Although recognizable motifs are workers, the industrial or natural environment, or sports, these photographs exceed the boundaries of a genre. Contrary to the rest of the analyzed photographs, where faces and figures dominate the composition, here people are shown as small figures in an industrial environment. They are not the main actors, but part of an atmosphere. More then just visual quotations of a motif, these de-contextualized pictures provide opportunities for different feelings and associations.

"The text *directs* the reader through the signifieds of the image, causing him to avoid some and reactive others; by means of an often subtle *dispatching*, it remote-controls him towards a meaning chosen in advance."[13] Without captions, as Barthes said, to "anchor" photographs, their meaning is ambiguous. A reader knows nothing about the intentions of the photographer (when, where or why the picture was made). A worker in the background may be associated with an ordinary person relied on for the whole production (which makes him/her important), or an unimportant individual, insignificant in the totality of the work process. Thus, it is possible to read the same pictures in many ways. "We saw that the code of connotation was in all likelihood neither 'natural' nor 'artificial' but historical, or, if it be preferred, 'cultural'."[14] The photographs in the *Delo* supplement call for interpretation. A viewer is active and the photographs do not impose the obvious or preferred meaning, they do not prove or declare anything. They are just a starting point for a chain of associations and connotations.

1980 – Holidays after Tito's Death

Tito died in 1980 at the beginning of May, and the event marked The Day of Youth editions. All front pages in the study contain both, visual and verbal reports about the holiday. *Delo* kept its traditional layout, whereas the holiday is the only topic on *Politika's* front pages. The visual representation intends to appeal strongly to emotions, but while *Delo* emphasizes the sorrow caused by Tito's death, *Politika* is overloaded with messages of love and devotion. Also, the amount of published photographs is significantly different in both newspapers. To remind readers of Tito and *"štafeta,"* *Delo* used 10 and *Politika* 53 images.[15]

Delo shows a line of people grieving in front of Tito's memorial center in each of the analyzed issues, twice on the front page (photographer, Dragan Arrigler). Readers witness on these pictures people's grief as a collective emotional reaction. The absence of close-ups prevents this message from becoming too personal. As a result, it suggests to a reader to understand the loss as the general feeling of society and not of any particular person on the photograph. *Politika* provided its readers with significantly stronger visual propaganda about Tito. It used photographs not to express the actual atmosphere in the county, but to construct and reinforce memories about Tito. Although the May 25 issue was not marked as a special edition, its content had significantly changed, the first 13 pages were dedicated to Tito and The Day of Youth. The imagery as well as the published stories convey favorable, pleasant memories of Tito. They glorify and depict him as a father figure, surrounded by happy children and young people, as documented by archival photographs on the front page.

The photograph from *Politika* presents Tito surrounded by young people.

The composition reminds the reader of photographs in a family album, e.g., classmates with a teacher, old people with their off-spring, or periodical gathering of a large family. Only here the fam-ily is too numerous to be placed in a photographic frame. Thus, faces on both sides are cropped leaving it to the imagination of the reader to speculate about how many of people remain outside the frame. Some photographed subjects glance to the side, indicating that someone else is there. It is easy to think of this group as having an indefinite number of members, leaving readers with the option to imagine themselves as a part of it. Belonging to this group was very important, as some (at the left) climbed up on objects (chairs?) to be included. They are all smiling in an atmosphere of joy and excitement, sharing their love and devotion to the leader, just as a large title suggests, *"Mladost s Titom u srcu"* (Youths with Tito in their hearts). Archival photographs are used to construct a vi-sual narrative about the unbreakable connection between Tito and young people. He is pictured dancing with young in *"kozaračko kolo,"* talking and laughing with pioneers, posing for photos with rally participants, visiting brigadiers building a highway. He is a hero and they are his followers.

Another type of pictures also has an important role in *Politika's* visual representation of this holiday. These are pictures of Tito used as an image within the image. His portrait, as part of photographs, is juxtaposed with young people visiting the memorial center or dancing in stadiums. Photographs of youths in front of his portrait, or with his face on their T-shirts, are a visual promise that they will follow in his footsteps; they are expressions of their love and devo-tion.

The complete visual representation in *Politika* disregarded his death (which would bring out his human nature) and constructed him as a symbol, an iconic figure, and as the person who created Yugoslavia and provided a good life and a promising future for the new generations. Consequently, the main visual message to read-ers of *Politika* is that Tito is present and immortal. Printed state-ments (present in many titles), that although he is not among us, he is in our hearts and that his deeds are everlasting, have numerous pictorial equivalents. Among others, participants forming a heart in front of his large picture in Šabac (photographer, Ivan Nikolić) or a picture of football players holding a sign before the beginning of the final match, *"Tito će večno živeti u nama"* (Tito will live within us forever, photographer, Z. Grujić). A dominant impression about young people is that they are following in Tito's footsteps and are devoted to the ideas of a socialist Yugoslavia. All photographs in *Politika* fit this description. In *Delo* some do not, like the cover photograph of *Sobotna priloga* (photographer, Miško Kranjec), which can only be understood in relation to others, it is meaningless without the wider context.

> The intelligibility of the photograph is no single thing; photographs are *texts* inscribed in terms of what we may call "photographic discourse", but this discourse, like any other, engages discourses beyond itself, the "photographic text", like any other, is the site of a complex "intertextuality", an overlapping series of previous texts "taken for granted" at a particular cultural and historical conjuncture.[16]

This photograph, contrary to the dominant pictures of young people, shows a couple (neither a group nor an exceptional individual), in a banal everyday activity – driving around and eating (not a socially significant activity), during their leisure time (not at work). They seem unaware of being objects of the photographer's interest and show no intention to send a message and deliberately represent themselves. They are not an example of young hard-working socialists. Moreover, signifiers, which are part of this visual syntagma, like jeans, a sandwich, and a motorbike, connote a western life style. This picture is an exception from the hegemonistic representation of young in the holiday's issues.

On the first Day of the Republic after Tito died, the newspapers were united in their effort to reassure readers that nothing had changed. On the cover of *Politika* the president of the federation announced, as restated in the title of his interview, that Tito's deeds are guidelines for further actions. *Delo* depicted a distinctive festive atmosphere at that time of the year with familiar motifs, street crowds and the induction of new members in the pioneer organization (photographers, Dragan Arrigler, Janez Pukšić). New factories and successful workers were still a central part of

Photographs published in *Delo* are assembled as a visual narrative of Yugoslavia , a country of common, hard-working people.

the visual narratives in both newspapers. To remind readers about Tito's thoughts, *Slavnostna priloga* (*Delo's* supplement) reprinted on its front page the part of his speech, which stressed the strength of Yugoslavia (in the working class, the policy of independence, and self-managed socialism). What is specific for this supplement is its visual narrative about Yugoslavia, consisting of 23 photographs from different parts of the country. They appear in a row at the top of pages, like frames of a film.

This layout suggests their importance (the sections is reserved for headlines and photographs) and links them with each other more then with the text below. The only inscriptions are the place names where they were taken and the names of the photojournalists (Miško Kranjec, Marjan Zaplatil, Janez Pukšič, Janez Zrnec, Dragan Arrigler, Bogo Čerin). This visual representation includes motifs from each republic and province. The most frequently depicted scenes are from the everyday life of workers and farmers, but there are also activities in streets, parks, by the river, at a bistro, in shop, or in a classroom. There are no well-known symbols, buildings or places. Without the name of a location it would be difficult to tell where the photographs were taken. Only small but significant details (like a Cyrillic inscription) provide a clue for some of them. These photographs tended to represent ordinary people in everyday situations. The visual narrative defines, in its own way, Yugoslavia as a country of common people, their jobs, and everyday life, and repeats a hegemonic message, which grounds the representation of socialism in the fact that the power of society lies in ordinary workers.

Another, yet less noticeable but very interesting visual narrative emerged from cartoons. They are visual comments mostly about the economic situation; they spotlight its main weaknesses and problems like inflation, uncoordinated regional politics, export deficits, and the national debt (artists, Milan Maver, Nikolaj Pirnat, Marij Pregelj, France Uršič, Marjan Amalietti, Aleksandar Dimitrijević, Branko Stefanović, Bine Rogelj, Dragan Lazić, Adi Mulabegović). While photographs show the everyday life in a country, where workers and farmers are the dominant production force, cartoons reveal more about the economic achievements of their production.

1987 – Different Approaches in *Delo* and *Politika*

In 1987 the central celebration of The Day of Youth was questioned in Slovenia: is it not too expensive for a country in a deep economic crisis? Does it have any purpose under changed circumstances? Opinion were openly expressed that this grandiose spectacle was obsolete and old-fashioned. These ideas were absent from the front pages, however. Both, *Delo* and *Politika*, still treated the holiday as an important subject. But while they published The Day of Youth photographs on their respective front pages, their content was more revealing.

A selection of scenes from *"slet"* indicates different editorial viewpoints. *Politika* readers see the red star formed by 5,500 people with Tito's portrait in the background. This kind of composition is very similar to one in previous years. The mass of participants arranged in the shape of well-known symbols, like the flag (in *Politika*) or the crest (in *Delo*) in 1980. Although title of the celebration, "Turn on the Light" pointed to problems, the front-page composition of *Politika* conveys a message about continuity. *Delo* published a more ideologically neutral visual message of participants holding hands (photographer, Tanjug). The caption explains that young people from all republics and provinces performed together. The chosen viewpoint (eye level, oblique angle) does not reveal any information about the mass character of the spectacle. None of the old, traditional signifiers are included in the frame. While *Delo* contains clues that this could be the last Youth Baton Relay, *Politika* readers get impression that the celebration will continue despite problems.

Politika's visual narrative, with the central celebration as dominant subjects, does not hint at impending changes. The newspaper shows the Youth Baton Relay at a rock concert to symbolically connect traditional values and modern trends as equally important aspects of young peoples' lives. Details from *"slet"* are small narratives about the joy of youngsters, the gracefulness of the performance, the excitement and happiness on the faces of majorettes, the discipline of participating soldiers (photographer, Emil Vaš). *Politika's* reporting kept readers under the impression that fundamental social values are not brought into question. The different approaches suggest that the media struggled to define the meaning of reality, which is constantly produced and transformed. The consensus between republics no longer existed, and the meaning of Yugoslavia had to be negotiated and reinvented with each republic (and newspaper) searching for its own definition and position.

> Within this framework, ideologies are not simply imposed by governments, business interests or the media as their agents – although this possibility always remains as institutional option through mechanisms of direct control such as censorship. Rather, media forms and representations constitute major sites for conflict and negotiation, a central goal of which is the definition of what is to be taken as "real", and the struggle to name and win support for certain kinds of cultural value and identity over others. "Realism", then, is a crucial value claimed by different parties to the contest.[17]

Indeed, Yugoslavia's reality was differently depicted by these two newspapers. Although Tito had been dead for seven years, *Politika* used the feuilleton section to explain his relationship with three powerful politicians, Churchill, Roosevelt and Stalin, to reinforce the impression of his historic role. On those photographs Tito looks like a monument. The low angle of the camera, his pose, and his serious facial expression stress his significance. The feature recalls the glorious past and shows Tito as the authority, whose actions and ideas should be treated as guidelines. *Politika* applied the same tactics for the Republic Day issues. It turned to the past when an economic crisis made a visual narrative about success inappropriate. Pictures of actors in the role of Tito in a TV drama and serial dominate the pages of *Sedam Dana*. This supplement has a double function, as a television guide and, at the same time, as a means to help (re)construct history. With its choice of historical themes and pictures, *Politika* tries to shape people's views of the past. While in 1987 readers were faced with visual reminders of Tito, the history of the Communist Party and partisan resistance in World War II, only topics from an earlier Serbian history were included in 1990.

Delo, on the other hand, remained focused on the present with no references to the past or to Tito. The layout is traditional and contains images of the usual holiday activities (photographers, Igor Modič, Aleš Černivec, Zoran Vogrinčič). A photograph of new production facilities in Iskra, together with a text about numerous new objects, was used as evidence of Slovenia's economic prosperity and it's keeping up with technological trends. A picture of a successful company shows that Slovenia's industry was efficient despite the crisis in Yugoslavia. This story of economic success is in contrast with reports (published on the same page) about federal state intervention being an obstacle to economy growth. Slovenia's approach to the economy was shown as being different and more rational than the federal one.

The visual representation of the Day of the Republic in *Politika* changed significantly; no pages were dedicated to the holiday, there were no pictures of any new subjects and no accounts of extraordinary workers. This shift from being a pillar of the socialist society to an almost invisible force reveals the lost of power and influence of the working class. The old construct of a powerful socialist country was not sufficient, although the new one was not in sight. *"Priloga ob dnevu republike,"* in difference to previous years, when workers were the main topic, now offered a visual narrative about politicians. Their facial expressions and gestures play the main role in these photographs. The specificity of this photographic narrative lies in its captions. Contrary to an earlier practice when supplements had no texts to guide the interpretation of readers, captions in juxtaposition to pictures offer a third, frequently ironic and witty meaning. The choice of politicians and comments were tightly connected to the actual economic and political situation. An exception is a picture used to announce the supplement. It shows a group of people looking at the sky. The composition from above only shows people but not the object of their gaze. They are in the position of observers (the camera angle stresses their passive position), expecting something (from above). A similar photograph is used on the first page of the supplement, but this time there is one individual, a veteran, with medals on his lapel looking beyond the frame with his hand shielding his eyes to see better (photographer, Joco Žnidaršič). Although these photographs were taken in another context and with a different intent, here they are open to a variety of interpretations. Readers are in the position of looking at people who look at something they cannot see, asking themselves: what are they looking at, what is so important but cannot be caught by the camera? It may suggest that their gaze is directed at the future, which remains beyond the reach of photography, which is always about the past. These photographs raise a question about what to expect, and this question implies uncertainties.

The divergence between the two newspapers in their approach to the subject emerges in the issues of this year. While *Delo's* readers faced the uncertainty of a future Yugoslavia and The Day of Youth, *Politika* ignored problems and offered an escape into narratives about the past.

1990 – The Last Year in the Life of Yugoslavia

The agenda setting of *Politika* changed and The Day of Youth is no longer newsworthy. Other topics have priorities and the holiday, as well as youth, in general, is marginalized. The only trace left is a report about the meeting between a politician, Borisav Jović, and a delegation of the Socialist Youth (Tanjug). On The Day of Youth the last congress of the Alliance of the Socialist Youth of Yugoslavia was held in Ljubljana. The alliance was dismissed; it was the first federal sociopolitical organization that ceased to exist. While the photograph on the front page of *Delo* showed an informal talk from the congress, a nearby cartoon is more revealing, conveying a message about its end. Two gravediggers are lowering a coffin with the Yugoslav crest on it.

A cartoon from *Delo*, entitled *Pokop iluzij* (*Burial of illusions*), symbolically shows the end of Yugoslavia.

This visual message does not only convey the end of the Youth organization, but more generally the end of the federal state. The crest, whose central part was a fire consisting of six smaller flames, turns into smoke, suggesting that the symbolic unity of different republic ceases to exist. Ribbons on the sides carry the names of events, which signify the beginning of an end (the 13th Congress of the Youth and the 14th Congress of the Communist Party). The title of the cartoon, "Pokop iluzij" (Burial of Illusions; artist, Franco Juri), takes the reader to a new ideological interpretation of Yugoslavia as a deception, which was not what it seemed. In *Delo* the meaning of Yugoslavia is clearly redefined; it is an illusion, which has come to an end, as stated by the cartoon.

The Day of the Republic in 1990 was at the time of the first multiparty elections in Serbia. The question of the future of the federation could no longer be ignored and it was mentioned in both newspapers, but they sent opposing visual messages to their readers. In *Politika*, a comment about the future of the federation appeared in the form of a cartoon showing the flames of the crest turning into fire with firemen trying to extinguish them (artist, Mića Miloradović). *Politika* used the same state symbol as Delo did earlier for The Day of Youth, only here the flame was turning into danger, e.g., fire, and was not disappearing in smoke. While the *Delo* cartoon stated that Yugoslavia was dead, *Politika* showed it in danger. The message was polysemic. Will the firemen succeed? Are they trying to prevent a disaster or to preserve Yugoslavia (perhaps inseparable moves)? And whom do the firemen represent? In the dominant discourse of *Politika* the comment may be seen as a warning that some republics are putting Yugoslavia in great danger, while federal and Serbian politicians (firemen) are trying to save it. But it can also be understood as pointing to a situation, which is potentially destructive but not beyond repair before it turns into a disaster (fire). This visual representation reflects the dominant opinion among the political elites in the Yugoslav republics. While *Politika* showed the disintegration of Yugoslavia as a great danger, for *Delo* it is a trouble-free political act.

An awareness that a gathering of the members of the federal presidency could be of historic importance resulted in a front-page photograph by *Delo* (photographer, Tanjug). Its title, "the last toast to the federation" implied a civilized farewell and that a disintegration of Yugoslavia was a done deal. This representation left the impression that the future of the federation was a question of a political agreement, which put the issue on the safe ground of political rules and procedures. Pictures showing politicians from different republics together assured readers that officials were willing to talk, there were still good relations among them and problems could be resolved by political means. It convinced a reader that there was no need to be afraid and that a breakup would be painless. This photograph, or any similar one containing any kind of reassuring message, was not published in *Politika*.

Conclusions

The visual representation of the holidays was coherent with the dominant ideology of socialist Yugoslavia. Photographs with its privileged relation to reality were used to show clearly that Yugoslavia was a good, just, harmonic, and happy society. Smiling faces, satisfied workers, young people, proud to continue in their ancestors' footsteps, and pictures of Tito portrayed success. This kind of representation sent a message to readers: we are a great country and there are no doubts that we are doing well. Published pictures, as well as the holidays themselves, were an integrative force. They took part in creating common memories and a feeling of unity among nationally, economically, and religiously diverse parts of the country.

In the holiday issues of the newspapers, Yugoslavia was represented through its people. Socialism was impersonated through a worker and brotherhood and unity through faces and figures of young people with different backgrounds, participating in the celebration of The Day of Youth. The whole country, its history, ideology, values, and achievements, is represented as tightly connected to one man, Josip Broz Tito. Yugoslavia was represented as socialism with a future (thanks to the achievements of the past). This approach left numerous groups of people out of the media constructed country. Emphasizing hard labor led to women being scarcely represented. They were shown as workers in the textile industry, but other professions dominated by woman (as teachers, nurses, sales-persons) are absent. Individuals with any kind of special need, problems, or a deviation from the norm were excluded. There was nothing to cast a shadow on the strong and happy society. Although the country was a geographical entity, the visual representation of Yugoslavia was not tied to its physical territory. There are no landscapes, well-known geographical locations, pictures of towns, different architectural styles, or maps. Only new factories, resulting from the efforts of the working class and the representations of progress and economic growth can be seen. The country was only represented as an ideological construction inhabited by (chosen) people.

Even though the country was burdened with different problems and by a deep economic crisis, its ideological foundations remained unshaken in the holiday representations until 1987, when manual workers, once the main actors on the pages of the holiday editions, vanished. The atmosphere of participating common people, especially strong in *Politika*, was replaced by pictures of formal and serious events. While *Delo* was focused on current affairs and a time to come, *Politika* used the holidays for returning to the past and collective memories about the successful leader, glorious moments, and better times. Its representation indicated an overall situation in Serbia, without a clear vision of the future, it was turning towards the past. At the beginning of the period examined in this study, state symbols were used to provoke identification with the community. A flag, a crest, a red star, but also *"kolo"* for unity, *"štafeta"* for devotion to the leader, with their established and well-known meanings, were used to depict Yugoslavia. In 1990 symbols offered a way to express the erosion of a common symbolic field. The crest with its flames, each one for one republic, was especially appropriate for cartoons, in which these flames became smoke or fire. This visual comments points to a painless disappearance of Yugoslavia or to an uncontrolled disaster.

The comparison of two different daily newspapers with similar profiles shows that *Politika* (Serbia) carried more emphasized and obvious visual propaganda of the values of the federal state. Some themes were frequently present in *Politika's* visual representation, but rarely if ever depicted in *Delo*. For example, pictures of ordinary workers as role models, mass approvals in the context of The Day of Youth, or an overemphasized expression of devotion to Tito. The choice of subject and composition, made an ideological photographic message in this newspaper straight and clear. By repeating the same motifs, *Politika* stresses an already obvious meaning. The possibility of polygamy of the photographic expression is not used. Repeated use of eye-level frontal shots creates a habit of looking from just one angle, without raising a question about how things would appear from another perspective.

The way of looking at things (and showing them to the public/ audience) indicates a way of thinking. A visual representation, which is narrowed to just one perspective, becomes a hegemonic gaze, which makes the depicted world seem natural. The visual construction of socialist Yugoslavia is an example. Focused on idealized normality, it omits to depict problems, doubts, or weaknesses. There was no suffering, unhappiness, even ugliness on these pages. The images were so beautiful, how could anyone believe in them? Maybe, because they trusted their eyes, or because they were looking for what they wanted to see? Power to arouse emotions made memories and become evidence at the same time making visual messages important for attempts to understand any period of history. Seeing is not divorced from the rest of consciousness. Therefore it is important to gain another perspective. Creative visual expressions raise awareness of media constructions of reality and provoke readers to think about their perception of the world. A changing viewpoint renders a different image in the frame and introduces the possibility that our picture of the world is just one among many.

Notes

[1] Stuart Hall, "The Work of Representation," in *Representation: Culture Representation and Signifying Practice*, ed. Stuart Hall (London: Sage, 1997), 25.

[2] Robert Bocock, *Hegemony* (London: Ellis Horwood Limited, 1986), 7.

[3] Christine Gledhill, "Genre and Gender: The Case of Soap Opera," in *Representation: Culture Representation and Signifying Practice*, ed. Stuart Hall (London: Sage, 1997), 348.

[4] Peter Hamilton, "Representing the Social: France and Frenchness in Post-war Humanist Photography," in *Representation: Culture Representation and Signifying Practice*, ed. Stuart Hall (London: Sage, 1997), 82.

[5] John Tagg, "Evidence, Truth and Order: Photographic Records and the Growth of the State," in *The Photography Reader*, ed. Liz Wells (London: Routledge, 2003), 260.

[6] For example, news report on Serbian television Pink, http://www.youtube.com/watch?v=Pflt0y888ws (accessed May 25, 2007).

[7] Jelena Đorđević, *Političke Svetkovine i Rituali* (Beograd: Dosije, 1997), 161.

[8] Momčilo Stefanović, *Titova Štafeta Mladosti* (Beograd: NIRO Mladost, 1988), 32.

[9] Zoran Majdin, "Sveti Kvorum," *Vreme*, November 29, 2001.

[10] Victor Burgin, "Art, Common Sense and Photography," in *Visual Culture: The Reader*, ed. Jessica Evans and Stuart Hall (London: Sage, 2005), 48.

[11] Victor Burgin, "Looking at Photographs," in *Thinking Photography*, ed. Victor Burgin (London and Basingstoke: The Macmillan press LTD, 1982), 146.

[12] Allan Sekula, "On the Invention of Photographic Meaning," in *Thinking Photography*, ed. Victor Burgin (London and Basingstoke: The Macmillan press LTD, 1982), 87.

[13] Roland Barthes, "Rhetoric of the Image," in *Visual Culture: The Reader*, ed. Jessica Evans and Stuart Hall (London: Sage, 2005), 38.

[14] Roland Barthes, "The Photographic Message," in *A Barthes Reader*, ed. Susan Sontag (New York: Hill and Wang, 1982), 206.

[15] *Politika* had three photo pages.

[16] Victor Burgin, ibid., 1982, 144.

[17] Christine Gledhill, ibid., 1997, 348.

4

Officers without an Army
Memories of Socialism and Everyday Strategies in Post-Socialist Slovenia

Tanja Petrović

Introduction

Nostalgic feelings towards the socialist past have spread "from Stettin in the Baltic to Trieste in the Adriatic."[1] They have attracted much attention among political elites and journalists, who usually consider such feelings as signs of moral weakness, irrationality, or inability of individuals to find their way in the ongoing social and economic transformation. Thus, nostalgia for socialism is seen not only as deviant, surprising, and unnatural, but also as threatening to still fragile democracies in the former communist states. From a historical perspective, the negative attitude towards nostalgia that follows dramatic political and social changes, articulated by ruling elites and those who shape media and public discourses, is not a novel phenomenon, but rather a rule. Svetlana Boym points to the fact that after the October revolution in Russia, nostalgia "was not merely a bad word, but a contrarevolutionary provocation. The word nostalgia was obviously absent from the revolutionary lexicon. Nostalgia would be a dangerous 'atavism' of bourgeois decadence that had no place in the new world."[2]

In the case of the former Yugoslavia, the end of socialism coincided with the breakdown of the federal state; therefore, post-socialist nostalgia among former Yugoslavs cannot be separated from another nostalgic object, a vanished country. Yugo-nostalgia, an expression of a positive attitude towards Yugoslav socialism, possesses a dimension that makes it additionally problematic and intriguing for journalists and others engaged in creating the popular discourse. The fact is that in the countries of the former Socialist Federal Republic of Yugoslavia, people are still not only sentimental about the system that is seen as thoroughly different from western democratic systems, but in this particular case "a wave of nostalgia is sweeping countries born from the bloody conflicts in the 1990s."[3]

Another reason for the negative perception of any expression of nostalgia towards socialism and a common, multinational Yugoslav state, resides in the constructive ideological potential of nostalgia. According to Boym, there are two kinds of nostalgia. "Restorative nostalgia evokes national past and future; reflective nostalgia is more about individual and cultural memory. Nostalgia of the first type gravitates towards collective pictorial symbols and oral culture. Nostalgia of the second type is more oriented toward an individual narrative that savors details and memorial signs."[4] Restorative nostalgia is a characteristic of collective identity strategies in post-socialist societies, where "nostalgia for earlier historical periods – different ones for different constituencies – is a pervasive aspect of making the post-socialist future."[5] Restorative nostalgia is widely present in former Yugoslav republics, where it is mobilized in evocations of pre-Yugoslav national values, and in reconstructing national identities, helping to fill the void left by the delegitimization of a supranational Yugoslav identity. In the Serbian restorative nostalgic discourse and symbolism, for instance, socialist symbols and rituals are being replaced by new ones, stressing national unity.

Ivan Čolović provides an illustration of the replacement of one of the Yugoslav socialistic rituals by new nationalist symbols. "Tito's Baton, or the Youth Baton (*Titova štafeta/štafeta mladosti*) was carried for the last time in 1987, the year Slobodan Milošević came to power in Serbia. Instead of the baton there would soon appear on our roads different symbols of political power and unity – the relics of saints and poets. Among these were the relics of Prince Lazar, which left Ravanica in June 1989 to arrive in Gračanica on June 28 the same year, the six hundredth anniversary of the battle of Kosovo Field. This put them on disposal of Milošević who, on that day in nearby Gazimestan, gave the infamous warmongering speech heralding the armed conflict in Yugoslavia which began soon after."[6]

Yugo-nostalgia, which often invokes the ideology of "brotherhood and unity" of the former multinational state, stands in sharp contrast to the nationalistic ideologies of the newly established states and hence "has often been resorted to as an accusation in ideological showdowns over the previous years."[7] This nostalgia was perceived by political and economic elites and in the public discourse of these countries, as well as in the West, as a rather unpleasant surprise, unexpected from societies, which had just started enjoying the benefits of a pluralistic democracy and capitalist markets and which, after more than 50 years of "artificial unity in socialism," had returned to their "real essence" and "historical roots." Accordingly, those who do not or cannot identify with new identity patterns promoted by national(ist) political elites, are condemned to nostalgia. Stef Jansen suggests that Croatian president, Franjo Tudjman, labelled as Yugo-nostalgics "children of the Yugoslav people's army's officers, red bourgeoisie, and children from mixed marriages."[8]

The phenomenon of post-socialist nostalgia is increasingly attracting worldwide attention from academics. A significant number of them have dealt exclusively with the political consequences of nostalgia for socialism and have focused on the relations between nostalgia for socialism and processes of democratization, and the impact of nostalgia on political developments, including election results.[9] Recently, however, there is a notable interest in anthropological aspects of post-socialist nostalgia. This interest reveals itself in the efforts of scholars to relate nostalgia in post-socialist societies to the concrete experience of people and to the ways in which their attitudes, values, and memories are shaped and discursive constructions of East and West, socialism and capitalism, totalitarianism and democracy are construed. These scholars mobilized themselves in an effort to apply some precision to nostalgia, "the most elusive of concepts,"[10] through the analysis of its discrete manifestations, discursive forms of its expression and its political and social implications.

This chapter deals with the ways in which the socialist past in Yugoslavia is remembered by former officers of the Yugoslav

People's Army (*Jugoslovenska narodna armija*, henceforth the JNA), who now live in Slovenia. They seem to be particularly prone to a longing for the Yugoslav socialist past, since the new, post-socialist circumstances are unfavorable for them in at least two ways.

First, the JNA officers, together with their families, were one of the most privileged and protected groups in socialist Yugoslavia. Since they were obliged to accept posts around the country, they were frequently moved with their families and lived in settings alien to them. Their social networks were, thus, limited to other officers and their families, while the state itself contributed to the creation of a "society within society" by providing officers and their family members with services and infrastructures parallel to and separate from civil ones, such as special social security, housing, education, and health care. Furthermore, they were subject to separate legal procedures and enjoyed hierarchically ascending privileges; there was also a separate Communist Party organization for JNA officers; they spent their holidays in special resorts and shopped in subsidized stores.[11] Cultural and entertainment activities, such as concerts, dancing evenings, holiday celebrations, or theater performances were also organized for them and their families in army cultural centers (*dom vojske*) that existed in larger towns. In this way, JNA officers did not only work in an essentially Yugoslav institution,[12] interacting on a daily basis with people from all parts of Yugoslavia, but remained within this Yugoslav network in their private lives as well. The end of socialism, followed by a breakdown of the Yugoslav federal state, left them not only without these privileges, the army and the country they had served, but also without a sense of their professional existence, which dramatically influenced their private and everyday lives.

Second, in Slovenia, these JNA officers are deeply stigmatized as those who opposed the country's independence and, thus, threatened the security of the young state. In addition, most of these officers were not of Slovenian origin,[13] and the combination of these facts made it impossible for them to have been included in the "Slovenian national body," that is, in the process of intense national homogenization that followed the country's independence.

Remembering socialism, like any kind of remembering, may be interpreted as a cultural practice and a discursive strategy, which gives meaning to social structures, values, beliefs, and actions of a society and its members. The process of remembering is always highly dependent on the moment, when the act of recollection (remembering) takes place.[14] The present moment gives shape to people's memories, and enables them to position themselves within an existing social reality, and to negotiate and justify their statuses and roles. Only by connecting the past with the present, or in positioning of what once was in relation to now, can the full meaning of memories reveal itself.[15] The ways in which socialism is remembered by these former JNA officers is, thus, deeply dependent on their current social status in Slovenian society, and their narratives of socialism are implicitly dialogical with the dominant public discourse in the country.

For this reason, I will first consider the position of these officers in Slovenian society and the prevailing attitudes towards them, followed by the ways in which they construe the narrative of their memories. Narration, as a form of remembering, is a way in which people attach meaning to their memories. As Kathleen Stewart argues, "[to] narrate is to place oneself in an event and a scene – to make an interpretative space – and to relate something to someone: to make an interpretative space that is relational and in which meanings have direct social referents."[16]

Despite the fact that the former JNA officers in Slovenia are among people, who are the usual suspects when it comes to nostalgia for socialism, I will argue that the sharp opposition between their high esteem in socialism and their current unfavorable social status notwithstanding, these officers do not verbalize their memories of socialist times through the discourse of nostalgia. I nevertheless insist on relating their narratives to the theoretical concept of post-socialist nostalgia in the analysis of their memories, because it is exactly the absence of the nostalgic discourse in the officers' narratives, which tells much about what nostalgia for socialism is as a discursive and cultural practice, and how to understand its performative potential. At this point it seems useful to borrow the argument from linguistics that the absence of a sign (zero-sign) bears equally relevant information as its presence. The following discussion not only aims to outline memories of Yugoslav socialism of a particular social and professional group, but it has another, more general ambition, namely to contribute to ongoing discussions about the nature, substance, and performative manifestations of the post-socialist nostalgia.

The analysis is based on the narratives of eight former JNA officers, representing a wide range of military ranks. The individuals now live in Ljubljana, Novo mesto and small towns across Slovenia. Some of them participated in 1991 developments that eventually lead to Slovenian independence, while others were pensioned and left army services before the beginning of conflicts on Slovenian territory. Most of them were pensioned prematurely, and all of them had no jobs after the JNA left Slovenia in 1991. Some of them live in mixed, others in ethnically homogeneous marriages; some have their families in Slovenia, while others have families in Belgrade and elsewhere in the former Yugoslav republics.

Burden of Unfitting Biography: Former JNA Officers in Slovenia

In 1997, "Outsider," a Slovenian film, directed by Andrej Košak, was released. The film, which was recognized by many as the first Yugoslav film produced after the fall of Yugoslavia, provides a typical portrait of the JNA officer: a strict individual with rigid principles, blindly but sincerely devoted to the ideology of Yugoslav socialism, living in an alien setting and in a mixed marriage (in this case, the officer was a Bosnian married to a Slovenian, who was a housewife). The officer comes into severe conflict with his adolescent son, who grows up under the influence of the Ljubljana punk culture at the end of 1970. The conflict eventually ends most tragically with the boy's suicide. The significant popularity of the film in the former Yugoslavia, and particularly in Slovenia (it was the second most popular Slovenian film ever made),[17] tells at least two things about its topic and the way it was cinematically shaped.

First, the JNA officers were a social group, perceived as "culturally relevant" in the Yugoslav context on daily and ideological levels. The Yugoslav army and its officers were considered one of the most important pillars of Yugoslav unity, simultaneously symbols and guardians of the Yugoslav socialist state. Their personal fate was highly influenced by the fate of the country. Second, the image of the JNA officer as depicted in this film was recognizable for most former Yugoslavs. This image, however, was to be largely replaced by a new one, created during the violent breakup of socialist Yugoslavia.

When the federal state broke down, and national armies emerged in Yugoslavia's successor states, the former JNA officers became the most problematic elements for the "national bodies" of these new states. In the former Yugoslav republics, which suffered from wars of independence, a negative attitude developed towards the part of the JNA officer cadre, which bore actual responsibility for violence and war crimes. It spread to include all individuals, who professionally served the JNA, even when they had not been active officers at the start of the conflicts. As a rule, the officers did not ethnically belong to the majority of the population, due to the JNA policy of sending both, recruits and officers, always to another socialist republic to strengthen the idea of unity among all Yugoslav peoples. Miroslav Hažić observes that even the same ethnic origins could not guarantee a stable position in the new national armies for the former JNA officers: as soon as they were not needed for war operations, they were relieved of their posts.[18]

Ideological mechanisms of restorative nostalgia characteristic of the collective identity strategies in post-Yugoslav societies also touched the newly formed national armies in the Yugoslav successor states, where restorative nostalgia works through efforts to establish a continuity of the pre-Yugoslav army traditions. In the process of building bases for ideology and identity of the armies that replaced the JNA, there was no place for a Yugoslav legacy, which was condemned or ignored in the public discourse. Consequently, the former JNA officers were left without the possibility of being incorporated into new social structures and, therefore, without social recognition, respect and authority, even when they did not have any active role in the violent breakdown of the country. Such perception of the JNA officers eliminated any possibility for their deeper social integration into the newly defined post-Yugoslav societies. Almost two decades after the breakdown of Yugoslavia and the start of ethnic conflicts on its territory, many of them still live in very difficult circumstances, struggling to gain basic social rights and security.[19]

The JNA was perceived as a principal impeder of Slovenian liberalism in the period preceding concrete actions that led to this republic's independence on June 25, 1991, when the Slovenian Assembly proclaimed independence, and the Yugoslav flags and symbols were replaced by Slovenian ones at border crossings. New border crossings were established between Slovenia and Croatia. On the same day, the Yugoslav Federal Executive Council in Belgrade issued a decree for the protection of the national borders in Slovenia. The JNA forces attempted to regain the border crossings, but on Thursday (July 4) "the ten-day war" ended with the withdrawal of JNA units to Croatia and to their barracks. Slovenia's territory was completely under the control of the Slovenian Territorial Defense forces.[20]

Almost two decades after Slovenia had gained independence, the JNA officers remain negatively marked in the still dominant discourse of Slovenia's victory against the JNA; they also did not fit into the image of the nation's unity, shaped by distancing from the Yugoslav socialist legacy. Together with their families, they were largely among the "erased," who represent one of the hottest issue in Slovenian politics, involving residents from the former Yugoslav republics. In 1992, about 18.000 permanent non-Slovenian residents disappeared from official records and faced serious complications regarding their legal status and life in an independent Slovenia.[21] According to Blitz, among the "erased" "were approximately five hundred officers from the JNA, many of whom did not see active service and had intermarried with Slovenes."[22]

It took years for many former JNA officers in Slovenia to obtain Slovenian citizenship and the right to receive pensions. Some of them only managed to gain the latter as late as November, 2006.[23] The process of creating an ethnically defined state in the 1990s was followed by increasingly negative attitudes towards non-Slovenes, particularly towards those from other former Yugoslav republics, expressed in various domains of social life.

Non-ethnic Slovenes reported considerably higher levels of discrimination, in both their public and private lives, which was expressed in two-tired employment practices that favored Slovenes, as well as difficult relations with the state authorities, limited opportunities for political participation, and unequal treatment by the police.[24]

In the domains of culture and the arts, people from other former Yugoslav republics were regularly depicted as uneducated and performing low level jobs. They were generally associated with backwardness.[25] Among those who did not fit into the Slovenian "ethnic body," former JNA officers were strongly stigmatized and "most commonly scapegoated in the media by the nationalist politicians."[26]

The negative aura of JNA officers and their image of a problematic and suspect social group, which does not deserve any support from the Slovenian state, since they had been fighting against its independence in 1991, are still present in society. This is well illustrated by a reader's letter published in the Slovenian daily, *Delo*, in 2004, which recalls the unjust treatment of former Yugoslav officers who found themselves in Slovenia when Yugoslavia broke apart.

> Those people voluntarily took the oath to defend Yugoslavia, and to give their lives for it, if necessary. This was a serious oath that deserves respect. It is something very different from the oath that young JNA soldiers were forced to take starting the obligatory service, or that one taken by immature Homeguards during WW2. If I had refused to take an oath to the JNA, while serving in the Serbian town of Kruševac in 1960, I would have been imprisoned; if a Homeguard would have done the same at the stadium in 1944, he would have been killed. Because of this, I would like to urge the new government not to treat sworn JNA officers equally with some problematic persons just because they served the JNA, and to give them Slovenian citizenship.[27]

An extremely negative image of the JNA and its officers is still maintained by some Slovene mainstream politicians and constantly exploited during renegotiations of power relations on the Slovenian political scene. As recently as in May, 2007, and in the context of a conflict between Slovenia's president, Janez Drnovšek, and prime minister Janez Janša, *Demokracija*, the journal of Janša's Slovenian Democratic Party, published the image on a billboard, which was meant to delegitimize Drnovšek and to present him as a politically and morally problematic figure. Drnovšek was depicted in a JNA

A billboard depicting Janez Drnovšek in the company of high-ranking JNA officers.

uniform, accompanied by Veljko Kadijević, minister of defense and commander-in-chief of the JNA during conflicts that resulted in Slovenia's independence. The image was a response to Drnovšek's statement that the "situation in Slovenia seems to be worse than it was at the end of 1980s," which was cited on the billboard and placed next to the photograph. Depicting Drnovšek in the company of JNA officers was meant to not only delegitimize his statement, but also to question his attitude towards Slovenia's independence and his role in gaining it.

The dominant political discourse that maintains the negative aura of JNA officers, who live in Slovenia, also maintains the myth of Slovenia's struggle for independence and the crucial role of the Slovenian Territorial Defense (*Teritorialna obramba, TO*) in the success of that struggle.[28] Indeed, the two military formations, TO and JNA, are defined by a set of sharply oppositional qualifiers, such as patriots : traitors, democrats : dictators, or defenders :

aggressors. Moreover, most of the leading Slovenian politicians have built their popularity and legitimize their actions based on this very myth. Janez Janša, who was Slovenian Prime Minister from 2004 to 2008, extensively uses military imagery to strengthen his political position. His own role of a peace activist on the eve of Slovenia's independence was replaced by the role of an officer of Slovenian army at the start of the conflict with the JNA. Moreover, he was the first defense minister of the independent Slovenia and "is the only Slovenian military hero apart from General Maister."[29] In the 2004 pre-election campaign, Janša appeared on billboards dressed in the uniform of the Slovenian army.

The centrality of the myth of the struggle for independence in the Slovenian national imagery makes this imagery, and the discourse through which it is reproduced, no less militarized than the ideology of the JNA officers. It comes, therefore, as no surprise that the Slovenian public discourse regarding JNA officers is exclusive and generalizing. All JNA officers are treated in a similar manner, regardless of their actual role in the ten-day war. This discourse functions only through the above-mentioned opposition, never considers more general values and never opts for a more individual treatment, called for by the author of the above-cited letter.

In spite of a generally negative attitude towards JNA officers, which proved to be very pervasive during two decades of Slovenian independence, the majority of them has, nevertheless, managed to resolve formal and existential problems and now lives as pensioners in Slovenia. However, as pensioners, they face another, equally challenging task, to organize their lives and give meaning to their activities and the values they live for in an independent Slovenia. With the breakdown of the federal state, brotherhood and unity as its basic ideological premise lost its sense and was replaced by escalating nationalisms. Their beliefs, ideals and the sense of their professional life became outdated and were condemned and ridiculed in the public discourse. Their side of the story is impossible to be heard in public, since it is incompatible with the dominant narrative of the victorious ten-day war and the unity of Slovenian people in gaining independence.

Those among them, who had occupied important and decision-making positions within the JNA, published their memoirs and offered their reasons for the breakup of Yugoslavia and the responsibilities for the tragic developments in the 1990s.[30] In Slovenia, their attempts to enter the public sphere were mainly ignored by officials and others engaged in creating public opinion. Colonel general Konrad Kolšek, commander of the Fifth Army Area that covered Slovenia and Croatia, published his memories of the last days of Yugoslavia in 2001.[31] This book, according to him, received minimal public attention, although interest among ordinary people was much greater, and the book sold out relatively soon after its appearance. In 2005, the book appeared in Serbian and was met with a similarly high interest by readers in Serbia and Croatia.

Honorable People in Shameful Times: Explaining the Breakup of Yugoslavia

A juxtaposition of two temporal dimensions, then and now, which usually provides a narrative framework for articulating the discourse of nostalgia, is infrequent in the narratives of former JNA officers. Their narratives are anchored in the past and principally concerned with how it was possible for the country to disintegrate in such a violent manner, and the moral and actual responsibility for that disintegration. They also speak about the aftermath of Yugoslavia's breakdown and their treatment by Slovenian authorities, and society in general, after Slovenia gained independence. Regarding the current situation, they are concerned about perceiving their own position and do not refer to broader social and political circumstances.

The former JNA officers see the violent breakup of the federal state as their personal drama and failure, regardless of their actual role in military actions during the Yugoslav wars; even those officers, who left active military service before 1991, expressed a kind of personal responsibility and shame for the way the country was torn apart. Colonel General Kolšek opens the Serbo-Croat edition of his book with the following sentence: "History will never forgive us that after 45 years of peace, building the country, freedom and development, we allowed the Yugoslav nations to be involved in a brutal conflict in the heart of civilized Europe."[32]

Another former JNA officer of a much lower rank (a 68-year old lieutenant colonel from Novo mesto) describes the burden of historical responsibility and guilt in a similar manner:

> Let us put aside what happened here in Slovenia in the "ten day war." We should only thank God that it finished in that way. However, what happened in Bosnia in Croatia... One may make a tactical mistake, or an operational mistake, if you can understand these military expressions. But making a historical mistake and being remembered in the country's history as a traitor and worthless person ... that is what happened to us. That is what happened to us.

Taking on so much personal and moral responsibility is not so much a consequence of guilt imposed on the JNA officers by the new national political elites, but rather a consequence of their deep personal investment in the army and the blending of their private and professional lives. This personal investment creates an emotional burden for the interpretation of the past, which is narratively expressed by linguistic means of repetition: "It was terrible, really terrible. We experienced that as horror. We could not believe that Yugoslavia is tearing apart," states a 65-year colonel from Nova Gorica (cf. the repetition of the last sentence in the statement quoted above).

Explicit metapragmatic comments by interviewees also underline this emotional burden:

> I talk about these things with emotions, because it is not easy to lose a country. We were educated in the Yugoslav spirit then, particularly those of us, who worked for the military. Also many civilians long for Yugoslavia. Not only those from other republics, but Slovenians as well (a 67-year old colonel from Ljubljana).

At the same time, speaking about responsibility for what had happened to Yugoslavia and Yugoslavs, they chose a strategy typical for most ordinary people in the former Yugoslavia, who speak about the responsibility of politicians and the naivety of people.[33] Similarly, the officers make a clear distinction between the highest army officials and the army, which includes officer corps and soldiers. Without denying that fatal mistakes had been made by the supreme commanders, they stress that the army had been naive but not guilty of the developments in the 1990s. A 64-year old colonel from Ljubljana points out that "the army had no responsibility for what happened. It was manipulated and used... There were individual extremists, of course. And the full responsibility was with the JNA headquarters. They made terrible moves."

Imagining a dialogue with the dominant Slovenian discourse about the JNA, they stress the patriotism of JNA officers and soldiers and the high values, which were promoted and maintained by this institution. The oath taken by former JNA officers to defend the country and give their lives, if necessary, becomes the moral foundation in their narratives for building and justifying their position and actions in the JNA, and the reason for demanding respect for themselves today. A 55-year old colonel from around Ljubljana emphasizes that

> officers were quite privileged in socialist Yugoslavia. They would be awarded apartments faster than civilians; their wives were easily getting jobs. Because the military profession was not easy. We promised at graduation that we would dedicate all we have to the country and the army. We could be sent anywhere, to any corner of Yugoslavia.

The professional life of JNA officers in Slovenia abruptly ended with Slovenia's independence and the withdrawal of the JNA forces from Slovenian territory, completed at night between October 25 and 26, 1991. The majority of them were left without a chance to continue their military careers in an independent Slovenia, even if they were Slovene by birth. At best they could be prematurely pensioned or obtain another job. These options were considered unsatisfying and humiliating, since they foreclosed gaining social recognition and respect and left no option to fully realize themselves professionally and invest their knowledge in Slovenian society. A lieutenant colonel from Novo mesto remarks, no JNA officer, not only we, who were born in the South [in other Yugoslav republics, TP], but also Slovenians, none of us obtained any important position in Slovenian society after 1992. And many people I know were worth such positions. In the headquarters of the republic were 30 Slovenian colonels. They had excellent qualifications, had obtained M.A. degrees and completed all military schools. But none of them was offered work in the Slovenian army. The authorities thought that it was more than enough that we received apartments and pensions.

Stressing the damaging consequences that the deterioration of their officer status had on their personalities, the 64-year old colonel from Ljubljana articulates the officers' expectation that the military value system should be applicable in the broader context of the Slovenian society. Accordingly, an individual with a high military rank, who had been respected and highly regarded in the army, should expect the same treatment outside the military context:

There are many officers among the "erased." They fight for their rights in European courts. It is sad that someone who had a high rank such as lieutenant colonel and remained here in Slovenia, that such a person could not find any decent job. A neighbor of mine works as a doorkeeper now. That was the only job he managed to find after a few years of looking for a job. There are many examples like this. Those people are ruined as personalities because of such treatment.

Such expectations originate in the ideology of the Yugoslav People's Army, which, similarly to other armies, emphasized high moral characteristics and professional skills of its officers.[34] Numerous privileges, institutions separate from civilian ones, and relatively closed professional and private networks during Yugoslav socialism resulted in self-perceptions of officers as highly important and respectful social agents with a high esteem and social recognition. Their narratives depict losing such sense of self as a personal drama, which cannot be alleviated by financially good circumstances in which they live. A 69-year old lieutenant colonel from Ljubljana provides some examples of an unrealizable professional life for former JNA officers in an independent Slovenia:

> My neighbor was a physician, a surgeon in the military. When the JNA left Slovenia, he worked for half a year without pay to keep his practice. They did not want to employ him, although he is Slovenian. Another Slovenian physician asked for a job in a hospital, but they demanded that he take additional exams to get employed. The very same man had operated on 20.000 Slovenians as a military surgeon. He could not find any job and eventually he opened a private practice. Isn't that a shame? They could have made great use of him. Another surgeon, who has also operated on me, was a Bosnian Muslim, a great man, he also had to open a private practice, because they did not want to take him. These people did not lose anything financially, they earned much money as private doctors, but money is not everything. One also needs to be content and be respected in society. And we are not met with that kind of respect.

Feelings of exclusion and obsolescence, usually companions of aging, are more strongly expressed in the narratives of former JNA officers, due to the abrupt and radical loss of the context and ideological network in which they could enjoy high social status and self-esteem. The lack of social recognition and authority based on age and achievements in their professional careers, expressed above, is one of the central aspects stressed by the former JNA officers when reflecting on their current position. A 63-year old lieutenant colonel from nearby Maribor explains self-perception in the following way:

> We are now forgotten in every way. First, we are getting old. We received pensions, our families live on, our children completed their education. But we are forgotten and abandoned, because things unfortunately turned out that way. We are forgotten both officially and privately. No one has done anything bad to me personally, but I nevertheless feel that something is wrong. It is not at all as it is supposed to be.

His wife adds, "I am Slovenian, and I am happy that we now live in an independent Slovenia. But it is not nice how our JNA officers, including my husband, are treated. They are cut off and ignored, and there is so much hatred towards them."

Her statement explicates a counter-discourse to a generally accepted assumption that loyalty to the Slovenian state excludes any positive evaluation of the JNA officers, their social and political roles and moral characteristics. The pervasiveness and the self-evidence of such assumption is also reflected in other statements, which contain or implicate a different attitude, and is indicated by a need of their authors to additionally justify their position, which they assume to be problematic for the audience and society, in general. The above cited letter of a reader begins with such positioning and justification: "Although I am aware of the risk that those who used to read my texts will not do so anymore, I have a feeling that I must write the following."[35]

No Present, No Nostalgia

As suggested, an explicit comparison of aspects of their social and political life in the past and in the present is rare in the narratives of the former JNA officers. They reach for this discursive strategy only when comparing the JNA with the professional Slovenian army, introduced in 2004, when the country joined NATO. According to them, the main disadvantage of the professional army, compared to the JNA, is the lack of patriotism, devotion, and moral values.

A lieutenant general from near Celje remembers,

some ten days before the ten-day war, there was a flood in Laško. And the JNA soldiers and officers went into the water to save people's property and to build dams. And where is the army now when it comes to an earthquake or a flood? They do not help anymore, because they are paid soldiers. JNA soldiers were not only there for carrying weapons; they were also helping people and building the country. Slovenians should not forget that.

A lieutenant colonel from Novo mesto describes the difference between the JNA and the professional army in the following way.

"I have a very bad opinion about the professional army. It is named professional army, but it is, in fact, a legion. There is no patriotism any more. This army is not dedicated to the well being of its own country, but to some global interests."

The officers speak of the present in positive terms only when they refer to the successful integration of their children into Slovenian society. Their only satisfaction is the fact that their children managed something that they could not achieve, to gain respect in society. The lieutenant colonel from Novo mesto emphasizes: "A new generation of young people born in mixed marriages grew up here. These people are university professors, state secretaries; they work in important institutions. There was even a minister who lived in our apartment block."[36]

The discourse of nostalgia, in general, and post-socialist nostalgia, in particular, is based on juxtaposing past and present, where the selectively remembered past is seen as better and laden with real qualities and values, which do not exist in the present.[37] The absence of explicitly positive evaluations of the socialist past and negative evaluations of the present in the narratives of JNA officers may be partly explained by the fact that such assessments would necessarily conflict with the dominant discourse in Slovenia. Since maintaining the myth of the struggle for independence and the essential role of the Slovenian army in this struggle still dominate the Slovenian political discourse, a positive stance towards the socialist past, articulated by former JNA officers, would be interpreted as an act of opportunism and confirm their disloyalty to the Slovenian state once again.

Typically masculine, ideological constructs of patriotism and honor (among officers) are important structural elements of both, the discourse of Slovenian politics and the personal narratives of the former JNA officers. The former, which possesses power and social control, inevitably excludes and delegitimizes the latter. As Nielsen points out, "patriotism is an ideology, like masculinity, that posits specific behaviors and beliefs as best for a nation and an individual."[38] Accordingly, individual acts of a patriot are always in accordance with collective interests, i.e., for the best of the nation. For this reason, former JNA officers stress so much their social marginalization and the reduction of their existence and activities to an individual level, without the possibility of gaining social recognition and respect through acting as social subjects, who contribute to the nation's well being.

Another important reason for the absence of positive assessments of the past in the narratives resides in the very nature of the discourse of nostalgia. Similar to other forms of remembering, nostalgia is about the production of the present rather than the reproduction of the past.[39] To be able to interpret and justify one's present position through the discourse of nostalgia, one must rationalize the past by attaching secondary meanings to memories and past objects and events. For that one needs to distance oneself from the past and to perceive it as finished and remote, as Gerald Creed persuasively argues, "the term nostalgia only resonates (…) when there is no chance of going back."[40]

For these former JNA officers, their past is radically disconnected from their present. Since there was no social world to replace the socialist one for this social group, their memories are fully mobilized for justifying what represented their social world before the end of socialism and Yugoslavia. Due to the lack of a substitute, one

Wall decoration in the home of a former JNA officer: recognition plaques for his service in the JNA, portrait of Tito in a marshal's uniform and an old photograph of Novo mesto.

in their new form
Borospherform are Almost unredemizable but As

may argue that socialism actually could never end for them and
their present becomes an extended past. Not surprisingly, virtually
all of the interviewees still keep Tito's portrait in their apartments.

This act of keeping the marshal's portrait in their private spaces
is not what we usually recognize as nostalgia for socialism. This
kind of nostalgia is possible exactly because socialism ended, and
there is no chance of its return. The awareness of irreversibility
makes objects from the socialist past, such as Tito's portrait, cultural objects that emanate nostalgia. Therefore, such objects leave the
walls of homes and institutions and appear on flea markets all over
the former Yugoslavia. As Pogačar notes, Tito's portraits are there

> often juxtaposed to items that have no connection to the
> former Yugoslavia. Thus, the remnants of the Yugoslav ex-
> perience blend into a wider picture of nostalgicising evoca-
> tions of the past, which goes to show that in this bricolage
> of various items, the precise origin loses its importance and
> they start to figure as fragments applicable to a particular
> person's interest and/or memory.[41]

The story is rather different for these former JNA officers. For
those, who kept Tito's portraits in their homes, these portraits did
not acquire any secondary function and, therefore, remained where
they used to be in socialism, on the apartment walls of citizens.
Although many Yugoslavs, regardless of their ethnic origins, have
a positive opinion about Tito and his role in the history of the Yugoslav peoples,[42] the former JNA officers are among those very rare
individuals, who have kept his portraits in their homes. They remained there, because there was no acceptable ideological substitute for the JNA officers to replace socialism.

Since the Slovenian society does not leave them any space in
which to act as social subjects and to reinterpret or justify their beliefs, views and decisions, the former JNA officers cannot transform
their memories and objects from the past into nostalgia. For the
same reason, they cannot distance themselves from their memories and to employ them in their demands for respect and acknowledgment from society. Having only the past as a space for making

sense of their social existence, these former officers maintain practices and rituals that are typical for that past and incompatible with
the present. They maintain connections with their colleagues and
classmates from the Officers' Academy and regularly meet them
in Slovenian resorts and travel to Belgrade for reunions. They re-
tell common memories and publish monographs for anniversaries
of their graduation, which do not differ in style and themes from
those published during the socialist period. They live in a continuous past, in which Tito's portrait on their apartment walls appears
to be the only natural decoration.

Notes

[1] This is a paraphrase of Churchill's words, "From Stettin in the Baltic
to Trieste in the Adriatic, an iron curtain has descended across the Continent" used by Mitja Velikonja, "Tistega Lepega Dne: Značilnosti Sodob-
nega Nostalgičnega Diskurza," *Balcanis* 12–16, 5, (2004): 37; cf. Maria
Todorova, "From Utopia to Propaganda and Back" (opening address at
the conference on Post-Communist Nostalgia, University of Illinois at Urbana-Champaign, USA, April 7–8, 2006).

[2] Svetlana Boym, *The Future of Nostalgia* (New York: Basic Books, 2002),
59.

[3] Harry De Quetteville, "As Poverty Bites. Former Yugoslavs Pine for
Tito Era," *The Daily Telegraph,* September 25, 2004.

[4] Svetlana Boym, ibid., 2002, 49.

[5] Susan Gal and Gail Kligman, *The Politics of Gender after Socialism*
(Princeton: Princeton University Press, 2000), 4.

[6] Ivan Čolović, "O Maketama i Štafetama," in *VlasTito Iskustvo: Past
Present,* ed. Radonja Leposavić (Beograd: Samizdat B92, 2004), 155.

[7] Dejan Kršić, "Work in Progress," in *VlasTito iskustvo: Past Present,* ed.
Radonja Leposavić (Beograd: Samizdat B92, 2004), 31.

[8] Stef Jansen, *Antinacionalizam* (Beograd: XX vek, 2005), 221–2, f. 1.

[9] Joakim Ekman and Jonas Linde, "Demokrati Och Nostalgi i Central-
Och Österuropa," *Nordisk Østforum* 17(1) (2003): 65–84; Kristen Ghodsee,
"Red Nostalgia? Communism, Women's Emancipation, and Economic
Transformation in Bulgaria," *L'Homme, Europäische Zeitschrift für Femi-
nistische Geschichtswissenschaft* 15(1) (2004): 33–46; David S. Mason and
Svetlana Sidorenko-Stephenson, "Public Opinion and the 1996 Elections
in Russia: Nostalgic and Statist, Yet Pro-Market and Pro-Yeltsin," *Slavic
Review* 56(4) (1997): 698–717.

[10] Maria Todorova, ibid., 2006.

[11] Miroslav Hadžić, *Sudbina Partijske Vojske [Destiny of Party Army]* (Beograd: Samizdat B92, 2001), 321, f. 40.

[12] The last American ambassador to socialist Yugoslavia, Warren Zimmermann, stresses the fact that the JNA was the most Yugoslav of all institutions, since "people from all parts of Yugoslavia were meeting there" (Warren Zimmermann, *Origins of a Catastrophe. Yugoslavia and Its Destroyers – America's Last Ambassador Tells What Happened and Why* (New York: Times Books, 1996), 64).

[13] The ethnic structure of the JNA officer corps was one of the largest concerns of state and army leadership. Despite the desire of state authorities that the JNA officer corps reflect the ethnic diversity of Yugoslav nations (there were legal acts regulating the number of officers from each ethnic group; the 242nd article of the 1974 Yugoslav Constitution also promotes the principle of equal representation of all Yugoslav republics and provinces relative to the number of inhabitants – cf. Mile Bjelajac, *Jugoslovensko Iskustvo sa Multietničkom Armijom 1918–1991* (Beograd: UDI, 1999), 49, f. 63), officers of Serbian origin prevailed; for instance, in 1985, 5.82 % of the JNA officer corps were Montenegrins (who made up 2.58 % of the Yugoslav population), 12.51 % Croats (19.74 %), 6.74 % Macedonians (5.98 %), 3.65 % Muslims (8.92 %), 2.64 % Slovenians (7.82 %), 57.17 % Serbs (36.3 %), and 1.09 % Albanians (7.72 %). More than 50 % of the Serbs among the officers were from Croatia and Bosnia-Herzegovina (ibid.). The national quota was successfully applied only for the highest positions in the JNA structure until 1982, when general Mamula became minister of defense, and the most important army leadership positions were occupied by Serbs. The prevalence of Serbs and the deficit of Croats and Slovenians in the JNA officer cadre was frequently explained by economic factors, since men from economically disadvantaged regions were most interested in military careers; hence there was a low interest of young people from urban centers, especially in economically well developed Slovenia (John Lampe, *Yugoslavia as History, Twice There Was a Country* (New York – Melbourne: Cambridge University Press, 1996), 337). The other explanation is grounded in Serbia's long warrior tradition and the high esteem for the military profession (Warren Zimmermann, ibid., 1996, 62).

[14] Maria Todorova, "Remembering Communism," *Centre for Advanced Study in Sofia Newsletter* 2 (2002): 15.

[15] Kathleen Stewart, "Nostalgia: A Polemic," *Cultural Anthropology* 3(3) (1988): 227.

[16] Kathleen Stewart, ibid., 1988, 227.

[17] "Več Kot 100.000 Gledalcev," *Mladina*, January 5, 2004.

[18] Miroslav Hadžić, ibid., 2001, 179.

[19] In Serbia, numerous families of officers, who left other Yugoslav

republics, still live in very difficult circumstances. They are settled in properties and hotels belonging to the Serbian army. Their existence is uncertain, and there is not much hope for improved living conditions; in October, 2006, Serbian daily newspaper, *Danas*, reported that between 800 and 1,000 former JNA officers and their families will have to leave improvised apartments in the Novi Sad garrison ("Bez Stana s Pregršt Rešenja," *Danas*, October 4, 2006).

[20] The territorial defense system had been set in 1968 and was organized on the level of republics, whose governments controlled Territorial Defense forces and weaponry (Sabrina Ramet, *Thinking about Yugoslavia: Scholarly Debates about the Yugoslav Breakup and the Wars in Bosnia and Kosovo* (Cambridge: Cambridge University Press, 2005), 115).

[21] Cf. Jasminka Dedić, Vlasta Jalušić, and Jelka Zorn, *Izbrisani: Organizirana Nedolžnost in Politike Izključevanja* (Ljubljana: Mirovni inštitut, 2003); Vera Klopčič, Miran Komac, and Vera Kržišnik-Bukić, *Albanci, Bošnjaki, Črnogorci, Hrvati, Makedonci in Srbi v Republiki Sloveniji, Položaj in Status Pripadnikov Narodov Nekdanje Jugoslavije v Republiki Sloveniji* (Ljubljana: Inštitut za narodnostna vprašanja, 2003), http://www.uvn.gov.si/fileadmin/uvn.gov.si/pageuploads/pdf_datoteke/Raziskava_Polozaj_in_status_pripadnikov_narodov_nekdanje_Jugoslavije_v_RS.pdf (accessed November 25, 2007). Slovenian sociologist Rastko Močnik termed this act of Slovenian officials the fourth ethnic cleansing on the territory of the former Yugoslavia (Rastko Močnik, "Kje Smo Zdaj, Ko Smo v EU?," *Mladina*, May 4, 2004, http://www.mladina.si/tednik/200417/clanek/slo-kolumna--rastko_mocnik/ (accessed November 25, 2007); cf. Martin Pogačar, "Traces of Yugoslavia: Yuniverse will B-last" (unpublished M.A. thesis, School of Slavonic and East European Studies, University College London, 2005), Brad K. Blitz, "Statelessness and the Social (De)Construction of Citizenship," *Journal of Human Rights* 5 (2006): 453–79.

[22] Brad K. Blitz, ibid., 2006, 462.

[23] "Pravo na Penziju Bivših Oficira JNA," November 2, 2006, http://www.b92.net/info/vesti/index.php?yyyy=2006&mm=11&dd=02&nav_id=218214&nav_category=167 (accessed November 25, 2007).

[24] Miran Komac, *Percepcije Slovenske Integracijske Politike. Zaključno Poročilo* (Ljubljana: Inštitut za narodnostna vprašanja, 2005).

[25] Mitja Velikonja, "'Ex-home': 'Balkan Culture' in Slovenia After 1991," in *The Balkan in Focus – Cultural Boundaries in Europe*, ed. Barbara Törnquist-Plewa and Sanimir Resic (Lund: Nordic Academic Press, 2002), 189–207.

[26] Brad K. Blitz, ibid., 2006, 469.

[27] Mihael Prijatelj, "Oficirji JLA v Sloveniji," *Delo*, October 20, 2004, 5. In 2001, the major general, Marijan Kranjc, in a letter to the president of the

Slovenian Parliament, Borut Pahor, demanded the introduction of a legal act to regulate the rights of high-ranking JNA officers. He warned that eight of these honorable individuals had died already before managing to claim their basic rights of pension, health insurance and Slovenian citizenship, and he urged that something must be done before the ninth of these "army pensioners without pension" will die (Marijan Kranjc, "Ne Čakajte, Da Pomro!," *Nedeljski dnevnik*, July 15, 2001).

[28] Politically motivated attempts to use the myth of the struggle for independence and the symbolic potential of the Slovenian army are constantly present in Slovenian politics, regardless of which political fraction is in power. Milan Zver, minister of education in the 2004-08 Slovenian government, often stressed the insufficient presentation of the formation of the Slovenian state in textbooks, while the Prime Minister, Janez Janša, often suggested that Slovenians are not sufficiently aware of the importance of the role of the Slovenian army in 1991. It seems that Slovenian politics is much more interested in maintaining the military myth than is the public. In 1995, on the occasion of the 50th anniversary of the victory against fascism, the minister of defense, Jelko Kacin, wanted to organize an army parade. The idea was met with strong public opposition. Members of the Slovenian government again proposed a military parade in 2006, during preparations for celebrating the 15th anniversary of Slovenia's independence, but it was also abandoned due to strong public opposition ("Parada? Ne, Hvala!," *Mladina*, February 27, 2006).

[29] "Parada? Ne, Hvala!," *Mladina*, February 27, 2006. General Rudolf Maister (1874–1934) fought for the Slovenian northern border within the Kingdom of Serbs, Croats and Slovenes after the First World War and is considered the most important figure in Slovenia's military history.

[30] In the 1990s and the early 2000s, there was a "flood of memories from principals in the Yugoslav drama" (Sabrina Ramet, ibid., 2005, 108). Ramet provides an overview of some of this memoir literature, stressing that publishing this kind of literature is welcome, "insofar it affords the opportunity to see how the participants themselves would like their roles and actions to be remembered, and provides fresh accounts from inside concerning what may have happened" (Sabrina Ramet, ibid., 2005, 108). The author also finds these memoirs and autobiographies vital "if one is going to capture the spirit of an age" (Sabrina Ramet, ibid., 2005, 132).

[31] Konrad Kolšek, *Spomini na Začetek Oboroženega Spopada v Jugoslaviji 1991* (Maribor: Obzorja, 2001).

[32] Konrad Kolšek, *Prvi Pucnji u SFRJ: Sećanja na Početak Oružanih Sukoba u Sloveniji i Hrvatskoj* (Beograd: Dan Graf, 2005).

[33] Michael Herzfeld points to the universality of this strategy, stating that "people ignore their own agency whenever they are offered a chance to do that" (Michael Herzfeld, *Kulturna Intimnost* (Beograd: XX vek, 2004),

186–7).

[34] Janowitz considers honor a basis of the "belief system" of the military establishment in the USA (Morris Janowitz, *The Professional Soldier. A Social and Political Portrait* (New York – London: The Free Press – Collier Macmillan, 1974), 215–6). According to the professional military ethics training guide of West Point Academy, "An officer's honor is of paramount importance, derived through history from demonstrated courage in combat. It includes the virtues of integrity and honesty. Integrity is the personal honor of the individual officer, manifested … in all roles. In peace, the officer's honor is reflected in consistent acts of moral courage. An officer's word is an officer's bond." (Bill McWilliams, a talk to the United States Military Academy Cadet Honor Committee, in Washington Hall, December 3, 2001, http://www.westpoint.org/academy/malo-wa/archive/McWilliamsTalk.html, accessed November 25, 2007). For the concept of honor among military professionals, cf. also Tomislav Smerić, *Sparta Usred Babilona? Sociologijski Aspekti Vojne Profesije* (Zagreb: Hrvatska sveučilišna naklada, 2005), 273–87; Mika La Vaque-Manty, "Dueling for Equality. Masculine Honor and the Modern Politics of Dignity," *Political Theory* 36/4 (2006): 715–40.

[35] Mihael Prijatelj, ibid., 2004, 5.

[36] Retired major general Marijan Kranjc, in his letter to Borut Pahor in July, 2001, mentions the case of General Jozo Kukavica, who has lived in Slovenia for 30 years and could not obtain the right to a pension. At the same time, his son, Dr. Igor Kukavica, contributes to the good reputation of Slovenia through his successful scientific work (Marijan Kranjc, ibid., 2001).

[37] Michael Herzfeld (ibid., 2004, 186–187) labels this phenomenon structural nostalgia.

[38] Kim E. Nielsen, "What's a Patriotic Man to Do?," *Men and Masculinities* 6 (2004): 240–53, here 240.

[39] Daphne Berdahl, "'(N)Ostalgie' for the Present: Memory, Longing, and East German Things," *Ethnos* 64 (2) (1999): 202.

[40] Gerald Creed, "Domesticating Discontent: The Work of Nostalgia in Bulgaria" (paper presented at the conference "Post-Communist Nostalgia," University of Illinois at Urbana-Champaign, USA, April 7–8, 2006).

[41] Martin Pogačar, ibid., 2005.

[42] A 2003 Croatian opinion poll showed Tito as one of the greatest Croatian historical figures, along with Nikola Tesla. In Slovenia, there has also been an increase in people, who consider Tito a positive historical personality. According to a public opinion poll, 63.9 % of Slovenes had a positive view of Tito in 1998, while in 2004, this number jumped to 79.5 % (Mateja Hrastar and Vanja Pirc, "Ljubi Diktator," *Mladina*, May 24, 2004,

23). Similarly, according to a TV poll in 2005, 77 % of Slovenes agreed that Tito was a positive historical personality, while 33 % viewed him unfavorably (Trenja, Pop TV, March 17, 2005). In 2007, 81.4 % of all Slovenian citizens considered Tito a positive historical personality ("Lik in Delo Tovariša Tita," *Mladina*, May 19, 2007, 46).

Part III

Popular Culture and Yugoslavness

5

European Sounds, Yugoslav Visions
Performing Yugoslavia at the Eurovision Song Contest

Dean Vuletic

At the 2004 Eurovision Song Contest, Serbia and Montenegro's entry "Lane moje" (My darling), performed by Željko Joksimović and the Ad Hoc Orchestra, was awarded the maximum number of twelve points by Bosnia-Herzegovina, Croatia and Slovenia. This was the first time since 1992 that Serbia and Montenegro had participated in Eurovision[1], as the international isolation imposed upon them – or, more exactly, the Federal Republic of Yugoslavia that they had comprized – in the 1990s for their roles in the conflicts in Croatia, Bosnia-Herzegovina and Kosovo had excluded them from such international cultural events. After the 2004 contest, Serbia's foreign minister Goran Svilanović told Croatian Television that the twelve points awarded by Croatia to Serbia could "help improve relations between the countries in the region,"[2] a notion which reflects the political value that some cultural and political elites in the former Yugoslavia have historically attributed to Eurovision. But the political effects of the contest should not be overstated; indeed, the support that the peoples of the former Yugoslavia have given each other at Eurovision in recent years is a manifestation of a shared popular culture that persists more on the basis of cultural connections, linguistic similarities and commercial ties rather than on flourishing political relations.[3] Furthermore, the popular memory of a common experience at Eurovision from 1961 to 1991 – when they all sent a common entry to represent them and when Yugoslavia was, in many respects, a cultural and political outsider in the contest – might in part explain their recent manifestation of cultural solidarity there. Indeed, where once they had few countries whose cultural and political affinities they could rely upon for votes, the successor states of the former Yugoslavia can now at least look to each other for support at Eurovision.

Now the world's largest and most famous popular music contest,[4] Eurovision began in 1956 as a manifestation of cultural cooperation among Western European countries which were at that time undertaking some of the first steps towards contemporary economic and political integration.[5] At its inception, the aim of the contest was to "stimulate the output of original, high-quality songs in the field of popular music by encouraging competition between authors and composers through the international comparison of their works."[6] Since then, Eurovision has been a stage upon which the cultural, political and social identities of Europe[7] have been performed and negotiated, and during the Cold War it provided sound bites that captured the essence of relations between Yugoslavia and Western Europe. In the 1960s and 1970s – that is, before the intensification of the economic and political problems that would spell the break up of the Yugoslav federation – Eurovision had a special significance in the cultural life of Yugoslavia for several reasons. First, Yugoslavia was the only socialist, Slavic and Eastern European country to take part in Eurovision during the Cold War, due to its nonaligned status in international affairs and its willingness to engage in cultural cooperation with the West. Participation in Eurovision therefore affirmed Yugoslavia's membership in a Western cultural sphere and portrayed it as the most culturally liberal, modern and open part of Eastern Europe – while, at the same time, masking some of the undesirable similarities that Yugoslavia had with other Eastern European states, such as limits on artistic and political freedoms. Alongside this political dimension, there was also a commercial aspect to Eurovision that allowed for the international promotion of Yugoslavia as a tourist destination and the development of its popular music industry through exposure to Western record companies and markets. Finally – and perhaps most significantly of all – Eurovision had a huge audience among the country's citizens: it provided entertainment for the millions of them who each year followed the preliminary contest for the Yugoslav entry, its preparation for Eurovision and then the final itself, when many of them would gather around television sets with their family and friends to watch it. They found Eurovision enticing as it had the status of a Western product, and because it was the West that initiated the most attractive global trends in popular music during the Cold War. Furthermore, they depended on Western Europe's evaluation of Yugoslavia at Eurovision to shape the image of their country abroad as well as their own cultural and political identities, as Western confirmation of the development of Yugoslav popular music through success at the contest could affirm how modern, prosperous and even fashionable Yugoslavia had become.

Among the images of Eurovision from the 1960s, 1970s and 1980s that are most ingrained in the popular memory of societies in the former Yugoslavia, it is the victory of Yugoslavia at the contest in Lausanne in 1989 – which earned it the right to host Eurovision in Zagreb the following year – that is one of the most powerful. This win came just before the disintegration of the Yugoslav federation in 1991; indeed, between the 1989 and 1990 contests, socialist regimes fell throughout Eastern Europe, and Slovenia and Croatia held their first multiparty elections that brought pro-independence parties to power (in Croatia, these elections even took place in the very month that Eurovision was staged in Zagreb).[8] Ironically, though, when Yugoslavia's internal political cohesion was stronger and its international prestige greater in the 1960s and 1970s, this had not translated into cultural success at Eurovision, and the low scores that Yugoslavia achieved there in those decades even prompted public debate on whether the contest was damaging the country's image abroad. This asynchrony highlights the cultural and political ambivalence that characterized Yugoslavia's participation in Eurovision in the 1960s and 1970s, when Yugoslav cultural and political elites – including artists, composers, lyricists, journalists, party officials and representatives of radio and television stations and record companies – pursued cultural exchange with the West, but at the same time wondered whether they were accepted by it on equal terms; tried to imitate Western trends in popular culture, but were also critical of the "capitalist vices" that accompanied them; and sought to use Western styles of popular music to promote a modern image of Yugoslavia, but also questioned how up-to-date they were with them and whether it was appropriate for a domestic variant to incorporate folk elements. These dilemmas were rooted not only in the ideological and political contradictions, predilections and suspicions of Yugoslav socialism – and, in particular, nonalignment as one of its distinctive features – but also in a conceptual predisposition originating in Western Europe that has, as the historian Larry Wolff demonstrates, since the Enlightenment considered the lands of Yugoslavia and the rest of Eastern Europe to be a "demi-Orient" occupying "an ambiguous space between inclusion and exclusion" in European cultural and economic affairs.[9] As Wolff puts it, "[a]lienation is in part a matter of economic disparity, the wealth of Western Europe facing the poverty of Eastern Europe, but such disparity is inevitably clothed in the complex windings of cultural prejudice,"[10] and it was this "cultural prejudice" that some of Yugoslavia's cultural and political elites thought was at play when their country fared poorly at Eurovision. Yugoslavia's Eurovision experience in the 1960s and 1970s was thus a more uproarious one than the narrative of victory from the 1980s might suggest: to be sure, Eurovision was an arena in which Yugoslavia's citizens shaped their own identities through their interaction with the West, but it showed that the country's cultural openness to the world – which was touted by the regime as a distinguishing feature of Yugoslav socialism, as opposed to the more restrictive systems in the rest of Eastern Europe[11] – was not unproblematic culturally, ideologically or politically.

Beaches and Brooches

Although an explanation of the relationship between Yugoslavia's performance at Eurovision and its international cultural and political relations requires a more detailed study of voting statistics, the content of its Eurovision entries and cultural and political discourses, it is a simpler task to demonstrate how Yugoslavia's participation in the contest during the Cold War was determined by its political character – and, most of all, its nonaligned position in international affairs. From 1945 to 1948, the Communist Party of Yugoslavia (CPY) modeled its cultural politics – as it did other affairs of state – upon that of the Soviet Union, and it privileged cultural cooperation with the countries of Eastern Europe.[12] As Cold War tensions intensified in these years, Western popular music was attacked by Yugoslavia's leaders as a cultural and political threat from the West, and radio programs were censored accordingly;[13] as Milovan Djilas, the Yugoslav vice premier at the time, declared in 1947, "America is our sworn enemy, and jazz, likewise, as its product."[14] However, the CPY softened its attitude towards Western popular music in the couple of years following the split between Yugoslavia and the Soviet Union in 1948: their alliance was severed in June of that year after Yugoslav leader Josip Broz Tito defied Soviet political domination, which resulted in Yugoslavia being expelled from the Cominform, the international organization of communist parties. Yugoslavia's leaders then sought economic and political support from the West, and from 1950 their rapprochement with it was accompanied by a growing openness towards Western cultural influences.[15] An early manifestation of this was Yugoslavia's participation in the European Broadcasting Union (EBU), which it joined in 1950 as a founding member.[16] Membership of the EBU was decisive for Yugoslavia's presence at Eurovision, as it is through the EBU that the contest has been arranged and only members of the organization can participate in it. During the Cold War, the EBU promoted cooperation among Western European public broadcasters, and Yugoslav Radio and Television (JRT, Jugoslavenska radiotelevizija) – the Yugoslav association of radio and television stations – was a member of it and not the International Organization for Radio and Television (IORT), which was the same sort of organization for Eastern European and other socialist states.[17]

With CPY – which was renamed the League of Communists of Yugoslavia (LCY) in 1952 – maintaining a less hostile stance towards the West than its Eastern European counterparts did, Western popular music developed more freely in Yugoslavia in the 1950s than anywhere else in Eastern Europe. An economic boom in that decade allowed for the investment – especially from 1956 – of more resources into the production of consumer goods and the development of entertainment and leisure activities, which resulted in huge increases in the rates of ownership of radios, record players and records and the expansion of radio and television services.[18] By the end of the 1950s, local popular music festivals were a major attraction in the cultural life of Yugoslavia and, according to the ethnomusicologist Ljerka V. Rasmussen, they were "the single most powerful public forum for the presentation, production and definition of Yugoslav popular music."[19] The most important among them was the Opatija Festival, which began in the Croatian town of the same name in 1958 and was organized by JRT, and from 1973 to 1976 Yugoslavia's Eurovision entries were chosen there.[20] That Yugoslavia did not already enter Eurovision at the time that the Opatija Festival was established was due not to any ideological or political suspicion of it but rather to technical issues: namely, television services – which were a prerequisite for participation in Eurovision considering that it was conceived as a televised contest – only started to develop in Yugoslavia from 1956.[21] By 1960, however, JRT believed that its technical capabilities as well as the quality of Yugoslav popular music had reached a standard that would allow it to take part in Eurovision, and in that year its board of directors and commission for music agreed that it should apply to enter the contest.[22]

In 1961, Yugoslavia made its first appearance at Eurovision with the love song "Neke davne zvezde" (Some distant stars); it was performed by Ljiljana Petrović, a well-known artist of the time who started her popular music career in 1956 and had since then appeared at international jazz festivals in Western Europe.[23] But although Yugoslav artists had already been participating in Western contests and festivals of popular music before Yugoslavia entered Eurovision, Petrović recalls that

> the performance of the Yugoslav representative aroused much interest. Of course, one must know that it was the time of the Cold War and that Yugoslavia was the first socialist country that appeared at this festival of European popular music.[24]

Petrović finished eighth in a contest of sixteen contestants, and she achieved a better position than did the entries of some countries whose popular music industries were more developed than Yugoslavia's, such as Austria, Belgium, Germany, the Netherlands and Sweden.[25] Petrović's result suggests that Yugoslavia was not so disadvantaged by its political character at its first Eurovision; indeed, while its entry may have intrigued some of its competitors, it was hardly a matter of controversy then or in subsequent decades. Furthermore, a study of the countries that entered in the 1960s and 1970s shows that the participation of some others stirred much more debate: these included Spain and Portugal, which were until the mid 1970s ruled by the right wing dictatorships of Francisco Franco and António de Oliveira Salazar, respectively; Israel, whose participation was criticized by other Middle Eastern countries and brought increased security measures to the contest; and Greece, Turkey and Cyprus, among which relations were especially tense after the invasion of Cyprus by Turkish forces in 1974.[26]

To be sure, Yugoslavia never really sought to be politically provocative through its participation in Eurovision in the 1960s and 1970s; instead, it used it to affirm its membership in a Western cultural sphere rather than an Eastern political one, and in doing so it often presented itself more as a Mediterranean country. This was also intended to advertise Yugoslavia's burgeoning tourist industry, as Yugoslav cultural and political elites considered Eurovision to be a prime opportunity for the promotion of their country as a tourist destination for Western Europeans – especially when, by the 1970s, the contest's audience numbered in the hundreds of millions and it was one of the most popular programs in Europe.[27] Maritime motifs consequently pervaded many of Yugoslavia's Eurovision entries, as was first seen in 1963 and 1965, when Vice Vukov sang "Brodovi" (Boats) and "Čežnja" (Yearning), respectively. Like Vukov, who is a native of Šibenik, other Yugoslav performers at Eurovision also hailed from the coastal areas of Croatia, with the group 4M being from Rijeka and the Dubrovački trubaduri (Dubrovnik Troubadours) and Tereza Kesovija coming from its most famous tourist resort, Dubrovnik.[28] Their success on the Yugoslav popular music scene was in part due to their performance of music influenced by the motifs and styles of the Adriatic region, which was itself developing into a major centre for the production of Yugoslav popular music, especially through the festivals of Opatija, Rijeka and Split.[29] This promotion of Yugoslavia as a Mediterranean country was thus not only geared towards international consumption, but also reflected major cultural, economic and social developments in Yugoslavia that took place in the early postwar decades along its coastline. Indeed, the maritime-themed songs were the soundtrack of a period of expanding domestic tourism when many citizens from Yugoslavia's interior saw the Adriatic for the first time, and they reflected a common cultural discovery of the sea that much of the country was sharing in.[30] Furthermore, the Adriatic region was a bridge between Yugoslavia and the West not only because it attracted many Western tourists, but also due to its proximity to Italy and historical exposure to cultural influences from there. These were particularly significant in the 1950s and 1960s, when the trends being set by Italian popular music – especially the sort featured at the Sanremo Music Festival that started in 1951, and which Eurovision was modeled upon[31] – were closely followed in Yugoslavia by artists, composers, lyricists and, of course, many fans.[32]

Together with these maritime themes, Yugoslavia's Eurovision entries tended to have friendship, love and peace as their subjects and did not differ significantly from the staple themes of the entries of other countries, nor were they as explicitly political as some of the songs of, say, Greece or Portugal.[33] However, there were some occasions when aspects of Yugoslavia's political identities influenced the style and themes of its entries. For example, when Yugoslavia appeared at the contest for the first time in 1961, Petrović was told by her entourage that she should appear "humble and worthy of the socialist country from which I come," so she performed in a simple dress decorated with a brooch.[34] The Yugoslav entry in 1974 was a more obvious product of the political context of its time, with Korni grupa (Korni group) – one of Yugoslavia's most popular rock groups in the early 1970s – singing "Moja generacija" (My generation).[35] Accompanied by the sound of bombs falling,[36] the song was about the generation born during the Second World War, and it referred to how much better life in Yugoslavia had become since then.[37] It was an example from a repertoire of pop and rock songs that some of Yugoslavia's most popular artists produced in the 1970s, and which glorified Tito, the Partisan movement and other historical themes promoted by the Yugoslav communists as sustainers of a pan-Yugoslav identity. These songs accompanied a resurgence of conservative ideological and political values in the LCY, which had been challenged in the late 1960s and early 1970s by liberal elements within it as well as in other areas of Yugoslav cultural and social life.[38] This had especially been the case in Croatia, which had from 1966 witnessed a national cultural revival that developed into a political movement known as the Croatian Spring; this was quashed in December 1971 because Tito believed that its calls to increase Croatia's autonomy threatened Yugoslavia's integrity. The suppression of the Croatian Spring forced Vukov – who had represented Yugoslavia at Eurovision and had afterwards become a prominent figure in the movement, in part because he incorporated Croatian patriotic themes into his songs – to seek exile in Paris to avoid being arrested or imprisoned like many of the movement's other leading personalities were. Thereafter, he was forbidden from performing in public in Yugoslavia until the late 1980s.[39] Indeed, the examples of Korni grupa and Vukov show that Yugoslavia's declared cultural openness had its limits. While its artists had – unlike their counterparts in the rest of Eastern Europe – the opportunity to perform at Eurovision alongside Western European competitors, they were not able to produce music that challenged the political status quo in Yugoslavia, and were more successful if they conformed to – and, even better, openly promoted – the ideology and politics of the regime.[40]

The political maneuverings behind Yugoslavia's participation in Eurovision were, however, not always so evident in the performances of its entries, and concerned instead the way in which they were selected and the regional interests that they represented. Of the sixteen Eurovision entries sent by Yugoslavia in the 1960s and 1970s – and using the languages of the lyrics, the television centers that sponsored the entries and the place of residence of the artists as guidelines – six of them were from Croatia (4M, Dubrovački trubaduri, Kesovija, Krunoslav Slabinac and Vukov – who appeared twice), four from Serbia (Zdravko Čolić, Korni grupa, Lola Novaković and Petrović), four from Slovenia (Berta Ambrož, Lado Leskovar, Pepel in kri (Ashes and blood) and Eva Sršen) and two from Bosnia-Herzegovina (Ambasadori (Ambassadors) and Sabahudin Kurt).[41] That most of the entries came from Croatia, Serbia and Slovenia reflected the fact that the Yugoslav popular music industry was concentrated in Zagreb, Belgrade and Ljubljana – although the songs were often produced by a multinational squad of artists, composers and lyricists, some of whom had moved to these cities from other parts of Yugoslavia in search of better career prospects.

In this sense, the national grievances and rivalries that marked the break up of Yugoslavia in the early 1990s were not explicit at the Yugoslav preliminary contest for Eurovision in the 1960s and 1970s – when participants were, in any case, aware that such expressions could gravely harm their professional advancement, as the example of Vukov demonstrated. Instead, rivalry at the preliminary contest was manifested in a more insidious competition between artists, record companies and television centers for the cachet, power and profit that a victory there – and, even more so, one at Eurovision itself – could bring. In the 1970s, some commentators suggested that television centers were sabotaging the preliminary contest by voting for weaker entries in order to better the prospects of their own nominees; others, meanwhile, complained that a tendency of giving different television centers the opportunity to provide the Yugoslav entry meant that a politics of rotation, rather than a competition based on merit, was at play and was nullifying the competitive function of the preliminary contest.[42]

A Popularity Contest?

Criticisms of the preliminary contest were part of a wider public discussion on Eurovision that peaked in Yugoslavia in the mid 1970s, and which was motivated by the poor results that it was achieving there. In 1962, Yugoslavia achieved the best position that it would have at Eurovision from 1961 to 1982, when Lola Novaković finished fourth with the song "Ne pali svetla u sumrak" (Don't turn on the lights at twilight). Novaković even tied with the United Kingdom entry and finished ahead of such popular music powers as Germany and Italy, which had sent their stars Conny Froboess and Claudio Villa, respectively.[43] She claimed afterwards that her result showed that Yugoslav popular music could "successfully contend with that created by songwriters in Western Europe."[44] But after 1962, Yugoslavia's Eurovision performances increasingly became a cause for anxiety rather than pride. In 1964, for example, Sabahudin Kurt finished last when he received the infamous *nul points* for his song "Život je sklopio krug" (Life has come full circle), and for the rest of the 1960s and into the 1970s Yugoslav entries tended to rank in the bottom half of the scoreboard. These results were perceived by some Yugoslav cultural elites as a cause for concern, particularly because Yugoslavia was submitting its most successful artists to Eurovision, including ones with established reputations in Western Europe. For example, in 1965 Kesovija began a successful career in France, and she even performed for Monaco at Eurovision in 1966 before doing so for Yugoslavia in 1972 – although in 1966 she, too, came last in the contest, while in 1972 she ranked ninth.[45]

Yugoslavia's track record at Eurovision prompted its cultural elites to question why Yugoslav popular music was not successful at the contest: was it because their country was just culturally and politically too different from Western Europe, or because its popular music production was just not modern enough – particularly when it incorporated folk aspects or was not keeping up with the latest trends – to suit Western tastes? Such inquiries reflected wider debates in Yugoslav culture, politics and society in the postwar era that sought to analyze the impact of modernizing phenomena on cultural and political identities, as well as to understand how these were being shaped by Yugoslavia's nonaligned position in the Cold War. Indeed, one of the complaints made in the Yugoslav media in the 1970s concerning Yugoslavia's poor results at Eurovision was that, as the only socialist, Slavic and Eastern European participant, and as one of the less prosperous ones, it could not depend on cultural and regional similitudes for support in the voting. As the journalist Maroje Mihovilović put it in the magazine *Start* in 1976,

> we are a proud nation, we know that some geographical and historical circumstances have apparently pushed us into the background of the European cultural and pseudocultural community, and that bothers us. But we know that some neopolitical events nonetheless have a major significance for national self-affirmation.[46]

That such cultural and political interpretations were used to explain Yugoslavia's low rankings at Eurovision was also demonstrated by the remarks made by Zdravko Čolić after he came fifteenth at the 1973 contest with the song "Gori vatra" (The fire is burning). This was a hit in Yugoslavia but clearly failed to appeal to Western European audiences, and Čolić believed that this was due to cultural, linguistic and musical differences, as "the Serbian language was so incomprehensible to them [Western Europeans, op.a.]" and ""Gori vatra" sounded more Turkish than European."[47] The notion that the incorporation of folk elements was an obstacle to the success of Čolić and other Yugoslav artists at the contest is also supported by the conclusions of the sociologists Gad Yair and Daniel Maman in their studies on Eurovision: they argue that entries needed to adhere to a "Western style" at the contest in the 1970s, as "local and primordial cultural tastes" would not attract votes from enough countries.[48] To be sure, most Yugoslav entries also conformed to Western styles of popular music and were not of the highly popular "newly composed folk music" variety, which was largely considered by Yugoslav commentators to be an "aesthetically inferior musical language."[49] Newly composed folk music was also perceived as "reinforcing perceptions of culture-core differences between Balkan and (western) European culture," as well as between Yugoslavia's "eastern" republics (Bosnia-Herzegovina, Macedonia, Montenegro and Serbia), where the genre's audience and production was more concentrated, and its "western" ones (Croatia and Slovenia).[50] That Western intellectuals had been using the study of folk songs to underline the "backwardness" of Eastern Europe since the eighteenth century[51] was thus not lost among Yugoslav commentators in the 1960s and 1970s, who also used musical terms to interpret an East-West duality in both a European context and a Yugoslav one.

By the 1970s, millions of Western European tourists were flocking to Yugoslavia every year, but there was not a corresponding relationship between the increasing number of international visitors and the country's Eurovision results – meaning that, even if Eurovision was playing a part in advertising Yugoslavia as a tourist destination, it was not having the same success in promoting its popular music. It must be noted, however, that in the 1960s and 1970s voting at Eurovision was done by juries from each country, so the results were not as much a reflection of public opinion as they have been in the contests of recent years, when viewers in all participating countries have been able to vote by telephone.[52] Furthermore, trying to ascertain voting patterns at Eurovision in the 1960s and 1970s is made more challenging by the fact that six different voting systems were used during that period, while from 1975 onwards one system has been in place (although it has variously involved voting by juries and the public).[53] Nonetheless, studies by Yair and Maman on voting patterns at Eurovision from 1975 to 1992 point to a "structure of international hegemonic relations," and they support the claim of some Yugoslav cultural elites that their country was marginalized at the contest. These studies identify blocs of Western, Northern and Mediterranean countries that systematically preferred to vote for each other; Yugoslavia is included in the Mediterranean bloc together with Cyprus, Greece, Italy, Monaco, Spain and Turkey,[54] which Yair sees as having been bound by "common experiences of sea and history, which helped to create similar cultural tastes for music, dance and sexuality."[55] The Western group maintained a position of cultural hegemony not only because it was the largest bloc and thus awarded itself many points, but also because it received points from other blocs, which tended to give few points to each other because of "different cultural tastes and from lack of cultural contact with each other."[56] Furthermore, the Mediterranean bloc is considered the weakest one for it received the lowest average number of points in the contest and was more diffuse and unstable than the others, with its members exhibiting less loyalty to one another than those of the other blocs did.[57]

Together with these cultural and political analyses of Yugoslavia's disappointing performances at Eurovision, JRT and Yugoslav record companies also complained that they could not compete against their more powerful and wealthier Western European counterparts, who were able to invest more resources into the production and promotion of their entries. Representatives of JRT and some commentators in the Yugoslav media even claimed that Eurovision had been hijacked by Western record companies that were influencing the voting and seeking to exploit the contest for their own profits. On this point, they shared the concerns of some Nordic countries, which – while they themselves were not awarding Yugoslav entries many votes – agreed that Eurovision had become too commercialized.[58] Yugoslav artists also often felt like poor cousins at Eurovision when they saw how much was invested into their Western rivals. For example, Kurt complained that his team went to Copenhagen in 1964 without any promotional materials, records and almost without money, while posters of the Italian Gigliola Cinquetti – who won that year with "Non ho l'età" (I'm too young) – were plastered all over the city and her records were available for purchase.[59] Kesovija had similar criticisms after her performance in 1972, when she said that she had felt "like a painter whom people had requested to paint a landscape, but they had left the artist without the color green."[60] Yet while Yugoslav cultural elites were criticizing the voting patterns in Eurovision and the role of record companies in the contest, their own juries were not acting much differently than Western European ones: indeed, they awarded their maximum points to the winning songs in seven out of sixteen years in the 1960s and 1970s,[61] and the top three recipients of their points were the United Kingdom, France and Italy – countries whose popular music industries were, with West Germany's, the most powerful in Europe.

In the early 1970s, the question of whether Yugoslavia should continue to participate in Eurovision began to be discussed by the commissions of JRT concerned with the production of music programming on radio and television. They were worried not only about Yugoslavia's low rankings at Eurovision, but also that the selection for it was dominating the Opatija Festival and detracting from that event's major aim – that is, the domestic production of quality popular music for a Yugoslav audience, rather than the promotion of it to a Western market that seemed to be showing little interest for it.[62] Although some members of the commissions claimed that Yugoslavia's participation in Eurovision was a pointless effort, others maintained that the poor scores should not be a cause for "national trauma" and that the contest remained an opportunity for Yugoslav artists to appear before such a large audience.[63] But by the mid 1970s, Yugoslavia was still not achieving much success at Eurovision, and in 1976 it again figured at the bottom of the scoreboard when the aptly named Ambasadori came second to last with the song "Ne mogu skriti svoju bol" (I can't hide my pain). As it happened, JRT could no longer bear the pain, too. In September 1976, its board of directors decided to withdraw from Eurovision on the grounds that the Yugoslav public no longer supported it and that record companies were unfairly influencing the contest.[64] There were still some board members who wanted Yugoslavia to continue participating, or who thought that it could join forces with other countries that shared similar criticisms of Eurovision or had not performed so well there in recent years – such as Nordic and Mediterranean ones – to pressure the EBU and other members into reforming the contest.[65] But these views were pushed aside by those who sought a withdrawal from Eurovision. Some claimed that Yugoslavia had been deliberately relegated to the bottom of the scoreboard because the voting was too politicized, and that it was more important for Yugoslavia to maintain its dignity and reputation rather than to continue appearing at the contest.[66] The representative of Ljubljana Radio and Television, Janez Vipotnik, said that a general meeting at his station had decided unanimously that Yugoslavia should no longer participate, as "a strong political revolt arose in Slovenia" after the 1976 contest and "[a] discussion started in the press about whom it benefits for Yugoslavia to cooperate in an organization like the Eurovision Song Contest."[67]

There was not a particular response from the EBU or other Eurovision participants to Yugoslavia's withdrawal from the contest, most likely because the Yugoslav move was not so original as several countries had entered, left and reentered Eurovision in the past two decades. Furthermore, JRT's criticisms of the role of record companies in the contest had also been made earlier by Nordic participants – which had even submitted proposals for reform – and these issues were being discussed by the EBU at the time Yugoslavia withdrew.[68] Indeed, the fact that the Nordic participants had not only been more vocal in their criticisms but also active in proposing solutions, together with the EBU's willingness to address its members' concerns regarding Eurovision, suggests that Yugoslavia's withdrawal was more an annoyed reaction to the dented pride of Yugoslav artists, composers, lyricists, record companies and JRT – and, indeed, the country as a whole – rather than a pioneering effort to reform the contest. However, while the EBU and its members did not respond in any notable way to Yugoslavia's exit, the Yugoslav public did. Discussions in the Yugoslav media and letters sent by Eurovision fans to JRT maintained that, whatever Yugoslavia's result there, it still provided a stage upon which the country could display its popular music and tourist attractions, and that it was a social event for many people who liked to gather around their television sets with their family and friends to watch the contest.[69] In 1978, popular entertainment magazines from all over Yugoslavia, led by the Zagreb-based weekly *Studio*, asked their readers whether Yugoslavia should reenter the contest: 107,181 votes were received, and 97.5 per cent of them responded affirmatively.[70]

Conclusion

In response to this wave of public opinion, JRT decided that it should apply to reenter Eurovision, and Yugoslavia consequently returned to the contest in 1981. But it did not make a noteworthy performance until 1983, when Daniel Popović and his song "Džuli" (Julie) – which was about a romance between a local man and a foreign tourist – came fourth and proved to be the best-selling song of all of the entries of that year.[71] A couple of other Yugoslav entries finished fourth and sixth in Eurovision in the late 1980s, but it was the victory of the group Riva (Boardwalk) in 1989 with the song "Rock Me" that was the country's biggest ever Eurovision success. Almost three decades after it had first entered the contest, Yugoslavia appeared to have discovered a recipe for success at Eurovision by sending songs that conformed to contemporary Western European styles of pop music. However, as the Cold War ended and the fissures between the Yugoslav republics grew, the political divisions among them were played out on the Eurovision stage. In 1991, the entry from TV Belgrade – a certain Baby Doll who performed the song "Brazil" – won the Yugoslav preliminary contest despite criticism from the television centers in Zagreb, Ljubljana, Sarajevo and Skopje, who claimed that the voting had been politicized in favor of the Serbian entry.[72] This was the last year in which all of the six republics and two provinces in socialist Yugoslavia chose a common Eurovision entry, for by the next contest in 1992 the federation no longer existed.

The 1980s are remembered as the apogee of Yugoslavia's success at Eurovision, but while its experience there in the 1960s and 1970s may not be as glorious, it is perhaps more fruitful in offering insights into what Yugoslavia's citizens thought about their relations with the rest of the world as well as their own cultural and political identities. Yugoslavia's geopolitical position in Europe did indeed make it a unique participant in Eurovision in the 1960s and 1970s, and this, coupled with the fact that Eurovision was an international contest, televised annually and followed by a huge audience, meant that Yugoslavia's experience there was subject to much analysis among its citizens and often perceived of in political terms. As the only socialist, Slavic and Eastern European participant in the contest, Yugoslavia's cultural and political elites exploited Eurovision to promote their country as the most culturally liberal and modern part of Eastern Europe, and they hoped that the contest would additionally advertise Yugoslavia's tourist potential and advance its popular music industry. But as Yugoslav entries in Eurovision in the 1960s and 1970s increasingly finished with poor results, Yugoslavia's exceptionalism there was perceived to be problematic. The low scores prompted Yugoslavia's citizens to reconsider the purpose of this cultural exchange and whether it was in their country's interests to engage in it; they wondered if participation in Eurovision was more a confirmation of Yugoslavia's cultural and economic alienation from the West than an affirmation of its nonalignment. Yugoslavia is usually recalled as the Eastern European country that was most open to cultural exchange with the West during the Cold War, but its experience at Eurovision shows that its relationship with Western Europe was a more ambivalent one due to cultural and economic differences that had defined Yugoslavia as "Eastern European" well before 1945. The glitter of every Eurovision was a mirror for Yugoslavia: as its artists failed to be as fashionable as their Western European counterparts and its record companies competed in vain against more powerful Western ones, the limits of its modernity and prosperity – as measured against a Western yardstick – were exposed to the millions in Yugoslavia and around the world who followed the contest.

However, in trying to explain Yugoslavia's experience at Eurovision by invoking paradigms of international politics, some Yugoslav cultural elites misplaced and exaggerated their country's exceptionalism: there were, after all, other countries – such as Mediterranean and Nordic ones – that were expressing similar concerns about their poor results at the contest in the 1960s and 1970s, and which also variously found themselves on the cultural and political periphery of Western Europe.[73] But this sort of mentality was chronic in a country whose international reputation, and even raison d'etre, was based on its in-between position between East and West – a trademark which permitted Yugoslavia to take part in Eurovision and, more significantly, brought it special economic and political support from the West, but which became meaningless after the end of the Cold War. In the end, Yugoslavia's entry into and continued participation in Eurovision in the 1960s and 1970s was determined by its political status in Europe, but its success there depended on it tuning itself to the cultural tastes of Western Europe. The irony of its experience at Eurovision was that it achieved its greatest success there just as the Cold War international order and Yugoslavia itself fell apart. This heralded a new era in which Central and East European countries – including six from the former Yugoslavia – would enter the contest and start supporting each other in their Eurovision voting in a way that Yugoslavia could never count on in the 1960s and 1970s. In 2006, this even contributed to Serbia's victory at Eurovision with Marija Šerifović singing "Molitva" (A prayer), which was awarded twelve points from Bosnia-Herzegovina, Croatia, Macedonia, Montenegro and Slovenia.

Notes

[1] In this chapter, the word "Eurovision" is used as shorthand for "the Eurovision Song Contest," although technically it can also be used to refer to the Eurovision Network created by the European Broadcasting Union (EBU), the organization through which the Eurovision Song Contest is arranged.

[2] Ana Petruseva, "Old Friends Serenade Serbia in Istanbul," *Balkan Crisis Report* 499 (2004), http://www.iwpr.net/ index.pl?archive/bcr3/bcr3_200405_499_2_eng.txt.

[3] Further demonstrating this shared popular culture, composers and lyricists from the region have produced Eurovision entries representing countries of the former Yugoslavia other than their own. For example, in 2006 the Belgrade-based Goran Bregović composed Croatia's entry "Moja štikla" [My stiletto], which was sung by Severina, while Slovenia's song in 2007, "Cvet z juga" [Flower from the south], sung by Alenka Gotar, was composed by Andrej Babić from Croatia.

[4] Philip V. Bohlman, *World Music: A Very Short Introduction* (New York: Oxford University Press, 2002), 89.

⁵ Cited in Robert Deam Tobin, "Eurovision at 50: Post-Wall and Post-Stonewall," in *A Song for Europe: Popular Music and Politics in the Eurovision Song Contest*, ed. Ivan Raykoff and Robert Deam Tobin (Aldershot, England, and Burlington, VT: Ashgate, 2007), 27.

⁶ John Kennedy O'Connor, *The Eurovision Song Contest, 50 Years: The Official History* (London: Carlton Books, 2005), 8. The format of Eurovision is as follows: each year, participating countries send an artist and song to the televised contest. After all of the songs are performed, a jury – or, as is the case nowadays, the public as well – from each country votes for and ranks its top ten songs (although it cannot vote for its own country's entry) by awarding them points from one to eight, ten or twelve. The scores are then tallied up to give the winner, and the victorious country earns the right to host Eurovision the following year.

⁷ The definition of "Europe" at Eurovision is based on membership of the EBU, which includes not only European but also some Middle Eastern and North African public broadcasters. This has allowed Israel to participate in Eurovision since 1973, while Morocco entered once in 1980, but apart from these two cases all other countries participating in Eurovision have been from the European continent.

⁸ For a discussion of Yugoslavia's participation in Eurovision after 1980, see Dean Vuletic, "The Socialist Star: Yugoslavia, Cold War Politics and the Eurovision Song Contest," in *A Song for Europe: Popular Music and Politics in the Eurovision Song Contest*, ed. Ivan Raykoff and Robert Deam Tobin (Aldershot, England, and Burlington, VT: Ashgate, 2007), 92–7.

⁹ Wolff considers "the construction of Eastern Europe as a paradox of simultaneous inclusion and exclusion, Europe but not Europe. Eastern Europe defined Western Europe by contrast, as the Orient defined the Occident, but was also made to mediate between Europe and the Orient. One might describe the invention of Eastern Europe as an intellectual project of demi-Orientalization." Larry Wolff, *Inventing Eastern Europe: The Map of Civilization on the Mind of the Enlightenment* (Stanford: Stanford University Press, 1994), 4, 7, 9.

¹⁰ Larry Wolff, ibid., 1994, 3.

¹¹ Petar Janjatović, "Pogled Unazad: Jugoslovenski Pop i Rok," *Novi zvuk* 13 (1999): 42.

¹² Ljubodrag Dimić, *Agitprop Kultura: Agitpropovska Faza Kulturne Politike u Srbiji 1945–1952* (Belgrade: Rad, 1988), 164. For an exposition on the relationship between popular music and politics in Yugoslavia from 1945 to the late 1950s, see Dean Vuletic, ibid., 2007, 84–7.

¹³ Petar Luković, *Bolja Prošlost: Prizori iz Muzičkog Života Jugoslavije 1940–1989* (Belgrade: Mladost, 1989), 12.

¹⁴ Cited in Petar Luković, ibid., 1989, 11.

[15] Ljubodrag Dimić, ibid., 1988, 261.

[16] European Broadcasting Union, "1950: The EBU," *Diffusion EBU*, (Winter 1999/2000), 15; Ivo Pustišek, *Istorija Zakonodavstva o Radio-difuziji u Jugoslaviji: Međunarodna Regulativa i Jugoslovensko Zakonodavstvo (1907–1986)* (Belgrade: Savremena administracija, 1987), 104.

[17] Eurovision was broadcast to some parts of Eastern Europe from 1965. However, Eastern European countries had their own version of Eurovision from 1961 in the form of the Sopot International Song Festival, which was held annually in the Polish town of the same name, and the Intervision Song Contest that was organized by the IORT from 1977 to 1980. Ivan Raykoff and Robert Deam Tobin, "Introduction," in *A Song for Europe: Popular Music and Politics in the Eurovision Song Contest*, ed. Ivan Raykoff and Robert Deam Tobin (Aldershot, England, and Burlington, VT: Ashgate, 2007), xvii–xviii. Central and East European countries began to enter Eurovision after the fall of their socialist regimes in 1989 and 1990, when the IORT merged with the EBU. The last one of them to participate in Eurovision was the Czech Republic, which entered for the first time in 2007. Note also that Yugoslavia also began participating in Eurovision before some members of the European Economic Community and the North Atlantic Treaty Organization did, including Greece, Iceland, Ireland, Portugal and Turkey.

[18] Igor Duda, *U Potrazi za Blagostanjem: O Povijesti Dokolice i Potrošačkog Društva u Hrvatskoj 1950-ih i 1960-ih* (Zagreb: Srednja Europa, 2005), 43–8, 50–6.

[19] Ljerka V. Rasmussen, *Newly Composed Folk Music of Yugoslavia* (New York: Routledge, 2002), 41.

[20] Krešimir Kovačević, ed., *Leksikon Jugoslavenske Muzike, Vol. 2* (Zagreb: Jugoslavenski leksikografski zavod "Miroslav Krleža," 1984), 101–2. The Opatija Festival was not, however, the first popular music festival to be established in Yugoslavia – the Zagreb Festival was established before it in 1954. Ljerka V. Rasmussen, ibid., 2002, 41.

[21] Television services did not start at the same time in all of the Yugoslav republics and provinces: TV Zagreb first conducted experimental broadcasts in 1956, and TV Belgrade and TV Ljubljana did so in 1958. Croatian Radio and Television, "Povijest HRT-a," Hrvatska radiotelevizija, http://www.hrt.hr/hrt/povijest/povijest_hrv.html. Television centers were established thereafter in the capital city of each republic and province.

[22] Archive of Yugoslavia, JRT (hereafter "AY 646"), 70, JRT, "Zapisnik sa sastanka Muzičke komisije Jugoslovenske radiotelevizije održanog 29 i 30 juna u Beogradu," Belgrade, June 29-30, 1960, 7.

[23] Krešimir Kovačević, ibid., Vol. 2, 1984, 167.

[24] Cited in Momčilo Karan, *Pesma Evrovizije: Od Ljiljane Petrović do*

Željka Joksimovića (Belgrade: Svet knjige, 2005), 7.

[25] John Kennedy O'Connor, ibid., 2005, 19; "Evrovizija," Globus, May 20, 1961.

[26] The participation of these countries proved controversial at several of the contests. Regarding Spain and Portugal, the 1964 contest was marred by a protester who jumped onto the stage carrying a sign with the slogan "Boycott Franco and Salazar." Furthermore, because of its opposition to the Franco regime, Austria refused to attend Eurovision in 1969 when it was held in Madrid. Turkey withdrew from the contest in 1979 when it was held in Jerusalem, under pressure from its Arab neighbors who threatened to cut off oil supplies if it participated. Turkey also did not enter the contest in 1976, when Greece entered the song "Panaghia mou, panaghia mou" [My Homeland, My Homeland], sung by Mariza Koch and Dimitris Zouboulis, which protested against the Turkish invasion of Cyprus in 1974. John Kennedy O'Connor, ibid., 2005, 24, 37, 53, 65–6, 76, 80–1.

[27] John Kennedy O'Connor, ibid., 2005, 31, 47, 51.

[28] Krešimir Kovačević, ibid., Vol. 1, 1984, 207–8, 212.

[29] Krešimir Kovačević, ibid., Vol. 2, 1984, 2, 340.

[30] Igor Duda, ibid., 2005, 130–41.

[31] Ivan Raykoff and Robert Deam Tobin. ibid., 2007, xvii.

[32] As Duda puts it, for many of Yugoslavia's citizens in the 1950s and 1960s, Italy was a "window to the West." This was especially the case for those who lived in coastal areas and could catch Italian radio and television programs, and for the ones who made shopping trips to Italy – most famously to Trieste – to purchase goods that were not available at home, or were more fashionable or of a better quality. Igor Duda, ibid., 2005, 69–71.

[33] For example, in 1974, when the Poruguese entry "E depois do adeus" [And after goodbye], sung by Paulo de Carvalho, was first aired on national radio, its broadcast was used as a signal for the mobilization of troops who went on to overthrow the ruling dictatorship. John Kennedy O'Connor, ibid., 2005, 59. In 1977, Portugal went on to enter the patriotic song "Portugal no coração" [Portugal in my heart], sung by Os amigos [Our friends], which honored the 1974 revolution.

[34] Cited in Momčilo Karan, ibid., 2005, 7.

[35] Krešimir Kovačević, ibid., Vol. 1, 1984, 450–1.

[36] John Kennedy O'Connor, ibid., 2005, 58.

[37] At Eurovision in 1974, Korni grupa vied with another group singing about war, although in a more metaphorical sense: that was the Swedish group ABBA, which went on to win the contest with the song "Waterloo."

[38] Zdenko Čepič, "Oživljanje Politične Revolucionarnosti," in *Sloven-*

ska Novejša Zgodovina: Od Programa Zedinjena Slovenija do Mednarodnega Priznanja Republike Slovenije 1848–1992, Vol. 2, ed. Jana Fischer, Nataša Kandus and Igor Zemljič (Ljubljana: Mladinska knjiga, Inštitut za novejšo zgodovino, 2005), 1118.

[39] Vice Vukov, *Pogled iza Ogledala* (Zagreb: Nakladni zavod Matice hrvatske, 1999), 7; Vice Vukov, *Tvoja Zemlja: Sjećanja na 1971* (Zagreb: Nakladni zavod Matice hrvatske, 2003), 79–80, 102.

[40] For criticisms of the relationship of Korni grupa and other pop and rock artists with the political establishment, see Aleksandar Žikić, *Fatalni Ringišpil: Hronika Beogradskog Rokenrola, Deo 1, 1959–1979* (Belgrade: Geopoetika, 1999), 128, 166, 176, 207–8.

[41] In the 1980s, Yugoslavia's Eurovision entries also came mostly from Croatia, with one each as well from Bosnia-Herzegovina, Montenegro and Serbia. Macedonia never contributed a Yugoslav entry to Eurovision; indeed, the first time an entry from Macedonia appeared at the contest was when it began participating in it independently from 1998.

[42] Momčilo Karan, ibid., 2005, 16, 33; M. Goluža, "Rezultati Nezdrave Klime," *Vjesnik,* March 22, 1965; Zvonko Kovačić, "Čestitke Prije i Poslije," *Studio,* February 28, 1976; Zvonko Kovačić, "Želja Jedna – Ukusa Sto," *Studio,* March 13, 1976; Tanja Petrović, "Sećanja Bisere Veletanlić: Biografija Pisana Notama," *Gloria,* December 20, 2006.

[43] John Kennedy O'Connor, ibid., 2005, 21.

[44] Cited in Momčilo Karan, ibid., 2005, 11–2. Novaković was overjoyed with this result, which she considered to be unexpectedly good because, as she later remarked, at that time "[w]e still did not exist on the European [popular music, op.a.] scene," and before the contest she had received no attention from the international media. Cited in Petar Luković, ibid., 1989, 107.

[45] Petar Luković, ibid., 1989, 151.

[46] Maroje Mihovilovič, "Jer Što je Nama Eurovizija?" *Start,* March 24, 1976.

[47] Cited in Živko M. Bojanić, *Čola* (Belgrade: Udruženje nezavisnih izdavača knjiga, 2001), 71.

[48] Gad Yair, "Unite-Unite-Europe: The Political and Cultural Structures of Europe as Reflected in the Eurovision Song Contest," *Social Networks* 17 (1995): 157; Gad Yair and Daniel Maman, "The Persistent Structure of Hegemony in the Eurovision Song Contest," *Acta Sociologica* 3 (1996): 321. For a similar perspective, see Alf Björnberg, "Return to Ethnicity: The Cultural Significance of Musical Change in the Eurovision Song Contest," in *A Song for Europe: Popular Music and Politics in the Eurovision Song Contest,* ed. Ivan Raykoff and Robert Deam Tobin (Aldershot, England, and Burlington, VT: Ashgate, 2007), 19–21.

[49] Ljerka V. Rasmussen, ibid., 2002, xviii–xix. Newly composed folk

music is "a hybrid genre drawn from local folk music sources (rural nostalgia) and commercial pop patterns (aspirations to progress)," and "a by-product of the migration of [the] rural population to the cities and the rapid process of urbanization after World War II." Ljerka Vidić Rasmussen, "The Southern Wind of Change: Style and the Politics of Identity in Prewar Yugoslavia," in *Retuning Culture: Musical Changes in Central and Eastern Europe*, ed. Mark Slobin (Durham and London: Duke University Press, 1996), 100.

[50] Ljerka V. Rasmussen, ibid., 2002, xix.

[51] Larry Wolff, ibid., 1994, 310, 324–331.

[52] Alf Björnberg, ibid., 2007, 17.

[53] John Kennedy O'Connor, ibid., 2005, 185; Daniel Fenn et al., "How does Europe Make its Mind Up?: Connections, Cliques, and Compatibility between Countries in the Eurovision Song Contest," *Physica A: Statistical Mechanics and its Applications* 2 (2006): 578.

[54] In these studies, the Western bloc includes the United Kingdom, France, Ireland, the Netherlands, Belgium, Switzerland, Malta, Luxembourg and Israel, and the Northern bloc Germany, Denmark, Sweden and Norway. Gad Yair, ibid., 1995, 153; Gad Yair and Daniel Maman, ibid., 1996, 315.

[55] Gad Yair, ibid., 1995, 156.

[56] Gad Yair and Daniel Maman, ibid., 1996, 317–9, 321.

[57] Gad Yair, ibid., 1995, 147, 156, 157, 159.

[58] European Broadcasting Union Archives, The Eurovision Song Contest (hereafter "EBUA, ESC"), "Concours Eurovision de la chanson 1976-1977," EBU, Executive Group of the Television Programme Committee, "Eurovision Song Contest 1976," Milan, October 23-25, 1975, 3.

[59] Cited in Momčilo Karan, ibid., 2005, 13–5.

[60] Cited in Petar Luković, ibid., 1989, 151. For similar complaints made by Kornelije Kovač, a composer and musician from Korni grupa, see Petar Luković, ibid., 1989, 228.

[61] John Kennedy O'Connor, ibid., 2005, 180.

[62] AY 646-72, JRT, "Zapisnik sa zajedničke sednice Muzičke komisije i Komisije za muzičku produkciju JRT i muzičkih urednika TV, održane 8. oktobra 1973. godine u Beogradu," Belgrade, October 8, 1973, 1-2; AY 646-72, JRT, "Zapisnik sa zajedničke sednice Muzičke komisije i Komisije za muzičku produkciju JRT, održane 14. decembra u Beogradu," Belgrade, December 14, 1973, 3.

[63] AY 646-72, JRT, "Zapisnik sa zajedničke sednice Muzičke komisije i Komisije za muzičku produkciju JRT održane 28. maja 1975. godine u Budvi," Budva, May 28, 1975, 3; AY 646-72, JRT, "Zapisnik sa sastanka urednika zabavne muzike članova radne grupe za izradu propozicija za festival Opatija 74.," Belgrade, September 27, 1973, 2.

144   *Dean Vuletic*

⁶⁴ AY 646-8, JRT "Stenografske beleške sa 127. sednice Upravnog odbora Jugoslovenske radiotelevizije održane 30.IX i 1.X 1976. god. u Vrd-
niku," Vrdnik, September 30-October 1, 1976, 183-5; EBUA, ESC, "Déci-
sions 1," EBU, "Minutes—56th Meeting Administrative Council," Geneva,
December 10-11, 1976, 1.

⁶⁵ AY 646-8, JRT "Stenografske beleške sa 127. sednice Upravnog odbora Jugoslovenske radiotelevizije," ibid., 1976, 186-7.

⁶⁶ It was even alleged at this meeting that Israel had been favored in
the voting in the 1976 contest for political reasons. Ibid., 184, 189. Concerning Israeli participation, JRT's withdrawal from Eurovision in the late
1970s saved it from the dilemma of whether or not it should attend the
1979 contest in Jerusalem, at a time when Yugoslavia did not have diplomatic relations with Israel (these had been cut off by Belgrade in 1967, as
it had supported Arab states in the Arab-Israeli War).

⁶⁷ Ibid., 183-4.

⁶⁸ EBUA, ESC, "Concours Eurovision de la chanson 1976-1977," EBU,
Television Programme Committee, "Eurovision Song Contest: SR/YLE
Proposal for Decommercialisation of the Contest," Toulouse, April 28-30,
1976, 1-3.

⁶⁹ Momčilo Karan, "Poraženi 'Ambasadori,'" *Oslobođenje,* May 5, 1990;
cited in Zvonko Kovačić, "Na Vjetrenjače ne Treba Jurišati!" *Studio,* April
2, 1977; A.V., "Što Kažu Stručnjaci? Da!" *Studio,* April 8, 1978; "Rekli ste—
Da!" *Studio,* April 1, 1978.

⁷⁰ "Većina ili 97,53% Rekla je DA!" *Studio,* April 29, 1978.

⁷¹ John Kennedy O'Connor, ibid., 2005, 94.

⁷² Zvonko Kovačić, "Jugovizija Umire od Stida," *Studio,* March 15,
1991; Mirela Kruhak, "Sve se Zbilo iza Kulisa," *TOP,* March 18, 1991; Mirela Kruhak and Damir Strugar, "Sve je Bilo Lažirano?" *TOP,* March 18, 1991;
Dražen Vrdoljak, "Yuga Umire Pjevajuči," *Večernji list,* March 12, 1991.

⁷³ For example, on the national reactions to the low scores received by
Finland, Norway, and Turkey, see Mari Pajala, "Finland, Zero Points: Nationality, Failure, and Shame in the Finnish Media," in *A Song for Europe:
Popular Music and Politics in the Eurovision Song Contest,* ed. Ivan Raykoff
and Robert Deam Tobin (Aldershot, England, and Burlington, VT: Ash-
gate, 2007), 71–82; Ivan Raykoff, "Camping on the Borders of Europe,"
in *A Song for Europe: Popular Music and Politics in the Eurovision Song Con-
test,* ed. Ivan Raykoff and Robert Deam Tobin (Aldershot, England, and
Burlington, VT: Ashgate, 2007), 9–10; Thomas Solomon, "Articulating the
Historical Moment: Turkey, Europe, and Eurovision in 2003," in *A Song for
Europe: Popular Music and Politics in the Eurovision Song Contest,* ed. Ivan
Raykoff and Robert Deam Tobin (Aldershot, England, and Burlington, VT:
Ashgate, 2007), 136; and Martin Stokes, "Islam, the Turkish State, and Ara-
besk," *Popular Music* 2 (1992): 224–5.

6

Džuboks (Jukebox) – The First Rock'n'roll Magazine in Socialist Yugoslavia

Radina Vučetić

The process of Westernization, or the acceptance of cultural influences from western countries, was encouraged in Yugoslavia as part of the cultural cold war. Cultural influences by way of cultural diplomacy were important and powerful instruments of foreign policy in East and West in the battle for "hearts and minds," and in the battle of political ideas. Yugoslavia, with its position between East and West, was an ideal field for this kind of cultural war in which the West had much more to offer – superb visual arts, jazz and rock'n'roll, Hollywood production, modern and avant-garde theatre and dance, modernist literature, consumer goods, and fashion. That is the reason why Coca-Cola, rock'n'roll, jeans and popular culture became powerful weapons in the cold war. Through the process of a gradual cultural infiltration, the United States and other West European countries were able to export symbols, lifestyles, consumerism, and the core values of their societies.[1]

American and British influences in music through jazz and rock'n'roll were the most obvious ways of westernizing Yugoslav society. In the initial post-war years, jazz was considered decadent and was not so popular in Yugoslavia. After 1948, the big historical NO to the Soviets became a YES to jazz. Thanks to the American embassy in Belgrade, Dizzy Gillespie, Louis Armstrong, Ella Fitzgerald and other prominent jazz musicians gave concerts in Yugoslavia. American and British rock'n'roll inspired numerous rock'n'roll bands in the 1960s; it was the final proof that the influence of American and British music had become dominant.

As Aleksandar Žikić, one of the leading researchers of Yugo-slav rock'n'roll argues, very soon, rock'n'roll surged with full force, penetrating all pores of life and becoming inevitable even in the strictly controlled media.[2] NATO strategists, recognizing the vola-tile nature of rock'n'roll, even speculated on the military potential of rock'n'roll. In October 1958, the NATO journal, *Revue militaire générale*, theorized that jazz, rock and other modern dance music could be employed in the war against Communism. The idea was that the more time a young person spent listening to Little Richard, the less time he or she would read Marx and Lenin.[3] In the case of Yugoslavia, it proved to be true.

Belgrade, Music and the 1960s

The 1960s in Yugoslavia were a special phenomenon, as in most of the world. It was a period of the liberalization (more cultural, than political) and modernization of everyday life. Belgrade in the 1960s experienced swift modernization and the acceptance of Western trends. In this turbulent decade, Belgrade also built its Museum of Contemporary Arts. Beside the fact that it was the first and only museum of the avant-garde and modern art in a Communist coun-try, this museum also became famous since it was modeled after the Museum of Modern Art in New York. Plays by some of the most famous American writers had opening nights in Belgrade in the same season as their Broadway premieres (e.g., *The Openheimer Case* and *After the Fall* by Arthur Miller). The musical, *Hair*, which had its fifth premiere in Belgrade, after New York, London, Paris and Munich, was one of the turning points in Belgrade's cultural life. In 1967 Belgrade won the privilege of becoming the venue of one of the leading international theatre festivals (BITEF), which was a meet-ing point of East and West. In its first years the festival, hosted the most prominent American avant-garde theatre groups (Living The-atre, La Mamma, Bread and Puppet Theatre) completely changing what had been a predominantly conservative approach to theatre. Also, numerous concerts of American jazz and rock groups were organized, and in 1961, the first jukeboxes were installed in restau-rants and clubs. In November of 1962, "Love Me Do" by the Beatles was aired for the first time on Yugoslav radio, less than one month after its release in London. Yugoslavs adored the movie, *Rebel without Cause*; they cried when Marilyn Monroe died, and they warmly welcomed the crew of Apollo 11 in Belgrade, only three months after their walk on the moon. In the same decade, Yugoslav factories launched the production of Pepsi Cola and Coca Cola.

Vladimir Janković Jet, a rock musician, described the new atmosphere in Belgrade in 1964:

> The already, rather loosened constraints fell altogether, and life was changing before one's very eyes. The post-war generation was already on the verge of adulthood. Behavior, dress, music and all the other activities of young people were slipping beyond the control of the "culture censors." Going abroad and returning were no longer abstract ideas, and foreign-made products began to shower the capital. Jeans, t-shirts, and the latest jackets became a common feature and the streets began to look quite differently.[4]

At that time, music was no longer only the privilege of wealthy and powerful individuals. The role of radio proved to be crucial. All over Yugoslavia, young people listened to Radio Luxemburg, Radio Free Europe, and the Voice of America. They knew the latest hits and closely followed the careers and lives of music stars, their positions on "the charts," and they knew all about the manufacturers of different musical instruments. In 1961, Yugoslavia introduced its first rock'n'roll broadcast, *Meeting at 9.05*, hosted by Nikola Karaklajić, the first editor of *Jukebox* and the first Belgrade DJ. According to his recollections, young people dedicated Saturday evenings to the top twenty on Radio Luxemburg. The very next day, they would gather to discuss records and music and the top twenty list, and then make up their own lists.[5] This fact also demonstrates the openness of the regime, as well as the wish of young Yugoslavs to become a part of the Western referent system.

By 1965, there were already 88 official rock'n'roll bands in Belgrade (among them, the Silhouettes, the Black Pearls, the Ellipses, the Golden Boys, and the Panthers).[6] Especially in urban communities, young people used to spend their evenings listening to rock'n'roll music from jukeboxes, records, and radio. Disco clubs opened all around the country, breaking new ground for spending one's leisure time[7], and a stronger division existed between the Beatles and the Rolling Stones than between East and West.

The Jukebox – Why, When and How

One of the best examples of Yugoslavia's Western orientation in music is *Jukebox*, the first rock'n'roll magazine in the Communist world.[8] With all the changes that occurred in the early 1960s, records, record players, guitars and musical magazines became status symbols. Magazines specializing only in music had appeared in Yugoslavia as early as 1962. The first one, *Ritam*, was published in Novi Sad (1962-1965) as a "Revue for jazz and popular music."[9] *Plavi vijesnik* was published in Croatia in the mid-1960s as a popular youth magazine, but *Jukebox* (1966-1969)[10] was the first one dedicated exclusively to rock'n'roll music. This was followed by *Pop Express* from Zagreb (from 1969) and partly by *Gong* (1966-1968).[11] The idea to launch the monthly rock magazine, *Jukebox*, emerged from *Duga*, a publishing house, which issued a film magazine, *Filmske novosti* (*Film News*), when people rallying around this magazine realized that while rock music was gaining more fans, there was no magazine to cover musical issues. However, there were no rock music "specialists" among journalists, and the decision was made to appoint Nikola Karaklajić editor in chief. He had been the first DJ and radio journalist, who had done much since 1961 to promote rock'n'roll music in Yugoslavia.

More than 40 years later, *Jukebox* is still regarded one of the myths of the 1960s in Yugoslavia and its opening to the West. The *Lexicon of Yugoslav Mythology* describes *Jukebox* as a musical magazine "that welcomed rock music to Yugoslavia through the front door in the sixties."[12] One of the first Yugoslav rock'n'roll musicians confirms that when *Jukebox* appeared on May 3, 1966, "We were utterly exalted. Finally, there was a magazine, completely dedicated to popular music."[13]

Jukebox magazine was printed in color and it contained numerous articles and photographs from the Western press (mostly from the *New Musical Express*). Colorful cover pages, posters and records as gifts, seemed to suggest a high standard and openness of the

Yugoslav socialist society and showed potential Eastern European readers a special version of Yugoslavia's modernity and liberalism.

The establishment of the time in the beginning viewed rockers as simple-minded "losers," who were trying to copy the dissipated idols from a decadent West, and then as exotic phenomena characteristic of youth. As time passed, however, a number of able young politicians realized that they had a wonderful means of profiting politically. They organized poetry evenings and political gatherings, which also featured rock'n'roll bands. In return, these bands were given rehearsal space. They were thrilled to have a room available in a local party office, Boy Scout or youth hall. Their activities earned the organizers "good marks," because they were regarded as being capable of rallying young people.[14] Both sides were satisfied. Given these new opportunities for young rockers to play for different official organizations and to record their music for state companies, their songs lacked rebellion, typical for rock'n'roll in the world. Some of them recorded rock songs dedicated to love and even to Tito.[15] The latter practice was typical for totalitarian regimes. Although the Yugoslav regime tried to present itself as a liberal one, representatives of the elite culture (painters, sculptors, writers, film workers and musicians) competed in this way as a show of loyalty to the system. Rock musicians may have wanted to do the same, but they also may have seen it as a way into the establishment and the elite culture.

Karaklajić remembers that one of the crucial events that led to the idea of a new magazine dedicated only to rock music was the first *Gitarijada* (rock festival) held in Belgrade in 1966. This event drew 10,000 young people, which was considered an unprecedented success and a completely new phenomenon. These were no longer young people dancing in the classical way; instead, they were "swaying" to the rhythm of the new music. Young men, stripped to the waist, had their pals sitting on their shoulders. There was a public outcry, and a good number of critics thought such events were a mistake and should be discontinued, because they were not beneficial to the youth. Even the Central Committee of Serbia debated the issue, but cleverly left it up to the Central Committee of the Youth of Serbia to show more understanding, shifting the discussion to the CityYouth Committee, which understood the new aspiration of the youth.

According to Karaklajić, Yugoslav politicians had acted wisely by not interfering in this matter and by "letting the youngsters have their fun."[16] It was as Sabrina Petra Ramet suggests. "The authorities came to the conclusion that if rock music could not be suppressed, perhaps it could be put to work for socialism."[17] It was easier to maintain control of young people by avoiding the underground scene, illegal clubs, and the black market for records, and by making it open and transparent. Visibility, with the approval of the regime, would help create a positive image of Yugoslavia. Young people in Yugoslavia felt more freedom, and spectators from the West had proof of the liberal Yugoslav system.

At that time, young people were often the focus of debates in the ideological commissions of the League of Communists of Yugoslavia. Some reports from their meetings showed concern over Yugoslav youth. The Croat politician, Mika Tripalo, warned that the histories of the national liberation struggle and the Communist Party bored youngsters. On the other hand, there were reports about illegal escapes across the borders by individuals under 30.[18] But, according to these commissions, it seems that rock'n'roll was not anything for the socialist regime to be afraid of or worried about. Although rebellion was the essence of rock'n'roll, by letting it be visible and approved in socialist society, the regime actually prevented rebellion in Yugoslav rock. Self-censorship, which was omnipresent among artists in socialist Yugoslavia, contributed much to this issue. By not challenging the system with rebellion and by rocking on other topics (mostly about love), Yugoslav rock stars could be on the cover pages of popular magazines (*Jukebox* as well), they could publish records in state owned houses and organize concerts all over Yugoslavia. So who could resist not to resist?

In hindsight, it is hard to understand from a Communist perspective and socialist practice that party interference in the editing process of a magazine that was dedicated only to rock, a completely Western creation, was hardly in evidence. The clue may be a complete change of the main problems in Yugoslavia's socialist society. In the 1950s, ideological commissions mostly worried about Western influences still regarded as decadent, but in the 1960s "danger of growing western and decadent influences" (which was a common phrase in the ideology commission's vocabulary during the 1950s) was rarely mentioned. Instead, frightening in the eyes of party officials was a growing nationalism and more dissidents, mostly among philosophers, who challenged "brotherhood and unity" and Marxist dogma. Therefore, a musical magazine addressing Yugoslav youth could prevent both threats hanging like dark clouds over a peaceful socialist society. Obviously, the regime was not afraid of long hair, trousers and rock sound as long as there was nothing to challenge "brotherhood and unity" or the communist dogma. Sensitive political issues, like student demonstrations in 1968, which would probably be of interest to young readers of *Jukebox*, were just ignored.

At the time when he became editor of *Jukebox*, Karaklajić was already a national chess champion and a member of the national chess team. According to his recollections, it was not important for him to be a party member. Moreover, when he was offered membership, he refused, explaining that he and his family celebrated religious feasts. Instead of being a party member, Karaklajić suggested that his achievements and a medal from Tito were sufficient and that "the system was liberal."[19] He remembers that when he started promoting rock'n'roll, he was suspected of being a "CIA hireling." Suspicions and major opposition to his work did not come from the politicians, but rather from conservative music circles, which considered rock'n'roll of lesser significance. The only political interference occurred after the first issue of the magazine. A representative of the city committee asked for a meeting with the editorial staff. He explained that he wanted to see "what was going on and to advise us to be cautious, so as not to be regarded as someone's agency."[20] This appears to have been related to a kind of battle among editorial staff members over whether the Beatles or the Rolling Stones should be on the first cover. The final decision was in favor of the Rolling Stones. However, the Beatles would be on the cover page of the next issue. But, following the suggestion that the magazine should not look like someone's "agency," the Beatles were left for the third issue, while the cover of the second issue featured the Belgian singer, Adamo.[21] This "compromise" also demonstrated the Western orientation of the magazine, when a good-looking

guy from Belgium, who seemed like a nice boy from the neighborhood and not like someone from the Eastern bloc, appeared on
the cover.[22] Moreover, indications that *Jukebox* was published in a
socialist country were hard to find – it might have originated in any
Western country. There was no glorifying of Tito and no mention of
the Communist Party, self-management, voluntary masses, or the
achievements of a socialist society. The absence of ideological pressures and statements was amazing. The magazine definitely did
not address young communists, but young people in general. Only
two issues of the magazine showed faint traces of the prevailing
ideology. In both instances they were connected to members of a
rock group, *Elipse* (*The Ellipses*). When they were asked in an interview about their most memorable experience, they answered, "We
experienced something that every musician of ours would want to.
We performed for Comrade Tito at an evening gathering of friends
at the Youth Hall in Belgrade, to mark The Day of Youth. We all had
terrible stage fright, but we played well and were satisfied. This
will certainly always be our most memorable experience together."[23] At another time, when three of the most popular groups were
asked about their most memorable event in 1966 and their wishes
for 1967, members of *Elipse* answered, "Our performance before
Comrade Tito at the official opening of the Youth Hall," while their
wish for 1967 was "to thrill the Soviet audiences as we thrilled our
own."[24] It is interesting to combine these statements with a picture
in *Jukebox*, which showed members of the same group in front of the
Yugoslav State Assembly, as a kind of support and guarantee, not
only for them, but for the whole generation. Other rock musicians
interviewed in *Jukebox* during the three years of its existence did
not make any similar statements, suggesting that "political correctness" at the time was left to individuals and their personal beliefs.
Since most members of *Elipse* belonged to the former bourgeoisie,
their statements could be understood as a wish to emphasize their
loyalty to the system.

The *Jukebox* editorial of the first issue also expressed the wish
to aid in the modernization of society and stressed the absence of
ideologization in launching the magazine.

We are witnesses of the accelerating modernization of life at every step. Life progresses at an increasing speed. These changes reflect on everything that surrounds us. We are witnesses of a quest for novelty in literature, theater, film, painting, sculpture and music. Popular music is especially susceptible to these changes and therein lies its charm... The new wave of popular music that began several years ago with the massive use of electrical instruments, met with different responses among listeners. In contrast to the bitter opponents of this music, enthusiastic girls and boys appeared, who were fierce supporters of the new rhythm. And that is how new idols were born: young men with guitars conquered the hearts of their peers, and their influence exceeded the framework of music long ago. We encounter the passionate admirers of this music in all countries and parts of the world; the enthusiasm is the same in all hemispheres. In feeling the lack of a publication that would satisfy the interest of the vast public in this kind of music, the editorial office of "Film News" is to launch its monthly supplement – the *Jukebox* magazine –with the desire to entertain and inform readers about events in popular music.[25]

It seems that this magazine dedicated to rock'n'roll was in high demand at the time, it sold its entire circulation of 100 000 copies in less than 20 days. Other youth magazines published in Yugoslavia (at seven university centers and in Maribor), which had about 150,000 students, reached a circulation of 85,000.[26] These magazines did not always cater to the wants of their readers, but used to reprint complete speeches from various meetings of student organizations, League of the Communists of Yugoslavia conferences, or party congresses, which repulsed young readers.

Letters to the editor indicated that young people all over Yugoslavia were delighted that a rock magazine would become a feature in their lives. Although politicians and the public at large did not react disapprovingly, one commentary in *Telegram*, a Croatian magazine for art and culture, suggested that there were, nevertheless, some "custodians of Socialist values."

I know that many people will object that everything published in this *"Jukebox"* is not harmful, that today's youth loves the music, electric guitars, and has its favorites. It appears to me, however, that favorites like these are not worthy of the youth of a Socialist country and that such pastimes cause damage by becoming dominant and even exclusive. Because, do not deceive yourselves, comrades: the loss of long hours, and even days, listening to such popular music is leading the youth into spheres that are everything but constructive, in the personal and in the socially beneficial sense. And, instead of teaching young people not to "worship" the Beatles or Đorđe Marjanović, instead of instructing them to accept their music-making only as a temporary amusement and to occupy themselves with things that have more enduring values, we are encouraging our youth, liberally, to idleness or, at least, to a spiritual commitment to utterly worthless things, and what is more, we are doing so by means of such responsible and powerful media as the press or television. And now, we even have this *"Jukebox"*.[27]

This appears to have been the only unfavorable commentary, and the editors of *Jukebox* were wise enough to publish it in their magazine as a kind of irony. A commentary like this, published in the party press, like *Borba* or *Komunist*, could have jeopardized the destiny of Jukebox. But by letting this kind of commentary appear in a cultural magazine with a small circulation, the regime satisfied party hard-liners without harming anyone. To demonstrate that Yugoslav rock musicians were good role models for society, *Jukebox* published a poll in the next issue. Members of *Smeli* (*The Brave*) had to answer the following questions: which was the last premiere in the Atelje 212 theatre, name three Shakespeare plays, who was Sophocles, who played the role of Thomas More in the National Theatre, and name a play in which the famous dramatic actress, Mira Stupica, has performed?[28] Their answers were mostly correct, contradicting the commentator in *Telegram* by demonstrating that they can also be occupied "with things that have more enduring values."

Western Orientation of *Jukebox*

The atmosphere in urban areas of Yugoslavia revealed that westernization was under way. Records were coming in from the West. By the late 1950s and early 1960s, Yugoslav record companies had already started releasing records, mostly by British and American rock groups. According to Vladimir Janković Jet, "wherever you look, someone is carrying five or single singles, LPs or even an album tucked under his arm. Everyone has his own theory about which is the best band." He also remembered that only a week or two after making the famous Top 20, songs could be heard on jukeboxes in youth centers around Belgrade, so "we felt as if we were in London, listening to our 'juke'."[29]

Since everyone referred to "top lists," Jukebox established its own "top lists" from the very beginning. Top Ten lists presented to Yugoslav readers were from the USA, Great Britain, France and Italy. Later "top lists" included Dutch, Belgian, Norwegian, and Brazilian charts, and even some from the Philippines and Singapore, but none from the East.[30] Adding the top list of Yugoslav rock groups, which followed Western ones, made it obvious in which part of the polarized world Yugoslav rockers and Yugoslav youths were located.

Interviews with Yugoslav rock musicians also showed their Western orientation. For example, members of *Samonikli* (*The Growing Wilds*) mentioned Sonny and Cher, Them, Searchers, Walker Bros and Hollies as their favorite groups and The Shadows, the Beatles and Jean Pitney as their role models.[31]

To avoid browsing the air waves, *Jukebox* used to publish a precise schedule of popular radio stations and their frequencies. "Sundays from 18.05 till 18.55 – the French "top list" (Radio Europe 1); Saturdays from 22:00 till 23:00 – new recordings from the European music centers (Radio Paris), everyday from 18:00 till 19:00 the world's greatest hits (Radio-Saarbricken); Sundays from 16:00 till 17:00 – Melody Maker's British Best Sellers' List (Radio Droitvitch)."[32]

Not only did *Jukebox* inform its readers about popular radio broadcasts, but it also glorified one radio station, which was not very appreciated in other East European countries, Radio Luxemburg. It was described as a station that "broadcasts pleasant, simple and cheerful programs, introducing lively tones in the dreary colors of everyday life."[33] The same article reported hat the English section of Radio Luxemburg's broadcast was the most popular one in Yugoslavia and that it featured more than 100 broadcasts per week.[34]

Besides suggestions for Western radio broadcasts, there were also advertisements from Western musical magazines. One of the world's most popular rock magazines – the *New Musical Express* played a special role for *Jukebox*. It supplied not only most of the articles, but *Jukebox* also advertised it.[35] Its "Small Lexicon" carried an entry on the *New Musical Express*. Yugoslav readers could learn that it was published every Friday with a circulation of 600,000 copies and, most importantly, that it had 4,000 subscribers in Yugoslavia. It was possible to subscribe to this and other Western journals through the *Jugoslovenska knjiga* (Yugoslav Book) publishing house.[36] There was also some kind of cooperation with the *New Musical Express*, apparent in *Jukebox's* quiz on pop music. The first prize was a trip to a London concert organized by the *New Musical Express*.[37] *Jukebox* also recommended to its readers the British musical magazine, *Rave*, which printed between 30,000 and 50,000 copies, and had about 200 subscribers in Yugoslavia.[38]

Other pages also showed the Western orientation of *Jukebox*. The color covers of the magazine featured the Rolling Stones, the Beatles, Donovan, the Mamas and the Papas, Sonny and Cher, Who, The Monkees, and Cliff Richard. Inside were interviews with major British and American rock stars and details about the celebrities as well as texts and musical arrangements of the world's greatest hits. It was certainly helpful for fans, but also for local rock musicians, since authors of histories of Yugoslav rock agree that not many local musicians knew English very well and their performances in English were often more than funny.[39] All of these editorial practices played a part in elevating Yugoslav rock to a much higher level.

A particular breakthrough, devised by *Jukebox*, was the special gift included in each edition of the magazine starting with its tenth issue. It was a record made of a specific kind of plastic and recorded on one side only. Thanks to this policy of the *Jukebox* editorial office, the record libraries of Yugoslav youngsters were enlarged with some of the following titles, Rolling Stones: "Have you seen your mother, baby, standing in the shadow," Who: "Happy Jack," Animals: "When I was Young," Cliff Richard: "I'll come running," Shadows: "Sons & Lovers," Paul Jones: "Darlin." A special record as a gift was, as a matter of fact, the first innovation and applied in practice what was common in the Western press. Decades were to pass for the continuation of this marketing practice.

The records were published by the *Jugoton* record company; they included only EMI authors, because *Jugoton* had a license agreement with this record house.[40] Connections with the West surfaced also in the "record policy" as seen in one of the advertisements in *Jukebox*. *Mladinska knjiga,* a publishing house in Zagreb, opened a special service for selling records from abroad. They started out by offering "Delilah" by Tom Jones, "Lady Madonna" by The Beatles, "Congratulations" by Cliff Richards, "Bend Me, Shape Me" by Aman Corner, "Fire Brigade" by the Move, "Guitar Man" by Elvis Presley, "Jennifer Juniper" by Donovan, "Valleri" by the Monkees, Eric Burdon and others.[41]

Another innovation was to introduce posters. The *Jukebox editorial* cited English sociologists, who explained the importance of posters for youngsters: "with their enthusiasm for posters, an interest is awakening among young people in the figurative arts… With its suggestiveness and objective effectiveness, the printed picture can become a new element in education and progress."[42] It is unknown whether these posters changed the attitude of Yugoslavia's younger generation towards the figurative arts, but one thing is certain – the rooms of these youngsters in the grey Socialist world changed when they installed colorful posters of the world's famous stars.

The "top lists", records, and posters surely changed the musical atmosphere all over Yugoslavia. Another event probably connected with these innovations pioneered by *Jukebox* was the opening of Belgrade's first disco club in 1967. It was described as one that "could be seen in New York, Paris and London."[43] The club was in an adapted basement of an old building in the city center. Although it had space only for about 100 people, according to descriptions, it seemed to have fulfilled the basic disco standards with a DJ cabin, a dancing podium, spotlights, and furniture especially designed for the club. The walls were painted green and red, and the amplifiers sounded, as someone wrote, "Like we have never heard before in Belgrade." The Disco Club was up to date with European disco clubs and had subscribed to five records weekly from Paris and London, even before they had entered the world's "top lists!"[44]

The changes could also be better understood through individuals who could hardly be connected with a socialist society. One of them was Todor Nedeljkov from Belgrade. According to *Jukebox*, the world press wrote about this young man, the winner of a "beat-nik" poetry competition in Italy. He was to be a member of a world delegation of twelve young people to Vietnam to promote his peace verses. He was described as a 25-year old man, who had already traveled all over the world, hung around with Mick Jagger, Keith Richards, Brian Jones, Eric Burdon, and members of the Mamas and the Papas and had the same tailor as the Beatles, the Rolling Stones, and the Kinks.[45]

This Western orientation was obvious even to *Jukebox's* readers at the time. One of them compiled her own survey and submitted it in the form of a letter to the editor. In the first 20 issues there were 257 photographs of foreign groups and singers, and 69 Yugoslav ones. The most frequent ones were the Beatles (24), the Rolling Stones (17) and the Beach Boys (16).[46]

Jukebox and the East

Was it possible for the East to compete with Western rock? Not at all. At that time, no one listened to Soviet rock music, Soviet rock records were nowhere to be found, and most Yugoslav youngsters were unable to name a single Soviet rock group.[47] However, the real situation collided with the dominant ideology. The editors of *Jukebox* faced a difficult task, trying to reconcile Communist ideology with what the youths wanted. As Karaklajić remembers, there was no pressure, but they had to bear in mind that the magazine could not look like a Western "loudspeaker" but had to have "something else." He decided to include some East European bands whenever suitable.[48] Nevertheless, according to *Jukebox*, there were not many opportunities to do so. Furthermore, it seems that some of the writings about East European rock groups and letters from East European readers played the part of showing how liberal, progressive and different Yugoslavia was.

Karaklajić recalls letters to the editor from the East European countries after *Jukebox* appeared. In them, young people from all over Eastern Europe lamented over the fact that there was no magazine of this kind in their respective countries.

It is not clear how *Jukebox* reached the Soviet Union or other East European countries, but according to Karaklajić, newsstands near the Bulgarian and Hungarian borders used to order more copies of the magazine; it is possible that *Jukebox* was smuggled into neighboring Communist countries. He also remembers one Bulgarian, who contacted him – the latter was supposed to go on a business trip to Germany – when his son asked him to travel through Yugoslavia to buy a copy of *Jukebox* and to give Karaklajić a recording of his group (*The Crickets*).[49] However, some of the letters from Eastern Europe, like one from Czechoslovakia, suggest that *Jukebox* could be ordered through the mail.[50]

Some of the letters from the Soviet Union, as well as some reportages in the magazine, would emphasize the enormous ideological gap concerning music between Yugoslavia and the Soviet Union. For example, one Soviet student of journalism from Leningrad, Nikolai Latkin, was full of praise for *Jukebox* and rock'n'roll in general. Nevertheless, he also stated, "One should not renounce symphony music or the classics, such as Menuhin, Rostropovich or the Bolshoi Theatre Ballet." He also asked Yugoslav readers to send him some records, because "he would like to have records of the British rock groups." In exchange, he offered "Soviet records or anything else."[51] Irina V. from Rostov-on-the-Don wrote, "I and my friends love your magazine a lot. We often gather at my home and read it together. We love Yugoslav and foreign groups very much and it is a pity that we do not have something like that."[52]

The musical image of the Soviet Union appears in an article about the guest performance in Moscow by the group, *Indexi* from Sarajevo. Its members recall that "during our first rehearsal, we performed a couple of our compositions, and then we played two songs from the Beatles' repertoire. Then, they asked us to play our own, Yugoslav music, commenting that if they had wanted to listen to the Beatles, they would have invited them."[53]

On the other hand, there were comparisons, or even tributes, of some rock groups especially from Czechoslovakia. "Neither did Prague resist the new wave of electric guitars. The capital of Czechoslovakia today has over 200 orchestras, formed in schools, culture centers and factories." In the same issue, there was an article about the most popular group in Bulgaria (*The Silver Bracelet*).[54] Writing about another Bulgarian group, *Staccato*, gave *Jukebox* journalists the opportunity to emphasize the differences between Bulgarian and Yugoslav rock. "They showed us some music, a mixture of beat and rock that used to be popular in our country three years ago, but today people no longer listen to it. With its outdated repertoire and concepts of arrangement *Staccato* left a very faint impression."[55] *Jukebox* also informed its readers about the Polish rock group *The Blue-Black*, which gave a concert in Belgrade[56] and about *Olympic*[57] and *Flamingo* from Czechoslovakia.[58]

However, letters from Eastern Europe and information about rock groups from the East started to vanish after the first year of *Jukebox*. The obvious idea of *Jukebox* was to emphasize the uniqueness and exclusiveness of Yugoslav society in the field of rock. Yugoslavia wanted to remain the "special case" with its "own road" to socialism, so some facts that were important for rock in the Soviet bloc remained suppressed. Unfortunately, the same applies to Yugoslav historiography today, which still insists on the Yugoslav uniqueness concerning rock music. Neither the histories of rock'n'roll in Yugoslavia nor the cultural histories of that period[59] mention, for example, that an East German record company had released an album of Beatles hit in 1965, that the Polish state concert agency brought the Rolling Stones to Warsaw in 1967,[60] or that 92 per cent of Budapest's young people had attended at least one rock concert in 1969.[61]

How *Jukebox* Changed Everyday Life

Everyday life in Yugoslavia showed dramatic changes in the 1950s and 1960s. From fierce suppression in the initial post-war period to a gradual and then stronger and open acceptance of Western trends, Yugoslavia created its own daily life, moving dramatically from the Russian drink "kvass" and Soviet films, to Coca-Cola, American movies, jeans and the hippie movement. The analysis of everyday life – models of behavior, fashion, giving nicknames

(Jack, Joe, Jimmy and Johnny were the most popular nicknames in the 1950s and 1960s) – illustrates how the Coca-Cola generation established itself in Yugoslavia.

Was it possible to win a diplomatic battle by exporting art, music, movies, books and theatre performances? Perhaps. Western cultural influences did not change Yugoslav ideology. However, those influences certainly shaped generations. Young Yugoslav communists did not listen to the hits of Alla Pugatchova, they did not include Soviet movies among their favorites, and "kvass" was not a popular drink. Instead of these Soviet offerings, Yugoslavs chose jazz and rock'n'roll music, Hollywood movies, Coca-Cola and Levis. They were the most sought after icons of American popular culture, and satisfied their need to belong to the West, at least in a cultural sense.

Writing about rock music in Eastern Europe and in the Soviet Union, Timothy W. Ryback wondered what Soviet-bloc authorities could have done about young people who, in the privacy of their bedrooms, tuned into the broadcasts of Radio Luxemburg and Radio Free Europe, or who paid black marketeers half a month's income for two Beatles albums or a pair of blue jeans?[62] Yugoslav authorities prevented different forms of private rebellion by letting rock out into the open and making it accessible. In fact, by sponsoring rock recordings, rock groups, opening disco clubs, organizing rock concerts, letting rock be visible through the media and through a specialized rock magazine, like *Jukebox*, they controlled the younger generation and enabled them to be part of the two different worlds. The primary role of *Jukebox* to promote rock'n'roll and to elevate Yugoslav rock proved to be successful. Thanks to this magazine, the rock culture spread all over Yugoslavia. Every single band, even in the smallest communities, could own records and texts of the most popular rock groups in the world. Yugoslav rockers equaled Western ones, not only by gaining the same editorial space in the magazine as the Rolling Stones or the Beatles, but by becoming part of the establishment and serving as the new idols of younger generations.

On the other hand, the magazine also had fulfilled a secondary role. Ways of dressing, learning English, changing interiors of flats and houses, or disco clubs, new ways of having fun, popularizing a

Western way of life, represented some of the other messages which *Jukebox* brought to young Yugoslavs.

The political effects were also significant, since politicians succeeded in making rock'n'roll work for the system and running into the world of rock'n'roll was better than running into politics, which was burdened with number of problems in that decade.

Jukebox and the social atmosphere, especially in the large cities, made young people different. Their idols were not only the heroes from WWII, but also rock musicians like Mick Jagger and others, and their rooms in a grey socialist world were covered in colorful posters, while rock music flowing from record players, jukeboxes, radios, concerts and television made them feel free.

Notes

[1] Walter L. Hixon, *Parting the Curtain. Propaganda, Culture and the Cold War 1945–1961* (Basingstoke: Macmillan Press LTD, 1997), xii.

[2] Aleksandar Žikić, *Fatalni Ringišpil. Hronika Beogradskog Rokenrola 1959–1979* (Beograd: Geopoetika, 1999), 35.

[3] Timothy W. Ryback, *Rock Around the Block. A History of Rock Music in Eastern Europe and the Soviet Union* (New York: Oxford University Press, 1990), 26.

[4] V. Janković Džet, "You Really Got Me (Jurili ga mi)," in *Beograd Šezdesetih Godina XX Veka*, ed. Bojan Kovačević (Beograd: Muzej grada Beograda, 2003), 218.

[5] N. Karaklajić, "Sećam se Euridike," in *Beograd Šezdesetih Godina XX Veka*, ed. Bojan Kovačević (Beograd: Muzej grada Beograda, 2003), 236.

[6] More in: Petar Janjatović, *Ilustrovana YU Rock Enciklopedija 1960–1997* (Beograd: Geopoetika, 1998).

[7] I. Lučić-Todosić, *Od Trokinga do Tvista: Igranke u Beogradu 1945–1963* (Beograd: Srpski genealoški centar, 2002), 126–7.

[8] In Yugoslav literature, it is always mentioned that *The Jukebox* was the first rock'n'roll magazine in the Communist world. Before that, the magazine for popular music *Ritam* was published in Novi Sad (Yugoslavia) from 1962 till 1965. Timothy Ryback mentioned Czechoslovakia's magazine *Melodie* for rock and pop that came out in 1963 (Timothy W. Ryback, ibid., 1990, 58).

[9] *Ritam*, I, No. 1, October 1, 1962.

[10] In this article, only the first series of *Jukebox* (1966–1969) was analyzed. The second series was published from 1975 to 1986.

[11] S. Škarica, *Kad je Rock bio Mlad: Priča sa Isočne Strane (1956–1970)* (Zagreb: V.B.Z., 2005), 51.

[12] *Leksikon YU Mitologije,* (Beograd: Rende, Zagreb: Postscriptum, 2004), 116.

[13] V. Janković Džet, ibid., 2003, 230.

[14] V. Janković Džet, ibid., 2003, 222–4.

[15] In 2006 a compilation of songs about Tito was published on CD "To majka više ne rađa". Among the musicians who dedicated their songs to Tito, there were following rock musicians: Dado Topić, Davorin Popović from the rock group Indexi, rock groups Teška industrija, YU grupa, Generacija 5, and a number of pop musicians, like Zdravko Čolić, Oliver Dragojević and Đorđe Balašević.

[16] Interview with Nikola Karaklajić, Belgrade, March 23, 2007.

[17] Sabrina Petra Ramet, "Rock: The Music of Revolution (and Conformity)," in *Rocking the State. Rock Music and Politics in Eastern Europe and Russia,* ed. Sabrina Petra Ramet (Boulder-San Francisco-Oxford: Westview Press, 1994), 8.

[18] Archive of Serbia and Montenegro, 507, VIII, II/2-b (132-146), K-8.

[19] Interview with Nikola Karaklajić, Belgrade, March 23, 2007.

[20] Interview with Nikola Karaklajić, Belgrade, March 23, 2007.

[21] Interview with Nikola Karaklajić, Belgrade, March 23, 2007.

[22] See cover of the *Džuboks,* June 3, 1966.

[23] "Usponi: Elipse," *Džuboks,* July 3, 1966, 6.

[24] *Džuboks,* January 3, 1967, 9.

[25] Nikola Karaklajić, "Uvodnik," *Džuboks,* May 3, 1966, 1.

[26] Archive of Serbia and Montenegro, 507, VIII, II/2-b (132-146), K-8.

[27] "Drugi o Nama," *Džuboks,* June 3, 1966, 18.

[28] "Smeli 'Smeli'," *Džuboks,* July 3, 1966, 9.

[29] V. Janković Džet, ibid., 2003, 226–8.

[30] For example, see *Džuboks,* April 3, 1969, 21.

[31] "Samonikli," *Džuboks,* May 3, 1966, 4–5.

[32] *Džuboks,* May 3, 1966.

[33] "Radio Luksemburg," *Džuboks,* November 3, 1967, 7.

[34] "Radio Luksemburg," *Džuboks,* November 3, 1967, 7.

[35] Interview with Nikola Karaklajić, Belgrade, March 23, 2007.

[36] "Mali Leksikon," *Džuboks,* July 3, 1966, 15.

[37] *Džuboks,* August 3, 1967, 3.

[38] "Mali Leksikon," *Džuboks,* October 3, 1966, 15.

[39] For example, see Aleksandar Žikić, ibid.,1999.

[40] *Džuboks,* September 3, 1967, 3.

[41] *Džuboks,* May 3, 1968, 13.

[42] V. Marjanović, "Vreme Postersa," *Džuboks*, October 3, 1968, 3.

[43] "Događaj Meseca – Naš Prvi Klub Diskoteka," *Džuboks*, July 3, 1967, 2.

[44] "Događaj Meseca – Naš Prvi Klub Diskoteka," *Džuboks*, July 3, 1967, 2.

[45] "Teodor – Kralj Bit Poezije," *Džuboks*, September 3, 1967, 6.

[46] *Džuboks*, March 3, 1968, 3.

[47] Sabrina Petra Ramet, "Making the Scene in Yugoslavia" in *Rocking the State. Rock Music and Politics in Eastern Europe and Russia,* ed. Sabrina Petra Ramet (Boulder-San Francisco-Oxford: Westview Press, 1994), 8.

[48] Interview with Nikola Karaklajić, Belgrade, March 23, 2007.

[49] Interview with Nikola Karaklajić, Belgrade, March 23, 2007.

[50] *Džuboks*, August 3, 1967, 3.

[51] "Naša Pošta," *Džuboks*, August 3, 1966, 30.

[52] "Krcko se Dopisuje," *Džuboks*, October 3, 1967, 3.

[53] *Džuboks*, March 3, 1968, 12.

[54] *Džuboks*, June 3, 1966, 24–5.

[55] *Džuboks*, August 3, 1967, 2.

[56] *Džuboks*, December 3, 1966, 25.

[57] "Pisma," *Džuboks,* September 3, 1966, 11.

[58] *Džuboks*, August 3, 1967, 2; *Džuboks,* September 3, 1967, 5.

[59] For example, see Aleksandar Žikić, ibid., 1999, or Predrag J. Marković, *Beograd između Istoka i Zapada 1948–1965* (Beograd: Službeni list SRJ, 1996).

[60] It is interesting to compare this with the fact that the Rolling Stones had their first and only concert in Belgrade in July 2007, and that it was commented as one of the best examples of Serbian road to democracy and its entering to the World.

[61] Timothy W. Ryback, ibid., 1990, 4.

[62] Timothy W. Ryback, ibid., 1990, 5.

7

A Tale of Two Subcultures
A Comparative Analysis of Hippie and Punk Subcultures in Slovenia

Gregor Tomc

Introduction

When it comes to youth subcultures, Yugoslavia lagged behind modern industrial societies in the post-Second World War period, but not nearly as much as other East European socialist societies. Slovenia as the most developed part of the Yugoslav federation of nation states was even closer to western societies. In the early 1970s, the student movement and the hippie subculture were important elements of Slovenia's social landscape, while punks appeared almost simultaneously with their English counterparts somewhat later. In Eastern Europe, youth subcultures were not a part of everyday life until the 1980s. What was so specific about Slovenia, in particular, and Yugoslavia, in general? There are at least two reasons: a contingent historical event (break with Stalin) and a congenial cult of personality (Tito's "bourgeois" tastes).

The conflict with the Soviet Union was not over ideological matters since Yugoslav Communists were, as a rule, dogmatic Stalinists and fervent advocates of Soviet policies. It was first and foremost a clash of nationalisms. The Yugoslav communists engaged in independent resistance against the Nazis in World War II, creating needed self-confidence to perceive themselves as significant players in the Balkan region. Stalin – not unreasonably – interpreted their desire for autonomy as potential competition for supremacy of the communist block countries and stigmatized their nationalism as a dangerous deviation from the teachings of Marx and Engels and as ideological revisionism that could not be tolerated. Excommunication from the church of communism in 1948 was inevitable. Since the Yugoslav economy was by then completely dependent on Soviet block trade, an economic crisis ensued. A very reluctant rapprochement with its ideological enemies in the West was a necessity for the Yugoslav elite, if it wanted to prevent mass starvation. For Western politicians, "keeping Tito afloat,"[1] as the policy was known at the time, involved obvious strategic interests (weakening the Soviet block, changing an enemy state into a neutral one, or luring potential new defectors from the Soviet camp). Yugoslavia was gradually thrust into the capitalist world economy.

From the 1950s on, the party elite was facing a never-ending dilemma: to make the economy more efficient and, in the process, make its own supposed avant-garde role in society redundant, or to persist in the role of an ideological hegemon leading society from socialism to communism and thus deepening the economic problems. The party elite was constantly shifting between two negative options: making the party redundant and making backwardness inevitable.

It is possible to divide the history of Yugoslav socialism in the period after the clash with Stalin into three periods: the 1950s and 1960s were a period of gradual "liberalisation" (a euphemism indicating a smaller role of the party in the economic life, in particular, and in society, in general). The 1970s became a period of renewed party interference (the so-called global self-management system in economy and society) and the 1980s, with the death of its charismatic leader, came a clash between "liberal" and "dogmatic" forces for supremacy, leading to the eventual disintegration of the country. In its social and cultural life, the "liberal" aspect of Yugoslav socialism enabled numerous innovations as the party elite relaxed its position on many public issues, when its official policy on questions of art disappeared. The larger role of autonomous civil society initiatives, however, was largely absent in other Eastern European societies until the 1980s.

Also, cultural diversity in Yugoslavia was made more likely by the personal aesthetic taste of its charismatic leader. In authoritarian/totalitarian states, the charismatic leader's personal opinions on public matters are significant, especially in periods of uncertainty, when official dogma is interpreted in different ways by members of the elite. Since Marx and Engles were not specific on questions of popular art in the post-World War II period, Tito's role became essential. He was by nature a bon vivant, a lover of fast cars and beautiful women with an aversion to highbrow culture. He genuinely enjoyed the company of pop stars (movie actresses or singers). He by no means liked jazz or rock music, which was a generational difference rather than a question of dislike of popular culture. He was not as hostile to a "decadent bourgeois" mass culture as could be expected from a man in his position.

In the first post-war years, personal spending in Slovenia was lower than before the war, dissatisfaction of the population, especially in the cities, was increasing and something had to be done. The party elite decided to put greater emphasis on consumer production and agriculture. The trend started in the 1950s and continued throughout the 1960s. As households in Slovenia were small (3.5 members on average), with both parents employed, the standard of living started to increase.[2] People were buying all kinds of household appliances – refrigerators, washing machines, TV sets, record players, scooters, or cars. In the 1970s, growing personal consumption continued despite a turn to a more dogmatic, hard-line party policy on economics. The party elite managed to achieve this goal with a growing indebtedness to foreign banks. An unintended consequence of the orientation to consumerism was that collectivist ideas of socialism were gradually marginalized at the expense of individual leisure time consumption. Nobody seemed to notice how the emphasis of socialism shifted from creating an alternative to capitalism to entering into a competition with it.

The liberal economic policy in the 1950s and 1960s led to higher unemployment. The party elite decided to solve this problem by opening the borders, enabling workers to find employment abroad. The euphemism for this category of workers was "temporary workers abroad," in everyday language they were known as "Gastarbeiter."[3] An unintended consequence was that practically anybody, except for the "enemies of the state" (a code phrase for individuals who dared questioning the party monopoly of power), could travel abroad, including young people, familiarizing themselves with western youth styles.

What impact did these changes have on the cultural life in Slovenia? In the first years of the revolution, socialist realism (a combination of traditional working class culture, art of Soviet block countries, and progressive art of Western artists) was the rule. But since the 1950s cultural life was relaxing. In the classical arts, poets in Slovenia wrote lyrical poems devoid of any revolutionary substance, existentialist plays were staged in private theaters (if state theaters were closed for their experiments), and painters had exhibitions of their abstract art. Even greater changes occurred in popular culture. A very popular humorist of the post-war period expressed this new attitude in favor of pop culture in 1954: "... a good circus is a good circus but bad Shakespeare is still only bad Shakespeare."[4]

In the more relaxed cultural climate, jazz, which had been banned immediately after the war, was again being played at public dances. It was a gradual process, however. Bands, for example, could not play certain styles still perceived as inappropriate, for example, "boogie-woogie." Unfortunately, police informers were not well versed in popular music and would sometime mistake a feeble German schlager for a counterrevolutionary boogie-woogie. In the 1950s, the problem with jazz was even discussed by the highest political echelon. As a top communist official stated at the time:

> It is meaningless to be against jazz in principle because it can – with its modern expressive means – positively influence the mood of the working man, his cheerfulness. We do not reject jazz as such but merely its unhealthy outgrowths which have nothing in common either with music or with dance.[5]

In the still more liberal 1960s, even the "unhealthy outgrowths" of jazz became acceptable. Its protagonists were also influential in creating two new forms of popular music in Slovenia. The first was the state-supported "popevka," a combination of schlager, canzona and swing influences, needed above all for air play on state radio. The other was Slovenian country music, "narodno-zabavna muzika," a combination of polka and waltzer, played by a modified jazz combo and performed at rural dance parties, called "veselice." It did not enjoy firm state endorsement and had very little radio airplay, because it was perceived as too primitive.

But the 1960s were also the time when rock'n'roll became popular in Slovenia, especially with The Beatles, The Rolling Stones and English beat music, in general. Initially the media ignored it and fans had to rely on foreign radio stations (above all Radio Luxemburg), buying records and going to concerts abroad. Numerous local bands appeared blindly mimicking foreign acts. At "guitariads" bands would compete doing better cover versions of current pop rock hit songs. Most importantly, party authorities had no official policy for this new popular music, which was, according to many communists, still a "decadent bourgeois import from the West." Although the older generation often complained, it rarely went beyond civil society conflicts and disputes. The media would occasionally publish opinions for and against the new musical fad, and school teachers would sometimes prohibit long-haired pupils from attending classes, sometimes having their hair cut by force by zealous party youths. But for most members of the rock subculture, this only made their affiliation with rock music and western life styles more attractive.

Hippies

In the beginning of the 1970s, a substantial affinity with the western youth subculture existed in Slovenia, but there was very little original, creative local response to it. This changed with Buldožer (Bulldozer) from Ljubljana, which soon became an ideal type underground, progressive rock band:

> In 1975, a group of long-haired, bearded hippies, a brand new attraction from Ljubljana in Slovenia, walked onto the stage at a pop festival and played their version of a big pop hit that year called "Day of Love," changing it into "Day of Sickness." The singer, Marko Brecelj, came on stage in a wheelchair, a group of the band's friends, each of them pretending to be handicapped in one way or another, sang the chorus out of key, while the guitarist, Boris Bele, walked the stage, shooting at anyone who took his fancy (with blank cartridges, of course). When a member of the chorus "panicked" and escaped, he took a shot at him, accidentally "killing" a member of the audience. He apologized and then

shot the escapee just before he managed to get out of the hall. This type of rock theatre became the band's trademark. This, and their music, which the musical media conveniently labeled "the Yugoslav answer to Frank Zappa," made them an instant rock'n'roll sensation, but also caused them numerous problems. The "Day of Sickness" performance was never aired on television, they had problems with record labels (their Belgrade label declined to re-release their first LP record Spit into the Eye of Truth after 13.000 records were sold in a month, also refusing to release their second LP record Stick No Posters altogether), and sometimes their concerts were banned.[6]

Their sarcastic, cynical lyrics full of black humor did not go down well with the moral majority; they were sometimes interpreted as subversive and anti-socialist. The band was a welcome target for ambitious officials, who thought to promote their careers at the band's expense.

While rock music was at the core of the hippie subculture, other forms of artistic expression were also important. Kostja Gatnik, a painter by profession, also created numerous comics. He stood out as an original and unconventional artist (known for his parodies of comics of a local superhero, Peter Klepec). He was art editor of the local student newspaper, *Tribuna*, which also published some of his work. In 1977 he published a book of underground comics called, *Magna Purga*.

Vojin Kovač – Chubby, the self-proclaimed poet laureates of the lumpenproletarian cultural revolution, became publicly infamous for his Manifest of the Cultural Revolution. It was published in *Tribuna* in 1968 and appealed to all downtrodden people to revolt and demolish the "bourgeois proletarian revolution." The favourite targets of derision in his poems were the middle classes and their newly found desire for consumerism: "ideals are cheaper in Trieste" is a verse form one of his songs (Trieste is an Italian border town that became the Mecca for numerous Slovenian and Yugoslav shoppers). His radicalism soon led him to the conviction that poetry must not be written but lived, and he stopped publishing altogether. His only book of poems was published posthumously.

Front sleeve cover of the first LP by Buldožer "Pljuni istini u oči".[7] (A magazine for daltonists, bicyclists, rock guitarists, children and mercenaries, patients nearing cemeteries, professors and grave wailers, strippers, psychopaths, conductors and sailors.)

A comic strip by Kostja Gatnik.[8]

I don't need LSD
I don't need Maryanna

With a bottle of hard liquor
I'm flying in Ljubljana

This is his introduction to an unwritten play:

i'd like to
piss on a lady preoccupied with canaries every morning
i'd like to
steal a neighbor's chair because i don't like baroque
i'd like stones to throw people
i'd like to
meet a rabid man who bites a dog
i'd like
a horse to gallop on me
i'd like
cats to devour all decrees on deratization
i'd like to
return the wreath which i stole from prešeren

i protest
because ink dries too fast
i protest
because the government didn't ban barking in the center of
town
i protest
because reports on murders are too scant in newspapers
i protest
because prostitutes don't have preservatives
i protest
because nails twist too quickly
i protest
because the government did not order frogs to have four
legs
i protest
because orange peels are too thick

i demand
the immediate suspension of cloudiness
i demand
the extension of pregnancy to twelve months
i demand

that fish immediately multiply in ljubljanica
please
turn off the lights

i call for a hunger strike
of all who are against the weather getting worse
i call for a hunger strike
of all whose dogs are in heat
i call for a hunger strike
of all whose hair is tousled by the wind
i call for a hunger strike
of all who walk on grey streets
i call for a hunger strike
of all whose grass grows too slowly
i call for a hunger strike
of all who think daisies are too small
i call for a hunger strike
of all who go for a piss under tromostovje[9]

The hippie subculture was an important part of what it meant to be young in Slovenia in the early 1970s, but the subpolitical student movement (using radical political methods of public activity, methods which were until then largely unheard of in Slovenia) was also crucial. Under the influence of Western student movements, students from Ljubljana University soon followed with their first trade unionist demands in 1968 (protesting against higher rents in student dormitories). They gradually became more politically radical (demonstrations against the war in Vietnam, the American invasion of Cambodia, Nixon's visit to Yugoslavia, for the rights of Slovenian minorities in Austria, or against the Soviet invasion of Czechoslovakia). They closed the street at the Faculty of Philosophy, because excessive traffic noise hindered the teaching process. After the demonstration, the authorities pressed charges against three student activists. One was a poet who was supposed to have said: "It's a pity that we did not put barbed wire on the streets and behind it our sharpshooters could shoot policemen right between the eyes." Another one was a student of sociology, who thought that the time for guerrilla warfare had arrived and shared his opinion with other students by exhibiting a poster at the faculty. The last case concerned a group of students, who, in a more abstract fashion, warned the public in a proclamation that traffic noise, environmental pollution, and destruction of nature were indicators of a "perverted politics in society where alienation rules."[10] Out of solidarity with their three colleagues, students decided to occupy the Faculty of Philosophy. But other reasons for the occupation were also given (inequality in society, lack of democracy, lack of solidarity with Third World countries, despite the fact that Yugoslavia was one of the leaders of the non-aligned movement). Although the students criticized the "red bourgeoisie" in power, they supported the socialist project in principle. The problem was that they were more radical than the party elite. A well-known student slogan at the time, which illustrates this problem, was: For communism against "communism."

Milan Dekleva was then a student at the Faculty of Philosophy. He was an editor of Tribuna and Radio Študent, a local student radio station. He was also a poet, a writer and an activist at the time of the occupation of the faculty. A reflection by Milan Dekleva on a revolutionary culture, first published in an internal faculty student newspaper in 1971:

> Revolutionary culture, is it not the adjective of action and culture is consequently its content? In the language of the contemporary world, conforming to the stairway of power, action implies climbing: it is obvious that from this position we are resigned to sadly gaze upwards. It is indicative that we somehow resist putting forward a simpler solution, since the only open road points downwards: to the basic position of a unified human being still understanding culture as "an organized means of solving existential problems" (...). The concept of subculture, which we are still well aware of, is in this sense imposed upon us: we first considered it after the literary marathon, in the same rooms in which a free university now dwells. Subculture cannot be counterculture, a counterbalance to official (mass) culture: its point of departure cannot be power. Quite to the contrary, its source is more elementary: a demand for a unified human being is

a demand for a transcendence of the division on producers and consumers of culture, a division forced upon us by the bourgeois world. In reality, we are dealing with descent from the throne of a "royal" culture, supposedly satisfying some "higher" needs. Which is not to say: burning revolution in the consciousness of petrified heads, because freedom is only possible as a higher quality of a transformed society. Our culture is currently bound – with every step we make – to all demands we are trying to realize in our free university. It is bound with our communal life, food and sleep, thought and gut, and – most important of all – with our love and friendship, which we tear from oblivion. The status of student would be an obstacle in the context of the official university. Our free university has once more opened the possibility of a free culture. Of a culture in permanent motion, improvisation, continuous becoming. Perpetuum of construction. We are all "poets", or in other words: we are all open to "poetry."[11]

Punks

In the mid-1970s, the student movement was banned by the party elite (more precisely, it was forced to merge with the official Alliance of Socialist Youth), while old hippie values increasingly bored urban youths. For a while it seemed that the rock subculture was withering away, if it was not already dead.

Punk in Slovenia began when Peter Lovšin, who played weird folk songs in the mid-1970s (ranging from vomiting to masturbation) on acoustic guitar, met Gregor Tomc, who had read about punk in an American magazine and later also heard about it in London. They decided to form a punk band, named Pankrti (Bastards). The band rehearsed its material for a month before a concert at a local high school gym (the last concert there for many years to come). Despite their conviction that there was "no future," it turned out that there was a considerable future in store for the band, which lasted for ten years and six LP records. Helped by the local student radio station and the student cultural center, they recorded their first double single, "Ljubljana is sick/Pretty and vacant" in Italy, since recording studios in Yugoslavia were state-owned. A contract with a record company was needed just to get through the door of a recording studio.[12]

Gradually, a whole punk subculture evolved, a homology of creativity and everyday life. On the one hand, there were other bands besides Pankrti, like Ljublanski psi (Ljubljana dogs), Kuzle (Bitches), Berlinski zid (Berlin Wall) and Grupa 92 (Group 92) in the first wave of bands as well as punk discos, fanzines, and graffiti. On the other hand, there was a punk life style appearing publicly, perhaps for the first time, on such a scale (image, slang, values). During the first couple of years, this subculture was perceived by representatives of the dominant culture only as a symbolic threat. Persecution of the subculture began in earnest when F. Popit, then at the top of the party elite, decided that punks publicly vomiting on socialism should be stopped. The authoritarian leader clarified the party position on punk. This was the sign police needed to start with its repression. There were raids on pubs and other meeting places, police violence against punks on streets, raids against graffiti writers, concerts banned, and censorship became more strict. The persecution of the punk image became more common (a favourite target of policemen were badges with swastikas and "Nazi punks fuck off" written over them). This repression gradually escalated into the so-called "Nazi punk affair." A populist weekly newspaper, with the help of police informers, connected two otherwise completely separate events. Some swastika graffiti appeared in Ljubljana (concerts or Goebbels' assemblies, the journalist wondered) and some pupils maltreated a classmate (who planted these seventeen-year old kids on us, the journalist added). The answer was obvious to him: Nazi punks.

A moral panic was created and spread across Slovenia's borders. The consensus among Yugoslav media was that there is no place for punk in a socialist society. Subsequently, three punks were arrested in Ljubljana and charged with secretly trying to organize a National Socialist Party of Slovenia. In the ensuing trial all charges against the suspects were dropped, but by then the damage had been done. The punk subculture was perceived by communist authorities as a real threat to socialism and was by and large forced from everyday life to withdraw into more private and exclusively artistic punk scenes.

For example, this is the song Berlin Wall by Berlinski zid:

I'm shut in my own damn room
I'm hitting my head against the wall
I can't rush through the window
Damn it, it's too bad
The brains would splash neatly
On the frozen sidewalk
People would pass by and smile
"Idiot," they would say and relish.[13]

The year 1980 saw Tito's death and the formation of a band, Laibach (the German name for Ljubljana, perceived by the authorities as provocative due to a long history of national antagonisms between the two nations). These two events were interlinked. The marshal's demise triggered social and political instability in Yugoslavia, which, in turn, produced an ideal climate for Laibach's political aesthetics. It began with the banning their first multimedia project in their hometown, Trbovlje (a concert of punk bands with Laibach as headliner, projections of short movies, exhibitions of paintings, and speeches) because of dubious black posters (supposedly alluding to Tito's death). Their notoriety culminated in 1983, when they appeared on a popular national TV show. They wore what appeared to be military uniforms, with armbands bearing the Laibach cross (inspired by everything from Malevich to Christianity), with military-style crew cuts, their stony, expressionless faces lit from below. There were Laibach posters of mass political rallies in the background, while the tv presenter showed a documentary of Italian fascists demonstrating in Trieste against the Slovenian minority. In such a context, Laibach recited its prepared answers, including this explanation of the suicide of their original front man: "Art is a noble mission, one that demands fanaticism, and Laibach is an organism whose goals, life and means are greater – in both their strength and duration – than the goals, lives and means of its individual members."[14] Laibach Kunst was part of an art collective, NSK (Neue Slowenische Kunst) that created some of the most recognizable visual art of the period.

A characteristic poet, philosopher and performance artist of the time was P. Mlakar. In the mid-1970s he was a student

A poster for the band Laibach by Laibach Kunst.[15]

of philosophy and a poet. He became president of the student cultural center, which was instrumental in editing a book of comics by Kostja Gatnik, and later issued the first single of Pankrti. His artistic interests were numerous – he had occasional bands, acted in movies, wrote pornographic literature (for some he is the Slovenian de Sade), as well as works of philosophy (e.g., *An Introduction to God*). From 1980 on he was closely associated with NSK, especially as a performance artist. As a performer he liked to provoke his audiences. In Belgrade he told an audience of the already shrinking Third Yugoslavia: "Why is Serbia so small? Because God has abandoned you, you sinners."

For example, these are the lyrics of Garten des Friedens:

First he shoved one mine into his ass, then
a dynamite cigar into his mouth, proceeding
with smaller mines but of the same quality
into both ears and nostrils. He fastened some
bundles of dynamite on the belly and back
side of his body and some he tied
around his legs and arms. Once all his holes were stuffed
and all more significant outer parts of his body
offered a place for setting off explosives
he made for my garden which I created and which
I cultivate for all who cherish freedom
above everything else in life.[16]

The most prominent activist intellectual of the punk scene (also active as a concert promoter and DJ) was Igor Vidmar. At the time of punk he was a social science student. He played rock music on national radio and on the local student radio station. He was also active in the student cultural center. As a radical new leftist, he had contacts with numerous official youth organization members, although he was also critical of them (a sort of a loyal opposition to the regime). This was important, because he was probably the politically best-connected person on the punk scene. It was, above all, through his efforts that private punk creativity came to the attention of the public, and became a public concern (of media, record companies, and public debates). This is his reflection on the Union of Socialist Youth (USY) of Slovenia and punk:

The approach to mass culture in the introductory speech could be viewed as symptomatic of something labeled "fear by communists of the loosening potential and mobilization possibilities of media and of mass culture in a wider sense of the meaning, in interaction with autonomous producers" by a German theoretician. This fear is one of the basic reasons for an old bourgeois culture, in different variations and with different masks but structurally unchanged, still ruling in socialist states. This was a one-sided approach from which an undialectical and traditionalist conception of mass culture as opium of the people was evident. Tendencies of a critical approach were visible, but the other side of this tension, its emancipatory potential, was never exposed. Marxist theoreticians were already aware of this potential before the Second World War, in embryonic form, like Walter Benjamin. Recent discussions on the subject obviously did not stray into a reflection of mass culture, which should also determine USY's relation to it.[17]

Interpretation

In terms of social theory, Slovenian youth subcultures have to be understood in the context of a gradual assimilation of capitalist production and its implications for social and cultural life.[18]

Person/Background Relation in Slovenian Socialism of the 1970s

The production background of capitalism (private property, market regulation, nation state, bureaucracy, or industrial technology) represents the social situation in which modern individuals and a modern cultural background interact, gradually generating democratic authority in politics, empirical values in cosmology (generating secular, utilitarian, pragmatic orientations to life) as hegemonic, and the symbolic exchange of one-sided mass media (from one center to many individuals with little possibility of feedback, e.g., newspapers).

The modern social situation represented a significant break with the tradition of pre-industrial communities, which were pre-industrial in production, authoritarian in politics, religious in cosmology and integrated on the local level.[19]

The socialist system of values was perceived by the party elite as a counter-hegemonic background to capitalist modernity, as a political avant-garde of the future, but it never came to be. As a system of production, it was significantly less efficient – greater energy inputs of many were necessary for smaller energy outputs of most. This, by itself, would not present a problem, if the revolutionary elite had succeeded in creating a new, counter-hegemonic cultural background with which individuals would interact on a daily basis, eventually shaping the New Man (a person prepared for material sacrifice, collectivism and ascetics in production as well as for alternative forms of reproduction, the withering away of private family life and new forms of aesthetic practice, known as socialist realism). But this totalitarian project of creating a new individual failed and was soon abandoned (in Slovenia after about a decade of communist rule). This failure implied the gradual abandonment of a socialist cosmology, leading to an increased inefficiency of (re)production, soon threatening the existence of the regime itself. Despite control over media (which became significantly less efficient with cable and satellite technologies of the 1970s and the 1980s), the differences in the ratio of energy input/output in production became more obvious to increasing numbers of individuals, thus gradually transforming the emergent phenomena of socialism. An asymmetrical social situation emerged in Slovenian socialism: modern individuals persisted in an only partially modern background. Socialism soon became a sterile hybrid. Individuals were not maintaining and promoting its background with their everyday activity. This created a strain on the socialist cosmology, demanding substantial coercive energy of party authority just to maintain the ceremonial normative background behind the organization of everyday public life. If capitalist (re)production is embedded in everyday paramount reality, socialist (re)production was significantly detached from it, sometimes even opposed to it. If a capitalist background was a taken-for-granted, hegemonic social reality for individual cognitive actors, a socialist background was largely perceived as cognitively problematic. A "great divide,"[20] (in a very different context used to distinguish modernism from popular art in contemporary societies), or a schism between private cultural orientations and public normative demands, was created and maintained at a costly expenditure of energy. As a result, two backgrounds gradually evolved in socialism, an official one, appropriate for state controlled ceremonial cognitive activities, and a private one, possible in spontaneous social situations not structured by the official background.[21]

The interaction of capitalist and socialist social situations is hierarchical, embedded in the capitalist cultural background. In the case of youth subcultures, the societal level describes modern mass media, which enable a cultural industry level of interaction (modern musical industry, Hollywood); on the intermediate social level phenomena, such as urbanization and school system stimulate the emergence of youth peer groups (membership in gangs, biker or rock subcultures); while on the level of cognitive orientation different forms of creativity of sociable individuals (radical cultural attitudes such as playing in a rock group, being active in the student movement or joining a commune) are present.

This cultural background of the modern youth exerted a hegemonic influence on the partially cultural background of modern youth in Slovenia with its state-run cultural industry, traditionally lower levels of urbanization, class-integrated neighborhoods, and party-controlled school system. The partially modern background of socialism did not promote the appearance of unique youth subcultures. These would be unimaginable without the impetus of immediate imitation of originals (western hippy and punk) movements. On the other hand, it did not prevent the emergence of numerous innovative interpretations of the originals.

Hippies
Some factors of the influential societal background for bringing about the hippie subculture in post-war America were a prolonged period of economic stability, rising prosperity and growing consumerism in the general population, with a trickle-down effect on the young generation, suggesting to an increasing number of young persons, especially from middle-class backgrounds with little or no experience in earning a living, that problems of production were to a large extent de-problematized for good, absence of an elaborate competitive ideological background (liberal vs. social-democratic), grounding the political debate in "the end of ideology" context,

thus opening the background of political cosmology for innovative radical ideas (the student subpolitical movement), rapid diffusion of new media technologies as extensions of bodies and senses (the movie industry, radio, record player, juke-box, electronically mediated mass concert, television) promoting new forms of integration at a distance and resulting in greater autonomy.

On the intermediate level of social interaction, numerous factors influenced the creation of a specific peer subculture of youths: non-traditional approaches to upbringing by some psychologists (e.g., Dr. B. Spock, known as the "father of permissiveness"), stimulating anti-authoritarian, self-centered, hedonistic values among youths who were increasingly brought up in such a fashion, the musical industry was increasingly becoming an expression of cognitive experiences of young rock artists interacting with the cultural background of the young (rather than being an art form for anonymous, non-localized, non-specific consumers, standardized creativity for profit and a promulgation of middle-age lifestyles), stimulating similar, less radical changes in other popular art forms (the Hollywood movie industry saw the breakthrough of numerous young innovative artists) and in the press with new media like The Village Voice or Rolling Stones magazine, the war in Vietnam integrated otherwise disparate concerns of the young generation, providing a common purpose on the community level while radicalizing their opinions, the student subpolitical movement, inventing numerous innovative strategies of radical opposition to mainstream politics (draft card burning, sit-ins, teach-ins, be-ins, occupation of faculties), the drug subculture, promoting mind altering drugs from cannabis to LSD by advocates like T. Leary ("tune in, turn on, drop out", "freaking out"), which facilitated the dissociation of drug users from the predominant cultural background.

On the level of individual sociability, numerous creative individuals were setting the standards of what it meant to be a member of the hippie youth subculture. The most influential among them were active in the music industry (The Beatles, Jefferson Airplane, Jimmy Hendrix, Van Morrison, Bob Dylan, The Doors, Frank Zappa, Grateful Dead) but also in fashion and movie businesses, comics, and drug culture. The ideal type of music to covet among consumers was progressive rock. It had to be authentic (expressing personal experience of the artist), express some deeper meaning (not commercial singles but conceptual albums), transcend simple entertainment (dance music as background for other activities), and complex (variations in rhythm, uses of sound effects). As Paul Willis suggested:

> The hippies wanted to experience complexity and variation but of their own kind, in their own mode, and of their own making. They wanted to experience life not as a logic and rationality unfolding itself over time, but as an immediate richness occurring outside the dimensions of time (…). (…) A music which both attempted timelessness and an abstract, complex shape was marvelously formed both to mirror and momentarily complete this promethean attempt to encompass a post-capitalist timeless mysticism.[22]

On the complex societal, social and sociable levels of interaction, numerous individuals internalized some basic aspects of these values, integrating them into unique personal outlooks. These outlooks interacted with societal and social backgrounds – and on the sociable level with other individuals of similar orientations – thus creating and maintaining the hippie peer group life style. The latter structured their individual cognitive practices in a relatively stable cultural feedback loop in time/space. Every individual, of course, internalized these orientations in his/her own specific cognitive manner and in a unique hierarchy of significance, but in recognizable patterns of activity. Value orientations were easily discernable among a population of individuals with similar activities and outlooks. A typical hippie exists only as an abstract interpretation (for example, in theories of social scientists) of collective phenomena and/or as a generalization of individual cases. But as an emergent social phenomenon, it, nevertheless, cannot simply be reduced to individual examples of hippie followers.

Some central values of such an ideal type of a hippie subcultural background include: hedonism (ideology of "free love"), individualism (ideology of "doing your own thing"), dissociation (ideology of "freaking out," above all with the help of drugs), exotic mysticism (ideology of "spreading your consciousness" with various non-western religious practices, mostly of Asian origin, or with heretical interpretations of religious traditions in the words of the "wandering prophet" Charlie Brown Artman in 1966: Let Baby Jesus Shut Your Mouth and Open Your Mind), chiliasm (optimistic ideology of "the dawn of a new world," The Age of Aquarius, a belief that all problems can be solved if not in the community as a whole than certainly among consenting adults in a commune), authenticity (ideology of being innovative and creative, of leaving a unique personal signature on the background with which one interacts, the desire not to succumb to commercial demands of the cultural industry).

The societal background in Slovenia in the late 1960s was significantly different, although not necessarily hostile to the adoption of a Western hippie subculture. In the 1960s, prosperity was lower than in America and Western Europe (but still high when compared to other socialist societies); consumerism was significantly less developed (but still developed by socialist standards, facilitating the purchase of "decadent" bourgeois goods). The latter was viewed by party authorities with great suspicion (as an escapist ideology of the "petit bourgeoisie," or the middle classes, it was, nevertheless, tolerated as was obvious from throngs of people shopping in Trieste and other border towns on weekends and holidays). Self-management ideology put greater emphasis on the distribution of goods than on their production, thus seemingly de-problematizing production; self-management was "closet-communism," with the party elite gradually shifting emphasis from a totalitarian creation of the New Man to the preservation of an authoritarian monopoly over political power by the Communist Party behind a screen of non-politics (nominally all working people were actively participating in matters of public significance), effectively creating the absence of an elaborate ideological background in politics, and encouraging, to a certain extent, innovative public initiatives (this was especially true between the mid-1960s and early 1970s). This was the so-called "liberalism" of party boss, S. Kavčič, who allowed a somewhat more relaxed political climate. In the 1980s, "liberalization" was the consequence of Tito's death and the following disintegration of centralized political authority in Yugoslavia (liberalism by authoritarian socialist standards). Slovenia lagged behind in terms of new technologies (number of television sets, telephones or record players per capita, for example), but the 1960s were, nevertheless, a period of their accelerated introduction into everyday life.

On the intermediate level of the peer background were, again, differences and certain similarities between these two socio-cultural backgrounds. Thus, upbringing was more traditional (because Slovenia is less urbanized), but a more paternalistic cultural climate was also the consequence of a socialist ideology in family socialization (the older generations found it easier to legitimize their superordination in families or school systems, by appealing to prevailing state norms as unquestionable; they were able to justify their personal values as superior by appealing to a dominant authority). The rock music industry was underdeveloped (there were, for example, only two record labels, both state owned, like all studios and distribution outlets, which made access for youths to cultural media of autonomous self-expression more difficult). Protest against the Vietnam war and against the invasion of Czechoslovakia by Soviet forces could not have a similar emotional or integrational impact on protesters as they did in the United States, for at least two reasons: both events did not directly effect the daily existence of Slovenian youths, and party authorities adopted a similar outlook as student protesters, thus making distancing from older generations more difficult. The student movement could not radically break with the official state ideology (self-management ideology in domestic policy, non-aligned movement of Third world solidarity in international relations), because it was embedded in a similar leftist ideological background. Besides, any resistance to official political dogma was only possible at a greater personal risk, thus making it more unlikely. The illegal drug culture was much more limited, because of stricter police control of drug traffic, making alcohol the only easily accessible drug.

On the level of individual sociability, a surprising number of creative persons interpreted the relevant backgrounds with their unique individual outlooks. They interacted with the western hippie background (mostly through the influence of western rock bands, student movements, movies, and comics) and elements of the domestic background not hostile to experimentation (self-management ambivalence between ideological tradition and innovation, its emphasis on distribution over production) to create unique personal artistic expressions of a hippie subculture.

The hippie subculture would not have been possible without the influence of international role models or "a hostile foreign import from the West," and an example of a "decadent bourgeois" culture, according to the official regime at the time, or of cultural borrowing, characteristic of human societies throughout history, according to a more neutral terminology today. But borrowing went beyond a mere import in the case of the Slovenian hippie subculture. It was a necessary precondition for creative individuals to transform, taking into account domestic societal and social backgrounds, to create unique Slovenian versions of what it was like to be a hippie. The model might have been global, but its application was local.

While some elements of the borrowed value system were less problematic in the context of the new environment (e.g., hedonism, individualism or creativity), others were more likely to be perceived as competing with a socialist ideological background; they were, as a result, more likely to be viewed with greater suspicion by official gatekeepers (party officials, journalists in media, school teachers). These manifestations of a hippie subculture were, thus, less apparent on the intermediate level of the youth subculture (mysticism, dissociation and chiliasm).

Punks

Characteristics of the social and political situation critical for bringing about the punk subculture in England in the late 1970s included, firstly, a period of economic recession, hitting hardest members of the working class and generating a climate of despair especially among younger people entering the work force for the first time. Secondly, a prolonged period of conservative political rule and M. Thatcher's liberal ideological and economic policy, perceived as being against the interests of the working class, in general (e.g., ignoring the demands of striking miners) and of lower class youths, in particular (limiting the role of local city authorities, such as Greater London Council, which was significant in organizing youth leisure time activities). Thirdly, the rebellion of the young, which was structured in traditional ideological class terms, because of elaborate ideological backgrounds and clearly defined political positions of left and right parties, and of Labour and Conservative supporters. The class dimension of the punk subculture could extend from explicit political positions, such as Rock Against Racism, characteristic of more politically conscious bands like The Clash, to more implicit, or personal political positions, such as anarchic life styles best personified by members of Sex Pistols.

Influential factors on the intermediate level of a peer subcultural background included the culture industry of the mid-1970s, which still reflected the withering hippie ethos, alienating working-class youths specifically and those youths who modeled an aggressive life styles for more personal reasons and who consequently felt culturally alienated from the rock subculture, tending to perceive themselves as cultural outcasts/outsiders (either in relation to their parent generation, to the dominant national culture or to a combination of both). No major contingent event on the level of the nation state could integrate the otherwise disparate concerns of the younger generation, implying that no countercultural movement on the societal level was likely to emerge (a social movement feeding on the macro climate of despair and resentment), the drug culture background was stimulated by promoting more efficient (amphetamines) and more traditional, fatalistic working-class (alcohol-related) attitudes towards the socio-cultural background.

On the individual level, numerous creative individuals were setting the standards for what it meant to be a punker. Most of them were centered in the music industry (Sex Pistols, Clash, Stranglers or Joy Division in England or Ramones, Dead Kennedys, Patty Smith or Television in America), but also in the fashion industry (Vivienne Westwood), among graffiti artists, as opinion makers (Malcolm McLaren), and in fanzines (Mark Perry's Sniffin' Glue).

Musically punk was very different from the progressive rock of the hippies. It was purposefully standardized, simplicistic (more closely embedded in rock'n'roll convention), populist (folk music of the desperate, angry urban youths), unpretentious (short songs with an immediate message) and democratic (open to all with the courage to publicly express themselves musically). Punk was an attempt to return to the imaginary roots of rock music as a musical youth rebellion in contemporary modern societies. Mike Brake describes punk as music made by working class kids who reject the virtuosity of superstars, the wealth of successful musicians and hippies:

> Its followers appear to be shocking which attracts those who feel that there is no future, that there is no work and that there are no prospects. The music is not unlike reggae; it has an emphasis on rhythm with melody in the background, which connects it to the punk image and anarchy. Lyrics talk of high-rise apartments, living on the dole and white riots and were attractive to working class kids.[23]

Brake's reduction of punk to a working class phenomenon is, to a certain extent, a simplification. While the first generation of English originators of the subculture were undoubtedly expressing working-class youth fatalism and resentment, the originators did not have to be working class youths to experience and express such attitudes. One could say that first generation of the English punk subculture depended on a working-class background for inspiration and that many, but not all, punks were of working-class origin. For many of them, identification with the lower class was not so much class affiliation as cultural affiliation. Class diversity becomes even more obvious in later generations of punk subcultures, when basic social orientations of punk become more aestheticized and available as "ready mades" for anyone with an adequate personal disposition to relate to. The same is true of all youth subcultures. The hippie subculture was similarly embedded in preoccupations of a middle-class American youth, but was soon appropriated by youths regardless of their class position, who could relate to the hippie world outlook and life style. If this were not the case Brake would not be able to talk of working-class hippies.

In a complex feedback loop of individual, social and societal levels, many members of the younger generation internalized significant elements of the cultural background of the punk life style, generating the punk subculture as a recognizable phenomenon. This punk background, in turn, structured the cognitive orientations of individual punkers, thus establishing a rather stable social situation recognized as a subculture, while individual members maintained it as a continuous phenomenon in space and time with their everyday activity.

Some central values of the punk subcultural background were the devaluation of values (things are not what they seem to be, they are always less, e.g., love is sex, free is ignorant, autonomous is naïve, political is corrupt); individualism (a nihilistic withdrawal, a cynical distance, a sarcastic attitude towards public commitment, a scepticism towards acceptable moral values, an ignorance of approved ways of doing things by the individual); anarchism (not on a public but rather on a personal level, not as a revolutionary anticipation of change, because that would be naïve, but rather as an individual choice, a nihilistic attitude of resentment of mainstream public life and of the dominant authority); realism (a this-worldly orientation, living in a world in which no meaningful ideological transcendence is possible); living for the moment (because there is no future, resignation to public pessimism, an orientation which makes sense when individuals feel disempowered, in principle, fatalism); accessibility of creativity (de-mythologisation of the creative process, open to the enthusiasm of all rather than to the virtuosity of the few, an authentic attitude as a precondition of punk art, a general contempt for idolization and fetishism of art).

However, the English social situation was significantly different from the Slovenian one. The late 1970s saw the beginning of an economic recession, but the specific socialist ideology led to a policy of "buying social peace" with loans from Western banks, thus, social differences were not nearly as pronounced and the climate of despair among the lower classes not nearly as articulated; a more authoritarian political rule led by the head of the party, F. Popit was perceived as legitimate by the moral majority (there were no dissident sub-political movements against the regime), while it merely generated a climate of boredom and indifference among the youth, because of a lack of an urban subcultural life; an extremely complex system of self-management made a meaningful political positioning almost impossible, promoting anti-political (personal anarchist) attitudes which were more attractive to the young; there was no major contingent event on the level of the nation state which could integrate the otherwise disparate concerns of the younger generation, implying that no counterculture could emerge on the societal level.

Some influential factors on the intermediate level of a peer subcultural background included the following. Due to a weaker market regulation, the culture industry was still state-controlled and too underdeveloped to reflect youth interests more than marginally; most domestic popular musical production was limited to Yugoslav versions of pop and country music, while record imports and concerts by foreign entertainers were rare and unpredictable; the only manifest youth movement was the state-controlled Alliance of Socialist Youth of Slovenia (ASYS), subordinated to the League of Communists of Slovenia (the party), so that autonomous public youth activities were predominantly sporadic, latent and local in nature, the only widespread drug culture was traditionally acknowledged alcohol consumption.

Due to the authoritarian nature of the regime on the societal level, there was less autonomy in the interaction between the subcultural peer level and young punks. This was more indicative of some orientations than of others. For example, expressions of resentment were tolerated to a lesser degree than expressions of boredom and indifference. Although the source of orientations might have been different for English and Slovenian youths, it served a similar purpose on the subcultural level – it was an important element of the punk attitude. Some elements of the borrowed value system were less problematic in the context of the Slovenian punk subculture (realism, individualism, living for the moment and accessible creativity), while others had to be expressed more subtly, because they could be perceived as potentially illegitimate by official gatekeepers, like party officials, servile journalists, indoctrinating teachers (devaluation of values, anarchism).[24]

The other crucial societal factor influencing punk in Slovenia was, comparatively speaking, a weaker market regulation of cultural production and consumption. As a result, assimilative tendencies – transforming authentic minority subcultural rebellion into fashionable mass trends – were insignificant in comparison to Western European movements. This had a curious side effect, in the societal vacuum of a largely absent market/culture industry a specific background evolved on the social level, generated by ASYS, made possible only in the context of a decentralized self-management system. It would be next to impossible to understand Slovenian punk without the politically marginalized ASYS in terms of its actual influence on dominant national public events, since it was no longer perceived as a significant political player by the aging communist leadership. But because it still retained its central political position in society in terms of political activity (access to media, public expression of opinions), ASYS could still make its views public. Its institutions (mostly Radio Student, RŠ, and the Student Cultural Centre, ŠKUC) became instrumental in transforming punk from the private sphere of creativity to a public cultural performance on the societal level. Either through its activists or through individuals with access to its media, ASYS opened the doors to punk (through radio airplay, concerts, recordings, publications). This proximity of punks to leftist subpolitics and their significant dependency on its political channels of public promotion also politicized Slovenian punk to an unusual degree. If western punk, above all, faced market and cultural forces of assimilation, and the danger of economically selling out, Slovenian punks faced a qualitatively different problem. They were expected to achieve high subpolitical standards, set by their new political mentors in ASYS, or by those closely associated with the organization, resulting in the danger of over-politization. The bands were expected, above all, to be politically incorrect in the prescribed manner. They were under great influence by leftist DJs and promoters at RŠ who decided, for example, who was appropriate enough (politically incorrect in the prescribed way) to perform at the Novi rock festival (an annual festival of promising new bands held in Ljubljana). Proximity to these alternatives, radical interpreters of political correctness became crucial for making it in the punk subculture of Slovenia. It also sometimes made Slovenian punk a very sombre, somewhat didactic affair.

Because of these specific societal and social backgrounds, which could be best described as "repressive tolerance," a climate which did not encourage the appearance of the subculture, but also did not thwart it, Slovenian punk witnessed original cognitive inputs on the level of individual creativity, which in turn helped create a subcultural background specific for the local social situation.

Comparisons

When American and Slovenian hippie subcultures are compared, significant differences become obvious. The long tradition of popular music (since the jazz subcultures between the two world wars) in America created a heterogeneous musical scene with strong tendencies of assimilation into a mainstream pop culture industry and consequently of integration into a parent/dominant world. Resistance to the Vietnam war was treated as deviance to be dealt with by the state apparatus of repression, which generated radical subpolitical dissent. Subcultural innovativeness interacting with subpolitical activism produced countercultural phenomena, such as communes. The domestic musical tradition in Slovenia, on the other hand, was more meagre and subdued. Progressive rock musicians could react only to state-run pop music (emerging pop rock and a traditionalistic folk music). Authorities were much more suspicious of any potential competition with socialist ideology, interpreting instances of subpolitical radicalism (mostly the student movement) as cases of deviance (in the terminology of D. Hebdige, interpreting symbolic threat to the symbolic order as a real threat to the real order), leading to the liquidation of the student movement with the implication that countercultural phenomena were less frequent and articulate and more transitive.

The different fate of both subcultures is also significant. T. Roszak's prediction[25] of the fusion of the subpolitical student movement and the hippie subculture in America, of the lunatic bohemian beatniks and hippies with the sober political activism of New Left students, never came true. The end of the Vietnam war and the gradual assimilation of authentic hippie attitudes into acceptable mainstream hippie fashions resulted in a gradual withering away of the countercultural potential of the American youth. In Slovenia, events that led to the eventual disintegration of the youth subculture were significantly different. With the demise of the "liberal" government of S. Kavčič, the autonomous student organization was prohibited and replaced by the party controlled Alliance of Socialist Youth. On the other hand, there was less pressure on the hippie subculture. Although over-zealous ASYS officials could ban rock concerts (for example, of Buldožer in Ljubljana), the subculture was mostly ignored and tolerated on the margins of everyday subcultural life. On the other hand, the underdeveloped culture industry had neither the potential nor the ambition to assimilate elements of hippie subculture into the dominant culture. As a result, the hippie subculture persisted in a marginalized and isolated position.

Differences are also apparent between English and Slovenian punk subcultures. In the case of the English subculture, the highly developed culture industry gradually turned creative innovation into popular fashion and thus exerted a strong influence on dominant cultural values and practices. In Slovenia, an undeveloped culture industry implied a greater influence of creative foreign influences and significantly lesser temptation of assimilation into the mainstream culture. This implied a smaller influence of youth subcultural practices on mainstream culture; while the more repressive climate generated by the interaction of punks and authoritarian socialism created and maintained more subdued expressions of resentment (clothed in irony, sarcasm, cynicism, or black humor), and stimulating a retreat into a realm of supposedly pure, self-sufficient artistic expression, whereas strong ties to ASYS created a very politicized, New Left orientation of numerous punk artists.

The rejection of an aggressive punk subculture was present in both political contexts, in the politically democratic system in England and the politically authoritarian system of Slovenia. But it was much more fatal for punks in Slovenia (e.g., a trial of supposed Nazi punks, raids of graffiti writers, persecution of punk image, or police interrogations). As a result, punk as a subculture had to retreat from everyday life in the early 1980s into new wave artistic expression and life style.

Conclusion

Hippie and punk subcultures are phenomena of young individuals and their activities. In the case of Slovenia they are the product of internalization of a subcultural Western life style (mostly on the level of subcultural borrowing), which interacted with a socialist ideology as a subordinated form of organization of industrial production, generating numerous specific creative outputs of individuals (hippie and punk subcultures).

The socialist background of Slovenia, too, was the result of interacting with Western superordinate backgrounds, which were gradually being assimilated by actors as taken-for-granted conditions of their creative activities, while the subordinate Soviet-type background of socialism, inaugurated after the Second World War, became a restricting factor of individual autonomy.

Two rock subcultures appeared in Slovenia in the 1970s, hippies and punks. The hippie subculture was more intimistic, disassociate, hedonistic, mystical and optimistic, whereas the subculture of punks was more extravert, aggressive, pessimistic and nihilistic in outlook. Their pronounced differences rest on the fact that they were first and foremost products of subcultural borrowing from Western sources and of appropriation by individuals, who were cognitively attracted to them.

These differences were to a lesser extent a product of interaction between youths and their domestic backgrounds. It does not imply, however, that individual members were necessarily less creative in comparison to their Western role models. Creative individuals were often able to interpret the global background from a specific local perspective and/or from a specific individual perspective, thus generating innovative, original cultural outputs, producing subcultural worlds that were as relevant and authentic as those which originally inspired them.

Notes

[1] Mateja Režek, "Spor z Informbirojem," in *Slovenska Novejša Zgodovina 1848–1992*, ed. Jasna Fischer (Ljubljana: MK, 2005), 933.

[2] Zdenko Čepič, "Zvišanje Življenske Ravni," in *Slovenska Novejša Zgodovina 1848–1992*, ed. Jasna Fischer (Ljubljana: MK, 2005), 1088.

[3] Zdenko Čepič, "Demografske in Socialne Spremembe," in *Slovenska Novejša Zgodovina 1848–1992*, ed. Jasna Fischer (Ljubljana: MK, 2005), 1130.

[4] Aleš Gabrič, "Približevanje Kulturnih Dobrin Širšemu Krogu Ljudi," in *Slovenska Novejša Zgodovina 1848–1992*, ed. Jasna Fischer (Ljubljana: MK, 2005), 1032.

[5] Gregor Tomc, *Profano. Kultura v Modernem Svetu* (Ljubljana: KRT, 1994), 171.

[6] Gregor Tomc, "We Will Rock YU," in *Impossible Histories. Historical*

Avant-gardes, Neo-avant-gardes, and Post-avant-gardes in Yugoslavia, 1918–1991, ed. Dubravka Djurić and Miško Šuvaković (Cambridge and London: The MIT Press, 2003), 451.

[7] Buldožer, *Pljuni istini u oči* (Beograd: PGP, 1975).

[8] Kostja Gatnik, *Magna Purga – Danes in Nikdar Več* (Ljubljana: ŠKUC, 1977), 22.

[9] Vojin Kovač – Chubby, *Chubby Was Here* (Koper: Lipa, 1987), 15–6.

[10] Aleš Gabrič, "Študentsko Gibanje," in *Slovenska Novejša Zgodovina 1848–1992*, ed. Jasna Fischer (Ljubljana: MK, 2005), 1065.

[11] Milan Dekleva, "Svobodna Univerza in Kultura," in *Študentsko gibanje 1968–'72*, ed. Ciril Baškovič et al. (Ljubljana: KRT, 1982), 157–8.

[12] Gregor Tomc, ibid., 2003, 456.

[13] Berlinski zid, "Berlinski Zid," in *Punk Je Bil Prej,* ed. Peter Lovšin et al. (Ljubljana: CZ, 2002), 100.

[14] Gregor Tomc, ibid., 2003, 457–8.

[15] Laibach Kunst, "Laibach," *Problemi*, 205/206 (1981): 64.

[16] Peter Mlakar, "Garten des Friedens," *Problemi*, 205/206 (1981): 21.

[17] Igor Vidmar, "Reflection on the Union of Socialist Youth of Slovenia and Punk," in *Študentsko gibanje 1968–'72*, ed. Ciril Baškovič et al. (Ljubljana: KRT, 1982), 157–8.

[18] The social situation may be observed on three interdependent levels of abstraction. The first depicts levels of substantive orientations (from individual cognition to primary group orientations and anonymous ideology) while the second depicts levels of formal structuration (from individual actions to group interactions and anonymous organizations). The three horizontal lines compare levels of abstraction of substantive and formal interaction. The lowest line depicts the concrete level of individual cognition and interaction, which is largely contingent, the middle line levels indicate a more structured primary social life that we recognize and take for granted, while the highest level depicts levels of interaction which demand metaphorical perception of self (person), others (society) and other (of natural and supernatural), and which are much more stereotypical. We can represent these levels schematically in the following fashion:

- ideology/societal
- orientation/social
- cognition/sociable

Some characteristic examples of cultural orientations/forms are on the societal level: state norms, market regulation or monogamy; on the intermediate level: family, peer group or subcultural values and knowledge; and on the level of individual cognition: sensations, feelings and thoughts some characteristic examples are a romantic pair, a teacher-pupil relationship or greeting a passer-by.

[19] But early modernity also witnessed competitive ideas of production background; the most ambitious one was probably socialism, embedded in romantic ideology. The socialist production background (state property, planned regulation, party state) moralized problems of industrial production. An alternative social situation was implied in which individuals were supposed to delay gratification of their needs and in which values were above all collective, ascetic, puritanical etc.

[20] Andreas Huyssen, *After the Great Divide. Modernism, Mass Culture, Postmodernism* (Bloomington and Indianapolis: Indiana University Press, 1986).

[21] Because of its inherent productive inefficiency and the failure of totalitarian attempts to redefine, re-traditionalize the individual, it soon became obvious that the socialist experiment was not so much a counter-hegemonic avant-garde to capitalism as its somewhat backward cousin. The relation between the two systems soon emerged as one of super-ordination and sub-ordination, where elements of the first system were gradually being assimilated into socialism.

[22] Paul Willis, *Profane Culture* (London: Routledge & Kegan Paul, 1978), xx.

[23] Mike Brake, *Sociologija Mladinske Kulture in Mladinskih Subkultur* (Ljubljana: KRT, 1983), 79.

[24] In this context, a comparison of punk scenes in different parts of the second Yugoslavia would also be of interest. It would show varying degrees of "repressive tolerance" (the term is borrowed from H. Marcuse) in different political backgrounds of the federal republic, generating to a certain extent different interactions of youths with respective dominant cultures, which in turn produced to a certain extent varying degrees of urban youth autonomy. Hypothetically speaking, the Slovenian scene was probably the most autonomous one, while the Sarajevo scene was the least autonomous one, with all the other scenes falling somewhere in between.

[25] Theodore Roszak, *Kontrakultura – Razmatranje o Tehnokratskom Društvu i Njegovoj Mladenačkoj Opoziciji* (Zagreb: Naprijed, 1978).

8

Yugoslav Past in Film and Music
Yugoslav Interfilmic Referentiality

Martin Pogačar

> The possible is therefore the mirage of the present in the past; and as we know the future will finally constitute a present and the mirage effect is continually being produced, we are convinced that the mirage of tomorrow is already contained in our actual present, which will be the past of tomorrow, although we did not manage to grasp it.
>
> *Henri Bergson*

Introduction

The chapter deals with the specific relationship between Yugoslav popular culture and the country's socio-historical context. Yugoslav popular culture (particularly film and music) was made unique by the country's geopolitical position (neither west nor east) and additionally characterized by the relatively low outflow of cultural products and a relatively high influx of western popular cultural "goods," which led to the emergence of a specific symbolic *Yuni*-verse.[1] The main question in the chapter focuses on how cinema, television and popular music may be used as complementary historical sources. In this respect, the primary interest is the relationship between cinema (and television) dealing with the past and the specific socio-politico-economic situation of Yugoslavia in the 1970s and 1980s. I investigate two cinematic texts – an episode of Srdjan Karanović's series *Grlom u jagode* [Reckless Youth] (1975) and Rajko Grlić's feature film *Samo jednom se ljubi* [You Only Love Once] (1981) – and two cinematic characteristics (typecasting and musical soundtrack). The main features that bind the texts are the same protagonist (Miki Manojlović) and the film's theme song, Ivo Robić's *Samo jednom se ljubi*.

First, I present the amusing feature of Yugoslav cinematography – the same actors in different films appearing in characteristically very similar roles. To this Yugoslav version of typecasting, I refer to as the *Yugoslav interfilmic referentiality*: a character does not only inhabit the cinematic dimensions of one film, but establishes an interfilmic "persona," which is built on references (not necessarily direct) to other filmic and TV texts. This phenomenon is widely present perhaps most notably in Hollywood (think of typecasting Bruce Willis, Sylvester Stallone, or the film stars of the 1940s and 1950s Hollywood). The difference, when compared to Yugoslavia is the former's global effect, while the latter only functioned in the rather limited territory of the former Yugoslavia and significantly contributed to the creation of *Yu*niverse. This, however, makes it no less interesting. Today, the emergence and spread of the internet sales enables people, who were in one way or another forced to leave the Yugoslavia, to find fragments of their country's past and their own pasts in films and series. This also enables people who only migrated in time (and today live in one of the newly formed states), or were not even born then, to experience through film and music excerpts of the times past. If popular culture once determined the shared field of common cultural experience, the latter now re-emerges through discovering forgotten or dismissed cinematic traces of the Yugoslav past.

The second cinematic element is film music (soundtrack), which plays an important role in the creation of "filmestrial space"[2] and significantly transgresses its boundaries. The soundtrack is an important feature that contributes to the creation of a convincing diegetic space, giving it the depth that a two-dimensional picture lacks. The popular genre of *popevka*,[3] a Yugoslav equivalent to German *Schlager* and Italian *canzona*, is here understood as a tool for underscoring Yugoslav typecasting, it is placed into the broader picture of producing a distinct cinematic reality that significantly contributes to the creation of the popular-cultural representations of the country's past.

Mediatized Past

The moving pictures in historical research may be understood in the way implied by Siegfried Kracauer: "Films come into their own when they *record and reveal physical reality* [...] [a]nd since any medium is partial to the things it is uniquely equipped to render, the cinema is conceivably animated by a desire to picture transient material life, life at its most ephemeral."[4] The audio-visual images thus reveal a certain physicality of an age and its inhabitants (the fashion, the interior décor of homes and offices, the cars, the kitchen appliances, and the landscape, to name a few). The material aspect of the past is therefore visually quite successfully preserved in its appearance and represented on screen (as ghostly as such representations are), which enables and predetermines the inhabitants of today to imagine and think about the past in a rather visual manner. Additionally, these images reveal certain characteristics of an age that go beyond mere depictions of materiality: the linguistic characteristics and idiosyncrasies of a certain period, the workings of an ideological apparatus, the very means of film production, the state of technology etc. On the other hand, it cannot be stressed enough that film, TV and (popular) music are heavily imbued with fictitious components and mythological connotations. It is only by considering all these aspects – and not taking Kracauer's statement too literally – that explorations in the cinematic past become feasible.

The 20th century particularly has been dominated by the visual; many other types of representation are loosing its role today due to the supposed incapability of accurate representation of events and periods, coupled with the irresistibility of the visual media, believed to give the "most accurate" image of events. Film (documentary or feature, newsreels, news etc.) tends to condense a period, an event or a person's life into a comprehensible narrative that can be consumed without much effort.[5] As opposed to dealing with the past that takes into account classical archives, investigating the mediatized past has some distinct features: first, the capacity to present the past in movement and sound makes the representations of the past appealing and informational. Yet, such procedures are necessarily abstractions and rather subjective generalizations prone to individual appropriation and internalization. Second, the mediatized past is deterritorialized and detemporalized,[6] fragmented and placed in new time–space settings. To put it differently, history on film may be inaccurate, false or manipulated, yet it is through the hints to the underlying historical contexts that a certain period may "become alive," in conjunction with historical sources.

Yugoslav Cinematic Past

Broadly speaking, the era of Yugoslav cinema coincides with the period between the end of the World War II and the collapse of the socialist regimes of Eastern Europe. At a more local level, the cinema of the second Yugoslavia started to develop at the onset of the reconstruction of the war-wrecked country in 1945 and abruptly terminated with the state's infamous demise in 1991. Today, the retrospectives of the film opuses of Yugoslavia's most renowned film directors, the reruns of ex-Yu films and TV series, and the growing sales of "the greatest Yugoslav movies on DVD" on the internet, indicate a growing public interest (of both younger and older) in Yugoslavia's cinematic past. Francois Truffaut once said, "When the shooting is over, the actor can die for all I care, I've got him on film."[7] If the "actor" is replaced by the "country," ("shooting" speaks for itself) then the statement attains a rather different meaning when talking about the dead country and its cinema. Cinematically speaking, Yugoslavia lives on.

The existence of the second Yugoslavia has been essentially intertwined with the production of moving images. The power of film and later TV, and their ideological potential did not go unnoticed by the regime which often used these features to its own ends – to disseminate and propagate the ideology and values of socialism, brotherhood and unity, non-alignment, the mythology of World War II, among others. These persistent themes of the Yugoslav quotidian and high politics found their place in many films and other mass media, most commonly in popular music, literature, fine arts; and also in architecture, and monuments etc.

Cinema

In the immediate post-war period, the Yugoslav Communist Party (KPJ) nationalized, centralized and accordingly orchestrated the entire film production industry. The initial post-war period left its mark on the field of cultural production with the authorities' insistence on "social realism," posing a demand on the artists to depict "reality" programmatically and idealistically.[8] However, before long the regime's grip over cultural production eased, especially after the break with the Cominform in 1948 and the implementation of the politics of self-management. Workers' councils were introduced as decision-making bodies overseeing film production, distribution and exhibition.[9] Ever greater numbers of films produced resulted in the rise of the popularity of Yugoslav cinema. For illustration only, in Slovenia, cinema attendance was constantly increasing from 1947 (6.570.000 tickets sold) to 1960 (17.189.000 tickets sold), with a slight decrease in 1951/52. From 1960 onward, attendance started gradually to decrease: to 10.456.000 in 1970, 8.651.000 in 1980, and 2.846.000 in 1990. Such dynamics may be attributed to the joint effect of the relatively low production of Slovenian films (17 feature films in the 1950s; 33 in the 1960s; 29 in 1970s; 42 in the 1980s),[10] the increasingly more popular and affordable TV. The cultural politics in the former Yugoslavia kept the ticket prices at a very low level, which ensured relatively large numbers of cinema goers despite the worsening economic situation (especially in the late 1970s and the 1980s). Yet, as Daniel J. Goulding maintains, due to the fact that cinema was mainly financed through ticket generated income, low ticket prices resulted in insufficient resources for any kind of sustained development.[11]

The 1960s, by many considered the golden age of Yugoslav cinema saw numerous quality films produced and the *new wave* emerge.[12] The latter was fashioned by authors (Boštjan Hladnik, Želimir Žilnik, Živojin Pavlović, among others) who "sought to free Yugoslav cinema from bureaucratic dogmatism and to promote free expression and experimentation. Inspired by Italian Neorealism and various new waves in European cinema, the filmmakers rejected the dominant style of socialist realism, with its officially sanctioned optimism and patriotic education of the masses, opting instead for exposing the darker side of the socialist state with its corruption and hypocrisy."[13] The enthusiasm of the 1960s, which characterized the political, economic and cultural situation of the former Yugoslavia during this period, nevertheless started to wane at the turn of the decades. The 1960s brought in its wake the so-called "leaden 70s"; the purges blew away the more liberal fractions within the Communist Party (Slovenian Stane Kavčič, Serbian Latinka Perović et al.) and dealt with the nationalist sentiments (Croatian Spring).[14] Repercussions of the 1970s also fell upon the sphere of cultural production, the cinematic *new wave* (*novi val*, also *novi film*) was labeled *black wave*; and film production in general was rather poor in numbers. The negative trend in film production and cinema going that begun during the 1960s continued well into the 1970, reaching the all times low in 1976 with only 16 feature films produced.[15] However, this period also witnessed an increased production of partisan epics that immediately achieved a cult status.[16] Moreover, towards the end of the 1970s, "Yugoslav cinema entered a period of decreased ideological turbulence during which the stylistic and narrative vocabularies of genre filmmaking substantially developed."[17]

The times of false tranquility and *social deafness*[18] seem to have ended with the death of President Tito. This was apparent in many areas of cultural production and politics: in the emergence of punk rock, the alternative movements, the questioning of the very foundations of Yugoslavia and its regime etc. In the sphere of film, the period of Yugoslav cinema that started in the late 1970s and continued throughout the 1980s, represents a period of increased interest in the immediate post-war period. The taboos were beginning to be addressed, the suppressed past disinterred. A group of directors, formed at the Prague FAMU (Film and TV School of the Academy of Performing Arts), started making films known as *new Yugoslav cinema*, also labeled a specific Yugoslav version of the "cinema of moral concern," which was emerging at the time in the Eastern and Central Europe.[19] Alongside the themes of contemporary social problematic, they were addressing the interpretations of World War II and the post-war political situation.

The 1980s directors rarely tried to undermine the existing socio-political order. Rather, they "critically questioned the official mythology of Yugoslav socialist foundation and evolution from the heroic partisan struggle, to early Stalinist orthodoxy, to the progressive break with Stalin and the creation of the 'self-managing' socialism" from within the ideological horizons.[20] In doing so, the directors used to typecast certain actors and actresses which helped the Yugoslav interfilmic referentiality to emerge.

Television

An important turning point in the history of Yugoslav cinematic universe was the bloom of TV. Ever since the early 1960s on, cinema going, a popular pastime of many Yugoslavs, was confronted with its blue-light-box substitute invading domestic privacy. Accordingly, images from the silver screen started to invade the private and influence the collective spheres: contributing to the emergence of what Svetlana Boym calls "a field of shared cultural experience."[21] Television became a commonplace quotidian experience.

Film and TV were recognized by the regime to be the most appropriate and appropriable, if not always the most accurate and straightforward media for dealing with the past, present and future. In this respect the "partisan films were popular with the Yugoslav regime as they had a powerful legitimizing function, providing a useful mental prod for people to remind the viewers what the alternative to Communism was."[22] More to the point, numerous TV series, procuring "easy-watching," humorous, soft-edged comedy depicted the sunny side of Yugoslav reality (Vruć vetar [Hot Wind], 1980). Yet, when dealing with some uneasy issues, these would be camouflaged with a good measure of irony and black humor. There were, however, certain series that overtly questioned the social situation, problems of youth (Sivi dom [Gray Home], 1984), and human trafficking (Dom za vešanje [Time of the Gypsies], 1988). Regarding the role of television, Velimir Stojanović's remark on "Retrovision" seems quite that amusing: "Well, look what this little screen has turned into – a little mirror that shows us, through the dust we raised ourselves, the characters and faces of the past."[23]

The dominant role of television in everyday life "dethroned" film to the level of ordinary everyday experience. Seeing a film was no longer a ritual (a ritual of going to the theatre, submerge into the darkness, and let the flickering beam take over), but instead became a part of the daily routine, with the viewer randomly glimpsing at the images and sporadically immersing into the story while performing everyday tasks. Television thus endowed the everyday life with a specific rhythm of continuous presence of "action," events and entertainment.[24] The direct broadcast intrinsic to television promotes the "aesthetics of the fact" and has the capacity to present itself not as a metaphorical representation, but as the presenter of the life itself.[25] To take this a little further, *simultaneous collective reception*,[26] most successfully realized precisely through television and cinema, enables the individual to participate, "quasi-actively," in the collective action only by sitting in front of the telly. If before the age of television one had to go "out" to participate in a collective experience, the TV brought this experience "in." In fact, TV made out of *Homo sapiens* another species altogether – one that incessantly zaps through the channels – *Homo zapiens*.[27] The incessant zapping through the programs, the "power" to change to a different program or to switch the telly off, gives the viewer a false sense of control, while on a deeper level nourishes apathy and general inability to critically asses or react to the mediatized contents. This is partly due to "television's tendency towards personalizing all social, cultural, and (for our purposes) historical matters within the highly controlled and viewer-involving confines of a well-constructed plot structure."[28] Regardless of the viewer's extent of superficial involvement, they may identify easily with narratives on screen.

The humanity had the luck and opportunity, Thomas Elsaesser says, to build a cultural memory of the ordinary, the quotidian, of what interests common people, what entertains them and what touches them, what they have seen on TV or in films: a history of pastime and the "killing of time" along with the history of all death fields on television.[29] And it is the characteristic of both film and TV in one way or another dealing with the past that the images they convey are "not tied to a specific time, but are exemplar of life at that period."[30] Mediatization of real and fictitious events thus essentially influences the workings of the processes of remembering, for it condenses the past into universally recognizable, continually repeated and replayed sets of images.

In this respect, Yugoslav films and TV series and their historical role have to be understood as examples of life in Yugoslavia in various periods of time. The inherent generalizations and social, cultural or political commentary they may convey enable us to construe a representation of the past. However, apart from the elements such as plot and narrative, one important factor in imagining the cinematic past is typecasting – Yugoslav interfilmic referentiality.

Yugoslav Interfilmic Referentiality

As indicated above, the cinematic remnants of the Yugoslav past bring to the fore the interesting phenomenon of more or less the same actors appearing in similar roles time and again: the unde-featable partisan, the nurse, the typical dysfunctional father and the strong mother to name a few. Thus, the field of a shared cultural experience attains commonly recognizable traits.

The basic characteristic of any cinematic text is that it creates its own space and time. These spatio-temporal dimensions pro-vide the basic set of determinants, coordinates of a filmestrial space within which a story unfolds. Yet, for a story to emerge fully, the narrative needs characters and events. The characters are involved in a plot and the actions they perform constitute a series of events.[31] It is only when events happen and characters act in the constructed space-time continuum (the cinematic universe) that a story is put in motion. Once the story is unfolding, the characters become "alive." Eventually, it is up to the viewer to comprehend, reconstruct and interpret the meaning. This process is based on what is presented on screen, on the supposed author's agenda, and the socio-cultural background of the viewer. The events and characters figure as the kernels and catalysts of meaning and demand suspension of disbe-lief in their ghostliness.[32] Thus, if we want to "enjoy" the film, we have to deny its fictional character and accede to inevitable sim-plifications and obvious errors. In terms of seeing a cinematic text historically, this means that the viewer has to "by-pass" (not dis-card) certain obvious historical inadequacies. Consequentially, this enables them to see the past in its metaphorical dimension.

The emerging filmestrial space is significantly defined by the physical representation of the filmestrial environment, and the "ap-pearance and personality" of characters. To use Maurice Merleau-Ponty's phrasing: "Another person, for us, is a spirit which haunts a body and we seem to see a whole host of possibilities contained within this body when it appears before us; the body is the very presence of these possibilities."[33] Physical traits often define per-sonality and in the process of watching a film endow the character with an aura of a living person. The character thus begets a filmic being, inevitably related to their appearance, image, to their "real" personality, public or private. Often they become fused.

The predominant aspect of any interfilmic referentiality, and of the Yugoslav one, is that the faces of ever-present characters do not inhabit one filmestrial space exclusively, but rather "migrate" from one to another. They co-exist in multiple fictional universes contributing to a common, trans-filmic symbolic universe to emerge. And this is the most important feature of interfilmic referentiality: it creates a commonly recognizable symbolic universe. In a certain historical period it functions as the common field of cultural experience mentioned above; in retrospect, it construes the symbolic universe of the past. Thus, this past can be seen indeed as a "foreign country," yet made close and familiar with the faces and characters.

In cinema, a set of predetermined "mythipical"[34] roles is often used and similar patterns are clearly discernible in Yugoslav film as well. This phenomenon is perhaps most conspicuous in the popular partisan epics that launched Bata Živojinović, Ljubiša Samardžić and Boris Dvornik as the role model liberation-war heroes.[35] Seriously outnumbered, they managed to defeat countless Nazis, Fascists and collaborators. This was the case in two particularly well known war-time films, Veljko Bulajić's *Bitka na Neretvi* [The Battle of Neretva] (1969) and Stipe Delić's *Sutjeska* [The Battle of Sutjeska] (1973).[36] The standard myth producing mechanisms were deployed, (re-)establishing and reproducing social cohesion and distribution of responsibilities (the care for the wounded and less able, the blind carrying the cripple, comradeship, righteousness, devotion to the cause, prospect of peace and better future for all etc.). This inevitably resulted in stereotypical representations of the Nazis and Fascists on screen and in everyday life.[37]

Perhaps the utmost exemplary occurrence of interfilmic referentiality is a scene from Goran Marković's *Specijalno vaspitanje* [Special Education] (1977). Cane (Ljubiša Samardžić) takes a young boy, Trta (Slavko Štimac), to a Belgrade correctional institution and when they get off a train he catches a fleeting glimpse of Vojislav Brajović (Tihi, a character from Aleksandar Đorđević's *Otpisani* and the sequel, *Povratak otpisanih* [The Written-off; The Return Written-off] (1974)). Cane, of course, recognizes the Yugoslav film star. Yet, pointing Brajović out to Trta, he does not use the actor's real name, but says, "Look, there's Tihi." This fleeting textual event figures as a typical case of interfilmic referentiality: there is Samardžić, a famous actor who impersonated a number of partisan characters (the mythipical partisan) in the role of a police officer, paying tribute to his fellow fighter. The viewer is thus invited into the symbolic universe of the Yugoslav interfilmic referentiality. Recently, Bata Živojinović, a Serb, and Boris Dvornik, a Croat, who spent the last 15 years politically active on the opposing sides of the Yugoslav conflict, made peace via video-link. The following blog entry illustrates the intertwining of their respective private lives with the cinematic realities: *They made it side by side through Sutjeska, Neretva, the seven enemy offensives, film festivals, Pula, Niš, Herceg-Novi, Beograd – the covers of all the magazines published in the SFRY – they were in every café ... Boris in* Bolji život [Better Living]*, Bata in* Srećni ljudi [Happy People].[38]

The phenomenon of Yugoslav interfilmic referentiality is not at all limited to wartime partisan films, but extends across the broader Yugoslav film and television production. For illustration only, Danilo Bata Stojković repeatedly appeared in the roles of a dysfunctional father, apparently firm in his views and principles, yet inherently submissive. For instance, in *Čuvar plaže u zimskom periodu* [Beach Guard in Winter], *Varljivo leto '68* [The Deceitful Summer of '68], *Maratonci trče počasni krug* [The Marathon Family], and also in the television series, *Grlom u jagode* [Reckless Youth], 1975.

The relationship between interfilmic referentiality and history may be somewhat obscure, yet it seems viable when approaching the cinematic past through the popular conceptions of the filmestrial space created and conveyed. The interfilmic referentiality assisted in creating a *Yu*niverse (albeit it may never have functioned very well) that hosted narratives of the heroic anti-Fascist past and ... These common identifiers (ideally) facilitated a creation of a transnational community that although ethnically, linguistically, and culturally different nevertheless related to these trans-national issues. Today, the referentiality contributes to nostalgic discourses that are often closely related or intertwined with identity-quests of people who lost their homeland, families and friends – people whose lives were marked by abolition of the common past and inhibition of the future.

Fictional Spaces and History

Let us now turn to Srđan Karanović's television series *Grlom u ja-gode* and Rajko Grlić's feature *Samo jednom se ljubi*. The series was made in 1975 and deals with the 1960s. In creating the series, the director was aided by his colleague, Rajko Grlić. The result was a ten-episode series, each episode presenting a year in the decade, a year in the lives of a group of friends as they come of age in Belgrade, the capital of Yugoslavia. Made and broadcast in the mid-1970s, the story had a strong nostalgic potential from the very beginning on and this sense of nostalgia has only grown ever since. Even today, the "audiences [...] seize upon, remember, replicate and transform elements [...] quote dialogues, emulate styles, and whistle tunes they had learned from television, radio, or movies."[39] Because of the popular-cultural representation of the 1960s, the series soon became one of the Yugoslav cult series. It tried to recreate and evoke, in the end quite successfully, the carefree time of youth, the careless vibe of the 1960s, the lingo, the architecture, and the prospect of a better future. The 1985 down-to-earth "anti-sequel" (as Karanović describes it), *Jagode u grlu* [Hard to Swallow], received fiery rejection.

Grlić's film, *Samo jednom se ljubi*, was made in 1981, shortly after the death of Tito and in a time of crumbling ideals and surfacing problematic events, which dated in the time of the World War II and its aftermath. The main narrative of Grlić's feature film is set in a small Croatian town immediately after the end of World War II. Three friends, Tomislav (Predrag Manojlović), Vule (Mladen Budiščak) and Mirko (Zijah Sokolović), are about to set up civil government, initiate and lead the reconstruction of the war-wrecked town, and safeguard the creation of a new socialist society. Manojlović becomes romantically involved with a ballerina and falls passionately in love with her. Alas, she is a bourgeois girl and he is a working class lad and a devout communist. They are even further divided by the ideological constraints imposed upon them by the new social order.

Investigating the series *Grlom u jagode* and the film *Samo jednom se ljubi*, certain differences are obvious. First of all, the former a TV series and the latter a film, the texts necessarily differ in stylistic arrangements, film language they deploy, and the very structure of narrative (*Bildungsroman* vs. downward spiral of individual decline). Moreover, the series much more plays the card of the collective (although it is quite individual in many respects) whereas the film puts the collective in the background and exposes the vulnerability of an individual confronted with the collective. Due to its format and style, the series proves a much more appropriate tool to construct continuity. Ever the same opening and closing credits in each episode create an impression that the story neither has a definite beginning nor an end. Thus, it creates a never-ending circle of repetition, which serves the story and its nostalgic character very well: the series (narrative) is thus positioned outside the "real" time and space, into the never-ending past open to endless possible futures.

The film, on the other hand, proves excellent to portray the decay of a man, lost in the devouring forces of a downward spiral. It presents Tomislav's decline from a highly-esteemed party official to a shell of a man. Yet, the inherent mythical structure of cinematic narrations detaches the story from its extra-filmestrial dimensions (postwar Yugoslav reality) and renders the narrative well applicable to the socio-political situation of the early 1980s. The differences between the film and the series could be interpreted as response to the social situation and indicate the socio-political unrest at two levels: first, the generation change and the sobering-up from the postwar enthusiasm resulted in the emergence of suppressed topics: the fragility of the Yugoslav state foundations, the growing nationalisms, the postwar killings. On the second level, during the 1970s, the illusion of development that fed on the growing economic factors and personal freedoms deteriorated considerably: in the slight of the failing modernization and urbanization (bitterly depicted in Dušan Kovačević's theater play, *Radovan III*, 1980), Yugoslav society awoke from the postwar delirium to face increasing social inequalities, political discord etc.

Both texts deal with the past, although each approaches a different past in a different way. One idealizes the golden 1960s and endows the period with an aura of innocence and joyfulness. Although this seems to be the most popular conception that is to some extent surely true, the implicit critique of the system nevertheless has to be acknowledged: the problematic of adolescence, finding a job, the spoils of consumerism. Yet, the very structure of the series marginalized its critique-potential, i.e. it made it easily negligible and only apparent when looked at the hidden messages closely. The film, especially in the latter part, lacks any mythical depictions of the new order, but realistically depicts the fall of man and his ineptness to secure a place in the new society. This is most bitterly depicted in a conversation, where Tomislav and his friend are discussing whether the latter, an important public figure, should be given a villa in the outskirts of town: "We didn't fight so that we all have nothing, but for everyone to have something." Disenchanted, Tomislav replies: "Yes, but everyone."

Manojlović

The binding element of the film and the series is Predrag Manojlović – Tomislav and Miki Rubiroza. Both Karanović and Grlić often cast Manojlović, finding him and his acting appropriate for the characters they wanted to create. Manojlović appeared in many films, often playing an outgoing macho type. The following statement found in the online *Leksikon Yu-mitologije* may be a good start: *My favorite in the series was Miki Rubiroza, the one hot cat among the rest of the group. In one episode Miki is leaving home to find better life abroad and Bane gives him his suit … Ten years later I saw my mates leave the country and before long I myself ended up leaving the country, just like Miki Rubiroza finishing up somewhere across the border.*[40]

In one of the episodes of *Grlom u jagode*, Miki and Bane have a discussion at a train station. Miki brings to attention the frequency of their use of words: "the world, in the world, from the world, of the world" and concludes "I'm going abroad after money and standard."[41] Bane replies that it is a much bigger thing to make your own world at home than move into a foreign one.[42] This account also provides a brief description of the character played by Manojlović – "laf i smekerčina," designating an impulsive, communicative, sexually emancipated man – implying a set of persistent traits of the most of the characters Manojlović impersonated.

In Grlić's film and in Karanović's series, Manojlović plays a stubborn and capable, sexually unrestrained youth popular with friends and girls. In addition to that, Tomislav is a leader of the three officials (male) with high ideological standards. Yet, when a woman whirls into his life he is willing to compromise both his friendship and his own ideals. If, regarding sexuality, the beginning of the film is according to Jurica Pavičić rather homoerotic (river-swim), the latter part of the film explicitly introduces heterosexual passion; if the official art and social environment are in socialism relatively "clean" sexually, Tomislav's lascivious behavior has certain ideological connotations. Carrying a bed across town for Tomislav and Beba, the "innocence [of the newly establishing regime] is destroyed in many ways: the partisans invaded the 'innocence' of a bourgeoisie villa, thus gave evidence to the people of erotic decay of the new elite, and let a woman enter the macho-brotherhood."[43]

In the series' tenth episode "Glava ili pismo" [Heads or Tails], the following scene takes place: Miki, Bane and their friend Svetlana are sipping tea in the garden at Svetlana's home. They have an argument over Bane's marriage, love and matters of the heart.

> *Svetlana (to Bane):* "What about love?"
> *Bane replies:* "Eventually, love will come. Usually people are in love in the beginning, and then it wanes later on. With me, it's the other way around. Now there is none, later it will surely come."[44]
> *Miki (singing a line from Robić's song):* "Samo jednom se ljubi, sve je ostalo varka [You only love once, all the rest is fake]" *and utters a criticism of Bane's hasty marriage:* "Now then Bumbar, your conduct is extremely panicky, almost childish. Have you ever heard of the saying: Marry in haste, sorry for ever? Good luck!"
> *Bane:* "You mean, don't rush into things?"
> *Miki:* "Yes, that's what I think."
> *Bane:* "Well, I rushed into it. Svetlana, forgive me."[45]

Offended by Miki's provocation, Bane punches him. To succumb temporarily to the spoils of interfilmic referentiality: what Miki does not realize is the prophetic implication of the words (both lyrics of Robić's tune and the proverb), to which he falls prey in Grlić's film. Compared with the characters he gave life to in other films, it could be concluded that the personality of

Manojlović's interfilmic character, although every time distinctly different, nevertheless bears certain comparable traits. Without much doubt it can be maintained that Manojlović represents a type of character that could easily be denoted a "proper Yugoslav." He invariably conforms to sometimes outright orientalizing depictions of a Balkanite, most notable perhaps in some of the more recent Kusturica's films (*Underground*, 1995), which can be without much reservation considered self-Balkanizing. Perhaps his physical appearance and I-don't-give-a-toss attitude sometimes correspond with a popular image of a wild, cunning, humorous and daring Dinaric man.[46] Considering the symbolic constructions of "Yugoslavs" and "Balkanites" in Yugoslav and post-Yugoslav cinema it seems feasible to ascribe the success of his fictional character to its exaggerated stereotypical image of an inhabitant of these parts of the world. His interfilmic character fits very nicely in the lines of a song by a band called Jugosloveni: "Who can't do without a pub, who's in there at the break of dawn, who swears an awful lot, who cheats and parties? Who can't do without a bean-stew and without strong slivovitz, without sauerkraut, garlic and bacon, who's protective of his own wife, but is doing everybody else's, who goes to the pub during working hours? Who achieved freedom in their own blood, and said no in '48? Who runs their own politics without the help of the Russians and Americans?"

Popevka *or Life – Sing Along or Die Trying*

Both texts are fundamentally marked by music. In *Grlom u jagode*, Zoran Simjanović's instrumental theme changes (basic structure remaining the same) in order to support a particular scene – it acquires the form of a partisan marching song to underscore the workers' brigades, or attains a romantic hue when giving depth to a romantic moment. This helps in developing recognizable characteristics of the filmestrial space. In *Samo jednom se ljubi*, Robić's popular number appears throughout the film, slowly revealing its form from initial instrumental until the fully realized song at the end. The latter song is discussed in more detail below.

Usually, a certain song can be without much trouble pinpointed to a certain period, basing the process on the stereotypical musical forms. Music tends to subsume the spirit of an age and to condense time (Zeitgeist). With considerable accuracy, one can thus recognize 1970s glitter rock, 1960s flower-power acidy musical maneuvers, 1950s rock-a-billy, and of course, *Schlager, canzona* and *popevka* that emerged in the late 1940s and survived the next four decades. Every period is marked by a set of distinct (dominant) popular musical expressions, mainly in terms of form and less of content, which with time become characteristic "musical representatives" of an age.

In terms of form, the popular music is primarily defined by, and hence reflective of, the state-of-the art in the field of recording and reproducing technology that exist at the time; the ways of playing the instruments and manners of singing, the prevalent use of certain instruments and amplifiers, etc. However, the audio memory is extremely malleable and prone to adjustments. In the absence of a first-hand experience that would help to validate the historical (in)adequacy of the Robić's *Samo jednom se ljubi*, the tune retrospectively overrides and therefore redefines the "real" music of the period by imposing a form that corresponds and concomitantly defines the popular imagination of what the music was like then. It therefore serves as a tool for establishing historical distance. In terms of content, the prevailing theme is, irrespective of style or period, love and disappointment.

How does Robić's tune work in a film? The Grlić film's theme song was originally recorded by Ivo Robić in 1957, twelve years after the historical time of *Samo jednom se ljubi* (sometime between 1945 and 1948). This does no damage to the film, let alone affects its credibility. To the contrary, the tune helps the story to unfold convincingly and contributes to the characters and places fully to emerge. Despite the tune originating in the late 1950s, it is perfectly applicable to any fictionalized time in the period between 1945 and 1960s. Why? It is a peculiarity of human audio-memory to periodize musical past: to devise a representation of the past closely related to the "genealogy of (popular) music" that is intertwined with the pace and ways of personal becoming along the sounds of particular music. Moreover, this intertwining of the history of (popular) music and personal tastes and preferences is often complemented by incursions of video materials and documents originating in or portraying a certain period. Thus, the individual mechanisms of imagination (often randomly) connect and relate the fragments of the possible past(s) in the framework of mediatized sound and vision.

One decisive characteristic of the tune is its pre-filmic existence. It has been around for twenty-four years before making appearance in Grlić's film. Therefore, a viewer may (already) have (had) a personal relationship established with the song, personal memories inscribed into its audioscapes. On the other hand, the tune as a "public property" also represents a "document" of an age in the sense that when listening to the song today it can trigger certain images and ideas about the past. The role of popular music in film can be explained in the following way: Duration of the sound in time, the melody and the lyrics, create specific audioscapes, a *geography of sound*. Michel Chion writes about the specific characteristics of a pop song – it is usually limited to the length of about three minutes, corresponding to the capacity of a circular single; it has an overture, a peak and an ending (dramatic structure); and, most importantly, it is repetitive. Repetitive (think of the very shape of the record) in the sense it can be played repeatedly, thus enabling words and melody[47] to be consumed ad infinitum.

The dramatic structure of the song is interspersed with a refrain, which breaks the temporal linearity and establishes an impression of circular repetition. Thus, the song becomes a "world" of its own, which absorbs the filmestrial space and gives it a spin. Most importantly, the absorbing quality of music is not only limited to the filmestrial spaces, it is also greatly susceptible to personal and collective images (from the news, TV, etc.) that enter its distinct architecture. The circularity folds space and time into a new dimension and the openness of structure allows the listener's feelings to inhabit this space-time bubble. Consequently, the song is inscribed in the memory of the listener. As a remnant of the past, with its malleability and flexibility of interpretation, the song transgresses from the individual level of the listener onto the level of a more common social experience.

Simultaneously a social and highly private experience, music captures, reflects and produces feelings. Music in film functions as a dimensional and emotional enhancer. Giving it depth, it fills the filmestrial space, making the distinction between the filmestrial space and the space of experiential reality ever more porous. To some extent it also subordinates the narrative to its own rhythms. It works through a set of cultural musical codes, which are exemplified by music that has come to be associated with a certain mood or state of mind, further canonized by the film industry into conventional expectations. The simultaneity of collective reception positions the music in a way as to translate the individual experience into the broader social picture.

It is precisely through this optic that one may interpret the role of Robić's song in Grlić's film. In the film, the song first appears after about a half an hour of film has elapsed, and only in its barely recognizable form – instrumental abstraction. Until then, the audio background consists of workers singing, children reciting revolutionary songs, and marching music coming from a record player. Over the next hour, the theme music starts to appear ever more often, until it eventually prevails in audio scenery. Different parts and phrases are played in different ways. Invariably, the song appears preceding a romantic scene, where, interestingly, the "romantic" refers to both the ballerina and the red star hung above the entrance into the town hall.

The passages gradually become longer and more pronounced. This effect reflects and underscores Tomislav's internal strife and personal decline. The song follows him from the moment he meets Beba until his very end. Tomislav, the war hero, grows increasingly disillusioned by his friends' socio-political misconduct and betrayal of ideals.

At the time of his hospitalization, the most explicit critique of the system and state-of-affairs comes to the fore. Under the pretext of needing peace and calm, Tomislav, the "disturbing element," is "institutionalized," disqualified, and thus appropriately removed. Particularly telling is the scene where Tomislav fires a gun against his reflection in the mirror. The mirror shatters, and his constructed social image with it. The time of ideals is definitely over.

After the personal, social and political, collapse of the protagonist, the song firmly holds the viewer in its grip, following Tomislav trying to find his love. And it is only at their final encounter in the basement of a jazz club that the song is realized in full. To terminate the sinister dreamy effect the song has created in preceding scenes and to pronounce the harsh reality of decline, the presence of the singer, Ivo Robić, could not be more effective. Walking into the jazz club, Tomislav's gaze meets Robić's.

Listening to Robić singing live, which features as an intrusion of the real, Tomislav is relieving memories of his lost love to the lines of the tune, "And then love returns to our thoughts, and everyone realizes its radiant glow. You only love once..." The lines the viewer has only anticipated are for the first time clearly and unmercifully pronounced: "You only love once, all the rest is an illusion." Tomislav, a shell of former strength and enthusiasm, runs a bullet into his head.

Up until this final full-on song performance, the film score is exclusively instrumental (apart from the few above mentioned exceptions), triggering and enhancing feelings, nostalgia, and memories of what could have been but was not. At the same time, it forces the viewer to add the words to the musical pattern (provided one knows the tune), to hum along the ill-fated personal and ideological romance. Thus, the viewer participates in the ideological catch of the film: subsumed in the (love) story, on the one hand, the viewer sympathizes with the protagonist, with the representative of "true" socialist ideals. Until the final encounter, the "allegiance" to the woman and the political system is preserved in a repetitive impasse of relatively open-ended prospects. This "suspension of disbelief" into the bitter reality ends when the band starts playing the tune. The music, thus far only existing as an extra-diegetic emotional enhancer intended for the viewer, invades the filmestrial space and necessitates the inevitable collision of fiction and reality. Fusing visual and auditory components of personal decline and tranquilizing momentum of the song, Grlić charges the filmestrial space, and consequently the entire postwar history of Yugoslavia, with inevitable premonition of debacle. In the end, the viewer is left with the song, playing over closing credits. The story encapsulated in the soundscapes of the song is ready for endless reruns. The shattered images of the prospects of the future are never to be reassembled again. Thus, it turns out that one was lured into humming along a tune that deceitfully led the protagonist toward his end. There is no remedy for a broken heart, deceived in love and politics.

Particularly if we consider the wider implications of the *popevka* genre as such. Namely, along with jazz, *popevka* was considered a product of the decadent capitalism denying and disrespecting the "true" values of the socialist "man." Thus, as maintained by Jurica Pavičić, the worse thing that could happen to Tomislav, the true revolutionary, was to see the new world into which the "new state evolved, a world where the rules are dictated by petit bourgeoisie and pragmatism."[48] A new world so bitterly anticipated by the tune lurking in the "underground" of the jazz club.

The tune therefore laces the filmestrial space with repeatability and endows it with historical accuracy (particularly in retrospect). In the series, the tune Miki whistled makes a reference to the pop-cultural setting of the late 1960s, alluding to inevitable fusion of the everyday life with the contents of popular culture and its further (re)appropriations. In the film, the song works as a positioning agent: knowing that the tune does not fit into the period depicted, the viewer is on the one hand positioned outside the filmestrial time, while on the other it is firmly set into arbitrary "once-upon-a-time." From such position the viewer may easily be misled to believe the narrative could unravel in any other time. In light of the situation in the early 1980s, when loyalty to the state, the idea and the party was becoming increasingly questionable, such flexibility of narrative was particularly detrimental (hence the fierce rejection of the film after first released).

The main effect of the song in the film and the doomed lip-servicing tranquilization of social order is that in postwar Yugoslavia the people would often sing (or at least hum) along and discard any doubt or premonition into the deceitful calm and prospect; such conduct discourages the viewer/citizen to ask questions.

Conclusion

Crossing film studies on the terrain of history yields additional understanding of the place and time through the spectacles of popular culture. Comparison of Karanović's series and Grlić's film foremost discloses a certain shift in terms of conceptions of the past. If the former is a rather nostalgic rendition of the 1960s, a period that figures as *golden* throughout the western hemisphere, the latter presents a disenchanted, reality-stricken account of the immediate postwar period. However, it should be noted that the series is not only an exercise in nostalgia. Particularly in the last couple of episodes it touches upon themes that demanded social attention (and still do today, although in different settings) such as the problematic of finding a home, social stratification, consumerism etc. These seeds of an overall disillusionment touched upon in the series nevertheless found its expression in the Karanović's 1985 feature film *Hard to Swallow*. The disillusionment expressed in Grlić's film, on the other hand, is more explicitly directed at the problematic of socialist ideology in the first years of the new state. The period is initially portrayed in terms of endless potential and enthusiasm, but it swiftly turns into a somber portrayal of a time of personal opportunism, betrayal of ideals and deceit of friendship. The problematic of the legitimization of the regime was present throughout the existence of Yugoslavia, but found most fertile grounds in the early 1980s, when the regime was no longer in a position to exert much pressure against the rising social movements and increasingly eloquent civil society. The period epitomized the search for new identities, which necessitated the addressing of a suppressed past. And this is the main theme of *Samo jednom se ljubi*: the very personal, intimate component of the regime in establishing, the personal struggle for survival and better life, the will and determination to go beyond one's beliefs in search for love, be it carnal or ideological. However, the film's two alternative English titles, *Melody Haunts My Memory* and *Melody Haunts my Reverie*, prove much more sinister. Here, the melody functions as the eerie visitor of dreams and memories. The beautifully mythologized glorious revolutionary past is but a reflection in a broken mirror.

Such representations, "fragmentary but specific, allow us to re-cover some of the psychological and emotional dimension of historical events embedded within them."[49] In the case of the series, although made five to fifteen years after the times depicted, one is able to sense the Zeitgeist of an era through most ordinary quotidian events of the youth in Belgrade, their joys and fears, losses and hopes. Much the same, *Samo jednom se ljubi* discloses the fears and problems of the past, and also of the present (1980s). It "allegorically depicts a society that swiftly swapped the uptight, intolerant, and puritan ideals for hedonism and pragmatism of the 'new class,' evicting on the way the cruel puritans as unwanted ballast."[50] Today, both film and series figure as narratives of an unfulfilled striving for a more just social order and better future. Even in the post-Yugoslav times when the "better and fairer" has supposedly substituted the previous "criminal" regime, the utopic ideals cherished in Yugoslavia are still valued today, albeit from a different setting. In many respects "today" is just as problematic as was "yesterday," with the public and political discourses using similar rhetoric and ideological disqualifiers.

Closing A (defeatist): Victor Serge in his *The Case of Comrade Tulayev* asks, "Shall we ever escape from falsehood?"[51]

Closing B (nostalgic): Arsen Dedić sang in "Sve bilo je muzika," "Loving her was like music, was it ever real, this blossom in my palm? Loving her was like music, like an enchanted moment, am I just writing this song, or was I truly hers? Now, many a long year parts us, people are different here, so is the town, is she still the one I used to know, has she given much love?"[52]

Closing C (realist): Srđan Karanović put it nicely in an interview, "Of course, I look forward to changes, but am also very cautious. I am afraid it is all about 'changing the looks,' whereas the 'workings' remain the same."[53]

Notes

[1] This is evident in the popularity of western music (at first predominantly of jazz, and later of the Italian, German, and later mostly Anglo-American popular music), cinema, frequent use of English words and phrases in slang, still apparent today. This latter feature expresses most overtly, I believe, the orientation of (predominantly) youth towards the West, and implies a mind-set that presupposed inclusion of the Yugoslav cultural universe into the western hemisphere.

[2] I use the term "filmestrial" (extra-filmestrial) as a cinematic analogue to "terrestrial" (extra-terrestrial) and use it to denote a film-created space, both diegetic and extra-diegetic.

[3] Here it should be noted that *popevka* is a distinctly Slovenian notion and does not have an analogue neither in Serbo-Croatian nor in English. But because the music referred to with this term stylistically corresponds

to *popevka*, I use it nevertheless. Besides, *popevka* has an interesting connotation for it expresses the easy-listening characteristic of such music and relative ease to memorize the tune and words and to sing or hum along.

⁴ Siegfried Kracauer, *Theory of Film: The Redemption of Physical Reality* (Princeton, New Jersey: Princeton University Press, 1997, 1960), xlix.

⁵ For a chronology of narrative practices see Tessa Morris-Suzuki, *The Past Within Us* (London: Verso, 2005).

⁶ On deterritorialization see Arjun Appadurai, *Modernity at Large: Cultural Dimensions of Globalization* (Minneapolis, London: University of Minnesota Press, 1996); see also Martin Pogačar, "*Yuniverzum*, Cinematično Ozvezdje," *Časopis za kritiko znanosti*, no. 224 (2006): 17–29.

⁷ Zdenko Vrdlovec, "YU Eighties," in *40 Udarcev, Slovenska Filmska Publicistika o Slovenskem in Jugoslovanskem Filmu 1949–1988*, ed. Zdenko Vrdlovec (Ljubljana: Slovenski gledališki in filmski muzej, 1988), 373.

⁸ Pavle Levi, *Disintegration in Frames: Aesthetics and Ideology in the Yugoslav and Post-Yugoslav Cinema* (Stanford: Stanford University Press, 2007), 15.

⁹ Daniel J. Goulding, *Jugoslavensko Filmsko Iskustvo, 1945–2001, Oslobođeni Film* (Zagreb: V.B.Z., 2004), 1–33.

¹⁰ Statistical Yearbook of the Republic of Slovenia 1996, "Culture," http://www.stat.si/letopis/1996/08-96.pdf (accessed September 2, 2007).

¹¹ Daniel J. Goulding, ibid., 2004, 155.

¹² Daniel J. Goulding, ibid., 2004, 64.

¹³ Bohdan Y Nebesio, "Yugoslavia, Novi Film," http://www.filmreference.com/encyclopedia/Romantic-Comedy-Yugoslavia/Yugoslavia-NOVI-FILM.html (accessed August 24, 2007).

¹⁴ See Jože Pirjevec, *Jugoslavija: Nastanek, Razvoj ter Razpad Karadjordjevićeve in Titove Jugoslavije* (Koper: Založba Lipa, 1995); Božo Repe, *Jutri je Nov Dan: Slovenci in Razpad Jugoslavije* (Ljubljana: Modrijan, 2002).

¹⁵ In 1960, 130.124.000 tickets were sold, the total dropping to 80.874.000 in 1971; moreover, attendance of films of Yugoslav production dropped from 21.075.000 in 1960 to 6.100.000 in 1971. See Daniel J. Goulding, ibid., 2004, 67, 149.

¹⁶ According to Janet Staiger, cult texts are texts that the viewers view repeatedly and texts to which they wish to initiate others. Janet Staiger, *Media Reception Studies* (New York and London: New York University Press, 2005), 125. Umberto Eco maintains a cult film (series) is one that provides a "completely furnished world so that its fans can quote characters and episodes as if they were aspects of the fan's private sectarian world." Eco in Janet Staiger, ibid., 2005, 126.

¹⁷ Pavle Levi, ibid., 2007, 57.

[18] Fran Tonkiss, "Aural Postcards: Sound Memory and the City," in *The Auditory Culture Reader*, ed. Michael Bull and Les Back (Oxford, New York, Berg: Sensory Formations Series, 2004), 304.

[19] Pavle Levi, ibid., 2007, 58.

[20] Daniel J. Goulding, ibid., 2004, 174; Pavle Levi, ibid., 2007, 58.

[21] Svetlana Boym, *The Future of Nostalgia* (New York: Basic Books, 2002), 64.

[22] Andrew J. Horton, "Lyric Landscapes and Living Hell," http://www.kinoeye.org/02/17/horton17.php (accessed June 15, 2007).

[23] Velimir Stojanović, *Osuđeni na Slobodu* (Novi Beograd: Sanimex, 2003), 261.

[24] Henri Lefebvre, *Rhythmanalysis, Space, Time and Everyday Life* (London and New York: Continuum, 2004), 64.

[25] Slobodan Novaković, *Čovek, medij* (Novi Sad: Prometej, 1998), 84.

[26] Victor Burgin, *In/Different Spaces, Place and Memory in Visual Culture* (Berkeley, Los Angeles, London: University of California Press, 1996), 158.

[27] Victor Pelevin, *Babylon* (London: Faber and Faber, 2002), 78.

[28] Gary R. Edgerton, Introduction to *Television Histories. Shaping Collective Memory in the Media Age*, ed. Gary R. Edgerton and Peter C. Rollins (Lexington: The University Press of Kentucky, 2001), 2.

[29] Thomas Elsaesser, "Prvi Vlak Morda Zakriva Drugega," in *Avdio-vizualni mediji in identitete*, ed. Melita Zajc (Ljubljana: Slovenska Kinoteka, 1996), 54–6.

[30] Janet Staiger, ibid., 2005, 188.

[31] Jakob Lothe, *Narrative in Fiction and Film. An Introduction* (Oxford: Oxford University Press, 2003), 73.

[32] Ibid.; see Janet Staiger, *Interpreting Films. Studies in Historical Reception of American Cinema* (Princeton, New Jersey: Princeton University Press, 1992).

[33] Maurice Merleau-Ponty, *The World of Perception* (London and New York: Routledge, 2004), 82.

[34] "Mythipical" implies a fusion of "mythical" and "typical" roles.

[35] On discursive construction of the "partisans" and "Germans" in Slovenian partisan film see Peter Stanković, *Rdeči Trakovi* (Ljubljana: Fakulteta za družbene vede, 2005).

[36] The impact of these (and other) war-time films also echoed in popular music: in the early 1980s Prljavo Kazalište sang: "I grew up along war films in color, constant school fights … I'm a truly happy child."

[37] In the *Lexicon of Yu-mythology* Dejan Novačić fabulously depicted the *"Germans"* as bloodthirsty creatures, wearing recognizable felt uniforms, which destroy all forms of life they come across, taking greatest

pleasure in killing wounded partisans. The life cycle of *Germans* unravels in two distinct and exclusive phases. In the first phase Germans freely move around in all directions and are extremely aggressive. In the second phase, though, after Bata Živojinović appears (occasionally in a cocktail with Boris Dvornik) there is massive extinction, panic retreat or sissy surrender of Germans. *German language* – in the first phase exclusively imperative ("hände hoch!," "schnell!," "loss!") in the second phase degrades into unarticulated cries of surprise and pain.

[38] Branislav Kovačević Cole, "Bata i Boris – Pomirenje, Oprostaj ili Nesto Trece?" Blog entry posted November 8, 2006, http://blog.b92.net/node/2787 (accessed April 2, 2007).

[39] Mark Allen Peterson, "Performing Media, Toward an Ethnography of Intertextuality," in *Media Anthropology*, ed. Eric W. Rothenbuhler and Mihai Coman (London: Sage Publications, 2005), 130.

[40] Mercator @ 2002-06-20, comment on "Grlom u jagode", Leksikon Yu Mitologije, comment posted on June 20, 2002, http://www.leksikon-yu-mitologije.net/read.php?id=708.

[41] Here it should be noted that the use of the world "svet" in the South-Slavic languages also corresponds to the world beyond the borders, usually related to better opportunities and higher standard of living.

[42] Srđan Karanović (Dir.), *Grlom u jagode [Reckless Youth]* (PGP RTB, 2003 [1975]), Glava ili pismo.

[43] Jurica Pavičić, "Žudnja Vlasti i Vlast nad Žudnjom," *Hrvatski filmski ljetopis* 40 (2004): 51.

[44] Srđan Karanović, ibid., 2003 [1975].

[45] Srđan Karanović, ibid., 2003 [1975].

[46] See Jovan Cvijić, "Studies in Yugoslav Psychology," *The Slavonic (and East European) Review* (1930–31): IX(26): 375–90, IX(27): 662–81, IX(28): 58–78; and Dinko Tomašić, *Personality and Culture in Eastern European Politics* (New York: George W. Stewart, 1948).

[47] Michel Chion, *Glasba v Filmu* (Ljubljana: Slovenska kinoteka, 2000), 196.

[48] Jurica Pavičić , ibid., 2004, 54.

[49] William Guynn, *Writing History in Film* (New York, London: Routledge, 2006), 175.

[50] Jurica Pavičić , ibid., 2004, 54.

[51] Victor Serge, *The Case of Comrade Tulayev* (London: Bookmarks and Journeyman (a joint publication), 1993), 22.

[52] Arsen Dedić, "Sve Bilo je Muzika," N/A.

[53] Srđan Karanović, "Ne Pripadamo Istoj Fioci," *Vreme* 523, January 11, 2001, http://www.vreme.com/arhiva_html/523/21.html (accessed July 10, 2007).

Part IV

Leisure, Work and the State

9

Flirting with Television in Socialism
Proletarian Morality and the Lust for Abundance

Maruša Pušnik

Introduction

In the 1970s, one of the largest department stores in Ljubljana organized a special promotion of color TV sets during the football World Cup. The store offered to lend a color TV set to any interested costumer, who could try it out for free and either return it or buy it after the World Cup ended. Although the 1970s were years of economic and cultural prosperity in socialist Slovenia, it was still hard to buy western technological goods in stores. People were at that time used to black & white TVs, and were naturally very interested in this new color technology. One of the informants described his experience:

> When I saw the advertisement I asked myself, "Why not?" I went to the Maximarket store and brought home a nice modern color TV. We really enjoyed watching football in color. My family was amazed, and when the World Cup ended I was facing a tough decision: to take it back or not? I knew it would be dull to watch black and white TV after we had experienced a month of color TV. It was expensive, but I was embarrassed to take it back to the store. Finally, I decided to buy it. I went to the store and made a deal to pay for the TV in several monthly installments.

This example indicates some of the typical dilemmas that people in the socialist times encountered and which significantly structured their everyday lives, such as the lack of modern technology, enthusiasm for new leisure practices, lower living standards, desires for a better and wealthier life, the promising images of the West, working morality, a great deal of resignation in daily life, feelings of inferiority and shame, etc. In other words, it tells about the translation of socialist ideology into everyday experience. These dilemmas will be addressed in the chapter presenting the rise of television in socialist Slovenia and people's experiences with this new media and communication technology. The massive penetration of television into Slovenian homes between the 1950s and 1980s had tremendous consequences for Slovenian socialist society, but also significantly affected the routines of people's lives: their leisure spaces, popular culture and their everyday habits, fantasies and values. Television was – from its very beginning – involved in the reproduction of symbolic power, of the most invisible, routine and everyday forms of power that structured people's lives in the privacy and intimacy of their homes.

Why did I choose television, something that at the first glance seems a bit marginal and not too important for the understanding of the socialist way of life? First, the investigation of the history of socialist technology may embrace the political, economic, cultural and social factors of the entire period of the country's existence, as Stokes argues.[1] This means to also reveal history about socialist innovation and the processes of economic and social development; such a study can shed light on the processes of failure and success of socialism. Second, the answer also lies in the biopolitics and in the technologies of the self through which docile bodies were being created by the politics of television. This Foucauldian concept[2] can be put in a very good use when analyzing leisure spaces such as television in the network of regulatory practices of socialist society. I argue that also through micro, everyday practices, such as TV watching, buying TV sets, furnishing home spaces with TV sets, etc., social life was regulated either by encouragements or limitations and in turn the subjectivities were also produced. To paraphrase Foucault, this would mean to observe each of these practices through an optic of biopolitics simply as "a practice, which is to say, as a 'way of doing things' oriented toward objectives and regulating itself by means of a sustained reflection."[3] Through such practices human beings were created as subjects of a socialist regime, who thought, lived, spoke, worked and loved in accordance with that regime. Technologies of the self that developed around the everyday practices of TV consumption in socialism allowed individuals to shape their own bodies and thoughts in a specific manner but also set the ways in which socialist society pacified, dominated and regulated these subjects, to put it in Foucault's words.[4] TV watching, for example, remained the silent private pleasure of people's domestic life, while the practices of TV watching and the building of national TV network were strongly encouraged and controlled by the socialist state apparatuses. Television, therefore, was accompanied by ambivalent attitudes. On the one hand, from its very beginning it was occasionally publicly condemned as being a bourgeois capitalist practice, sometimes it was even considered as idle practice; and as a material product it was condemned as being in conflict with the socialist modest attitude regarding the possession of commodities. But on the other hand, people as well as the propagating authorities always found ways around their own constraints that had been inspired by socialist ideals and encouraged mass participation in the consumption of television as a modernizing force, a socialist educator, and a symbol of progress.

The rise of television in Slovenia can be considered a strong boost to the westernization of the everyday socialist life, which introduced alternative visions of socialist modernity and hybrid democracy incorporating both socialist and western capitalist ideas.[5] Williams argued that television changed our world forever, implying that from its very beginnings television was closely connected to the social environment.[6] Television initiated the fostering of a specific discursive order in Slovenia that started structuring a peculiar socialist reality from the 1960s onwards when transforming people's homes into information and entertainment tool sheds and disseminating specific discourses, lifestyles and perceptions of reality.

This chapter is based on an ethnographic microanalysis and is structured as an oral TV history project, presenting people's history of television. The analysis is based on 80 interviews with ordinary people of different social statuses from various parts of Slovenia, aged between 40 and 85. The interviews were used to gather their perceptions, memories and understanding of the advent of television in socialism and their personal experiences with watching television as a leisure practice. Their memories and testimonies of the uses of television in the routines of everyday life thus help disclose the transformations of the social and political space, cultural practices and material conditions in that period.

The Rise of Television in the Socialist Landscape

Television sets were first demonstrated in the 1920s. In 1929, the first experimental television service was launched with BBC, who pioneered the world's first regular public electronic television service in London in 1936.[7] However, due to several disputes over the mechanical and electronic TV technology and World War II, the transformation of television into an instrument of mass communication was postponed and rose only after 1945. Also in Slovenia, Baron Anton Codelli had experimented with television technology in the 1920s, but television appeared in Slovenia only after World War II.[8] Its massive arrival was dependent on the electrification of the Slovenian homes, which was a general prior project of the socialist state to rebuild and to urbanize the country after the war. The electrification was extensively completed by the middle of the 1950s, when almost 87% of Slovenian settlements or 75% of Slovenian households had the electricity.[9] Therefore, when television was rising in the 1950s, the majority of the Slovenian homes were already equipped with the electricity.

The introduction of the public television service in Slovenia started in the early 1950s and, since Slovenia was a part of a federal multiethnic Yugoslavia; its television service had also been developing from its very beginnings as a part of common Yugoslav television. The television laboratory at the Institute for Electric Connections organized three public demonstrations of television technology in Slovenia: the first one in 1953 and the next two in 1956 when the first experimental television broadcasts were launched from the exhibition centre in Ljubljana. This channel was transmitted to a few existing televisions set up in public spaces in

Ljubljana (shop windows, coffeehouses, etc.). In 1957, Radio Ljubljana was renamed Radio and Television (RTV) Ljubljana, and in the same year the first regular television channel in Yugoslavia was launched by TV Zagreb. A year later, on 11 October 1958, TV Ljubljana started transmitting its own regular television channel; since then, TV Ljubljana was developing as a part of common Yugoslav television.[10] In November 1958, all three existing television studios in Yugoslavia – Zagreb, Ljubljana and Belgrade – merged to form a common television network, Jugoslovenska Radiotelevizija (JRT – Yugoslav Radio and Television) with an agreement that Ljubljana and Zagreb would each contribute 30% of the channel's content, while Belgrade would contribute 40% due to the central news program "TV dnevnik" (TV news) that was prepared in Belgrade in the Serbo-Croatian language for the whole of Yugoslavia.[11] However, television in Slovenia, which was developed in the times of the strongest creation of the socialist system, regularly transmitted western European TV channels – Austrian ORF and Italian RAI – from 1957 (despite severe oppositions of federal Yugoslav authorities) and was bringing images of the western world to the socialist landscape in that early stage.

Although Slovenia/Yugoslavia was among the last countries in Europe to introduce television – all of its neighbors except Albania and Bulgaria already had their own channels at the time – television entered a great number of Slovenian homes in the next decade. If in 1959 there were 778 television sets in Slovenia and around 4,000 television sets in Yugoslavia, in America nearly almost 90% of all homes already had television sets.[12] However, in the 1960s and 1970s television in Slovenia grew rapidly. At the end of the 1960s there were around 200,000 TV sets in Slovenia or one TV set per eight inhabitants, but at the end of the 1970s there were already around half a million TV sets or one TV set per three inhabitants. These were the times when television became a part of the typical inventory of households in Slovenia and when the majority of the Slovenians became acquainted with TV technology and made it part of their households. It is not a coincidence that the massive diffusion of television started in the 1960s, since these were also the years of political relaxation, liberal economic reforms, student movements and demonstrations, shortening of the working hours and the creation of more leisure time, and also of the considerable improvement of the living standard, when Yugoslavia also opened to the western trends and products. These were the times of abandoning of previous orthodox and more rigid socialism. In the 1960s, Slovenian families started to purchase household appliances and other electrical apparatuses on massive scale, such as kitchen ranges, irons, washing machines, boilers, radio and TV sets and others. Moreover, personal consumption and buying power were the highest in the 1960s because salaries rose enormously, on average by 600% from 1960 to 1970.[13] The diffusion of television coincided with several transformations of the Slovenian society that were accelerated, reproduced and strengthened with television.

Already in the 1960s when Yugoslavia was restructured into a federation of republics, various intellectuals and cultural critics in the Slovenian society warned that the Communist Party was indirectly influencing the television broadcaster's policy and its broadcasts.[14] Despite this anxiety, the censor's declarative and direct interventions were rare and TV Ljubljana remained relatively autonomous. But still, there were several indirect interventions into the TV's policy and its channel. Both, Lado Pohar, the first director of TV Ljubljana, who also built first television studio and started with TV broadcasting in Slovenia after he learned about TV in western countries, and France Perovšek, the first director of RTV Ljubljana, told me that there were many silent rules that this institution had to follow. For instance, it was not allowed to show crucifixes on TV and they did not broadcast any religious programs. It was also generally desirable, if not a necessity, that employees be members of the Communist Party. Otherwise, they both declared that they did not feel any direct pressures from the state authorities when managing the institution or directing the channel.[15] Perovšek and many other employees at RTV Ljubljana were also very tightly involved with various cultural or political state functions and into the Party activities. In this manner, the operative logics of socialist power structures were reproduced on the scale of each individual who lived and worked by the socialist morality without any strict state interventions. In this regard, Pohar's memory of one of his first contacts as a director of TV with the prominent and highly influential Slovenian Party official is illustrative:

I remember once a man in black leather coat came to my office and ordered me to immediately come with him. I just had to leave the studio in the middle of the work and a car was waiting for me in front of RTV. We silently drove to a private yard when I realized that this is a house of an influential politician. I was so scared. They took me to his living room and he was standing there in front of the TV set and started to yell at me, 'What are you doing to me, Pohar, what are you doing to me?' I was shaking with fright and I suddenly started to think what I did wrong that authorities here in Ljubljana or down in Belgrade might be so furious. Then he pointed with his finger on the screen and I saw that instead of still TV picture there were stripes flying down the screen. I got my breath back and told him, 'Comrade, no problem, I'll solve this in a moment.' I rotated a TV knob until the picture stood still and everything was ok. He was happy and they drove me back to the RTV building.

Perovšek's story of how he treated those employees who were not obedient to the ruling system is also similar. Once, when a radio producer broadcast religious songs on Christmas Day, Perovšek received a telephone call from the furious leading circles with a complaint and a warning that he needed to take care of this problem seriously. He explained that he would never fire the employee because he was raised in such Christmas tradition, even if he had been a Partisan during the WWII and a member of the Party. He called this man to his office, "taught him a lesson," as he said and did not do anything else. But it helped that this was never repeated later, he told me. The system of obedience and docility to the socialist power structures was reproduced on the level of individual's negotiation with such small, daily practices in the public life. Perovšek as well as most of other informants argued, for instance, that they constantly performed various "forbidden practices, for which we were all aware that they should not be expressed loudly and on the street" in the privacy of their homes and in the circle of family members or friends.

Predsednik republike Josip Broz Tito je pred kratkim sprejel iz Ljubljane TV sprejemnik delo Inštituta za elektrozveze

One of the first television sets made in the country, in Ljubljana and donated to the president of Yugoslavia, Josip Broz-Tito (second from the right).[16]

Moreover, from the perspective of the socialist regime, the television technology itself was also problematic in this early period of television, because the TV sets themselves symbolized western production, consumption and capitalist industrialization. The socialist authorities tried to overcome this discomfort with the domestic production of entertainment electronics, which meant that almost every republic of Yugoslavia had its own local producer of TV sets (e.g. Elektroindustrija Niš – EI in Serbia, Gorenje and Iskra in Slovenia, Elektroindustrija Rudi Čajevec in Bosnia and Herzegovina). "There was no free selection of TV sets in the stores at that time, they usually had one or two types of Yugoslav TVs, and we all had same televisions all over Yugoslavia," is how the informants repeatedly described their practices of buying TV sets. High-tech-nology projects, as Stokes argues, were often touted as the solution to the country's persistent economic problems in socialist coun-tries.[17] Yugoslav planners and leaders favored the high-prestige technology products and wanted to tailor the production according to socialist ideas. In 1956, the Yugoslav Federal Executive Council granted half a billion dinars and one million dollars for the intro-duction of television in Yugoslavia in three stages – for the building of television network and of television broadcasting centers across Yugoslavia, and also for the development of domestic production of TV sets. The main concern of domestic television industry was how to incorporate as much as possible of domestic products into foreign television technology, such as Siemens, Grunding, Thomp-son Houston, which had penetrated the Yugoslav TV production at that time. "Due to technical advantages, our television equip-ment will have to be as uniform as possible – standardized. This standardization, which will be foreign in its basis, will have to be organized in such manner that this coproduction will leave at least some nice, bright space also to our production companies."[18] In this regard the advertisement in one of the Slovenian daily papers from 1957 is very informative: "A company for the marketing and sale of radios, tapes, televisions and other radio material, Radiocenter in Ljubljana, has already imported and sold off more than 70 TV sets. Unfortunately, the company has no more foreign funds for the im-port of new TV sets and therefore we will have to wait for domestic production. As it seems we will get our first Yugoslav-made TV sets this autumn."[19]

The late 1950s and early 1960s were also times of considerable economic reforms. Yugoslav national industry, and especially the electronics industry was on the rise, and there were state plans of how to accelerate the export of Yugoslav industrial products to western markets.[20] The socialist authorities wanted to build an in-dependent system through its own industrial production of vari-ous material products. In the 1960s, Yugoslav domestic television production flourished and its aim was to "come closer to the level of companies in the industrially developed countries as quickly as possible," as the dailies reported. For instance, in 1968, domestic companies already produced, displayed and sold "a rich selection of TV sets, about twenty types or more for different tastes and pockets," among which were also luxury models, fully automated TV sets and battery-powered TV sets.[21] However, before that increasing production, in the early and in the middle of the 1950s, it was a common practice to smuggle these electronic apparatuses to Yugoslavia from western markets since there was a total lack of TV sets in Yugoslavia. Pohar remembered how one such early TV set was brought from Italy for President Tito to fill him with enthusiasm for television technology so that he would later support the development of domestic television production: "On the Italian border the customs officers said that it was totally impossible to bring this device to Slovenia and that they would confiscate it. When the Party commissioners told them, 'Comrades, don't play with us. You don't know for whom this TV set is, it is for the president himself,' they immediately allowed us to cross the border."

TV Screen of Realism and Dreams:
Between Paternalist Instruction and Fantasy

Soon after its arrival, television watching became one of the most popular and time-consuming leisure activities and entertainment practices.[22] In contrast, the socialist perceptions of television emphasized mostly its educational role and the socialist authorities tried to promote and use television as an apparatus of enlightenment. Television on one hand disciplined its consumers when instructed and educated them according to the working morality in very paternalist manner, but on the other it allowed for the converting and resisting of these dominant socialist practices when offering TV consumers the space of the western consumer-oriented morality. The broadcasted western values and images of the West on the screens challenged the socialist ordering of daily life, its morality of modesty and temperance and, in turn, also people's needs. All this also resulted in the (re)structuring of the socialist regime and subjectivity of that time.

The domestication of television in the 1960s served as an urban cultural practice; television urbanized the rural Slovenian landscape and brought images and promises of the industrialized, modernized and developed socialist land. Television immediately started

TELEVIZIJA: ob torkih zaprto

Cartoon from the Slovenian newspapers in the 1960s, announcing that there was no television broadcast on Tuesdays. The caption below read, "Television: closed Tuesdays."[23]

to strengthen faith in social development and reinforced the belief that it directly contributed to industrialization, progress, evolution and civilization. This was in accordance with the socialist ideas of collective building of the country in the post-war period. The growing urbanization of the country was evident in the restoration of infrastructure by the work brigades, the building of new industrial plants, de-agrarization and migration of farmers to industrial centers, the growth of cities, the building of new industrial places and workers' residential neighborhoods, the electrification of homes, and in the rising living standard.[24]

The socialist power structure built a discursive regime in which urbanization was a synonym for education and dissemination of working morality. Also, Slovenian newspapers reported about television in such manner and presented it to thousands of Slovenian people in such a way that television would bring universal development to the society, that it would inform people and also educate them. For instance, one of the earliest news articles on television entitled "Socialist society ensures the right place to television" presented the meanings of television for the socialist society in a very solemn tone:

> In the struggle for liberation of television – this child of tomorrow from the embraces of old society, in the struggle, which is a part of the general battle for the new society, television in advanced countries could contribute a lot. And for this reason, television should be implemented and expanded as soon as possible in the socialist countries and especially in Yugoslavia.[25]

Also, the leaders of RTV Ljubljana institution were concerned mostly with the question of reaching masses of viewers in Slovenia in the first decade of television. The main mission of RTV's politics, as it is also written in the founding papers, was not only to reach as many Slovenian people as possible, but also to enrich their lives and to culturally instruct them with the help of television, especially those people in rural areas. In practice, this meant that they intensively started building a network of transmitter stations and, in the 1960s, with the help of work brigades most of the transmitter stations were built and set to cover the whole Slovenian territory with radio and TV signals. As the data show, such policies of RTV's leadership was also evident in the growth of the TV-transmitter power – from 1.35 kW in 1960 to more than 2000 kW in 1975 when almost the whole of Slovenia was covered with TV signals.[26] With the TV signal, to use the words of Perovšek, the first director of RTV Ljubljana, "Slovenia became nothing but one city and one countryside."[27]

The building of transmitter stations in Slovenia was closely connected with the dissemination of television sets around Slovenia and both projects were primarily socialist political projects to urbanize the country and to modernize the life of Slovenia. In 1965, the newspaper *Borba*, for example, announced that 163,000 television sets had been sold in the whole of Yugoslavia in comparison to only 103,000 vacuum cleaners and 90,000 water heaters.[28] Also, most of the informants' stories confirmed that they were equipping their households with television sets earlier than with washing machines or vacuum cleaners. As one informant stated, "We were watching television, when our mother still washed dirty linen on a washboard." With the growing number of television sets, the state demonstrated the higher living standard of people and the urban status of the whole country. Television and its discourses imbued rural areas with the urban mental schemata based in a technologically determined environment. Even after television became an ordinary everyday commodity, it still maintained the character of an urban and modern apparatus. People would often express pride in their TV sets and would usually show them to visitors entering their home, as they were reporting in the interviews.

The TV sets possessed an influential image of prestige that seriously challenged the value system and the relation between the urban and rural lifestyles, as an informant's statement shows: "My father, who owned one of the first television sets in my village, sold a vineyard and bought a black and white television set for that money." In the symbolical view, this act represents the processes of transition from rural to urban. Television in this sense overtook the traditionally most valued thing in the rural Slovenian mental schemata: land. Accordingly, this act also characterizes the transition from a traditional, agricultural to modern, industrial socialist society. Television as a technology and as a discourse became involved in the processes of transforming rural areas by bringing urban values, lifestyles and perceptions of the urban, industrial world to the rural population. This was also the plan of the socialist state to industrialize the country, to enlarge the working class and to increase the industrial production in large factories, mines, and ironworks. However, the interviews revealed that people were in a way still stretched between traditional patterns of life and modern, urban styles. They could not fully become accustomed to modern conditions but neither could they hold on to their tradition anymore. There were many stories about workers who managed small farms at homes in their free time or about new tenants in block of flats who still raised chickens in their cellars, yards or even in the bathrooms. People also explained how hard they wished to watch television since the practices of watching television demanded more and more time but they were at the same time feeling guilty because there was so much to do in or around the house:

> We always wanted to watch television until the end of the broadcasting in the evening, no matter what was on, but I felt so unpleasant because I knew I had to wake up at 5 in the morning and go to work. Before television, we usually went to bed very early and this was not a problem. We had two pigs at that time and chickens and we needed to take care of them before we went to work. Later, we abandoned chickens and pigs because both didn't work anymore – job and farming, I mean.

The mere practice of television watching was perceived as a leisure activity, but was also confirming the socialist idea that with the technological progress and industrialization of the country people would have more free time than ever before. Such socialist discursive ethics and aesthetics were visible in the programming, too. The programming tone was rather instructive and authoritative, but the informants, as they described, were not bothered by this and still enjoyed watching. One of them explained, "If I compare that program with today's programs, it was so boring, but it was interesting for us and we kept watching it. I even watched TV transmissions of those long meetings of the Central Committee of the Communist Party." In the early years of television, the programming schedule included many cultural programs, TV plays, produced from literary works, and movies mostly of the Soviet and domestic Yugoslav movie production. The socialist ideology was built into the programming; the notion of socialist progress was constantly put into speech; such as through the popular documentaries of the economic progress of the country, Partisan movies, TV coverage of speeches of Party officials, etc. In the biopolitical sense, people were educated by television, and such programming disseminated the knowledge about modesty, humbleness, diligence and other virtues of socialist working people. This power mechanism was so efficient, because people enjoyed watching TV and had fun while being educated through this new communication technology.

Although the socialist political system influenced the development of television in Slovenia, its structure and program, it would be wrong to argue that television served only as a propagandistic apparatus of disciplining and subordinating the citizens. According to Pence and Betts, it is important to bridge popular experience and communist politics if we want to understand socialist modernity, because socialist countries were not closed societies, but they were circumscribed fields of interaction, characterized by a surprising amount of texture and conflict, whereby western influences also played an important role.[29] In this regard, the TV channels in socialist Slovenia were supplemented and slowly overshadowed by more and more western production. TV screens with images of the West were also intensively contesting the socialist discursive order. Already in the 1960s, television had become a window to the desired western reality in Slovenia. Its social impact was connected to the popular western genres broadcast on TV Ljubljana but also to the programs of the Austrian ORF and the Italian RAI television stations that were opposed by the leadership of TV Belgrade and communist authorities who, for example, criticized RAI's news program for bringing the politics of the NATO and western values to the Slavic peoples.[30] Despite these reproaches, TV Ljubljana continued its co-operation with the Italian channel RAI and did not stop transmitting its programs. In the 1950s and early 1960s, there was a lot of Italian TV program and one of the main Slovenian dailies enthusiastically reported, "Although it was the 'Ljubljana TV week' they transmitted Italian TV programs every day, sometimes even too heavily. Do you understand Italian? I don't, unfortunately. But anyway, it is sooooo very interesting!"[31]

Moreover, TV Ljubljana transmitted more programs produced by western European TV stations (Eurovision) than by eastern European TV stations (Intervision). In 1966, it transmitted 100 hours of Eurovision programs and only 14 hours of Intervision programs; ten years later, in 1976, there were 526 hours of Eurovision programs and only 40 hours of Intervision programs.[32] Television screens enabled Slovenians to inspect and experience the western world. The gap between the reality of socialist everyday life and the televised imagery of the virtual western life created a rather absurd situation in which Slovenian viewers' cultural capital superseded their economic capital. On one hand, the TV discourse was paternalizing and creating them as modest workers, but on the other it accelerated the daydreaming about the worlds, objects and practices from the West they saw on television. This coincided with the times of minor transformations of socio-economic and political system in Yugoslavia, when socialism in its liberal dress was introduced, as Ramet says, and when Yugoslavia gradually opened itself to the capitalist western world.[33] In the 1960s, Yugoslavia fully opened its borders and allowed the free migration of its citizens to other countries but also foreign citizens were allowed to come to Yugoslavia without visa requirements.[34] Slowly but persistently in such a context TV discourses also produced a specific discursive order based on the formation of a new consumption culture and on the challenging of socialist values. More and more popular genres were coming from the West. Most of the informants in the first place recalled western broadcast shows such as detective shows, game shows, westerns, situation comedies, soap operas and dramas. People were also fascinated by various goods and practices seen on television. Almost all informants mentioned that this was the first time they saw the Eiffel Tower "live," as well as New York, convertibles, microwave ovens, improved mascaras for eyelashes, and other wonders of the modern household. Television promised mobility to its viewers; in their imagination, it offered them to travel to the western worlds through the consumption of televised images, which they received every evening in their homes. Western, especially American fictional television like films, situation comedies, soap operas and adventure shows presented images of sophistication, abundance, wealth and leisure. Moreover, informants who received Italian or Austrian TV signals reported they usually watched those programs even if they could not understand the language. They were also enraptured with their advertisements: "I was mad about ads. Our television at that time didn't have many of them. Italians have advertisements for everything they were selling. From toilet paper, alcohol, cigarettes to detergents. These ads were big stories." A few informants reported that they regularly visited their relatives who lived close to the Italian border at the time of the Italian music festival San Remo, with the purpose of watching TV broadcasts of this festival. Some people living close to the borders, for instance, described that they rotated and pointed their antennas toward Italy or Austria to receive their television signals and there are many anecdotes about moving the antennas "to receive western signal," as they used to say.[35] The continual consumption of western TV programming enabled the recodification of socialist values and their merging with the western ideas that produced a particular socialist structure of feeling in socialist Slovenia. Beside other factors, TV in this regard also made Slovenian or Yugoslav socialism a bit different from more orthodox and rigid models of socialism, such as those in Czechoslovakia, Poland, Hungary or Soviet Union. This also testifies that socialism has been experienced differently by millions of people living in different socialist countries.[36]

Television screens with western programs started to bring to and build up a western psyche in socialist Slovenia, to paraphrase Morley and Robins.[37] The televised western imagery broadcast western cultural capital across the socialist Slovenian media landscape. Television equipped people with a formula of leisure, freedom, democracy, consumption, wealth and goods. In this regard, it stimulated imagination and people started to contest socialism through visual images. But also as a technological apparatus the television was treated as a western product; informants reported they believed that the TV set itself could bring them a nicer life:

> In the middle of the 1950s, I traveled to Rome with a Yugoslav political delegation and there I saw a television set for the first time in my life. One evening, I saw a couple sitting on the terrace, having dinner and looking into the television set from the hotel room in which I stayed. It impressed me so much and I said to myself, "Look how nicely they live in the West." This image of the couple, having dinner and comfortably watching television, haunted me for years. In Slovenia, this would be perceived as a very bourgeois practice, but I think there was nothing wrong with this.

Such a western lifestyle was consumed and celebrated in people's intimate worlds. Many informants described how they imagined living in these worlds and how they identified with the actors. The most common TV show mentioned in this respect was the American soap opera "Peyton Place"; informants reported that they were fantasizing about these worlds and all that goods they could not buy at that time. Television offered some kind of escape from socialist everyday and fostered specific types of daydreaming consumerism that was nevertheless converted into forms of real, socialist consumerism. These kinds of televised images introduced material goods as desired objects and shopping as leisure activity, which was not in accordance with prevailing socialist views and was at the same time very limited because of various mechanisms that prevented such leisure and consumerist practices. The limitation was an insufficient supply of western goods to the Yugoslav socialist markets and the migrations to the neighboring western countries were also limited by various mechanisms. For instance, during the oil crises in the 1970s and later in the 1980s, there were severe limitations of fuel that prevented long trips and consequently the spending of money abroad. However, people still found their ways to purchase the western goods either by daily shopping trips to Italy or Austria or by the migrant workers' (gastarbeiter's) weekly or monthly supplies from Germany, Switzerland, Italy or Austria. One informant whose husband worked in Germany from the late 1960s onward explained: "I remember seeing a special blender on television in an American show and my husband bought it in Germany and brought it next time he returned home." Television broke the perception of the unnecessariness of such goods and made them desirable and accepted. It started to shape people's desires and to loosen the stiff socialist control over their needs. It brought images of a wealthier and more leisurely life and mediated new desirable lifestyles and the accompanying mental schemata.

Specific elements of the televised western world thus slowly penetrated the socialist homes and television started to shape a specific discursive order in Slovenia that was not completely in line with socialist values and the socialist ordering of the world that demanded disciplined, well-trained, modest and immaterially-oriented bodies. Socialist television caught its viewers in a kind of harmony between instruction through very authoritative, paternalist voices and pleasurable fantasies that viewers started to seek on the screens. Television thus contributed to the reformulation of the gap between the socialist East and the capitalist West. The prevailing common perception of the dominant socialist values (like modesty, industry, diligence, class equality) slowly started to change and television consumption was to a certain degree a corrosive agent of the then dominant socialist morality. Fang maintains that the tools of mass communication have power first to shake and then to shape national policies; he gives an example of a collapse of communist rule in Poland: "Asked what caused the fall of communism in Eastern Europe, Polish president Lech Walesa pointed to a TV set. 'It all came from there,' he said."[38]

On the Governing of Living with Television: Television and the Socialist Subject

The notion of the governing of the living with television is being understood in the broad sense of biopolitical techniques, discourses and politics through which television in socialism managed, governed and regulated human behavior and consciousness in the course of people's daily life, to put it in Foucault's words.[39] This means to explore what television did to human subjects in socialism, how television discourses, ideologies and its institutional practices produced, controlled and regulated the self and, accordingly, also how individuals shaped their own bodies, thoughts, minds and behaviors in accordance with the socialist television regime. Featherstone warns that such leisure activities as television watching can be regarded as a source of pleasure, but also personal transformation should not be ignored, while individuals might find varying degrees of expressivity and self-control in them.[40] The appearance of TV sets in homes changed living habits and restructured traditional domestic life, family culture, mentalities, behaviors and people's identities. Television invaded and conquered the domestic sphere in the 1960s by promoting "the need for their permanent presence in the lives of individuals," as Hardt would maintain.[41] In 1960, there was only one television set per 500 Slovenians; in 1968 there was already one television set per seven Slovenians.[42] Television, therefore, changed the way of acquiring information and entertainment in socialist Slovenia and promoted changes in its social and political life, but also started to redefine the meaning of the self and to introduce new technologies of the self through which people developed knowledge about themselves and used to understand themselves.

One of the most important changes that television introduced in the individual's private sphere was the reorganization of the home space. People started to spend more time with television, which changed their traditional living habits and restructured traditional family functions. The interviews confirmed that in the 1960s television became a status symbol of the household. Informants reported they placed their TV set in the most visible space in the home, that they viewed it as an altar and treated it with some respect: "We were not allowed to touch it all the time, especially not children, and that is why it was placed in a higher position. We walked around it very carefully. We decorated it with lace and crocheted napkins and put flowers and family pictures on it."

With the watching of television becoming a popular practice, the home space was restructured to achieve the best setting for the pleasurable habit. Although in the 1960s television design programs and interior design experts[43] were already something quite normal in western countries, they were still not accessible to viewers in socialist countries. However, it can be assumed that the televised western domestic life on the screen gave people in socialist Slovenia ideas on how they could rearrange their traditional domestic space, which was in pre-war times connected to agricultural and pre-modern life-style. TV sets produced a new kind of domestic space – the living room was ordered around the television and not vice versa and the living room became a leisure centre of the home. At first, in the late 1950s and early 1960s, television sets were in most cases placed on the refrigerators, small tables, kitchen cabinets or dining tables in kitchens where families spent most of their time and which were the centre of housework, domestic economy and production. Older informants confirmed that before the 1960s, middle-class city dwellers and rural entrepreneurs in particular arranged a kind of parlor in their houses or flats, which was strictly separated from kitchen and other household activities; it was a place for leisure activities, for sitting, reading and relaxing, for chatting and greeting neighbors, friends and other guests. However, with a few exceptions most of the informants did not have such spaces in their homes before they purchased their first TV set. The majority of informants stated they began to rearrange their rooms and equip them with furniture and these conversation spaces were transformed into living rooms. A middle-aged village informant reported: "We put the television in the kitchen. We actually did not have a living room at that time. Only a few years later, when my father said that we could not watch television in the kitchen anymore and that we needed more space for that, we arranged the room next to the kitchen, where my brother and I were sleeping before that, and we bought stands and armchairs." People started to spend more time in the living rooms and they organized these spaces to be as comfortable and convenient as possible. The living room slowly became central leisure area in the private sphere.

In this respect, television changed trends in homemaking styles and fashions in the "western way" since it modernized Slovenian homes, turning them into comfortable leisure spaces for the desirable activity of television watching. There were plenty of illustrative statements how informants were buying cozy sofas, couches, armchairs and tables at that time. An older city informant remembered: "Simple chairs were not enough anymore, because your back started to hurt if you sit on them for too long in front of the TV." People in this sense started to "live through television," to use Fang words,[44] and made it an important factor of their everyday socialist reality. But access to diversified range of furniture was very limited on the Yugoslav market and there was no significant import of foreign, western-designed furniture. The domestic wood industry started to produce a few standard and very typical models of living room furniture, with which almost the majority of the Slovenian homes were equipped at that time. Although this furniture was designed in accordance with the western fashion trends it still kept a touch of ascetic working morality and modesty in its design. Moreover, the comfortable leisure practice of television watching was in this regard codified and normalized through the standardized furniture in the socialist way. However, the home industry was also given impetus when started to massively produce and sell the furniture. This branch of industry was also increasing the national income.[45]

Such socialist appropriation of television had at least two important consequences for people. First, the massive penetration of television into people's homes helped to develop domestic

Yugoslav socialist economy, which resulted in the rising of the living standard and in the acceleration of consumption. Second, television changed the styles of habituation of people in their private sphere. The practice of television watching became an important part of domestic life that was equal to other household and leisure activities inside home, like cooking, reading etc. People started adjusting their time in their home space according to the television schedule. The feeling of the home started to be structured around television that promoted the ideas of comfort, convenience, happiness and leisure. The audiences thus became "members of a leisure class" according to Hardt,[46] whose comfort and convenience are parts of the definition of television, but as well as of western capitalism. Every naturalization and normalization of technology by various folk cultures in the history of humankind, as Bausinger would argue, shifted the spatial, temporal, social and also psychological horizons of people's lives: "But it is a product of the technical world, an indirect result of technology, which creates not only a new world of objects but also new social and spiritual realities."[47] Television in the times of socialism thereby disintegrated certain horizons that were valid for pre-modern and pre-urban societies and created new horizons, that were based on the mixture of socialist as well as western, capitalist culture.

Moreover, the growth of television in Slovenia coincided with the growth of industrial block settlements with specific socialist architecture that was based on the idea of giving a home to every individual working family. During the first housing reform in the early 1960s, the number of new apartments in Slovenia doubled and in 1971 there were 470,000 apartments, which coincided with the number of households in Slovenia; a ratio of one apartment for each family.[49] The mode of living in a block was considerably

The common set up of television in the socialist home space in the 1970s and 1980s. One of the most common models of television sets, as shown above, was usually put in the living room together with the usual furniture.[48]

different from the traditional way of living. Living in such an apartment required less work around the house, creating more non-work, free time that could be fulfilled by various leisure activities. The apartment functioned as a place of rest and television further changed it into a comfortable nook. But in the socialist perspective, coming home from the work in a factory or state office also meant the start of rehabilitation and rest. Television watching as a socialist leisure activity, therefore, was not perceived only as fun, distraction, pleasure, but also as a kind of do-something-for-the-society activity. In this regard, Featherstone warns when providing a definition of leisure in general that the component of a routinized work should be treated as an important component of all non-work, leisure activities.[50] The trick of the socialist regime was that its television programming also offered the images of successful socialist progress and of the working morality of modern socialist Yugoslav industrial society, which turned people into docile bodies in their free time to make them even more productive. Informants stated how in those early years of television they liked to watch TV reports about the industrial complexes, new factories, new equipment and machines in those factories, new mechanized agriculture etc. from different parts of Yugoslavia. The trick of biopolitics is the capturing of people into an environment in which they feel comfortable and at home while at the same time it subjects them to various social functions, which was the promotion of working morality, based on the values of diligence and modesty, in socialist Yugoslavia. Since television started to structure and control the ordering of time, space, habits and mentalities, and thereby, also the socialization and acclimatization of private, domestic spheres and intimate worlds, it could be argued that television sets had specific technical and societal control built into them, which was a mixture of socialist and capitalist sets of rules, prohibitions and codes.

Along with the physical restructuring of the home, television provoked mental and psychological changes. One of the key features that the advent of television introduced was television becoming a companion. Television reduced and replaced communication with other people. With the rise of new media like television, opportunities for personal contact decreased dramatically, "because technologies of communication, with their incessant demands on time and place, isolate individuals."[51] In this regard, television slowly started to propel the processes of alienation, isolation and individualization inside the collectively oriented socialist society. These typical characteristics of western capitalist societies and western psyche that promote individualism, freedom and free will of the individual,[52] started to face and corrode the socialist order of things based on the notion of collectivity and on the sense of community spirit that provided also the foundation of the specific social organization of Yugoslavia. The interviews revealed that television started to change the patterns of people's personal and societal communication. An older informant stated: "When my wife and I were younger, we used to go for long walks with our friends. But then, I remember, I started apologizing to my colleagues for the shorter walks because I wanted to catch a TV show. And we also met our friends less frequently and didn't play cards or go to the cinema as often as we did before television." Many informants also reported that they avoided visits during the time of TV news and explained that visits at that time of the day were simply not appropriate.

If one important characteristic of socialist period was its connectedness to work, the other one was its communal nature that constantly displayed the sense of collectivity. Although in the first years of television there was a widespread practice of collective watching, first in public spaces (public houses, coffee houses, milk bars, cultural societies, bus stations, police stations, restaurants, community centers, etc.) and later in people's homes – since many people did not have their own television set and watched them at their neighbors' or friends' homes – this only seemed to be a collective practice. Those early collective uses of television might be confirmed by the structure of TV subscribers. In 1959, there were 184 television sets owned by different collective associations and only 594 by individual users, which means that 24% of all TV sets were in public spaces. However, this ratio changed rapidly over the next few years in favor of individual subscribers; by 1966, only 1% of TV sets were owned by collective associations.[53] The practices of collective watching did not promote interpersonal communication. Many informants confirmed that when they watched television with other people there had to be total silence so they could concentrate. "We stared at the screen rather than to each other," according to the statement of an older man describing this practice. An older woman who was among the first in the village to own a TV set and often hosted her neighbors, described this practice: "People gathered at my place. Usually they also brought their own chairs, but many of them were also standing or sitting on the floor. There was such a crowd in my kitchen. We watched television and we could sit for three or four hours saying nothing to each other, just to the screen." People really did gather around TV sets in the same space, got involved in watching the same thing but this did not significantly increase their interpersonal communication. However, with the growing number of TV sets, the practice of television watching moved into the privacy of people's homes and became growingly individualized. Very similar patterns of individualized watching were repeated in family circles. Conversations were slowly removed from the living rooms when television communication started to dominate inside the home space.

Television technology was perceived as subservient to its individualized use from its very beginning. Family members actually started spending a lot of their time together in the same room and in close physical vicinity, but not with one another. Their isolation increased because television started to replace conversations with others and became a new friend who demanded an intimate relationship only between the viewer and the screen/program. In this sense, television introduced and strengthened changes in peoples' mentality that had serious consequences for the socialist regime, its morality and mentality. Although people felt connected to the world more than ever before with television, they became isolated and alienated from others, and this was not in accordance with socialist idea of collectivity. Television in socialism introduced

Television became an indispensable companion of people in their homes from the 1970s onwards.[54]

a specific kind of governing of souls; it developed and launched new technologies of the self with people as subjects caught between the socialist collective spirit experienced in their everyday life and the western capitalist individualized ethics experienced in their contact with TV screen.

Conclusion:
Television as (Un)Controlled Leisure Space in Socialism

The advent of television in socialist Slovenia affected the entire Slovenian society and also started to test and modify socialism itself. Television brought changes that influenced political and economic structures, cultural practices, communal activity, personal behavior and the meaning of self. It started to shape a specific discursive order based on a mixture of urban western mental schemata and modest, working socialist ethics. Although the disposable income of Slovenians in the 1960s and 1970s was much lower than the disposable income of their western contemporaries, sales of TV sets were on the rise and were comparable to the sales in western countries. Television in the 1960s already started the processes of social change that a few decades later culminated in the disintegration of Yugoslavia, the fall of the communist system, and change from the socialist self-management to capitalist market economy. The social change influenced by television was not only triggered by western contents that persistently eroded or reshaped the socialist ideology but also by the mere uses of television and practices of television watching which reshaped people's organization of their leisure time, domestic rituals, consumer practices and social spaces. The role of television in socialist Slovenia can be correctly defined as a propagator of social change as well as a defender and reproducer of the existing social and political order. Television played an important role in the opening up of the domestic socialist space to the external consumer capitalist space and, in this sense, made room for the recodification of socialist reality. However, television functioned also as a socialist surveying apparatus, which disseminated discourses of socialist progress and values of production oriented working morality.

Television watching became an important leisure practice of people's everyday life in socialism. Featherstone suggests that we should not confine leisure only to rational recreation (e.g. organized practices), but we also need to include among them more mundane activities, such as "the big five," i.e. television, drinking, smoking, betting and making love. The term "leisure" suggests fun, distraction, pleasure, but also includes routine work, productive component and routinized maintenance pursuits.[55] In this regard, socialism appropriated and colonized television as a leisure space in a specific way, in a way of prescribed meanings its discourses granted to television. Leisure tried to be simply adjusted to socialism and was often put in function as a prerequisite of work. However, at the same time, television subverted and corroded the socialist ethics. Therefore, television materialized and reproduced socialism and made it into a self-evident everyday condition of life, but it also subverted it when bringing western, capitalist discourses and practices to Slovenia. On the nominative and practical level, leisure was coded in socialism as a productive and instructive practice. Watching television was often seen as an educational activity and in such a way it functioned as a part of a socialist disciplining network, when disseminating the discourses of socialist progress and producing docile individuals who spent their leisure time in an educative and productive manner. The analyzed examples of the uses of television show that socialist leisure practices in Slovenia were not too different from similar leisure practices in western capitalist countries. The practices were almost the same; the only difference was that in two different systems they signified a bit different things – in the first, television leisure was also coded as an educative, productive space and was turned from consumptive into productive practice; in the second, it was coded more as an entertaining, idle, consumer practice. In the case of television in socialism, there is strong evidence of the intertwining of leisure practices with production. But among people television still remained in the space of pleasure. Such "leisure pleasure" as television watching in socialism was constantly emphasizing the pleasure of working for socialist community, but at the same time emphasizing the role of educational relaxation of the practice of watching television.

The socialist system was not static and even not predestined to failure. The ways socialism was put into everyday reality through various micro-practices and how everyday citizens asserted their subjectivity and made meaning in their own immediate social world when they were allowed individual action and autonomy tell more about the ultimate failure of socialism than simple references to the economic and technological backwardness of the socialist areas and to the communist dictatorship. Or to use Pence's and Betts' words, such an analysis can reveal the true limits of communist dictatorship.[56] Television that was used and practiced in concordance with socialist collective ideas offered some space of resistance, although not necessarily in the sense of rebellion and radical changes, but rather in the sense of recodification and adaptation of hegemonic socialist ideas.

Notes

[1] Raymond G. Stokes, *Constructing Socialism: Technology and Change in East Germany, 1945–1990* (Baltimore: The Johns Hopkins University Press, 2000), 3.

[2] Michel Foucault, "The Birth of Biopolitics," in *Ethics: Subjectivity and Truth, Essential Works of Foucault 1954–1984*, ed. Paul Rabinow (London: Penguin Books, 2000), 73–9.

[3] Michel Foucault, ibid., 2000, 74.

[4] Michel Foucault, "Technologies of the Self," in *Ethics: Subjectivity and Truth, Essential Works of Foucault 1954–1984*, ed. Paul Rabinow (London: Penguin Books, 2000), 223–51.

[5] It should be noted that the Yugoslav Radio Television (JRT) – unlike television stations in other Eastern European socialist countries, which until 1993 were members of the Union of Eastern European Broadcasters (called Intervision from 1961 on) – became a member of the European Broadcasting Union (EBU or Eurovision) in 1960, which was established in 1950 by Western radio and television stations.

[6] Raymond Williams, *Television: Technology and Cultural Form* (London: Routledge, 2003).

[7] Asa Briggs and Peter Burke, *A Social History of the Media: From Gutenberg to the Internet* (Cambridge: Polity Press, 2002), 175–8.

[8] Melita Zajc, "Televizija v Sloveniji pred Uradnim Začetkom: Med Koncem 19. Stoletja in Letom 1958 [Television in Slovenia Prior to Its Official Beginning: Between the End of the 19th Century and 1958]," *Javnost/ The Public* 15, supplement (2008): 79–93.

[9] Zdenko Čepič, "Urbanizacija in Življenjska Raven [Urbanization and Living Standard]," in *Slovenska Novejša Zgodovina 1948–1992 [Slovenian Recent History 1948–1992]*, ed. Jasna Fischer (Ljubljana: Mladinska knjiga in Inštitut za novejšo zgodovino, 2006), 1009–15.

[10] For detailed information on the history of the Slovenian television see Lado Pohar, ed., *Televizija Prihaja: Spominski Zbornik o Začetkih Televizije na Slovenskem [Television is Coming: Memory Reader on the Beginning of Television in Slovenia]* (Ljubljana: RTV Slovenija, 1993). See also Ljerka Bizilj, *Slikarji Stvarnosti: Podoba Slovenskih Medijev [Painters of Reality: The Image of Slovenian Media]* (Ljubljana: Modrijan, 2008).

[11] TV Ljubljana started to produce its own regular news program in the Slovenian language only on April 15, 1968.

[12] Lado Pohar, "Televizija Prihaja v Slovenijo [Television is Coming to Slovenia]," in *Televizija Prihaja: Spominski Zbornik o Začetkih Televizije na Slovenskem [Television is Coming: Memory Reader on the Beginning of Television in Slovenia]*, ed. Lado Pohar (Ljubljana: RTV Slovenija, 1993), 21–48. And see also Asa Briggs and Peter Burke, ibid., 2002, 240.

[13] Zdenko Čepič, ibid., 2006, 1015. And see also Zdenko Čepič, "Zvišanje Življenjske Ravni [Rise of Living Standard]," in *Slovenska Novejša Zgodovina 1948–1992 [Slovenian Recent History 1948–1992]*, ed. Jasna Fischer (Ljubljana: Mladinska knjiga in Inštitut za novejšo zgodovino, 2006), 1087–93.

[14] Marjan Rožanc, "Slovenska Televizija – Dezinformacija in Propaganda [Slovenian Television – Misinformation and Propaganda]," *Ekran* 62/63 (1969): 4–9. See also Ljerka Bizilj, ibid., 2008.

[15] France Perovšek, *Interview with the author* (Ljubljana, July-August 2007) and Lado Pohar, *Interview with the author* (Ljubljana, July–August 2007).

[16] Source: *Življenje in tehnika* 8, 1 (1957): 1.

[17] Raymond G. Stokes, ibid., 2000, 2.

[18] JK, "Vprašaji nad Televizijo: Ali Bomo v Tuje Ogrodje Lahko Vključili Domačo Tehniko [Questions About Television: Will We be Able to Include Domestic Products Into Foreign Technology?]," *Življenje in tehnika* 8, 1 (1957): 2.

[19] "Televizija Domače Proizvodnje ali iz Uvoza? [Domestically Produced or Imported Television?]," *Ljudska pravica* 23, 112 (May 14, 1957): 4.

[20] Jože Prinčič, "Razvoj Gospodarskih Panog [Development of Industries]," in *Slovenska Novejša Zgodovina 1948–1992 [Slovenian Recent History 1948–1992]*, ed. Jasna Fischer (Ljubljana: Mladinska knjiga in Inštitut za novejšo zgodovino, 2006), 1081–2.

[21] Igor Prešeren, "Očiten napredek naše elektronske industrije [Obvious Progress of Our Electronics Industry]," *Delo* 10 (October 10, 1968): 3.

[22] In the first months, the television station was only broadcasting on Saturdays and Sundays that were conveniently non-working days; only in the 1960s did it broadcast on most of the days in the week.

[23] Source: "RTV 1," *Delo*, March 8–14, 1964, 6.

256   *Maruša Pušnik*

[24] For detailed information see Zdenko Čepič, ibid., 2006, 1009–15.

[25] JK, "Iz Obrobnih Beležk o Televiziji: Socialistična Družba Zagotavlja Televiziji Pravo Mesto [From Marginal Notes on Television: Socialist Society Ensures the Right Place to Television]," *Življenje in tehnika* 8, 1 (1957): 1–2.

[26] Statistično gradivo SR Slovenije [Statistical Yearbook of the Socialist Republic of Slovenia], *Kulturno-umetniška dejavnost 1961–1979 [Cultural and Artistic Activities 1961–1979]* (Ljubljana: Zavod SR Slovenije za statistiko, 1982).

[27] France Perovšek, "Radio Ljubljana in Rojstvo Slovenske Televizije [Radio Ljubljana and Birth of Slovenian Television]," in *Televizija Prihaja: Spominski Zbornik o Začetkih Televizije na Slovenskem [Television is Coming: Memory Reader on the Beginning of Television in Slovenia]*, ed. Lado Pohar (Ljubljana: RTV Slovenija, 1993), 20.

[28] Melita Zajc, *Nevidna Vez: Rabe Radiodifuzne Televizije v Sloveniji [Invisible Connection: Uses of Television Broadcasting in Slovenia]* (Ljubljana: Znanstveno in publicistično središče, 1995), 111.

[29] Katherine Pence and Paul Betts, eds., *Socialist Modern: East German Everyday Culture and Politics* (Ann Arbor: University of Michigan Press, 2008), 6–7.

[30] France Perovšek, ibid., 1993, 15–6.

[31] P.K., "Televizija – Tukaj Sem [Television – I'm Here]," *Večer*, December 12, 1957, 5.

[32] Statistično gradivo SR Slovenije [Statistical Yearbook of the Socialist Republic of Slovenia], ibid., 1982.

[33] Sabrina P. Ramet, *Nationalism and Federalism in Yugoslavia, 1962–1991* (Bloomington: Indiana University Press, 1992).

[34] Zdenko Čepič, ibid., 2006.

[35] Similar trends were noticed in The German Democratic Republic (East Germany). Before the Berlin Wall crumbled and the two Germanys were re-united, residents of the Dresden area were five times as likely to seek permission to leave than other East Germans. They complained that life under communism was intolerable without television from West Germany. Dresden was too distant from the border of West Germany to receive television signals over the air. After discussion local authorities of the city of Dresden decided to bring West German signals in by cable. See Irving Fang, *A History of Mass Communication: Six Information Revolutions* (Boston: Focal Press, 1997), xxx.

[36] See more about various models of socialism in a volume, edited by Chris M. Hann, *Socialism: Ideals, Ideologies and Local Practice* (Abingdon: Routledge, 2005), especially Katherine Verdery's chapter on ethnic relations, economies of shortage and the transition in Eastern Europe,

Ladislav Holy's chapter on socialism in Czechoslovakia, Frances Pine's chapter on women's domestic economy in rural socialist Poland, and Michael Stewart's chapter on the ethnic minorities, the work ethic and socialism in Hungary.

[37] David Morley and Kevin Robins, *Spaces of Identity: Global Media, Electronic Landscapes and Cultural Boundaries* (London: Routledge, 1995), 27.

[38] Irving Fang, ibid., 1997, xxiii–xxxi.

[39] Michel Foucault, "On the Government of the Living," in *Ethics: Subjectivity and Truth, Essential Works of Foucault 1954–1984*, ed. Paul Rabinow (London: Penguin Books, 2000), 81–5.

[40] Mike Featherstone, "Leisure, Symbolic Power and the Life Course," in *Sport, Leisure and Social Relations*, ed. John Horne, David Jary and Alan Tomlinson (London: Routledge & Kegan Paul, 1987).

[41] Hanno Hardt, *In the Company of Media: Cultural Constructions of Communication, 1920s–1930s* (Boulder: Westview Press, 2000), 3.

[42] Statistično gradivo SR Slovenije [Statistical Yearbook of the Socialist Republic of Slovenia], ibid., 1982.

[43] For more about this, see Deborah Philips, "Transformation Scenes: The Television Interior Makeover," *International Journal of Cultural Studies* 8, 2 (2005): 213–29.

[44] Irving Fang, ibid., 1997, 141.

[45] The wood industry was rapidly growing from 1955 to 1975 in the socialist Slovenia, when the number of employees doubled from 15,000 to 35,000. See more about this in Zdenko Čepič, "Demografske in Socialne Spremembe [Demographic and Social Changes]," in *Slovenska Novejša Zgodovina 1948–1992 [Slovenian Recent History 1948–1992]*, ed. Jasna Fischer (Ljubljana: Mladinska knjiga in Inštitut za novejšo zgodovino, 2006), 1129.

[46] Hanno Hardt, ibid., 2000, 139.

[47] Hermann Bausinger, *Folk Culture in a World of Technology* (Bloomington: Indiana University Press, 1990), 32.

[48] Source: Private archive of the author.

[49] Zdenko Čepič, ibid., 2006, 1092.

[50] Mike Featherstone, ibid., 1987, 113.

[51] Hanno Hardt, ibid., 2000, 2.

[52] For more on the processes of alienation, isolation and individualization as sociological phenomena, see Anthony Giddens, *Modernity and Self-Identity: Self and Society in Late Modern Age* (Cambridge: Polity Press, 1991), *The Transformation of Intimacy* (Cambridge: Polity Press, 1992), *Runaway World: How Globalisation is Reshaping Our Lives* (London: Profile Books, 1999), or with Ulrich Beck and Scott Lash, *Reflexive Modernisation* (Cambridge: Polity Press, 1994). See also Peter Miller and Nikolas Rose,

Governing the Present: Administering Economic, Social and Personal Life (Cambridge: Polity Press, 2008).

[53] Statistično gradivo SR Slovenije [Statistical Yearbook of the Socialist Republic of Slovenia], ibid., 1982.

[54] Source: Private archive of the author.

[55] Mike Featherstone, ibid., 1987, 113–4.

[56] Katherine Pence and Paul Betts, ibid., 2008, 5–6.

10

Sportsmen of Yugoslavia, Unite
Workers' Sport between Leisure and Work

Gregor Starc

> [T]his space of sport is not a universe closed around itself.
> It is inserted in a universe of practices and consumption,
> which are structured and constituted as a system. There
> are good reasons for dealing with the Sport practice as a
> relatively autonomous space, but one should not forget that
> this space is the place of forces that are not applied only at
> it. I simply want to say that it is not possible to study the
> sport consumption, if we want to call it that, independently
> from the food consumption or the leisure consumption in
> general.
>
> *Pierre Bourdieu*[1]

Introduction

"Look at her. She's running around like she's got nothing better to
do," was a common remark made about a young physical education teacher who moved from a city to a small town in the late 1960s
socialist Slovenia and who brought with her the obviously disturbing recreation practice of jogging – totally alien to the local townspeople. Not only was she violating the code of work ethics, which
demanded from people to work, eat, sleep, and work again, but also
the code of the traditional gender roles, translated into ex-agrarian
and now proletarian townspeople's vernacular, demanding that
adult women stay at home and take care of the family when not at

work in a factory or an office. From the reaction of the townspeople, it seems that leisure time in that period was still understood, by a considerable part of the Slovenian population, as time devoted to very limited, non-profitable activities, such as knitting, social-izing with neighbors and friends at home, gardening, and going to pubs. Leisure, and certain leisure sports in particular, were in this regard especially problematic, and it took some interesting discur-sive maneuvers and dissemination practices to turn leisure sports into an acceptable popular and mass everyday practice of socialist men and women.

The quality of everyday life of average modern people – ex-cept of the small number of super-privileged who do not have to work at all and the underprivileged ones who cannot afford not to work all the time – is commonly characterized by two parts: <u>work</u> and leisure. The common understanding of leisure is therefore un-avoidably linked to work as its antipode. This is obvious also in the classical definition of leisure time, which states that this is the time free from work and other necessary activities, such as eating and sleeping; i.e. "play" activities which are outside normal routines; and experiences which are intrinsically rewarding.[2] In the socialist ideological milieu, however, such a definition of leisure time would be considered incomplete because the emphasis of the socialist economy was put more on production than on consumption.[3] In the above definition, leisure time belongs to the realm of unfavorable consumption, but the socialist regime found a solution to justify lei-sure time, and especially leisure sports, by propagating them as if they were in the service of work and were, in this sense, improving production. To combine "pleasantness with usefulness," became a characteristic feature of the socialist understanding of leisure time sports and this changed the classic economic understanding of rela-tion between leisure and work, according to which one can simply choose between more work or more leisure[4] and transformed this choice into choosing between more leisure for higher work produc-tivity or not.

It is not surprising, then, that the Yugoslav state and the social-ist regime, in its effort to prove to the capitalist states that social-ist production is more productive than the capitalist one, tried to implement a "hands on"[5] approach when it came to systematically controlling leisure and leisure sports in particular. In contrast to British experience in which sports and games were "historically low on governmental agendas,"[6] in socialist Yugoslavia, leisure sport always held an important position on political agendas and was subjected to governmental control. This means that people's leisure sport in the socialist period was positioned between state control and individual choice. It was not that people were forced to take up sport or that they were sanctioned if they did not take care of their physical well being – this remained their choice – but the state interventions directly influenced those who chose to participate. To illustrate this, I used different sources and methods and the analysis in this manuscript is in this regard based on the analysis of archive materials – mostly official documents, newspaper articles on sport and sport leisure in particular, and personal histories and narratives of 42 ordinary people aged between 36 and 80 from various parts of Slovenia and ex-Yugoslavia who were living and growing up in socialist Yugoslavia. In the epistemological sense, I used Foucault's methods of the archaeology and genealogy of knowledge[7] to first identify the existing discourses on leisure sport in socialism and afterwards trace their transformations at different times and occasions. I tried to follow Foucault's methodological advice to "grasp the statement in the exact specificity of its occurrence; determine its conditions of existence, fix at least its limits, establish its correlations with other statements that may be connected with it, and show what other forms of statement it excludes."[8]

Institutional Ideals:
Regime's Quest for a New Physical Culture

The end of WWII brought along considerable changes in the social and political life of people in Yugoslavia. The functioning of the socialist regime was different from the pre-war regime of the Kingdom of Yugoslavia with its parliament,[9] its monarch and its privileged elites who tried to rule predominantly illiterate agrarian populations, but it also shared many similarities.

Pre-WWII Yugoslav industrial towns and cities were populated by a smaller portion of the population whose everyday life and leisure possibilities were greatly exceeding those available in rural areas. Leisure sport in the period between both world wars became a very popular pastime activity among townspeople and school youth, but was, nevertheless, under the relatively strict control of the state. The largest gymnastic association, the *Sokol Association of the Kingdom of Yugoslavia*, was the privileged mass sport association that functioned under the personal protection of the Yugoslav king.[10] This association nurtured the idea of mass participation in sports but the lack of sporting traditions and poor sporting infrastructure in the rural areas and also in some urban settlings was a major drawback.

After WWII, members of the *Sokol Association* became very active in establishing *Physical Culture Committees*[11] – temporary committees with the task of establishing a permanent organization that would encompass all of the pre-WWII gymnastic associations as well as sport clubs. However, this proved to be a very hard task. Since in the pre-WWII Yugoslavia there was a strong and sometimes hostile rivalry between the privileged *Sokol* associations and sport clubs, this struggle continued within the *Physical Culture Committees* where two opposing sides with two different agendas confronted each other – the first one argued for the *Sokol*-like general physical education with massive participation while the other side argued for top-level sport. Since the first side was more influential and had stronger support from the socialist regime, it was decided that everyone who wished to perform in top-level sport should also be involved in prescribed regular general training.[12] Through *Physical Culture Committees*, the regime was trying to prescribe what kind of exercises were appropriate for the mass leisure sport and elite sport training; such interventions resulted in a power struggle between the regime's ideals and everyday reality. Instead of being directly involved in the sporting programs of *Physical Culture Committees*, people started establishing *Physical Culture Actives* in institutions, factories and schools; in these *Actives*, the prescribed program of general training was not followed. Additionally, the devotees of elite sport found the demand for top athletes to be involved in some general training absurd and constantly fought against this rule. This resulted in the breakup of *Physical Culture Committees* in 1952 when the followers of the mass general exercising established the *Partizan Association for Physical Education* while the top-sport followers established the *Association of Sports*.[13] *Partizan* afterwards functioned as the main mass sporting institution under the strong patronage of the socialist regime.

Like *Sokol*, *Partizan* also functioned effectively mostly in the urban areas, but the idea of the socialist sport politics was to give an opportunity for leisure sport to all citizens of Yugoslavia, regardless of their location, age or gender. In this sense, the *Partizan* movement put more effort into including wider masses of people. The highly unreliable statistics of the socialist propaganda claimed that in 1939 only 273,622 people or 1.78% of the whole Yugoslav population was involved in organized leisure sports while in 1953 this share has reached 2.97% of the population or 502,862 people and in 1957 exceeded 3% with 588,027 people.[14] The goals of such propaganda were clear and focused on popular mobilization. One of the key and much propagated socialist ideas was equal opportunities for all and this was demonstrated in the popularization of leisure sport in Yugoslavia. The socialist regime supported the idea that all people should have access to leisure sport, but at the same time the regime wanted to control it; the regime therefore encouraged people to get involved mostly in organized recreational sporting programs – especially the *Partizan* mass sporting programs.[15]

The regime never denied its political engagement with leisure sports and even publicly emphasized this fact, which would be very odd if viewed through the eyes of Westerners, who have always perceived involvement in leisure sports as a totally independent choice, free of political influences.[16] The involvement of politics in the new physical culture was openly expressed already at the first meeting of the *Slovenian Committee of Physical Culture*:

> The physical culture of our people is not and cannot be separated from the political and cultural life. The movement needs to be unitary in its purpose and organization, devoted exclusively to one common goal; it cannot be divided like before; it has to include all strata of the nation.[17]

In the early post-WWII years, the new socialist regime constantly emphasized the mass sporting movement and the improvement of national physical strength in connection with the rebuilding of the destroyed state infrastructure and the ability to defend the country against foreign enemies. This was also visible in numerous documents about the function of physical culture in socialist society:

> In the year 1946, we have to finally realize that physical education does not serve only its own purpose, and that individual sporting successes only have some value if they grew out of mass movement. Every organizer of physical education has to be certain that physical education should in the first place serve the interests of our people's state. We have to educate and prepare our youth for building and defending our homeland.[18]

Increasing urbanization and industrialization resulted in the expansion of free time, i.e. time off work. The one thing that was seen as undesirable was idle time that was non-productive and thus also morally harmful to the socialist system. This is what made leisure sports such an important tool that could capture people in their free time and prevent them from being idle. In order to avoid any reproaches about the idleness of leisure sporting practices and sport as whole, socialist propaganda tried to persuade people that sport in socialism had nothing to do with capitalism and that active participation in sport was a kind of struggle against capitalism, pictured as a "dark empire" of manipulating moguls and manipulated workers devoid of their rights:

> Physical culture and sport in all capitalist countries are suited to fit the capitalist social arrangement. This means that in those countries physical culture serves only its own purpose, it is subjected to uncontrolled development and is a tool in the hands of various exploiters, financial tycoons and politicians. The purpose of physical culture in capitalism is to keep masses of people in the dark regarding political problems and to keep them away from the progressive revolutionary struggle... This is how our physical culture looked too in the old, pre-April Yugoslavia... With the establishment of people's governance of our state, we not

only changed the socio-political establishment but also the character of sport and physical education… In our new state, which in the first place takes care of the working man, it is in the state's interest to have a worker, a farmer and a working intellectual enjoying all the goods provided by physical education.[19]

After the dispute between Tito and Stalin,[20] the Yugoslav socialist regime also ceased to follow the Soviet models of physical culture and tried to persuade people that when the development of the socialist physical culture was in question Yugoslavia had to find its own way without copying other countries and their experiences, since this could "hinder its normal development."[21] Care for people's physical activity was one of the most emphasized tasks of the socialist order. Sporting practices were seen as tools for the production of physically, mentally and morally fit men and women. The socialist revolution was, in fact, based on the idea of producing a new man that would be able to work and produce. The politics itself was very concerned with physical education, as one of the highest ranking Slovenian Communist Party politician Edvard Kardelj admitted:

The characteristic of our struggle, of our revolution, is precisely the care for every individual, the care for well being of individuals and the nation. The care for physical culture derives from this. We cannot imagine neither the wellbeing nor the security of the nation, nor the wellbeing nor a happy life without the physical growth of people, without improving health and physical resistance.[22]

Such discourse flowed through all spheres of social life. It could be found anywhere: in work organizations, schools, media and in people's private lives. It was so obvious and domesticated that it became invisible and was reproduced through people's everyday practices. In this sense, this was a very effective biopolitical[23] project that disciplined people's morality and mentality through their bodies. The main principles of the new, socialist physical culture were constantly reproduced in official discourses and emphasized principles of universality, utilitarianism, health and mass participation.[24] According to the first principle, it was recommended that people to take up various sports in order to assure the development of the entire person, not only of the body or only its individual parts. This idea was by no means new and was derived from the pre-WWII *Sokol* idea, expressed in the writing of one of the most influential leaders of the movement, Miroslav Ambrožič:

> There are sports that are above all or even exclusively in service of entertainment and boasting bravery, while they have little or no influence on human physical development. Such sports are for example hunting, fishing, boastful tourist climbing, horse racing, tennis etc. Other kinds of sports function only one-sidedly on the development of particular limbs while they have little or no influence on other organs, such as bicycling and football. Sokol should not take interest in those two kinds of sport and should not include them in its working plan, because they are unfit for the physical education of the nation.[25]

Derived from these kinds of ideas was the idea of a harmonically developed person, which was strongly emphasized in the worldwide Communist Party propaganda regarding physical education of the socialist masses:

> Bringing up, from earliest childhood, a physically strong young generation, whose physical and spiritual energies are harmoniously developed, is regarded by the Party as one of our most important tasks. This calls for the utmost encouragement of all types of mass sports and physical culture, and a physical culture movement, which embraces ever-wider sections of the youth.[26]

The second principle of utilitarianism was one of the most influential and grounded the idea that leisure sport cannot be understood as *l'art pour l'art* but has to fulfill other goals such as moral upbringing or increased work abilities. In this view, two main goals have been especially emphasized:

First, physical culture is a constitutive part of our youth's education, and second, through physical education we have to raise physical fitness of our workers. These are two demands which fully describe the importance of physical education and position it into social processes in our country.[27]

The principle of health additionally legitimized leisure sport as an activity, which contributed to the improvement and preservation of health. The official discourse constantly emphasized the health aspect, and connected it to the notion of productivity:

It is, of course, understandable that a sickly and feeble man will not be able to work like a man who is healthy and strong. This is why our people's government puts so much attention to physical culture, because it knows that with physical culture our working masses improve their health and strengthen their mental and physical abilities, which enable them to fulfill the task of our five-year plan and contribute to the rise of socialism in our state [...].[28]

Lastly, the fourth principle of mass participation proposed that all capable individuals should become involved in organized leisure sports programs in various sport associations. The weakness of this principle, however, was its failure to also include unorganized leisure sport, which accounted for the majority of leisure-time among people.

The health and productive force of the nation was further emphasized by widespread iconography of healthy, muscular, strong and productive bodies, which provided also the symbolic power to the new physical culture. This biopolitical hygienist nationwide project used the muscular iconography in a specific way: muscular bodies were not the bodies of sexual attraction but bodies that proved the productive force of the nation. Leisure sport was in this sense viewed as a preventive measure for the preservation of high production that can compete with any economy in the world. The call for physical culture was based on the belief that sporting physical activity would reduce the number of ill people and injuries at the work places. They calculated that because of people who called in sick or were injured at their work the number of lost working days went from 26 million at the beginning of the 1950s to 39 million at the end of the decade. The official statistics claimed: "The growth index of injuries at work grows much faster than the index of employed people. From 1952 to 1956 the number of employed rose for 29% while the number of work injuries went up for 346%."[29]

Physical-cultural workers, as professional sport workers were called in that period, worked hard to improve the physical and health status of the population and tried to build the system of sport organizations and the network of sport facilities that would enable masses of people to take up various sporting physical activities during and after work. Sporting infrastructure presented one of the biggest limitations to the organized leisure sport, since at the end of WWII in Yugoslavia there were only 2,000 sporting facilities, but with the strong state support this number was four times bigger by 1957[30] and continued to rise afterwards. The mere organization of leisure sport space itself was reflecting the hegemonic socialist values. The state intensively invested large sums money into the building of sporting facilities, into the education of sport experts, and into the organization of mass sport recreation programs. Leisure sport tended to be organized in an industrial manner: it was institutionalized, planned[31] and supervised. Various organizations organized *All-Yugoslav Congresses of Physical Culture* and similar events that aimed at popularization and massification of leisure sport. All these events were accompanied by slogans from people whose opinions were always held as the truth,[32] especially Tito: "Sport in Yugoslavia develops nicely and it is right to be so! I like sport and it is especially good if it is mass sport."[33]

Sport was seen as a tool that could build the working community, because it was pleasurable and educational, it had great socializing potential and the potential to attract masses of people. In 1976, when Yugoslavia adopted a new constitution and its so-called self-management became the prevailing form of managing its industry and economy, the *Executive Committee of the Assembly of the Physical Culture Community of the Socialist Republic of Slovenia* proposed a self-management treaty of physical culture in which it stated that:

Fundamental task of all supporters of physical culture activities is to provide opportunities for active and regular participation to masses of working people and citizens in various forms of physical culture activities. The number of participating people should be the main criteria when evaluating success in this area of activities.[34]

This treaty introduced the term "physical-cultural minimum," which was understood as a level of development of organized leisure sport and access of people to it in regard of infrastructure, professional guidance and physical abilities of individuals.[35] In other words, the state actively supported the education of professional physical culture workers, the organization of sport associations and financed the building of sport infrastructure, but it also tried to prescribe sporting activities, appropriate for masses and even certain norms of physical abilities of its citizens. However, this idea was not invented in 1976, but was only a re-articulation of earlier hygienist ideas. For example, as early as in 1959 the *Yugoslav Congress of Physical Culture* tried to introduce minimal norms that indicated the appropriate physical status of citizens. Although it was utopian and never fully realized, it served as a guideline:

The norms for the fulfillment of tasks are defined for different categories. An average exercising person between 18 and 34 ought to run 100m in 14 seconds and 1000m in 3:45 minutes, jump 130cm high, throw a weight 7.5m, climb a rope 3m high in 10 seconds and perform a cartwheel over two kneeling persons.[36]

These norms that were prescribed as minimal were far from easy and the goal of the leisure sport programs was to include the whole population, targeting not the development of individual but the development of the whole nation.

Nevertheless, the regime would have been able to control this only if leisure sport was institutionalized, which meant that it encouraged people to become involved in the organized leisure sports where they could exercise under the surveillance of sport experts. The programs were implemented in various sporting organizations, such as the *Partizan* sporting organization, but also in factories that employed sport experts who were called "organizers of sport recreation" and in schools. The never-ending project of various socialist sport organizations was to increase the number of active members. The *Partizan* sport organization, for example, addressed people with the slogan "A good citizen should be physically strengthened in our organizations!"[37] This emphasized the moral dimension of a good citizen who could be a good citizen only if he or she took care of his/her physical status.

Personal Realities:
Leisure Sport in Workers' Everyday Lives

The everyday reality of ordinary people's leisure sport, however, was often in opposition with the regime's ideals. Many people refused to get involved in any forms of organized leisure sporting activities at all and practiced sport on their own. Many people did not take part in any leisure sport at all. This was often the case with people who lived in the rural areas and especially with women. One of the women who lived in a rural area, as did more than a half of Yugoslav population in the 1960s and 1970s, explained why she did not take up any leisure sport: "After school we could not take up sports because we did not have time for it. We had to work on the farm. We also never went to the seaside and there were no swimming courses available, which is why I still cannot swim."

Other people got involved in leisure sports but only within their companies or "work organizations" (as they were called), not within the state-sponsored physical culture associations. Leisure sport within work organizations was usually organized by workers who had experience in certain sports, but in 1959 the *Sport Association of Slovenia* organized the first seminar for the organizers of sport recreation in working collectives,[38] who were later employed by factories and other companies to organize all leisure sport activities for the workers. A year earlier, in1958 the *Yugoslav Congress of Physical Culture* accepted the idea that the whole society and not only the *Partizan* associations, and that Sport Associations should be responsible for making physical exercising a mass practice. This stimulated the introduction of the so-called physical education into work organizations, families, kindergartens, military, scouts, holiday and other organizations.[39] This act seemingly softened the regime's grip on the control of people's leisure sport but was not fully realized since in all newspaper articles, research reports and official statistics on the participation in leisure sports from the socialist period I could find, only information on people who were involved in organized leisure sports was included. Despite great effort, I could not find a single document that even mentioned any kind of data or even professional guidance (except descriptions of gymnastic exercises that could be performed at home) on how to get involved in leisure sport independently, outside sport programs that ran under the patronage of the state. Obviously, what was not documented tells more about this phenomenon than what was propagated. The hegemonic discursive reality purposefully ignored people's independent everyday leisure sporting practices, because these kinds of practices did not fit the idea of controlled, productivity-enhancing, goal-oriented leisure in service of work.

Furthermore, work organizations were also very autonomous with regards to the sporting activities of their workers and did not follow the official guidelines on the selection of leisure sports or the organization of leisure sport programs. In most cases, work organizations organized physical culture actives, which should have evolved into organized leisure sport organizations within work organizations. However, as a sport historian Drago Stepišnik writes, physical culture activities did not follow administratively guided compulsory exercise plans, but became involved in non-regulated leisure sport practices, also called "wild practice."[40]

Regarding workers' personal choices, the regime proved to be powerless. The workers themselves decided which sport they would practice and in most work organizations leisure sport was implemented also in various forms. One form was regular sport practice after work, which was organized in different sections according to sports. If a company had its own volleyball, football, basketball, skiing or any other team, this team was usually the one representing the company when, for example, the so-called syndicate games were organized. These games were usually organized within a certain branch of industry; the paper-producing companies from all parts of Yugoslavia, for example, organized the Paper-workers' Games, which were usually held once a year in the form of tournaments or other form of competition. If such tournaments were organized during work time, the participating workers were excused from work, all their traveling costs were covered and they received full salary even if such tournament took several days. As one of the workers, who regularly participated in these kinds of games, explained:

> Our paper-producing work organization used to organize syndicate games. Once we went to Jajce in Bosnia to compete with other paper-producing work organizations. We had a football and a volleyball tournament and a huge party afterwards. It was good fun and the competitions were not too serious either.

The second form of leisure sport in work organizations, which became very popular in the late 1960s were active breaks during work time. As one of the informants, who worked in a factory in the late 1960s, described: "I worked in a large company that had some kind of sport association. Almost all the workers were a

Participants of a Woodworker's syndicate skiing competition in 1960s.

part of it and then we exercised." The idea of active rest was very popular and was grounded in the scientific experiments of the Soviet scientists who proved that physically active rest resulted in quicker regeneration than idle rest. Active rest was in the function of maximizing productivity and the main idea was that all the parts of the body that were not used during work should be activated in order to reestablish the physical equilibrium and avoid asymmetrical physical development. Work organizations that implemented the idea of active breaks usually had one active break per shift during which the workers would gather in the yard or in the hall and perform gymnastic exercises or play football or some other game.

Other forms of workers' leisure sport tied to their work were different syndicate trips, organized for the workers during weekends and holidays. These trips often included sightseeing but also hiking, swimming and picnics with various sport games. The workers themselves saw such activities as a sign of work organizations' care for their employees' wellbeing. One of the informants expressed his nostalgic view of these trips: "At my work organization they organized outdoor trips. We walked a lot and I miss this. We lived much healthier in socialism." During our conversations, the informants were constantly expressing this kind of nostalgia and a

Typical work organization's syndicate trip in the late 1960s.

romanticized view of the relationship between the companies and the workers. They were also expressing strong senses of belonging to their companies; however, this belonging did not include only themselves but their families as well. This was especially evident in their remembering of their family vacations that most often took place in the work organizations' holiday facilities.

In these workers' holiday resorts, the workers and their families could get involved in the fourth form of leisure sport in work organizations, tied to their summer or winter family vacations. Most work organizations built their own holiday facilities at the seaside or in the mountains, from cottages near skiing resorts to complexes of bungalows or camping trailers, equipped with pools and outdoor football, basketball or tennis courts, bowling rinks and children playgrounds. Holiday-making itself was not sponsored by work organizations and workers had to pay for it but such holidays were usually inexpensive and affordable since workers themselves (in)voluntarily funded[41] the building of holiday infrastructure or even physically helped in its construction and maintenance. A lumberjack who worked in wood cutting company in the 1970s explained:

> Every year, before the summer season started, four workers from our company went to the seaside to set up the company trailers in the camp and prepare them for the season. We always volunteered for the job, because it was nice to have a paid day off at the seaside.

The practical functioning of all these quasi-organized forms of workers' leisure sport shows that the "totalitarian" Yugoslav socialist regime – as it is popularly described in contemporary Slovenia and other ex-Yugoslav republics – was not able to control the totality of everyday life, and that it left a lot of space for resistance and independent decision making. When the control of leisure sport is in question, the regime's ideals and goals have never been even remotely realized; the regime itself was quite aware of this. There was, however, one state intervention into leisure-time sporting activities in Slovenia that was successful and even survived the downfall of the socialist regime.

In the early 1970s, the *Partizan Sport Association* launched a sport recreation project called *Trim* and the name itself reflected its main idea – to trim peoples' bodies like ship sails and to get them in a certain equilibrium by reducing the negative effects of physical or sedentary work. The project, however, avoided the prescription of exact training programs and instead focused on the building of widely accessible sport infrastructure and mass sport events. Numerous "trim paths," equipped with wooden training equipment were built in the forests and parks to be used by joggers and walkers as well as specially equipped "trim cabinets," small gyms (or fitness centers) with assorted fitness equipment, which were set up in schools, work organizations, medical institutions and community centers. The trim paths and trim cabinets were equipped with information posters, describing possible exercises that could be performed with certain equipment, but, nevertheless, enabled people to invent their own way of exercising. In this way, people who used this infrastructure were not encouraged to become members of clubs or associations; they did not exercise according to prescribed training program, but the infrastructure itself subdued and disciplined them into something very similar to the regime's ideal of an active, responsible socialist man. In the Foucauldian sense,

Trimček, the mascot and logo of the *Trim* recreation project.

this was a triumph of power because it showed that power is most effective when it is invisible, when it works "at its extremities, in its ultimate destinations, with those points where it becomes capillary; that is, in its more regional and local forms and institutions."[42] This also showed that in a seemingly totalitarian socialist regime, people were neither its target nor the points of its application but rather its vehicles of power. This is why the idea of trim paths survived through peoples' leisure practices despite the collapse of the regime.[43]

The socialist idea of leisure sport presupposed active participation, there was yet another, although physically passive, aspect of it that cannot be ignored, because it started occupying ever larger parts of worker's leisure time – the consumption of televised sport.

Parallel Realities: The Rise of Mediated Spectator Sport

Before television entered socialist everyday reality, the only way to see a sporting event was to visit a match and read the newspaper reports; my informants confirmed that until the 1970s even local matches attracted entire communities. However, despite its popularity, it was very difficult for the regime to exploit this kind of spectator sport in any propagandist or educational way. Sport propaganda has always been an important part of the socialist regime's power mechanisms and many official documents testify that when the social role of sport was in question, its propaganda always occupied one of the central positions, and it tried to fulfill the goal of mass participation by agitation. There were even ideas of setting up special propaganda teams which should include "a propagandist, a journalist, a psychologist, a sociologist, a teacher of physical culture, an organizer of sport recreation, a medical doctor…,"[44] in order to effectively persuade people to get involved in organized leisure sports. The propaganda machinery was needed especially because elite competitive sport was a dubious phenomenon in socialism and needed to be put into ideologically acceptable frameworks. Professionalism was especially problematic in this regard because of its anti-socialist nature; this was an open secret throughout the whole socialist period.[45] Moreover, there existed another problem of elite sport – exclusivism and elitism – which was addressed just as often. This ideological conflict was constantly disturbing the socialist sport and as early as the 1940s and '50s many public and academic debates revolved around it. In one of the typical sport propaganda publications, Igor and Mitja Prešeren wrote about the conflict between narrow elitist participation in sport and mass participation:

> Physical culture, especially of the kind we have so far known as sport, should not be the privilege of the selected ones... In order to develop an all-national character of physical culture, we need mass initiative, understanding of authorities, inexpensive equipment, state support and state control.[46]

State control, nevertheless, proved to be ineffective if not even nonexistent with sport and this is also why mediated sport, as a part of sport propaganda, was for the socialist regime a curse and blessing at the same time. It was a blessing because the international sporting successes of Yugoslav athletes could always be praised and used as a proof of the superiority of the socialist social order.[47] However, it was at the same time also a curse because publicly focusing on individual athletes instead of focusing on collective sport was in contradiction with socialist values and – even more embarrassing – because mass leisure sport was not attractive to the audiences and the regime could or would not control this in any way. In one of his interviews, the first Slovenian television sport journalist, Mito Trefalt, acknowledged this problem and answered the journalist's criticism that television should report also about mass physical culture:

> The show "On the Seventh Track" should talk about the fundamental problems of physical culture... but we now pile up reports that do not belong there. Unfortunately, Slovenian television for now recognizes only sport event broadcasting, and in "On the Seventh Track" we only present a short filmed report of the competition. We do not deal with international sport or sport recreation or sport medicine... In our sport editing at RTV Ljubljana, we have been trying

to implement weekly 20-minute specialized shows. The first would be focused on physical education, the second on elite sports, the third on international sports, the fourth on recreation, rehabilitation and sport medicine. But this is only wishful thinking, which is not realistic at this moment with only two journalists working in sports and in the current economic conditions.[48]

In the same interview, Trefalt also exposed the role of politics in the coverage of different sports and revealed that because there was a shortage of film stock in those days, journalists were allowed to use only 11 meters of film per match, which produced one-minute report in the news; football was in a much better position because Croatian and Serbian politicians ensured that their television stations (RTV Zagreb and RTV Belgrade) had the privilege of using up to 240 meters of film.[49]

A cartoon from the *Vodnik* newspaper, depicting the infamous view of the pre-WWII Yugoslav capitalist and exclusivist elite sport: "Sport club was often a 'limited liability company'. They only accepted talents; champions have been praised as gods as long as they served them. Nobody cared for the education of young athletes or mass participation."[50]

To cover this unpleasant truth, the socialist regime tried to publicly criticize commercialism and other "capitalist vices" but at the same time continued to finance and support elite sport broadcasting, allowing people (Communist Party functionaries included) to enjoy sinful[51] idle watching of televised matches and competitions. The *Slovenian Socialist Association of Working People* for example criticized elite sport and its representations:

> Widely known deficiencies and distortions cause also deviations in morality and values... [T]here is a false presentation of sport in which noble play, combativeness, camaraderie, respect, work habits, etc., are substituted by the worshiping of idols, "gladiatoria," the illusion of fast enrichment and other characteristics of commercial pseudo-culture. This creates (also with the "help" of the means of public information [the media]) specific moral norms, foreign to our society and its goals, which are based on the thesis of easy money...[52]

However, such verbal attacks on the broadcast sport had no effect on peoples' everyday practices and could not stop the growing number of television sets becoming indispensable parts of every household, nor could they prevent elite sport becoming one of the most important parts of the television programming in Yugoslavia as well as one of the most viewed. The only people who seemed to have problems with televised sport were probably of older generation from rural areas, who saw sport in general as an idle practice which was in contradiction with the work ethics and was a sign of laziness, as a number of my informants confirmed. One of them explained his father's strong opposition to sport:

> I was a sport enthusiast ever since I was a kid but my father was strongly against it. All he saw was work and he did not let me to take up sport. When I bought my first sport shoes, he threw them in the fire... He also controlled the television and whenever a sport broadcast would start, he would turn it off because he just could not stand sport.

It should be noted here that sport became part of television in socialist Yugoslavia at its very beginning, because the first experimental television broadcasting in 1956 was nothing but a football match between Yugoslavia and England in London.[53] Also, the first Eurovision broadcast,[54] produced in Slovenia, was a sport broadcasting of ski jumps in Planica in 1960. It was not surprising that the majority of my informants mentioned sport when we talked about their early experience with television.

In its early days, television watching was a peculiar practice on its own because television sets were expensive and inaccessible. People would gather at their neighbors or relatives who owned a TV set or would watch it in public spaces. The practice of public viewing of sporting events was similar to the practice of public listening to sport radio broadcasts outside, which was a popular socializing practice in some parts of Yugoslavia. Among my informants, there were also two who lived in Bosnia and they explained how this public listening looked. The first one explained:

> In our street, we had a radio and when there were any sporting or political events, somebody would put it on a high place and set the volume to maximum so everybody could hear it. This was necessary in order to get the information to as many people as possible in a short time.

The second one, in contrast, explained how this public listening looked when the radio was not loud enough:

> We used to follow the Yugoslav football league, which was on every Sunday at 3 p.m., but we had only a small battery radio transistor with a very weak speaker. This is why we asked the loudest person to listen to the radio and repeat the radio commentary as loudly as possible.

At the beginning of televised sport broadcasting, even the technicians were using a similar technique in order to equip the televised images with commentaries. In the late 1950s, for example, two high frequency technicians, who were maintaining the main television transmitter in Slovenia, provided off-tube Slovenian language commentaries to international sport events broadcast on television.[55] People, on the other hand, would practice group viewing of sporting events and most of the informants reported that when a certain match was on as many as forty people would crowd into one living room to see it. An older female informant, who lived in a village, for example, described what happened during the boxing match between Muhammad Ali and George Fraizer in 1971: "Almost 40 villagers came to my place to see this match. When we saw this event live, with all this action, blood, all these sporting clothes, those scantily-clad girls, the crowd, the men with cigars wearing fancy suits, all those black people, it was amazing."

The popularity of televised sport was so high that even work stopped when something important was on. One of my informants lived one floor above his office and he explained that when skiing, as the most popular televised sport in Slovenia, was on: "My colleagues and my boss would stop working and we all went to my apartment to watch the race." Another one, who lived in rural area, similarly explained not only the practice but also the solemn spirit that accompanied it:

> The first TV set appeared in my village in 1966 at my friend's Daniel farm. Many people went there whenever they were broadcasting ski jumps or alpine skiing. I remember Daniel's father who used to say that we have to dress nicely because people in the television can see and hear us.

> When I was a child in the 1980s, I also remember that when an important skiing race was on, school classes would stop and all children and teachers would gather in the classrooms that were equipped with TV sets to watch it.[56] Such events evidence the viewing of televised sports as a leisure practice was linked to work, interfered with it, but was seen as unproblematic. The regime itself did not try to combat this, despite the economic losses that were caused by the pause in production.

Conclusion

In one of his most famous works *Discipline and Punish*, Michel Foucault stated that human body is directly involved in a political field and that power relations have an immediate hold upon it because they "invest it, mark it, train it, torture it, force it to carry out tasks, to perform ceremonies, to emit signs."[57] When leisure sport is in question, Foucault's statement is in place, and it would be a very hard task, even to an eager proponent of western democracy, to prove differently. If we compared everyday leisure sport in socialist Yugoslavia to everyday leisure sport of the same period in western countries, we would probably come to the conclusion that on the level of individual choice the difference was minimal. The motives of individuals in both regimes, in both economies, were probably very similar. Their decisions to get involved in leisure sport were probably motivated by their care for health, physical fitness, their need for socializing, etc., and the state in both cases was equally interested in people's physical activity as well. People's motivation was, in fact, seen as their individual choice but this choice was actually made on the basis of knowledge which was reproduced in schools, in the media and other institutions, involved in the reproduction of society. The only difference was that each regime approached people's leisure sport differently. The socialist regime tried to directly influence people's involvement in leisure sport and admittedly tried to control it while democratic capitalist regimes did not want to get involved in such openly biopolitical projects due to ideological restraints.

Despite its efforts, the socialist regime was not very successful in its agitation for organized and thus controlled leisure sport. No matter how hard it tried to attribute work effectiveness, moral upbringing, social equality, collectivity and other socialist values to leisure sports, most of the people practiced it as pleasure. The regime, however, helped to bring leisure and work closer together on the discursive level and disseminated specific knowledge about it, which was very similar to the discursive maneuvers of sport enthusiasts among English Puritans, who, according to Max Weber, "saved" sporting practices from public condemnation by presenting them as a tool of physical efficiency:

Sport was accepted if it served a rational purpose, that of recreation necessary for physical efficiency. But as means for the spontaneous expression of undisciplined impulses, it was under suspicion; and in so far as it became purely a means of enjoyment, or awakened pride, raw instincts or the irrational gambling instinct, it was of course to be strictly condemned.[58]

In the puritan England as well as in socialist Yugoslavia a few centuries later, the dissemination of this knowledge turned leisure into more than consumption and gave it a productive dimension of psycho-physical-educational relaxation that contributed to higher work efficiency. At the same time, it turned work into more than just mere production and gave it a consumptive dimension by constant emphasis on the pleasure of working for community – protestant or socialist. The meaning of leisure was in this way transferred to work and work itself started to signify something pleasurable. In other words, this phenomenon proved that even the socialist Yugoslav regime, which is today identified as totalitarian, did not distribute its power in a pyramidal form. Its power functioned in a net-shaped way, and in this network people were empowered with choice. They were able to confirm the regime's ideas and got involved in organized leisure activities, but they were also allowed to oppose them without any sanctions. Furthermore, even the regime itself, if we can judge it upon the acts of Communist Party functionaries and administration in the work organizations, was not true to its own ideology, since it supported professionalism in sport, encouraged the development of elite sport-oriented television programming and even failed to sanction or control the disturbances in working process that occurred because of absence of workers from their working places due to televised sporting events. However, the regime, despite its failure to control leisure space, contributed to the development of mass leisure sport in socialist Yugoslavia, by enrolling people to believe in the usefulness of physical activity, by dissemination and by the control of this knowledge to remain more or less the same in time and space.[59]

Notes

[1] Pierre Bourdieu, *In Other Words: Essays towards a Reflective Sociology* (Cambridge: Polity, 1990), 210.

[2] Stanley R. Parker, *The Future of Work and Leisure* (New York: Praeger Publishers, 1971). See also Kenneth Roberts, *Leisure* (London: Langman, 1981).

[3] Henry D. Dickinson, *Economics of Socialism* (Manchester: Ayer Company Publishers, 1971). Since, in the socialist utopian ideology, the state provided everything, there was little room for consumption in the classical sense.

[4] Henry D. Dickinson, ibid., 1971. Dickinson's book was first published in 1939 and describes the functioning of socialism in a rather naïve way by emphasising the workers' power to decide on their own how much time they wish to allocate to leisure in contrast to capitalism where the production itself determines how much leisure time the workers can afford.

[5] Peter Borsay, *A History of Leisure:The British Experience since 1500* (New York : Palgrave Macmillan, 2006). Peter Borsay describes the interference of governmental control with personal leisure pastimes as a "hands on" approach which was alien to British experience but rather common in continental Europe.

[6] Peter Borsay, ibid., 2006, 43.

[7] Michel Foucault, *The Archaeology of Knowledge & The Discourse on Language* (New York: Pantheon Books, 1982).

[8] Michel Foucault, ibid., 1982, 23.

[9] Because of nationalist tensions, the Yugoslav parliament was dissolved on 6 January 1929 and King Alexander I Karadjordjević assumed absolute power.

[10] Vinko Zaletel, *Zgodovina Telesne Vzgoje in Sokolstva [History of Physical Education and Sokol]* (Ljubljana: Učiteljska tiskarna, 1933). On 5 December 1929, the Yugoslav King Alexander I Karadjordjević signed the *Law on foundation of the Sokol in Kingdom of Yugoslavia.* All non-Sokol associations operating in the field of sport for all were banned but sport clubs which operated in the field of elite sports were not affected by this act.

[11] Physical culture was a socialist synonym for sport in its broad definition and included elite sport, sport recreation and physical education.

[12] Drago Stepišnik, *Oris Zgodovine Telesne Kulture na Slovenskem [Outline of History of Physical Culture in Slovenia]* (Ljubljana: Državna založba Slovenije, 1968), 291.

[13] Drago Stepišnik, ibid., 1968, 269.

[14] Pera Djetelić and Dragan Maršičević, *Narodna Omladina i Jugoslovenski Kongres za Fizičku Kulturu [National Youth and Yugoslav Congress for Physical Culture]* (Beograd: Mladost, 1959), 7.

[15] The process of organising new, socialist physical culture, which was in the first post-WWII period strongly influenced by the Soviet models of physical culture, was similar in all Yugoslav republics although in Slovenia organisation of mass sport as a whole was before and after WWII much more developed than in other parts of Yugoslavia.

[16] "Keeping politics out of leisure is one of the few stances on which

Britain retains a broad political consensus," is a claim that would in this regard be confirmed in many western countries. In Mike Huggins, *Flat Racing and British Society, 1790–1914: A Social and Economic History* (London: Frank Cass, 2000), 15.

[17] Drago Stepišnik, ibid., 1968, 287.

[18] Rato Dugonič, "Naloge Naših Fizkulturnikov v Letu 1946 [Tasks of Our Physical Culture Workers in the Year 1946]," in *Nova Pota Fizkulture [New Paths of Physical Culture]*, ed. Rato Dugonič, Zoran Polič and Vojan Rus (Ljubljana: Mladinska knjiga, 1946), 3.

[19] Igor Prešeren and Mitja Prešeren, *Fizkultura in Šport [Physical Culture and Sport]* (Ljubljana: Mladinska knjiga, 1950), 3–4.

[20] The relations between Yugoslavia and the Soviet Union (and other states of the Warsaw Pact) deteriorated dramatically in 1948 and, as the result of that, Yugoslavia started opening itself to the western countries. The core of the dispute was the demand by the Russian bureaucracy in Moscow for complete and absolute control over the satellite states, even to the smallest detail of internal policy, and Tito's hostility and opposition to complete subjugation to Russia.

[21] Leopold Krese and Drago Stepišnik, *Deset Let Športa na Svobodi [Ten Years of Sport in Freedom]* (Ljubljana: Zveza športov Slovenije, 1955), 9.

[22] Pera Djetelić and Dragan Maršičević, ibid., 1959, 11.

[23] Michel Foucault, "The Birth of Biopolitics," in *Ethics: Essential Works of Foucault 1954–1984*, ed. Paul Rabinow (London: Penguin Books, 2000). Biopolitics should be understood in Foucault's sense as an intervention of the state into people's private everyday life: "By that I meant the endeavor, begun in the eighteenth century, to rationalize the problems presented to governmental practice by the phenomena characteristic of a group of living human beings constituted as a population: health, sanitation, birthrate, longevity, race…" See Michel Foucault, ibid., 2000, 73.

[24] Drago Ulaga, "O Razvoju Splošne Telesne Vzgoje in o Posebnih Nalogah Pomladne Sezone [On the Development of General Physical Education and Specific Tasks of the Spring Season]," *Vodnik: Časopis za poljudno fizkulturo* 2, 1 (1950).

[25] Miroslav Ambrožič, "Sokolstvo kot Velika Narodna Inštitucija za Telesno in Nravstveno Vzgojo [Sokolhood as a Grand National Institution for Physical and Moral Upbringing]," in *Sokol: Glasilo Slovenske Sokolske zveze [Sokol: Gazette of the Slovenian Sokol Association]*, ed. Engelbert Gangl, Ivan Bajželj and Stane Vidmar (Ljubljana: Slovenska Sokolska zveza, 1919), 18.

[26] Fred Albin, ed., *Education in the USSR: A Collection of Readings from Soviet Journals Vol. 1* (White Plains, NY: International Arts & Sciences Press, 1963), 131.

[27] Zoran Polič, "O Nalogah Fizkulturnih Organizacij [On the Tasks of Physical Culture Organizations]," *Vodnik: Časopis za poljudno fizkulturo* 4, 1 (1952): 3.

[28] Igor Prešeren and Mitja Prešeren, ibid., 1950, 3–4.

[29] Pera Djetelić and Dragan Maršičević, ibid., 1959, 8.

[30] Zdravko Šadl, ed., *Društveno-ekonomski Problemi Daljeg Razvoja Fizičke Kulture [Socio-economic Problems of Further Development of Physical Culture]* (Beograd: Jugoslovenski savez organizacija za fizičku kulturu, 1967), 53.

[31] After WWII the development of physical culture was subjected to identical five-year planning as industry or education.

[32] Michel Foucault, "Truth and Power," in *Power: Essential Works of Foucault 1954–1984*, ed. Paul Rabinow (New York: The New Press, 2000). Foucault invented the term "regime of truth," by which he meant the "general politics" of truth – that is, the types of discourse it accepts and makes function as true; the mechanisms and instances that enable one to distinguish true and false statements; the means by which each is sanctioned; the techniques and procedures accorded value in the acquisition of truth; the status of those who are charged with saying what counts as true. See Michel Foucault, ibid., 2000, 131.

[33] Evgen Bergant, Marko Rožman and Tone Bančič, eds., *Poletov Športni Kolendarček 1954 [Polet Sport Calendar 1954]* (Ljubljana: Polet, 1954), 36.

[34] Telesnokulturna skupnost SR Slovenije, "Samoupravni Sporazum o Uresničevanju Nekaterih Pomembnih Vprašanj Nadaljnjega Razvoja Telesnokulturne Dejavnosti v SR Sloveniji [Self-management Treaty on the Realization of Some Important Questions of Future Development of Physical-cultural Activities in SR Slovenia]," in *Razprava o Temeljnih Usmeritvah Telesne Kulture v Sloveniji [Discussion on Fundamental Guidances of Physical Culture in Slovenia]*, ed. Izvršni odbor skupščine telesnokulturne skupnosti SR Slovenije (Ljubljana: Telesnokulturna skupnost SR Slovenije, 1976), 3.

[35] Telesnokulturna skupnost SR Slovenije, "Koncept Množičnosti [Concept of Mass Participation]," in *Razprava o Temeljnih Usmeritvah Telesne Kulture v Sloveniji [Discussion on Fundamental Guidances of Physical Culture in Slovenia]*, ed. Izvršni odbor skupščine telesnokulturne skupnosti SR Slovenije (Ljubljana: Telesnokulturna skupnost SR Slovenije, 1976).

[36] Pera Djetelić and Dragan Maršičević, ibid., 1959, 29–30.

[37] Evgen Bergant, Marko Rožman and Tone Bančič, eds., ibid.,1954, 1.

[38] Franc Pediček, "Športna Rekreacija v Ritmu Modernega Dela in Življenja [Sport Recreation in the Rythm of Modern Work and Life]," *Ljudski šport* 11, 1–2 (1959).

[39] Leopold Krese, "Delo Naših Organizacij po Kongresu Telesne Kulture [Work of Our Organizations After the Congress of Physical Culture]," *Ljudski šport* 10, 12 (1958).

[40] Drago Stepišnik, ibid., 1968, 293.

[41] Work organizations could decide (with the support of workers' council) to raise funds for such projects by taking a small part of workers' salaries (the so-called self-contribution) or to organize special workdays in which all the profit was contributed to a project. Although most of this infrastructure was built with workers' money and belonged to them, the majority of this infrastructure was bought by managers and upper administration after the collapse of Yugoslavia.

[42] Michel Foucault, "Two Lectures," in Power/Knowledge: Selected Interviews and Other Writings 1972–1977, ed. Colin Gordon (New York: Pantheon Books, 1981), 96.

[43] In the late 1980s and early 1990s, many trim paths ceased to be maintained and the wooden equipment in the forests deteriorated but in the late 1990s some trim paths have been rebuilt and local authorities in various parts of Slovenia are today renewing or building new trim paths.

[44] Herman Berčič, "Osnutek in Idejna Izhodišča za Razvoj Množičnosti v Telesni Kulturi in Posebej na Področju Športne Rekreacije [A Draft and Starting Points for Development of Mass Participation in Physical Culture and Especially in Sport Recreation]," in Razprava o Temeljnih Usmeritvah Telesne Kulture v Sloveniji [Discussion on Fundamental Guidances of Physical Culture in Slovenia], ed. Izvršni odbor skupščine telesnokulturne skupnosti SR Slovenije (Ljubljana: Telesnokulturna skupnost SR Slovenije, 1976), 14.

[45] Professionalism in sport was officially recognized only in the late 1970s. For a more detailed discussion on professionalism in Yugoslav football, see Gregor Starc, "Bad Game, Good Game, Whose Game? Seeing a History of Soccer Through Slovenian Press Coverage," Journal of Sport History 34, 3 (2008).

[46] Igor Prešeren and Mitja Prešeren, ibid., 1950, 15.

[47] This was an important "feel good" at home factor for the people, as this phenomena is often referred to. See Lincoln Allison and Terry Monnington, "Sport, Prestige and International Relations," in The Global Politics of Sport: The Role of Global Institutions in Sport, ed. Lincoln Allison (London: Routledge, 2005), 13.

[48] Marjan Rožanc, "Razgovor z Mitom Trefaltom," Ekran 62/63 (1969): 10.

[49] Marjan Rožanc, ibid., 1969, 10.

[50] Drago Ulaga, ibid., 1950, 23.

[51] Especially in the 1970s when the spread of television was most intensive, physical education workers were often condemning such idleness: "'Let's get all Slovenians again back on their feet!' (out if their cars, away from television, away from sitting in pubs, away from 'suicides with a spoon' etc.," as was expressed in Miha Potočnik, "Pripombe in Predlogi h Konceptu Množičnosti [Comments and Suggestions to the Concept of

Mass Participation]," in *Razprava o Temeljnih Usmeritvah Telesne Kulture v Sloveniji [Discussion on Fundamental Guidances of Physical Culture in Slovenia]*, ed. Izvršni odbor skupščine telesnokulturne skupnosti SR Slovenije (Ljubljana: Telesnokulturna skupnost SR Slovenije, 1976), 13.

[52] RK ZSDL, "Nekatera Aktualna Vprašanja Razvoja Telesne Kulture v Sloveniji [Some Current Questions About the Development of Physical Culture in Slovenia]," in *Nekateri Aktualni Problemi Telesne Kulture v Sloveniji [Some Current Problems of Physical Culture in Slovenia]*, ed. Rajko Šugman and Krešimir Petrović (Ljubljana: Univerza "Edvard Kardelj", Visoka šola za telesno kulturo, 1979), 29.

[53] Marcel Štefančič, "I Nebo Plaće [Even the Sky is Crying]," *Mladina* 9 (2009).

[54] Yugoslav television was the only television of the ex-socialist European states that was a member of the European Broadcasting Union.

[55] Lado Pohar, "Televizija Prihaja v Slovenijo [Television is Coming to Slovenia]," in *Televizija Prihaja: Spominski Zbornik o Začetkih Televizije na Slovenskem [Television is Coming: Memory Reader on the Beginning of Television in Slovenia]*, ed. Lado Pohar (Ljubljana: RTV Slovenija, 1993), 36.

[56] I gave a more detailed description of this event in Gregor Starc, "Skiing Memories in the Slovenian National Mnemonic Scheme: An Anthropological Perspective," *Anthropological Notebooks* 12, 2 (2006).

[57] Michel Foucault, *Discipline and Punish: The Birth of the Prison* (New York: Vintage Books, 1995), 25.

[58] Max Weber, *The Protestant Ethic and the Spirit of Capitalism* (London: Routledge, 1997), 167.

[59] For a detailed description on the dissemination of knowledge, see Bruno Latour, *Science in Action: How to Follow Scientists and Engineers Through Society* (Cambridge: Harvard University Press, 2001).

11

Adriatic for All
Summer Holidays in Croatia

Igor Duda

In the decades after the Second World War socialist Yugoslavia went through a series of rapid economic, social and cultural changes. Processes that normally had lasted up to a century in the most developed parts of Europe were condensed into slightly more than a couple of decades in Yugoslavia. Forced postwar industrialization both attracted and pushed peasants to leave rural areas and move closer to industrial centers. In the late 1950s, the country went through an economic miracle, with the industrial growth rate reaching as much as 17 percent in some years.[1] Between the early 1950s and 1980s the share of the agrarian labor force dropped from two thirds to a quarter, while the number of urban inhabitants grew to nearly 50 percent of the total population. Real personal income doubled during the 1960s and tripled between the early 1950s and the late 1970s. As usual, rural flight, industrialization and urbanization acting together triggered an all-embracing modernization of society. What used to be a predominantly agrarian economy and a country heavily destroyed by war, only two decades later was to be transformed into a consumer society to become a fairly developed country, whose population enjoyed the amenities and troubles of modern life. Being a tourist was one of them.

Seaside tourism, spas and mountaineering have, of course, a pre-socialist history in Yugoslavia. But only after the Second World War did circumstances favor a tourist industry that attracted millions of domestic and foreign guests. The modest pre-war number of one million registered tourists grew to peak in the late 1980s at more than 20 million guests, including 40 per cent foreigners of mainly West-German, Italian and Austrian origins.[2] Four factors had a leading role in this development. Firstly, during the Golden Age of the European post-war period, mass tourism became a general trend: more and more people started showing an interest in spending their holidays away from home; they had sufficient incomes to be able to afford what used to be a luxury. Secondly, Yugoslavia was not part of the Soviet bloc, which eased border crossings and travel inside the country. Thirdly, following European trends established in the inter-war period, Yugoslav socialist authorities showed their predilection for a tourism-for-all concept, which initially provided a strong impulse for domestic tourism and its dominant social character. Fourthly – and perhaps most importantly – beach holidays were the most popular summer recreation. The Yugoslav Adriatic coast, mostly belonging to Croatia, perfectly fitted the picture of a Europe looking forward to a swim in the sea after hard years of disasters and scarcities. Therefore "Adriatic for all" and "Summer holidays in Croatia" may be perceived as fabricated slogans, which describe well the history of tourism in socialist Yugoslavia.

Based on statistical and narrative sources, this essay traces the development of mass tourism in Croatia from the late 1940s to the late 1970s and the growing popularity of summer holidays at the Croatian seaside. It starts with the legal regulation of holidays with pay and provides an overview of the domestic tourism history in its social and commercial contexts. Since the data clearly show the leading position of the Adriatic seaside in the tourist industry, the following narrative provides answers to the meaning of the Adriatic, its perception, and its place in Croatian and Yugoslav tourist mentalities. Finally, this contribution tackles the importance of tourism as a symbol of well-being.

Holidays with Pay and Tourism

The history of holidays with pay in socialist Yugoslavia starts soon after the war. The right to at least a two-week holiday with pay had been introduced by July 1946, when the Paid Annual Leave Ordinance was passed by the federal government.[3] In 1953 Yugoslavia ratified the Holidays with Pay Convention.[4] The document, also known as Convention 52, had been passed by the International Labor Organization already in 1936 and guaranteed at least six days off. It was a product of a new era in the development of the welfare state. After a century of fighting for shorter work hours across industrialized Europe, the political focus shifted in the 1930s towards holidays with pay.[5] The days off needed a content, hence they were an ideal opportunity for tourism, which – already known for its recreational and patriotic benefits – begun counting on the working class as well. However, it was not until after World War Two that vacations became widely accepted. At that time "capitalist and Communist regimes promoted travel as both ideology and social right."[6] After the initial steps of 1946 and 1953, the Yugoslav legal system continued supporting holidays with pay. According to the federal Labor Act of 1958, Yugoslavs were entitled to 12–30 days of vacation, depending on age and years of service.[7] The Labor Act of 1965 extended the minimal annual leave to fourteen days. These were not the only measures taken by the authorities: the agrarian background of the population, low personal incomes and socialist ideas called for much more.

In this context, the introduction of a 1950 travel guidebook to Dalmatia is a remarkably good source for explaining the emergence of domestic mass tourism.[8] Aiming towards "social and national harmony," the text is an excellent combination of the ideals of the international holiday-with-pay movement, Yugoslav socialist ideology, and patriotism.[9] It is written for co-nationals, but its ideas are totally in line with the general trends of the time. The author explains that compared to its prewar predecessor, tourism in socialist Yugoslavia was fundamentally different. Seaside resorts and hotels had been "places out of reach of the worker before the liberation, when they were meant only for the bourgeoisie," but now every worker has the opportunity "to go on holidays wherever he wants in his own country, in order to continue to work after the holidays using his renewed strength." Much organizational and construction work has been completed "in order to make the stay in Dalmatia useful, comfortable and pleasant, so that in following years a larger number of the holiday-making working masses would visit those beautiful parts of our country."

In order to achieve these goals wide actions were taken by the federal and republican governments, the tourist associations, the trade unions and other mass organizations. They included a variety of measures from tourist vouchers to tourist exhibitions and fairs, from investments in construction of new accommodations to improvements of the public transportation system, from education and enlightenment to political and economic propaganda and persuasion. Among these actions, the most important, initial trigger for attracting the masses was social tourism, i.e., tourism organized and subsidized by the state or the organizations it controls. For a country with a lacking travel culture and a lack of financial resources – where low family incomes were often an obstacle to enjoying commercial tourism – social tourism was a perfect way out.[10] Its development included two basic measures: financial benefits for workers and the construction of subsidized holiday centers *(odmarališta)*. The federal and regional administrations, the party administration at all levels, the army and police, the trade unions, factories, firms, and different associations became founders of such centers.

The trade union, in particular, played an important role in social tourism, and its central organization in Zagreb, where the Association of Trade Unions of Yugoslavia had its main office for Croatia, coordinated the action. Practically everybody was a member. In 1965, for example, its membership included 97 percent of 959,000 employees in Croatia. Already in 1946 the union had provided 1,200 Croatian workers with free summer holidays.[11] The union always maintained a council, department, or office for holiday policy and holiday centers. The participants of a union conference in 1960, for example, concluded that leisure, rest and entertainment were very important, because they effected job productivity and health, and improved personal and general consumption.[12] However, the trade union was only an exponent of state and party policies, thus, steps taken by the federal and republican authorities towards mass tourism were crucially important.

In 1952 the federal government issued an order – similar to a previous one in 1947 – qualifying members of the trade union, army and police forces, students and pensioners, and their families, for a 40 percent discount on the full-board rate during the high summer season and 60 percent at other times of the year.[13] During holidays they enjoyed a thirty-day discount on railways and a 50 percent discount on plane fares, based on a voucher issued by their union branch.[14] The system differed from the postwar one, because prices for accommodations and catering were now "freely formed according to the market, i.e., supply and demand."[15] Still, prices had to be registered in advance and were not allowed to change during the year. Workers were able to claim these benefits for accommodation facilities approved by the authorities. Accordingly, a list was published annually in *Narodne novine* (the Croatian Official Gazette), which also included units not exclusively catering to social tourism. In 1952 the document contained about 150 hotels, villas and boarding houses, about 40 holiday centers owned by the trade union and different companies, and four military and five police resorts. However, to obtain more refunds from the state budget, some hotels reported longer stays of their guests, and some workers found a way of using discount vouchers for longer periods and excessive train journeys. Because of these irregularities and a slow growth of worker interest, the system of benefits was abolished in 1954. The new circumstances pushed the union into more intensive promotion, targeting especially smaller and touristically undeveloped places, private accommodations, camping, and shorter excursions. Although the concept of tourist saving accounts – well known in some European countries – was not accepted, it was now possible to apply for a holiday bank credit.

In the meantime, Yugoslav borders were opened widely for foreign commercial tourism. Soon investments were channeled into more expensive accommodations and promotion abroad to attract foreign visitors, especially from Western Europe. A construction boom of new hotels and tourist apartments started in the early 1960s. However, regardless of increasing interest in rising foreign tourism and hard currency, the state could not completely abandon domestic or social tourism. In 1956 the Tourist Association of Croatia founded the Commission for Domestic Tourism, and in 1957–1961 the Development Plan of Croatia characterized the progress of domestic tourism as "the element of social standard."[16] In 1958 the Holiday Centers Act was accepted by the federal parliament. In 1959 the Croatian parliament issued a recommendation for the improvement of tourism and called for larger investments.[17] Finally, in 1956–1961, the years of the economic miracle, domestic overnights doubled. Thanks to economic success and rising standards of living, the role of social tourism was expected to diminish. Therefore, social accommodations were to be built with future commercial tourism in mind.

In the sphere of social tourism, ten-year-old acts regarding transportation benefits were replaced in 1961 by new instructions.[18] A holder of the newly introduced K-15 card had the right to a 50 percent discount on airline fares and 75 percent on other means of transportation. The discounts applied to one round-trip ticket. The years of the economic miracle ended with a crisis in the early 1960s. Higher prices and a slow growth of real income effected leisure travel, but the summer of 1963 brought a new, three-year rise of domestic tourism. The social tourism network spread significantly between 1962 and 1965, and some factories even opened travel agencies on site. The union urged companies to pay more attention to holidays and labor force recreation. However, another poor showing of domestic tourism in 1966–1967 resulted in the cancellation of transportation benefits, and the operation of social holiday centers moved much closer to a commercial logic. Furthermore, the 1966–1970 Development Plan of Croatia gave unprecedented priority to foreign tourism. Indeed, 1966 saw more foreign than Yugoslav tourist overnights in Croatia for the first time. After 1968 domestic travel grew again, although not as fast as planned: 11.5 million domestic overnights in 1970 fell 2 million short of expectations. What followed was a large and constant growth until 1980. The 1971–1975 development plan did not pay much attention to domestic tourism, but suggested to raise the general quality of the tourism industry, accommodate a larger number of guests in already existing units, and build new facilities primarily in areas appropriate for summer holidays.[19] The plan for the period between 1976 and 1980 was programmed for a more rational construction of new capacities and better bookings for existing ones.[20] Contrary to the previous plan, much was said about domestic tourism, which was expected to grow more rapidly thanks to organizational improvements. These measures were expected to secure 24.9 million domestic and 33.8 million foreign overnights in 1980. However, at

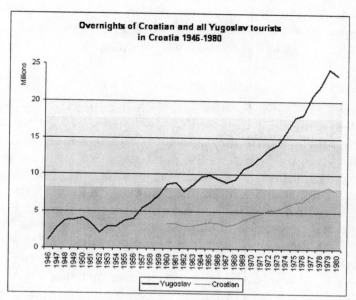

Overnights of Croatian and all Yugoslav tourists in Croatia 1946–1980.[21]

the end of the decade the real numbers were slightly lower – 23.5 million domestic and 30.1 million foreign overnights – but altogether double compared to 1970 and fivefold compared to 1960.

In the late 1960s the share of worker holiday centers in total domestic overnights in Croatia fell under 50 percent and reached less than 30 percent by 1980. However, the capacity of the centers continued to grow and was of vital importance for a constantly rising number of workers and their families. In 1980 social tourism was able to offer 93,970 beds in Croatia, but still not enough to accommodate all interested tourists. Others were able to choose among 700,000 beds in other types of accommodation and indulge in commercial tourism. They lodged in hotels and private accommodations, like rooms and apartments in private family houses. In addition, there was an increasing number of private summer cottages (*vikendica*).

A more expensive form of holiday-making marked the shift from collective to individual tourism. It seemed that the early encouragement by the authorities, the union and the tourist association, and the later promotion by tourist companies, succeeded in creating a domestic tourist, who felt the need to get away, preferably to the Adriatic beaches.

Destination: The Adriatic Seaside

Why was the Adriatic seaside an ideal holiday destination for all? Firstly, the popularity of the Mediterranean kept rising from the late nineteenth century, and by the 1960s southern European beaches were confirmed as the most attractive areas for summer holidays. Yugoslavia was a Mediterranean country, and as such an inviting destination for foreign and domestic tourists. Secondly, the image of the Adriatic Sea had a distinct place in the national identity and self-perception of Croatia and, in broader sense, Yugoslavia. Hence, the sea was a matter of national pride and swimming in it a must for domestic holiday makers. Thirdly, building tourism facilities and seaside holidays was cheaper than elsewhere, e.g., in the mountains. It was possible to sleep under the open sky or in tents, to lodge in different and inexpensive accommodations, and the only equipment a tourist really needed were a bathing suit and a towel – and sometimes not even that. Summer holidays at the seaside were, therefore, a financially most acceptable option, especially when a large portion of the population already lived there, had no reason to abandon its local beach during the summer season, and could host friends and relatives from the interior. It took a while for the seaside to gain popularity in Europe.

The coastal populations often feared and respected the sea because of its dangers. The sea was traditionally a sphere of work and meant for wars, trade, and fishing. But many fishermen never learned to swim and did not enjoy contemplating a maritime panorama.[22] Children and young people were the only ones to use the sea for play. In the mid-eighteenth century physicians started to believe in the health benefits of breathing sea air, drinking sea water, and taking short dips in the sea.[23] The aristocracy and royal families were pioneers of this new fashion, and the cures were believed to improve physical and mental conditions, while the scenery was expected to calm the troubled nature of a fragile individual. Earlier, "river or sea bathing was considered to be an immoral pastime better left to the ill-mannered lower classes."[24] It was not until the very late nineteenth century when swimming became part of adult leisure and recreation. The first seaside resorts were constructed, and the coast soon became the most desirable destination for spending the hot summer months. For tourists it was the favorite picture of paradise.[25]

The Croatian Adriatic coast also had its Mediterranean charm. During the Habsburg monarchy the existence of a swimming school in Rijeka was documented as early as 1826.[26] From the mid-nineteenth century on there were steamship lines and excursions, hotels and restaurants, bathing establishments and travel guidebooks, tourist and sport societies. In 1939 nearly one million tourists were registered in the Kingdom of Yugoslavia; foreigners spent 1.5 million and Yugoslavs 4 million overnights. The tourism value of the Adriatic coast rose incredibly in the second half of the century with the expansion of mass tourism. Although the straight coastline (northwest to southeast) of Yugoslavia was not longer than 750 km, its real length was 6,616 km. As much as 95 percent of this coastline, together with more than thousand islands, was part of Croatia, a fact which made its seaside, in particular, the leader of the Yugoslav tourist industry. As early as 1950 there were 8.6 million domestic (all Yugoslav) overnights in the socialist federation, with 4.1 million reported in Croatia. Through the decades, Croatia's share continued to be near 50 percent. By 1980 the domestic overnights in Yugoslavia increased to 50.1 million, with 23.5 million in Croatia (see graph 1). Statistically it meant that every Yugoslav citizen spent at least one night in the republic most oriented to tourism. Croatia's most attractive place for holiday makers was the seaside: it accounted for nearly 90 percent of domestic overnights and held a share of 80 percent domestic and about 90 percent foreign overnights for the Yugoslav coastline. Both, geography and the general democratization of travel caused an increase of foreign overnights in Croatia from 2.5 million in 1960 to 30.1 million in 1980, meaning that as much as 75 percent of foreign overnights in Yugoslavia occurred in Croatia. The data also show the massive scale of the tourist industry at the Croatian Adriatic coast – in the regions of Istria, Kvarner, Hrvatsko primorje, Dalmatia, and Dubrovnik. It was a rare occasion to come to Yugoslavia and not visit Croatia, and it was even more unusual to stay in Croatia and not being accommodated at the sea. Hence, holidays at the Croatian Adriatic seaside may be termed the conspicuous tourist practice in Yugoslavia.

The Croatian coastal areas were presented to foreigners as "a fragment from the Garden of Eden, where islands and ancient cities were linked together by a golden thread of history."[27] Croatia was a "happy blend," a "Mitteleuropa-in-the-Balkans." Two words sufficiently described Istria: "suntan and history;" while Dalmatia was described more poetically as "the golden coast and its tiara of islands." In the mid-twentieth century travel guidebooks expressed great expectations from Croatian tourism. "Croatia is a land of many and infinitely varied attractions, and promises to become one of international tourists' favourite playgrounds. The explanation lies perhaps in the fact that this region somehow achieves a happy blend of the beauties of most of the countries that surround it. The supreme attraction of Croatia is obviously the Adriatic Sea which borders it on the southwest."[28]

The domestic market was also not immune to tourist propaganda regarding the seaside. The Adriatic beaches became the major playground of Yugoslavia, but they were more than just a stage for pastime activities. The meaning of the magic sea ran much deeper with its roots in national, social, cultural, historical, natural, or geostrategic contexts. The sea was a national pride and important for the identity of the coastal republics – Slovenia, Croatia, Bosnia and Herzegovina, and Montenegro – although not everywhere with the same intensity. In Croatia the sea was incorporated into the republic's socialist coat of arms with the historical red-and-white checkerboard rising from the sea, surrounded by two sheaves of golden wheat topped by a red star. The landlocked republics of Serbia and Macedonia also developed a strong attachment to the Adriatic Sea, cultivated as a common element in the supranational identity of Yugoslavia. It became "our sea" and as such a strong argument in nation-building. School children were taught about its natural beauty, its colors and sounds, its islands, peninsulas and bays. History lessons always emphasized the importance of defending the sea against invaders, like the Venetians and later the Italians, most dangerous because of their proximity. The coastal towns were praised for their cultural heritage, architecture and literature. The Adriatic was a precious jewel also for Tito. "I said that our coast was the most beautiful in Europe. It really is very beautiful. I traveled a lot and have not yet seen a coast so beautiful as ours."[29] He liked the sea, sailed around the world, and established his residence and Yugoslavia's "second capital" on the Brijuni Islands of Istria, where he used to spend much time, regardless of the season.

On the other hand, the masses of tourists usually came to the seaside mostly during the summer. According to a 1974 survey of the Croatian Bureau of Statistics, 41.1 percent of the interviewed respondents went on vacation, 74.9 percent took vacations in July and August (usually their total vacation time), and 61.4 percent stayed at the seaside.[30] Since vacationers needed to be informed about tourist prospects, the press paid special attention to the Adriatic during the summer months. Its blue waters often appeared on the front pages of daily newspapers, or on the covers of weekly and monthly magazines (see figures 1 and 2), while the inside pages contained many photographs, articles and special sections on living by the sea, holidays at the seaside, the cuisine of the Adriatic regions, the biology of the sea, sailing, shipbuilding, or fishing. The weekly magazine, *Vikend*, the first specialized leisure magazine, published in Zagreb by Vjesnik since 1968, encouraged its readers to submit short comments on different topics, including how they were spending their leisure time, or what they liked most. In their reactions to the first topics (*How do you relax, how do you have fun*, 1969, *The prettiest, the dearest*, 1970–1972, *How do you get ready for holidays* and *What does it mean to come back from holidays*, 1973) readers showed a great interest in commenting on their seaside holidays. A dozen comments, mainly from Croatia, were published every week. In line with statistical surveys, readers were enthusiastically describing their summer holidays. For instance, Marijana Novosel from Zagreb had a plan for the summer of 1969: "I'm going to spend this summer at the beaches of Cres, one of the most beautiful islands."[31] Mile Jelača, a student in Opatija, was getting somewhat impatient and looked forward to his leisure time: "After I'm done with exams, there are the sea and the sun waiting for me."[32] Ivica Cerić from Lipovljani in Slavonia wrote: "I like it best when I ride on my motorcycle to our Adriatic, and spend my holidays there."[33]

Motorcycles were popular and, in fact, cars outnumbered them in Croatia for the first time only in 1964.[34] However, according to a 1974 survey, it was not so common for holiday makers to travel on two wheels: one half reached their destinations by car, while the other half depended on public transport and time tables; one quarter traveled by train, a fifth by bus and only 6 percent by air. Despite rapid motorization, only three years earlier there still had been 20 persons per car in Croatia, while 24 was the Yugoslav average.[35] Regardless of their means of transportation, the 1974 survey confirmed that as much as 41 percent of the interviewees stayed with relatives and friends. Likewise, the comments by *Vikend* readers prove the importance of family ties for tourism. Thus, it was common for grandchildren to spend the holidays at their grandparents' home or for locals to have their inland friends and relatives for summer visits. For instance, Zdravko Stjepanović from Sisak enjoyed visiting his grandfather in southern Dalmatia. "I like it best to spend my holidays in Makarska. I stroll down the old olive-groves and vineyards, and I often go fishing with my grandfather."[36] Nina Satas from Osijek shared the same experience. "I like it best at the seaside, at my grandparents' in Kaštela."[37]

In all accounts the leitmotif was an admiration of the sea. Marina Rupe from Čazma in Slavonia wrote, "I liked it best when I saw the Adriatic Sea for the first time."[38] Barbara Kirin from Zagreb was not less excited, "summer is what I like the most. The dearest thing is when I'm at our beautiful Adriatic."[39] Hrvojka Kružić from Kaštel Stari in Dalmatia shared the same opinion. "The blue Adriatic is the most beautiful sea. A summer spent there is the best."[40] She lived at the coast and enjoyed the sea throughout the year like Milena Rupčić from Rijeka. "I work morning and afternoons, so have almost no free time. Therefore I spend every free moment at the beach, where I usually take all kinds of newspapers. In the evenings, of course, I watch TV."[41] Ljubomir Mulan, a local from Dubrovnik wrote, "Since we live on the coast, we go to the beach early in the morning. We enjoy swimming and sunbathing. We come back home late in the evening. We take the maximum of our days off, and we accumulate the energy for the coming week."[42]

Swimming – often mentioned by *Vikend* readers – was probably practiced by all holiday makers. Josip Risek from Varaždin in north

Vikend magazine, cover 1974.

Vikend magazine, cover 1977.

Croatia swam while on holidays. "The dearest thing is when I see our blue Adriatic seaside, and what I like the most is swimming there."[43] Jelena Palijan from Zagreb was also a swimmer. "I'm having holidays in Poreč. I swim, sun-bathe and read a lot."[44] A 1979 poll shows that 61 percent of the interviewed Yugoslavs over 18 were able to swim.[45] Men (73 percent) were more likely to be able to swim than women (51 percent). The younger an individual the more likely he or she was a swimmer: 71 percent among those aged 18 to 24 were swimmers. Nationality was important, because republics with access to the sea or with a more active leisure culture had more swimmers: Montenegro, 85 percent, Slovenia, 76 percent, Croatia, 75 percent, and Bosnia and Herzegovina, 63 percent. The other republics and autonomous provinces fell below the federal average. Many non-swimmers were turned into swimmers during holidays at the seaside. Hence, swimming may be added to the magic formula of twentieth-century mass tourism, which includes the sea, sun, sand and sex, and for some perhaps also spirits.[46] Maybe there could be another s-word: vacationing at the seaside as a symbol of well-being.

Tourism as a Symbol of Well-Being

The 1950s and 1960s – the years of the Golden Age, economic miracles and high hopes – were watershed years and provided the final impulse for a democratization of tourism and holiday-making in Europe. "By the late 1960s, then, paid vacations had become an object of mass consumption, a subject of mass culture, and a right of citizenship linked to notions of entitlement and a just standard of living within an emergent social welfare state."[47] Tourism was understood as symbol and motor of consumerism,[48] not unlike in Yugoslavia, where it happened in three different ways: the investments in tourism accelerated the modernization of infrastructures, the development of domestic tourism created the need to escape, and western tourists with their lifestyles and hard currencies boosted Yugoslav consumerism. Tito was well aware of the double role of tourism and its significance for both, the economy and national well-being: "Both tourism and catering are extremely important fields of our economy. Not only because they bring high foreign income, but also because they need to provide our own citizens with tourist and catering services. Both of these fields are also very important for raising the level of living standards."[49]

For the first time in 1966 there were more foreign (non-Yugo-slav) than domestic tourists in Croatia. The following year was pro-claimed the year of international tourism, thanks to an initiative by Mexico and Yugoslavia at the United Nations. The domestic tourist market was growing, but not as fast as the interest of foreigners, who were outnumbered again shortly in the late 1970s. In Croatia the top 10 originating tourist nations in 1970 were: West Germany (6.5 million overnights), Croatia (4.4 million), Serbia (3.4 million), Austria (2.8 million), Slovenia (2.0 million), Italy (1.6 million), Bos-nia and Herzegovina (1.5 million), United Kingdom (1.0 million), Czechoslovakia (0.9 million), and France (0.8 million). Westerners came with colorful beach equipment and Easterners came to meet the West in a country with a suspicious form of socialism. On the other hand, Yugoslavs, according to popular belief, lived better than their counterparts in the Soviet bloc, and they did not need all of the attributes of the West, because they had found a balance be-tween these two extremes. The beaches were crowded, and during the 1960s and 1970s the shops remained well-stocked. "Yugoslavia, especially the more well-to-do Slovenia and Croatia, reflected a sort of 'Western oasis' of supply."[50] The cornerstones of the oasis were tourism and a consumer culture.

As tanned bodies were conquering the seaside, the official statistics, the trade unions and the press started inquiring about the participation of different income groups in the new summer culture. Yugoslav society was considerably leveled, but definitely not immune to class differences. In 1957 the share of blue-collar workers in total overnights realized in Croatia was 17.4 percent, the share of white-collar workers reached 34.1 percent, and the share of children 36.9 percent.[51] The underrepresentation of the working class was noticed at the time, together with the slow impact of so-cial measures supposed to motivate travel. Surveys by the Federal Bureau of Statistics in 1960 and 1961 show that slightly more than one half of four-member working-class Yugoslav families took hol-idays, only a quarter went to the coast and more than a third to the countryside.[52] Among those who headed for the seaside, as many as 55.8 percent stayed with relatives, only 2 percent took hotels, while about 16 percent stayed in holiday centers and in private accommodations, respectively.[53] On the other hand, 69.5 percent of white-collar families decided to travel, and a third of them went to the seaside.

Among working-class families, who stayed at home, only 10 percent stated that they did not wish to travel, while two thirds did not travel for a lack of finances. In 1960 the average monthly Croatian working-class pay was 16,950 dinars. Full board in a workers holiday center cost 500–860 dinars, although a worker paid only 350–500 dinars. If the mid-range rate of a week-long stay was 2,975 dinars, it was less than the weekly pay (4,238 dinars). This meant that social tourism had reached Butlin's British ideal from the late 1930s: a week's holiday for a week's wage.[54] A more detailed analysis of a 1974 survey by the Croatian Bureau of Statistics shows that better educated persons were more likely to travel, as well as those who lived in towns with populations of over 15,000, far away from the seaside, and in small families.[55] The permanent place of residence had a clear impact on mobility; thus, while almost two thirds of the inhabitants of Zagreb left on vacation, only one third of the coastal population did so. Living in a tourist area at the seaside, or very near to it, clearly diminished the chances for traveling during hot summer months. Everything one needed was already there!

According to the same survey, the seaside sojourn was very long: while 41.6 percent stayed for one or two weeks, 32.2 stayed for two or three weeks. Yet only 0.5 percent of the holiday-makers had to take out a bank loan! On average Yugoslavs were spending 688.10 dinars per week, which was only slightly more than the average weekly pay (655.75 dinars). One explanation may be that 41 percent still stayed with relatives and friends, others rented private rooms (19 percent), stayed in workers holiday centers (16 percent), hotels (11 percent), their own houses (7 percent), camps (4 percent), or other places. The most educated strata were less likely to stay with relatives or friends, but even for them it was still the most common solution (not less than 30 percent); their interest in private rooms and hotels was slightly higher than the average, while their turnover in workers holiday centers was somewhat lower (13 percent). Nearly one half of the participants in the poll had medium salaries (20 percent more or less than the national average), and there were no significant differences in holiday practices among the more or less similar income groups. However, generally a higher income meant fewer summer troubles for one's friends or relatives. The most distinctive group (about 3 percent) of people earned at least twice as much as the average income; they usually lodged in private rooms (42 percent), hotels (16 percent) or their own houses (15 percent), and showed less interest in other accommodations.

Different types of accommodation offered totally different vacation experiences. In 1969 the lifestyle magazine, *Start*, sent a small family (father, mother and daughter) to Opatija on a three-day holiday in a five-star hotel, followed by reporters, wanting to check the quality of the service during the low season, without knowledge of the staff.[56] Upon arrival at the Hotel Ambasador, the family's Volkswagen 1600 was parked in the hotel garage. The guests had a room with a view of the sea, but without television. They were able to use the swimming pool, visit the hotel's hairdresser, dance in the bar, and use the hotel's taxi service. The chambermaid was very kind; she sewed a button on father's shirt and provided headache pills. The husband ordered flowers for 30 dinars from the reception for his wife's birthday and a bottle of whiskey, for which he paid 240 dinars. *Start* covered these expenses, because in 1969 the average monthly pay equaled four bottles of whiskey. Although the magazine often covered luxury and posh lifestyles, and targeted better educated or wealthier readers, at the end of their stay neither the family nor the reporters complained much, since they had "agreed to be modest, as it suits a Yugoslav tourist family."

Five years later a different story was published by *Radničke novine*, the trade union weekly, whose reporter visited the workers holiday center in Vodice, Dalmatia, owned by Tempo, a Zagreb construction company. "The center is very nice. Every room looking at the sea has a balcony. The rooms are clean, bright, with three or four beds. In the corridor there is a shared bathroom, while every room has a sink."[57] Surrounded by oleander, rosemary and pine trees, 150 workers and their families stayed in the facility for two weeks in August. The children were happily playing, while some workers were resting on deck-chairs on a spacious terrace. The dining hall was clean, had a tv-set and a record player, and was a fun place in the evenings. There was also a bar offering inexpensive drinks and cigarettes. For Franjo Pijanec, an automobile electrician, his wife and two sons the center provided the only chance for a summer vacation. The family income was 3,500 dinars, and the family's two-week holiday cost 2,400 dinars. He had received additional 600 dinars from his company to supplement some savings. Back home the family was building a small house, and the husband was hoping for a loan from his company. They had been returning to Vodice for years showing that holidays can be great in their simplicity. Such a family would never lodge at the Hotel Ambasador in Opatija. Even if sent there as a reward, the family would probably feel uncomfortable.

At the same time, a two-week holiday in the luxurious Hotel Croatia in Cavtat, south of Dubrovnik, cost 2,520 dinars per person, or 180 dinars per day, while full board in a workers holiday centre, like the one in Vodice, cost only 43 dinars.[58] Hence, the average monthly pay (2,623 dinars) sufficiently covered 61 days in *odmaralište* and 15 days in a "de luxe" hotel. Moreover, the main advertising slogan for Hotel Croatia was: "You take summer holidays once a year" (*ljetujete jednom godišnje*). Following the logic that a vacation is a luxury that happens only once a year, some domestic guests used to spend more money than foreigners. They never cared if they had ordered one or three glasses a day; when they wanted two cups of coffee, they would simply indulge themselves.[59] While a foreign hotel guest often used to buy wine in a supermarket, the domestic guest – who was able to afford a hotel – always ordered wine from the hotel bar, and was ready to shorten the stay by a couple of days to completely enjoy being a tourist.[60]

The workers holiday centers and luxury hotels were two extremes on each side of cheaper hotels and private accommodations. In any case, the press qualified summer holidays as "the most important unimportant thing in the world."[61] According to first-hand accounts by *Vikend* readers, some were able to travel around the country or even visit fashionable European destinations, like Ruža Helbert from Zagreb. "The best thing to do on holidays is to travel. I've seen the most beautiful places, lakes and our wonderful coast. I visited Italy and Switzerland. I'll have nice memories in the future."[62] Others, like Ljubica Supančić from Zagreb, thought more about finances than nice memories: "I'm paying my debts until the next holidays."[63] Not everybody was equal, but large numbers of workers were turned into tourists and consumers. Not everybody was happy, although one's personal happiness was "the highest goal of socialism."[64] Not everybody was able to be a holiday-maker, although care was to be taken of one's "needs and supplies, leisure and fun."[65] However, the increasing prosperity was not an illusion. Yugoslavia went through extensive social and cultural changes. Thanks to the Adriatic Sea, tourism was both officially and unofficially recognized as a shortcut to social and personal well-being. New needs and habits were created, and a tanned body acquired the importance of a status symbol. Unlike foreign travel guidebooks, the socialist secular discourse did not openly claim that the Adriatic littoral was like the Garden of Eden, but some paradise-like features had to be acknowledged. Perhaps Croatian seaside resorts symbolized at least a preview of Marx's Kingdom of Freedom.

Notes

[1] See Dušan Bilandžić, *Historija Socijalističke Federativne Republike Jugoslavije. Glavni procesi 1918–1985 [History of the Socialist Federative Republic of Yugoslavia. The main processes 1918–1985]* (Zagreb: Školska knjiga, 1985), 232; Fred Singleton and Bernard Carter, *The Economy of Yugoslavia* (London and New York: St. Martin's Press, 1982), 129.

[2] *Statistički Godišnjak Jugoslavije [SG], Statistical Yearbook of Yugoslavia]* (Beograd: Savezni zavod za statistiku, 1990), 343. If not pointed out differently, all other statistical data on tourism are also taken from the official series *Statistički Godišnjak Hrvatske [SGH, Statistical Yearbook of Croatia]*, yearly published by Republički zavod za statistiku [Republican Bureau of Statistics], Zagreb, or from SGJ.

[3] "Uredba o Plaćenom Godišnjem Odmoru Radnika, Namještenika i Službenika," *Službeni list (SL)* 56 (1946).

[4] "Odluka o Ratifikaciji Konvencije o Plaćenom Godišnjem Odmoru," *SL* 2 (1953), Dodatak: Međunarodni Ugovori i Drugi Sporazumi.

[5] On the working time issues see Gary Cross, ed., *Worktime and Industrialization: An International History* (Philadelphia: Temple University Press, 1988); Gary Cross, *A Quest for Time: The Reduction of Work in Britain and France, 1840–1940* (Berkeley: University of California Press, 1989).

[6] Rudy Koshar, *German Travel Cultures* (Oxford: Berg, 2000), 4.

[7] "Zakon o Radnim Odnosima," *SL* 53 (1957).

[8] Jerko Čulić, *Dalmacija: Pregled Turističkih i Kupališnih Mjesta* (Split:

Povjereništvo za turizam i ugostiteljstvo Narodnog odbora oblasti Dalmacije, 1950).

[9] On social and national harmony see Shelley Baranowski and Ellen Furlough, "Introduction," in *Being Elsewhere: Tourism, Consumer Culture, and Identity in Modern Europe and Northern America*, ed. Shelley Baranowski and Ellen Furlough (Ann Arbor: University of Michigan Press, 2000), 16.

[10] On the postwar social tourism, leisure and consumer culture see Igor Duda, *U Potrazi za Blagostanjem. O Povijesti Dokolice i Potrošačkog Društva u Hrvatskoj 1950-ih i 1960-ih [In Pursuit of Well-Being: On History of Leisure and Consumer Society in Croatia in the 1950s and 1960s]* (Zagreb: Srednja Europa, 2005).

[11] See Zdenko Radelić, *Savez Sindikata Jugoslavije i Hrvatske: Kronologija (1945–1985) [Trade Unions of Yugoslavia and Croatia: A Chronology (1945–1985)]* (Zagreb: Institut za historiju radničkog pokreta Hrvatske, Vijeće Saveza sindikata Hrvatske and Radničke novine, 1986), 23.

[12] See Zdenko Radelić, ibid., 1986, 72.

[13] "Naredba o Povlasticama u Ugostiteljstvu za Vrijeme Korištenja Godišnjeg Odmora," *SL* 28 (1952).

[14] "Naredba o Povlasticama na Zrakoplovima za Osobe Koje su na Godišnjem Odmoru," *SL* 48 (1950).

[15] "Uputstvo o Naknadi (Regresu) Popusta od Prodajnih Cijena Pensionskih Ugostiteljskih Usluga i o Postupku pri Korištenju Povlastica za Vrijeme Godišnjeg Odmora," *SL* 28 (1952).

[16] "Društveni Plan Privrednog Razvoja Narodne Republike Hrvatske za Razdoblje od 1957. do 1961. Godine," *Narodne novine (NN)* 1 (1958).

[17] "Rasprava o Turizmu i Ugostiteljstvu u Saboru NRH; Preporuka Sabora o Unapređenju Turizma, Ugostiteljstva i Društvene Prehrane," *Turizam* 3 (1959): 1–2.

[18] "Uputstvo o Povlastici u Vožnji Prilikom Korištenja Godišnjeg Odmora," *SL* 18 (1961).

[19] "Društveni Plan Razvoja Socijalističke Republike Hrvatske za Razdoblje od 1971. do 1975. Godine," *NN* 1 (1958).

[20] "Društveni Plan Socijalističke Republike Hrvatske za Razdoblje od 1976. do 1980. Godine," *NN* 35 (1976).

[21] See *Statistički Godišnjak Hrvatske* (Zagreb: Republički zavod za statistiku).

[22] See Orvar Löfgren, *On Holiday: A History of Vacationing* (Berkely: University of California Press, 2002), 123.

[23] See Alain Corbin, *The Lure of the Sea: The Discovery of the Seaside in the Western World, 1750–1840* (London: Penguin, 1995), 65.

[24] Alain Corbin, ibid., 1995, 59.

310   *Igor Duda*

[25] See Fred Inglis, *The Delicious History of the Holiday* (London: Routledge, 2000), 113.

[26] See Boris Vukonić, *Povijest Hrvatskog Turizma [History of Croatian Tourism]* (Zagreb: Prometej and HAZU, 2005), 211.

[27] *Fodor's Modern Guides: Yugoslavia* (London: Newman Neame, 1958). On the guidebooks see Igor Duda, "Dokono Mnoštvo Otkriva Hrvatsku. Engleski Turistički Vodiči kao Izvor za Povijest Putovanja na Istočnu Jadransku Obalu od 1958. do 1969. [The Leisured Masses Discover Croatia: English Travel Guidebooks as a Source for the History of Travelling to the Eastern Adriatic Coast in the 1950s and 1960s]," *Časopis za suvremenu povijest [Journal of Contemporary History]* 3 (2003): 803–22.

[28] *Fodor's Modern Guides: Yugoslavia* (London: Newman Neame, 1958), 129.

[29] Tito's words to the tourist managers in 1969 quoted in Ante Živković, "Pri Vrhu Svjetskog Turizma," *Turizam* 11–12 (1978): 7.

[30] See "Korištenje Godišnjeg Odmora Zaposlenih u 1974. Godini," *Dokumentacija* 313 (1977).

[31] "Kako Se Odmarate, Kako Se Zabavljate," *Vikend* 61, 1969.

[32] "Kako Se Odmarate, Kako Se Zabavljate," *Vikend* 58, 1969.

[33] "Najljepše... Najdraže...," *Vikend* 93, 1970.

[34] SGH-71, 142.

[35] Calculations based on SGJ-72, 438.

[36] "Kako Se Odmarate, Kako Se Zabavljate," *Vikend* 62, 1969.

[37] "Najljepše... Najdraže...," *Vikend* 179, 1971.

[38] "Najljepše... Najdraže...," *Vikend* 193, 1972.

[39] "Najljepše... Najdraže...," *Vikend* 198, 1972.

[40] "Najljepše... Najdraže...," *Vikend* 207, 1972.

[41] "Kako Se Odmarate, Kako Se Zabavljate," *Vikend* 64, 1969.

[42] "Kako Se Odmarate, Kako Se Zabavljate," *Vikend* 59, 1969.

[43] "Najljepše... Najdraže...," *Vikend* 175, 1971.

[44] "Kako Se Odmarate, Kako Se Zabavljate," *Vikend* 68, 1969.

[45] See "Vještine Stanovništva Starijeg od 18 Godina," *Tržišne informacije* 1–2 (1979): 54.

[46] See Sue Wright, "Sun, Sea, Sand and Self-Expression: Mass Tourism as and Individual Experience," in *The Making of Modern Tourism: The Cultural History of the British Experience, 1600–2000*, ed. Hartmut Berghoff et al. (New York: Palgrave, 2002), 181; Orvar Löfgren, ibid., 2002, 173.

[47] Ellen Furlough, "Making Mass Vacations: Tourism and Consumer Culture in France, 1930s to 1970s," *Comparative Studies in Society and History* 2 (1998): 265.

[48] See Hartmut Berghoff, "From Privilege to Comodity? Modern Tourism and the Rise of the Consumer Society," in *The Making of Modern Tourism: The Cultural History of the British Experience, 1600–2000*, ed. Hartmut

Berghoff et al. (New York: Palgrave, 2002), 168.

[49] Tito's words at the 5th Congress of the Socialist League of Working People of Yugoslavia (Socijalistički savez radnog naroda Jugoslavije), held in 1960, quoted in Ante Živković, ibid., 1978, 2.

[50] Ivan T. Berend, *Central and Eastern Europe 1944–1993: Detour from the Periphery to the Periphery* (Cambridge: Cambridge University Press, 1996), 216.

[51] See "Turistički Promet Hrvatske u Godini 1957.," *Turizam* 6–7 (1958): 3–5.

[52] See Melko Erak, "Korištenje Odmora Radničkih i Službeničkih Obitelji," *Turizam* 6 (1963): 6–9.

[53] At the time in Britain one in three families spent the holidays at their friends' or relatives'. See Julian Demetriadi, "The Golden Years: English Seaside Resorts 1950–1974," in *The Rise and Fall of British Coastal Resorts: Cultural and Economic Perspectives*, ed. Gareth Shaw and Allan Williams (London: Mansell, 1997), 64.

[54] See Alan Tomlinson and Helen Walker, "Holidays for All: Popular Movements, Collective Leisure, and the Pleasure Industry," in *Consumption, Identity and Style: Marketing, Meanings, and the Packaging of Pleasure*, ed. Alan Tomlinson (London and New York: Routledge, 1990), 221.

[55] See "Korištenje Godišnjeg Odmora Zaposlenih u 1974. Godini," *Dokumentacija* 313 (1977).

[56] See Aleksa Vojinović, "Ambasador pod Povećalom," *Start*, February 12, 1969, 4, 5, 13.

[57] See Željka Valentinčić, "Tempo u Vodicama," *Radničke novine*, August 23, 1974, 19.

[58] Hotel Croatia Cavtat, advertisement, *VUS*, July 24, 1974, 22.

[59] See Zdenka Marok, "Ljetovanje: Najvažnija Sporedna Stvar na Svijetu," *VUS*, July 18, 1973, 36–7.

[60] See Mirko Galić, "Jednima Hoteli, Drugima Lavori," *VUS*, August 27, 1977, 10–2.

[61] See Zdenka Marok, ibid., 1973, 36–7.

[62] "Kako Se Odmarate, Kako Se Zabavljate," *Vikend* 59, 1969.

[63] "Što za Vas Znači Povratak s Godišnjeg Odmora?," *Vikend* 276, 1973.

[64] *Program Saveza Komunista Jugoslavije. Prihvaćen na Sedmom Kongresu Saveza Komunista Jugoslavije (22–26. travnja 1958. u Ljubljani) [Programme of the League of Communists of Yugoslavia]* (Zagreb: Stvarnost, 1965), 132.

[65] Ibid., 202.

12

"SOBE"
Privatizing Tourism on the Workers' Riviera

Karin Taylor

The tourism boom that unrolled in Yugoslavia in the mid-1960s significantly changed ways of life in the resort towns and villages. Apart from the socialist hotel developments, peasants and workers opened their doors to holidaymakers and reinvented themselves as tourism hosts. The sign *"sobe"* (rooms for rent) popped up alongside private homes all over the country's prime tourism regions. For people who had grown up tending livestock or working in the fields in the 1940s and 1950s outside the main cities, the tourism sector offered a new and appealing way of making a living. In the assessment of an elderly woman born on the Croatian island of Pašman, hosting tourists was preferable to agricultural labour,

> Some people say it's hard work with the rooms, but I say is it easier to hack maize in the baking sun?

The population in the increasingly popular tourist destinations saw a rise in living standards in direct correlation with the size of their homes. As more domestic and foreign visitors arrived, family houses were adapted and extended to cater to demand. Particularly extensive changes to the geographic and economic landscape of Yugoslavia took place along the Adriatic coast, from the Slovenian port towns in the north to the dramatic, steep coastline of Montenegro in the south. Croatia, with the longest Adriatic littoral and a number of established resorts from the interwar period, maintained a clear lead in tourism capacity and overnight stays.[1]

Tourism statistics for Croatia from the mid-1950s already showed "private rooms" as a key factor in tourism capacity, reflecting not only the political swing of that era away from centralization but an economic reality on the ground.[2] In the following decades, private accommodations vied with social tourism for the higher number of overnight stays in Yugoslavia after the combined figures for hotel and camping capacities. By the 1980s, private households were clearly ahead. This may suggest competition within the nominally "socialist" tourism sector, and indeed elements of market competition did emerge in practice, but into the 1980s Yugoslavia's self-management system fostered both social and home tourism as the League of Communists sought to meet ideological demands on the one hand and to satisfy the expectations of domestic and foreign guests on the other.

This article looks at the development of private tourism accommodation in two resorts on the Adriatic: Biograd na Moru in Central Dalmatia, and Petrovac na Moru on the Montenegrin coast. The fact that both resorts share the name "na moru" – on the sea – is coincidental and not common to Adriatic towns and villages, but it does underline their resort character acquired in the 20th century. The two small trading centres had already catered to a small number of visitors before World War II. While any number of similarities and indeed differences between them may be found, the intention here is to compare the circumstances under which private tourism accommodation evolved in two towns that had not belonged to the smart upper league of destinations like Opatija or Dubrovnik prior to socialism. Both towns saw significant investment from the system of social tourism and prospered from the holiday trips organized by trade unions and self-managing enterprises. By the 1980s, the Biograd municipality boasted a high concentration of over 50 social tourism facilities.[3] Since the resorts lie in neighbouring former Yugoslav republics (Croatia and Montenegro today), they offer the opportunity to compare how the structure and features of the Yugoslav tourism industry influenced the social texture in two Mediterranean regions with diverse national histories and specific political contingencies under the Yugoslav umbrella.

Despite significant state investment, one of the ailments of the Yugoslav tourism sector was the chronic lack of capacity for the masses of visitors who annually flocked to the seaside. By providing much-needed accommodation and services, private households helped to enable the consumption of the seaside experience by guests of all types, whether organized vacationers or individual travellers. At the same time, the hosts themselves became increasingly proficient consumers as earnings from tourism accumulated. In a book on the sociology of leisure and tourism[4], sociologist Simo Elaković underlined the consumer behaviour and spending power of the population of the Adriatic coast. According to a study in 1985, 73.4 percent of respondents in the "developed tourist regions" owned a foreign currency account in comparison with 37.3 percent in "smaller, continental non-developed settlements". But even in the latter case, people profited from their proximity to the tourism zones. Elaković noted, "The relatively rapid transition from wage labour to a tourism economy has enabled a leap towards realizing the so-called standard consumption package of the modern middle class that buys technical consumer goods from household devices over hi-fi equipment to better cars, as well as more recently boats, and at the same time enjoys significantly better housing conditions".[5] Elaković concluded with a rather scathing critique of excessive consumer behaviour and the new types of "parasitism" Marxists associated with the service sector in general and, in this case, the tourism industry in particular.[6] While the kinds of purchases listed above in the 1980s demonstrate profound changes in lifestyle, they did not materialize overnight for individual families but were the result of years of work, gradual home improvements and savings, often over two generations. However, the evident rise and differentiation of a consumer culture in the tourism resorts and the specific practices of people engaged in providing private accommodation reflected the deep transformations in society from which a Yugoslav consumerist "new class" emerged.[7] Tourism was just one element in a complex of transformative factors that included industrialization, urbanization, a degree of political democratization, the self-management venture, the full integration of women into employment and free education. Generally, a higher level of education was acknowledged by the socialist governments of Eastern Europe as a "politically correct" indicator of social stratification while the sphere of consumption remained suspect.

But this key factor in social difference was insufficient to explain the advantaged lifestyle seemingly enjoyed by tourism hosts in the Yugoslav coastal resorts. Many of the first generation hosts had only basic schooling and while they enabled higher education for their children – when they could – this was not the rule or was realized later by the generation of grandchildren in the post-Yugoslav states. The "new class" in tourism regions was not marked by educational levels, but by the efforts of the population to earn supplementary incomes and acquire the kinds of consumer goods that foreign guests from Western countries either owned or required. However, while the behaviours and attitudes bound up with the "bed and breakfast" livelihood appeared to contradict the stated goals of socialist policy on the one hand, they actively expressed the idea of a better life for all on the other.

In order to understand to what extent and just how work in the tourism business changed ways of life in the resort communities I suggest taking a look "backstage", as proposed by anthropologists and theorists of tourism.[8,9] In 2006, I recorded the testimonies of people who provided – and still provide – private tourism accommodation on the eastern Adriatic coast. Their lives were rift by the wars that tore Yugoslavia apart in the early 1990s and brought the collapse of family economies as domestic tourism caved in and foreign tourists sped to alternative destinations. People in Biograd na Moru who managed to rebuild or renew their properties after the war launched themselves into the new market economy, precariously burdened by loans. In Petrovac, on the other hand, my interview partners no longer worked in tourism. Either retired or in other jobs, they had left the business to "newcomers" who built apartment houses and rent out accommodations by impersonally depositing the key for customers without further communication.

In both towns, people's recollections of involvement in tourism during the socialist era dwelt on experiences of growing prosperity and feelings of having enjoyed a "good life" without the worries and fierce competition of the contemporary business. Nostalgia for a time when catering to tourists had seemed a secure, congenial and almost matter of course activity invariably washed over critical recollections of the organisation of tourism in socialism. It is an axiom of oral history that the process of remembering reframes the past in the light of the present. As my interview partners recollected how they had started out in tourism, the emotions and images evoked by remembering invited insight into past events, perceptions and meanings at play in the space of the "worker's" seaside resort.

Seaside Resorts in the People's Republic (until 1963)

In 1945, Biograd na Moru was a small town which had made a soothing impression in the late 1930s on an Austrian tourist passing by steamboat for its lack of a packed seafront and bustle. "Biograd does not actually make the impression of a town (or even) a larger settlement, but with its twinkling row of houses and splendid parks more closely resembles an inviting spa".[10] Although the town had briefly flourished as a seat of the medieval Croatian kings, it was destroyed several times over the centuries in the military tug-of-war between Venice and the Ottomans. Unlike other coastal towns such as nearby Zadar or Split, it had none of the prominent archaeological sights that had attracted travellers especially from the Austro-Hungarian capitals since the mid-19th century. However, its pleasant climate and attractive location with easy access to the many islands of Central Dalmatia made it a favourable spot for developing sport, nature and health tourism. A tourism association, "Soline," was founded in 1928. Shortly afterwards, an Armenian émigré engineer from the Soviet Union, Vagan Melik Karaganjan, decided to construct a modern luxury hotel on the south-eastern periphery of the town. The "Hotel Ilirija" was opened with much local publicity in 1934 and soon afterwards impressed the Austrian tourist with its stylish flair and neat surroundings.[11]

World War Two and the rise to power of Tito's partisans put an end to the plans for Biograd by hotel owners and entrepreneurs. The showcase "Ilirija" and smaller properties like the family hotel "Velebit" were nationalized. For a short time, the neon initials of the Ilirija's owner that had crowned the hotel building – VMK – were replaced by the name, TITO. Even the word "hotel" was replaced by the more socialist-sounding epithet, *Dom odmora* ("rest house").[12] From an establishment aimed at serving wealthy patrons, the former grand hotel was now opened to cater to ordinary citizens and foreign tourists. The owners of the nearby Hotel Velebit, the

A bed-and-breakfast in Biograd na moru with a *"sobe"* sign in Croatian, German and Italian (2006). In socialism, the ground floor served as a canteen for a number of enterprises.

Jelić family, were forced to see their entire furnishings confiscated by the new communist authorities and the premises functionally divided. The ground floor went to the hotel enterprise running the former Ilirija hotel for use as a restaurant. The second floor was reserved for housing workers and employees on collective summer vacation, i.e. was transformed into a social tourism facility (*odmaralište*). In the collective memory of this family, the formation of the system of social tourism that promised "paid holidays for all" was associated with violence and grave injustice.[13]

While the ideological agenda of the Yugoslav communists promoted recreation for workers instead of leisure for the rich, the state of tourism resorts and facilities in Yugoslavia after World War Two, in any case, were inadequate to offer more than the most rudimentary accommodations. Cities and infrastructures had been

badly damaged and there were shortages of almost all goods needed to serve tourism including basic foodstuffs and beverages.[14] In
a report submitted to the head office of tourism and catering of the
Croatian government in 1951, two officials dispatched from Zagreb
to investigate tourism services in the major resorts between Opatija
and Dubrovnik painted a dismal picture. Repeatedly, they noted
the run-down state of formerly exclusive hotels, criticized insipid
food, sloppy or entirely lacking services and poor management.
Their conclusion singled out examples for urgent improvement,
"Opatija, for example, at night-time resembles one of the most common villages on the coast of Europe".[15] The tone of the comments
suggests that the officials had pre-war memories and even rather
bourgeois expectations of what Adriatic resorts should offer, at
least to foreign tourists. But in the 1940s, tourism was a low priority in Yugoslav national development. Resources were thrust into
industrialization and production. By nationalizing hotels and larger properties on the coast belonging to the so-called "bourgeois"
class, the communist authorities provided makeshift lodgings for
the new worker holidaymakers without the necessity of immediate
investment.

Like Biograd na Moru, the town of Petrovac south of Budva
in Montenegro, saw tourists arrive during the interwar period, although on a smaller scale. Today's town was scarcely more than
a village at that time with a seafront made up of a double row of
stone houses overlooking the long sandy curve of the beach. In
1961, the population of Petrovac numbered 523.[16] The historical settlement, *Lastva* or *Kastel-Lastva*, named after its Venetian castello,
was renamed Petrovac na Moru after King Peter of Serbia at the end
of World War I. A local man recalled that in the 1930s students from
Belgrade had gathered in the summer at a "students' colony" in a
house close to the castello. A tourism association was founded in
Petrovac in 1925.[17] Two small hotels had opened on the eve of World
War II: "Palas" on the neighbouring Lučića cove in 1937 and "Petrovac" in 1939. Two guesthouses also offered lodgings.[18] According
to local people, the existing hotels in Petrovac were nationalized after 1945. A woman who visited her grandmother in Petrovac every
summer remembered listening to live music drifting across from
the terrace of Hotel Sutjeska, named after the failed Axis offensive

against partisan forces in Bosnia in 1943. Bands in the 1950s played the kind of Italian ballads and dance music popular during the interwar period and flowing into Mediterranean soundscapes in the post-war decades.

The same woman, born in Belgrade and whose merchant great-grandfather had built the most prominent houses on the Petrovac seafront, said that in the 1950s several families from the capital had regularly spent their holidays there in private homes. She described the visitors as "highly intellectual and good families": doctors, architects and professors. The guests had stayed in the old stone houses with no running water or modern toilet facilities. Each house had a well in the yard that supplied the household with water. "They had no bathrooms. Ours was the only house in Petrovac that had running water from a tap and an English toilet," she said. The guests from Belgrade had a long journey to their summer destination. Petrovac is some 500 kilometres from Belgrade. Until the Belgrade-Bar railway to the main port south of Petrovac was completed in 1959, holidaymakers from Belgrade travelled by train to Sarajevo and then on to the northern Montenegrin port of Herceg Novi. There they boarded the steamboat that travelled twice daily between the Croatian city of Dubrovnik and Montenegro's southernmost port, Ulcinj. On its way south, the steamboat stopped in Petrovac. Until the mid-1950s, Petrovac had no pier and the tourists could only disembark during calm weather, the woman remembered. The steamboat would stop a way out to sea and blow its horn to signal its arrival. Two fishing boats would go out to the steamboat and lash themselves to its side. "Then people jumped down with their suitcases, bags and everything, children (...) When there were waves it was really dangerous!". The fishing boats took the guests to the beach where they disembarked on the sand. Once the construction of the harbour was completed, the steamboat stopped directly in the town and disembarkation after the journey of "a whole night and a day" was easier.

While the established urbanites from Belgrade apparently savoured the "natural" feel of coastal Montenegro, workers from the growing industrial centres in Serbia also came to the seaside, but on organized holidays. The Belgrade-based building company Metalservis built and operated an *odmaralište* for its workers in

The Petrovac beach today with old stone houses on the seafront (2006).

Petrovac. The employees spent their holidays at rates subsidized by the firm. A former manager of Metalservis described the *odmaralište* as "self-sustainable": it ran its own farm producing food products in the nearby village of Buljarica. But although the Yugoslav social tourism system had the merit of making holiday travel possible for workers and their families, the actual operation of the facilities was ridden with problems. In the 1950s and 1960s, authorities and trade unions admitted setbacks and weaknesses in persuading workers to use the holiday offer.[19] Even at full capacity during the summer months, structural problems persisted since the *odmaralište* buildings remained empty for the rest of the year. In the case of Metalservis, the management decided to sell the facility to the municipality in the late 1960s and used the revenue from the sale to purchase a new company headquarters in Belgrade. In the self-management system, the firm's workers were required to agree to such decisions by referendum.[20] The former *odmaralište* was transformed into the "Hotel Riviera" around 1967 and joined Hotel Oliva, opened in 1964, as Petrovac's prime accommodation. Both category B hotels were operated by the "Hotel-Palas" tourism enterprise.[21]

Adjustments to Yugoslav economic policy from the introduction of self-management in 1953 to the new constitution of 1963 and subsequent economic liberalization correlated with a series of restructuring operations in tourism resorts. Documents from the Croatian state archive show that hotels and other properties turned into *odmarališta* during the post-war years were soon recommended for transformation into commercial-style tourist accommodations to boost capacity and improve services in general.[22] In Biograd, the classy name "Ilirija" was revived in 1957 for the tourism enterprise that ran the pre-war hotel and later the hotel buildings constructed around 1970 that made up the Biograd hotel complex. However, this did not mean that the *odmarališta* disappeared from seaside resorts. Instead of trade unions and firms retaining capacities that could be sold more advantageously to foreign tourists, the new tourism policy required them to seek alternative summertime accommodations for their workers and employees. Officials began to eye private homes.

After World War II, household tourist accommodations (*kućna radinost*) had remained part of the seaside picture. Despite communist rule, citizens had either continued to privately rent out accommodation or began to do so in the post-war years as tourism gradually picked up in the new Yugoslav state. Locals with space to spare would hail tourists at bus and train stations to rent their rooms. This untidy practice attracted criticism in the new Croatian tourism and catering journal, *Glasnik*, in 1953.[23] The journal called for regulation and proposed that tourism enterprises and households should cooperate. Against the background of the new Yugoslav decentralization policy, administrators officially recognised the potential of private households to accommodate both foreign and domestic tourists. In a further article, *Glasnik* drew attention to the fact that although domestic holidaymakers were offered larger state discounts before and after the main season, most consumers still wanted to be on holiday in the summertime.[24] But hotels simply could not cope with demand. "Guests start off on their summer holiday with big uncertainty whether they will be able to get accommodations or not. And once they have them, of course they pay on the basis of a free agreement with private individuals and are very often not registered as tourists". The journal announced that a proposal put forward by the Croatian Chamber of Catering and Tourism had recently been approved by the federal government. The tourism enterprises would be able to lease accommodations from private households during the summer season and receive the standard state rebates. "Rooms leased from private households are considered as an integral part of the capacity of the catering enterprises in these cases". The article concluded by emphasizing that according to the Chamber of Catering and Tourism, some 8,700 beds were already being offered by private households on the Croatian Adriatic coast every year.

The inclusion of private accommodations in the system of social tourism favourably influenced the official stance on small-scale business in general. In 1955, the Tourism Association of Yugoslavia declared its goal to increase accommodation offered by private households and proposed tax benefits with the aim of "extending capacity and enabling cheaper holidays for our people".[25] At the same time, efforts were made to put a stop to a "number of anomalies" such as direct rental to tourists, tax evasion and the failure of many households to register their guests.[26] These problems remained a feature of "bed and breakfast" accommodations and inconsistent tourism administration in Yugoslavia in the decades to come.

Guests in the Stable: Improvising Tourism (1960s)

Travellers to towns like Petrovac and Biograd saw considerable changes in the 1960s in transport infrastructure as the coast was developed for motor travel. Into the 1950s, visitors to Biograd had arrived by steamboat like in Petrovac, although with the benefit of landing at a stone pier. A man from Biograd remembered the excitement when the steamboat arrived twice a day and unloaded female tourists, "At 1 p.m. everybody was at the *riva*, all the youths, everyday". Some visitors also came by train to the nearby town of Benkovac and travelled on to Biograd along a gravel road. According to a man whose work on the Yugoslav Adriatic Highway project brought him to Biograd at the end of the 1950s, there was not a single asphalt road in the town although about ten *odmarališta* were based there at that time.[27] Everything changed when the Adriatic Highway (*Jadranska magistrala*) reached Biograd in 1962. Motorized tourists began to arrive en masse without making previous holiday bookings, especially from abroad. In 1963, the number of overnight stays recorded by foreign visitors to Biograd leapt by 53 percent over the previous year.[28] With a low hotel capacity of only three percent before the opening of the new Ilirija hotel in 1970, municipal households offered 36 percent of capacity ahead of *odmarališta* with 27 percent and camping sites with 22 percent.[29]

Until the tourism boom, the vast majority of local people in Biograd had worked in agriculture and fishing. In 1948, this was some 85 percent of the population.[30] Many were taken by surprise by the rush of holidaymakers. A woman from the village of Tkon on the nearby island of Pašman said that when she had married in 1954 and came to live in town, there had been "no tourism". "We worked in agriculture… we went to sell potatoes in Split, Hvar, Brač and so on…". Little by little the couple built its first house on the periphery of town. They shared the house with the husband's brother and his wife. The woman remembered that when the first tourists had appeared in Biograd looking for accommodations, local families began to make space, "People started to move for the summer into the kitchen to sleep or whatever, and gave the rooms to the tourists". Her brother-in-law was impressed by the apparent benefits of taking in tourists and suggested that the family offer its premises. Despite the lack of furniture and even sufficient rooms, they had no problem finding customers. The first guests were put up in the stable. Until the family bought beds for their visitors in the mid-1960s, the guests slept on airbeds they had brought along. "The tourists came and slept anyhow, just to be able to go to the sea," the woman said. She remembered that people from inland Yugoslavia, in particular, had been crazy for a seaside holiday, "They even came in tents… the neighbour had tents in her garden".

At that time, most homes in the neighbourhood did not have modern toilet facilities or a bathroom. Guests generally showered in the yard with the help of a rubber pipe joined to the water supply.

But the yard often became the heart of hospitality and communication between the hosts and their guests. The woman remembered, "In the yard we kept the hay, the tourists came and drank wine, we had plenty of wine… they drank, and sang, that was something!". Some two years after the family had taken in their first guests, representatives of a Zagreb enterprise arrived looking for rooms for their employees. By then the house was completed, but the three or four rooms available for summer guests were still unfurnished. The enterprise provided money for basic furnishings like chairs and beds. "But we didn't buy wardrobes, there was no money for that," the woman said. From then on, the family regularly rented accommodations to a series of Yugoslav enterprises starting with the newspaper company, *Vjesnik,* from Zagreb. "It wasn't much [money] immediately, but it was an income," she said. Another couple in the neighbouring village of Filip i Jakov, part of the Biograd municipality, started building their home in 1959. The husband

A guesthouse extended over the years perches below the Adriatic Highway in Rijeka Reževići, Montenegro (2006).

was a trained mechanic and worked as a driver, the wife did agricultural work. They had also not reckoned with tourism, but when
their single-storey house was completed in 1963 it was the newest
in the immediate neighbourhood. Tourists passing by car began to
stop and ask whether there were rooms to rent. The motorists were
mostly Germans, but also some Czechs and holidaymakers from
Belgrade. Once the few available beds were occupied, guests stayed
in the garage with blankets, on a bed of straw or on their own airbeds. Others were happy to sleep in the garden, the wife said. The
garage already had two residents: "I had two pigs in the garage and
during the night I heard them grunting… it made me laugh!".

With time, the house was converted in the summer months to
accommodate guests in three rooms. They shared a single bathroom and kitchen. "They would eat after one another, one lot at 12,
another at 1 o'clock… There was not enough room in the kitchen",
the couple's daughter-in-law said. "It was true partisan style!", the
wife joked. Her first guests from Germany, like others in the years
to follow, regularly spent their holidays with the family and made
them presents of fashionable clothing from German stores: nylon
blouses and T-shirts, sometimes new, sometimes second-hand.
According to the family, all guests were registered with the local
tourism bureau, but the bureau rarely sent them other visitors. Although they did not take in "social" tourists, they cooperated with
the social tourism network for some time. The wife, who according
to family lore cooked so well that once a guest put on 11 kilos during a three-week holiday, prepared dishes for the social tourism
organizations. But this family had no special canteen space and in
the long-term preferred to invest in improving their house for private tourists.

The involvement of these two families in tourism "came about"
rather than resulted from intention. But people with more insight
into the development of tourism gave earlier consideration as to how
they could profit from the growing industry. The man who worked
in engineering the Adriatic Highway (mentioned above) said he
had planned to engage in tourism from the start. "Everything was
going southwards… I reckoned that working with tourism would
be a good basis for living." He saw how the northern coastal resorts
had begun to flourish as the highway slowly unfurled down the

Adriatic coast. A native of continental Croatia, the young man fell in love with an 18-year-old girl from Biograd and decided to stay there. The couple purchased a plot from her uncles, took a loan for constructing a house and began to build in 1960. Since the man was a deputy manager in the road building company, he was able to buy materials at purchase price and had workers to transport the material for free. The two-story house was completed in 1961 and had ground floor space designed for use as a canteen. This was offered to the social tourism organisations that occupied the surrounding buildings in the summer and leased accommodations from private homes. In Croatia, this kind of lease for catering space, and the right of citizens to rent accommodation to tourists in accordance with the municipal authorities, was specified in a 1965 law.[31]

The couple's first contract was with the bakery enterprise *Žito Produkt* from Zagreb. For three months a year, the kitchen and dining space were utilized to cater to workers and employees on collective holidays. "We didn't cook, we just gave the space to the *odmaralište,* and they brought their own cooks, waiters (...) They brought cookers... chairs, tables, pans, everything," the man's wife said. Thus, 200 meals per day were cooked and served for either lunch or dinner, with people eating in three or four shifts. After the season, the entire inventory was returned to the firm's home destination. Although the couple leased the canteen space until the end of the 1970s, they extended their house and began to take in foreign guests earlier in the decade. Their last guests via the social tourism system came from a Bosnian textile company in Bihać. The wife recalled, "They said they had nothing. So we bought 50 plates – it was for 40 people – all the chairs, tables, everything possible. What we earned that summer we spent on the inventory." However, in the next season the couple used the dishes and furniture to offer breakfast to individual tourists and so completed the transformation of their premises into private bed-and-breakfast accommodations.

When the Adriatic Highway reached Montenegro around 1963, it similarly heralded a new era for the coastal communities. Montenegro had a particularly high rate of home accommodations, with households covering 43.9 percent of overall capacity in 1960.[32] Like in Croatia, many private households in the existing resorts were incorporated into the social tourism system in the 1960s and 1970s.[33] But the new highway allowed households in the poorer and more isolated settlements to tap into the flow of tourists for the first time. In the village of Rijeka Reževići, some five kilometres north of Petrovac, the first house to offer accommodations belonged to a couple who until then had lived off their olive plantation and spoke no foreign languages. Their son, a painter, remembered that the first guests had been introduced by a Czech engineer already familiar with the village, "He asked around where his best man could stay… We were ashamed to invite someone into our house without having good conditions for him or her… We realised that we had to improve the house for the guests, in order to cater for their needs". As a result, this family was the first to install running water and inside bathrooms in their house. The stone building was converted so that finally five rooms offered capacity for up to 18 guests who took their home-cooked meals on a terrace shaded by vines. Most of the tourists came from abroad: Germans, French, Italians and Austrians.

In the early days, the village was linked to the highway only by a steep track so that the guests were met up on the road and their luggage taken down by donkey. This was the son's task. "We used to get Christmas cards and New Years greetings from our guests, and on these cards there was a little message – My father's name was Mitar – 'Dear Mitar we are coming on the second of August'. And then what happened? We had a little donkey with a saddle, and we mounted it and went up to the top of the village, where the shop is now, and in the letter the man has specified, 'I'm coming at five p.m. on the second of August'. And we're late! We're late going up with the donkey, and the guest from Munich isn't… he's already there waiting for us!", he laughed. Relations with guests were amiable, according to the man. "We just did things the way we felt the guests would like." Communication with the local tourism association was limited to establishing prices; the family received neither expert advice on how to run the business nor a loan. But money came in and represented a crucial addition to the parent's pensions, enabling the son to study in Sarajevo. "We lived a little above the standard. But in any case renting out helped everybody to improve the standard of living. When people made money one season, they invested it to buy a fridge, a TV, or to fix their bathrooms", he said. The same man who recalled swimming as a child among the heavy woollen winter clothes that the village women then washed in the sea, as a teenager swam in the same bay with plastic flippers, a mask and a harpoon gun given to him by a tourist from Belgrade.

Tourism, mobility and the expansion of urban leisure practices not only impacted on consumer culture in the resort communities but changed social behaviour and expectations. In Petrovac, the first bikini worn on the beach around 1960 symbolized a new lifestyle and identity claimed by young women. According to the woman with family roots in Petrovac, she was the first girl aged 16 to sport a bikini in public, "I had a little Brigitte Bardot model, with bows on the side". When she headed towards the beach, her grandmother was aghast, "I said, 'I don't care, I'm going to the beach. Should I put on some bathing costume right up to my neck?'. After ten minutes, all the women looked down and of course they saw me, and asked my grandmother... 'Oh Sofia, have you seen that naked lady down there, that young woman, ooh I'm too ashamed to look, I've closed my shutters'. And my grandmother was a lady and said, 'Yes of course I know. That's my granddaughter, my Nada, and she's so pretty and can wear that'". And so, according to Nada, the discussion was ended and local girls began to mix in with tourists as part of the self-confident young beach population. By the time the Adriatic Highway was completed to Ulcinj in 1965, tourism had become a mass phenomenon down the entire Yugoslav coast.

Fish Picnics and Filter Coffee:
Professional Hosts (1970s and 1980s)

The 1970s were marked by improvements to private accommodations as people adapted and in many cases rebuilt their homes. The family of the woman from Pašman (above) started to build a new house on the same plot in 1974. The house was completed in 1978. Now it was specifically designed to accommodate tourists. The "tourist" floor had its own bathroom and toilet. The couple offered four rooms to guests; the in-laws also had four. In the mid-1980s, the rooms were adapted so that each acquired its own bathroom.

The extent of home reconstruction demonstrated that hosts were becoming increasingly proficient in the business of selling private accommodations to tourists. It also reflected changes in legislation. In 1963, loans from communal banks had become available to home owners for increasing and improving tourism capacity.[34] Interview partners in Croatia said it had been easy to obtain loans in the 1970s and 1980s. Furthermore, legislation reiterated and extended the rights of citizens to let capacity to tourists and specified accommodation categories in more detail than before. The constitutional amendments of 1971 transferred the regulation of the tourism and catering sector from the federal level to the republics. According to the 1974 Croatian law on "catering and tourism activities", citizens could rent out not only rooms but also apartments or buildings, or provide full meals as a "household guesthouse".[35] However, the scope for private business remained limited despite some adjustments, causing problems for people wanting to develop commercial tourism services. The 1974 Croatian law permitted a capacity of up to 14 beds. This was extended to 20 in 1978.[36] Legislation in the other republics varied.

A couple celebrates with German guests of 25 years at a ceremony organized by the Biograd tourism association and the municipality in 2001.

The second significant change of this decade concerned the role of foreign tourists. Statistics from the 1970s for Yugoslavia as a whole consistently show that households catered to more domestic guests than foreigners.[37] But in the perception of hosts on the Adriatic, foreigners seem to have constituted a dominant aggregate. The man who started out with social tourism in Biograd and turned to offering half-board private accommodations indicated that attitudes changed from a degree of scepticism to even preference. At first, direct advertising to foreigners had not been welcome by the community. "At the beginning it was somehow shameful to have a 'Zimmer frei' sign", he said. But with time, a more commercial stance was generally accepted. Host families built up relationships with foreigners who returned year after year. This man's regular German guests – four families – even gathered funds to privately loan him 20,000 German marks in 1976 for adding a new storey to his house, he recalled with reverence. In exchange, his guests consumed the equivalent of their loan over five years by making use of his holiday accommodation.

Regular guests from abroad also left behind various consumer goods after their stay with their hosts. A woman from Biograd who offered rooms from the mid-1970s in a new building right next to her birthplace, said "My guests brought me everything!". German guests brought colourful towels, for example, that were unavailable in town. One family even contributed a fridge they had transported all the way from Germany. But for this woman, the most important item was the filter coffee machine. "Before I used to make breakfast for the guests, for each room... I brought everything as each guest wanted it (...) I made sliced pršut, pancakes, as everyone wished... just for breakfast!", the woman said. But with a single coffee machine in the kitchen and a job in a nearby company, she wanted to lessen her morning tasks. She acquired her first filter coffee machines from German and Austrian visitors who cooked coffee in their rooms. "Sometimes a guest would give one as a present, sometimes we ordered them," the woman said. Finally, all the rooms were equipped for self-service. For this woman, the imported coffee machines represented both the kind of modern convenience her guests expected and her own personal liberation from the time-consuming routine of providing breakfast.

Young people who grew up in a family that accommodated tourists were acquainted early with the everyday contingencies of having strangers in the house. "In the summertime you migrated in your own house," a man from Petrovac said, referring to how his family had moved into the living room to free bedrooms for guests until they built a larger house when he was 18 years old. The family catered mainly to Yugoslav enterprises that booked accommodationy in 10-day blocks for their employees. For this man, sharing his social life with tourists had been fun. He recalled the tantalizing abundance of girls between his home and the beach, and that tourism had brought him a summer job every year. "I started to work at the age of 14 or so, selling newspapers to the German tourists – *Bildzeitung, Welt* – on the beach... I didn't have to, but I enjoyed it... something happened, something new". Another year he sold icecream, then tickets for a parking lot, and later worked as a hotel porter. With plenty of pocket money to spare, he enjoyed the cafes and the discotheque by the castello until the bars closed down for the winter. Then he would travel to visit friends in Belgrade until his money finally ran out some time in February.

Another opportunity for men in Petrovac to earn some extra money was a boat ride for foreign tourists to eat fish. The "fish picnic" included travel to a small cove or bay, grilling fresh fish over an open fire and a good dose of *rakija* brandy. This man sometimes accompanied his uncle or friends who had boats. "It was very funny when they [the tourists] came home, all drunk! They just dropped from the boat onto the pier". The man said the "domestic" plum brandy offered to tourists in the heat of the day was usually just an industrial product bought in the supermarket. Likewise, frozen mackerel on occasion figured as fresh fish. The locals, who fished with dynamite, also served "exploded" fish, but the tourists preferred the mackerel that was evidently still in one piece. "I ate it myself," the man said, "drinking wine on the beach, no problem... it was normal, no hard feelings... There was a lot of money and everybody was happy, the tourists and the locals." Although tourism brought perennial prosperity, the number of permanent jobs created by the tourism sector in Petrovac was limited and employment remained seasonal. Political connections were crucial to obtaining steady employment, the man said, and young people counted themselves lucky if they were able to get any kind of non-seasonal job.

Because tourism on the Adriatic coast was largely limited to the summer months and due to the legal restrictions on developing private businesses, families were unable to live from renting rooms alone. Both men and women, as was usual in Yugoslavia, were employed in other sectors, while the older generation often still cultivated private agricultural plots for the rest of the year. Even in tourism centres, the tourism industry was not a top employer. A 1980s report from the Biograd municipality released figures for employment in "social production", i.e., in self-management enterprises: 29.4 percent in agriculture, 28.2 percent in trade, 19.2 percent in tourism and 11.1 percent in industry in 1981.[38] The extra earnings from private tourist accommodations, however, contributed to a feeling of well-being and personal success. The families I interviewed in Croatia had purchased their first car by the early 1970s. Some underlined that their earnings from tourism had directly paid for the automoblie. The economic slump that hit Yugoslav society some ten years later was least felt in the tourism regions. People in both Petrovac and Biograd recalled the second half of the 1980s as a "golden era", when the number of foreign tourists shot up again, appearing to promise increasing wealth. Despite a slight drop in the capacity offered by households in Yugoslavia as a whole during the 1970s, private tourist accommodations again provided over 32 percent of capacity in 1987, followed by popular camping sites.[39]

The apparently privileged position of Adriatic resort communities generated criticism from the representatives of a socialist viewpoint. Discourse in the 1980s moved from supporting citizens in the provision of tourist accommodations to the type of comments voiced by Elaković who remarked on "self-enrichment" and even the "restoration of petit bourgeois relations".[40] But ideological critique meant little to most people making a living on the coast. Especially the older generation which had seen tangible improvements in living standards integrated its experience into a reassuring imagination of Yugoslavia that evaded evidence of inequalities. An English teacher in Petrovac organized her pupils to perform this image for foreign tourists until the 1980s. Gathered on a hotel terrace in national costumes, the children sang their teacher's English adaptation of the hymn-like song *Jugoslavijo* set to a Macedonian folk melody. One of the verses she sang to me went like this:

I like your pretty woods and sea,
The green fields, the lakes and valleys,
Your people are friendly and kind,
I'm proud and happy that I live in such a country,
Yugoslavia, Yugoslavia.

Conclusions

The *"sobe"* sign on the Adriatic coast symbolized both the social and economic achievements as well as the shortcomings of socialist Yugoslavia. Households in Biograd and Petrovac offered tourist accommodations right from the early years of the socialist state. The need to attract foreign tourists and, in addition, fulfill the promise of "holidays for all" encouraged political leaders and economists to integrate small-scale private business into the socialist project. An important effect was that the efforts of citizens to realize extra earnings from tourism, as had been common before socialism, were soon approved as a legitimate activity and contribution to the socialist endeavor. The *"sobe"* sign did not represent a commitment to unbridled capitalism – at least until the late 1980s – but participation in the Yugoslav way of managing the tourism economy. Although the share of private households providing capacities for tourism fluctuated somewhat over the decades, there was no dramatic change from the mid-1960s on. Change was more evident in consumption by these households and the way people went about catering for tourists. Generally, lifestyles along the Adriatic coast became more homogenous as the tourism industry and urbanization extended away from the former elite resorts to encompass fishing villages and small trading towns. But people who offered rooms to tourists made extra efforts to improve the comfort and conveniences in their homes. Hosts cited "foreign tourists" as the main trigger for investment. Foreign tourists were seen to have higher expectations than domestic holidaymakers, and as hotels and camping sites improved their facilities it was necessary to attract guests with at least a similar standard.

By catering to tourists, private households contributed to the holiday experience of consumers. Hospitality included preparing special meals for guests – grilled fish or meat – and supplying a steady flow of domestic wine and brandy. Authenticity is now a contested term in tourism studies, but in their memories people (re)constructed their role as hosts as genuine and motivated by real sentiment for their guests. Most interview partners felt that this sentiment had been lost in the post-socialist era. Today tourism seemed predicated on impersonal relations – symbolized by the substitution of the room in the family house with the tourist apartment – and the principle that "money rules".

When hosts put up tourists in their own homes they created a specifically "Yugoslav" holiday feeling for both domestic and foreign guests. Post-World War II Yugoslavia was never the province of elite tourism. Rather, the country offered holidays to ordinary folk who expected modest comforts and unostentatious recreational opportunities in naturally beautiful surroundings. Being able to buy leisure artifacts like beachwear and sports equipment (e.g. masks and flippers) was part of that package. For domestic vacationers, the practice of tourism reinforced the feeling that in the realm of holidays the majority of Yugoslavs could participate in a consumer culture that resembled that of foreign guests. Although the 1980s economic crisis made hotels clearly too expensive for most Yugoslav citizens, with a bit of luck they could still find lower-priced private accommodations and enjoy an affordable, if shorter, holiday. For their part, locals engaged in tourism enjoyed some higher status commodities, but also used them to entertain tourists during the season. New boats, for example, certainly figured as status symbols but were also used for taking tourists on fishing or sightseeing trips, thus boosting the offers of tourism. By mastering small-scale private businesses in the tourism sector, the "new class" that emerged in the Adriatic resorts contributed significantly to shape Yugoslavia as a tourist destination. The higher living standard they achieved was less exclusive than an important element in mediating an agreeable "holiday for all" over the decades that was a core value of the Yugoslav socialist program.

Notes

[1] Stevan Stanković, *Turizam u Jugoslaviji (3ʳᵈ edn.)* (Belgrade: Stručna literatura, 1990), 144–5.

[2] "Promjene u Strukturi Prometa i Korištenje Raspoloživih Kapaciteta," *Turistički pregled* 5–6 (1955): 3.

[3] *Pregled Stalnih Odmarališta na Području Općine Biograd na Moru*, dated 1985.

[4] Simo Elaković, *Sociologija Slobodnog Vremena i Turizma. Fragmente Kritike Svakodnevlja* (Belgrade: Savremena administracija, 1989).

[5] Simo Elaković, ibid., 1989, 114.

[6] Simo Elaković, ibid., 1989, 122.

[7] Patrick Hyder Patterson, "The New Class: Consumer Culture under Socialism and the Unmaking of the Yugoslav Dream, 1945–1991" (PhD dissertation, University of Michigan, 2001).

[8] Dean MacCannell, *The Tourist. A New Theory of the Leisure Class* (Berkeley, Los Angeles and London: University of California Press, 1999); John Urry, *The Tourist Gaze. Leisure and Travel in Contemporary Societies* (London: Sage, 1990).

[9] Critics of the backstage theory point out that the term suggests that a tourism façade separates a "constructed" tourism world from the "authentic" world in which tourism workers live. Here, I use the term to denote the position of the hosts while agreeing that realms of experience and meaning cannot be divided or graded in terms of authenticity.

[10] "Biograd na Moru, Stadt am Meer," *Dalmatien*, undated, 1.

[11] "Svečano Otvorenje Velikog Modernog Hotela 'Ilirija' u Biograd na Moru," *Jadranski dnevnik*, May 7, 1934, 4.

[12] Photographs (1950) in the Croatian State Archive (HDA).

[13] Interviews with the Jelić family, August and November 2006, and February 2007.

[14] Various documents in: HDA, fond *Glavna Uprava za Turizam i Ugostiteljstvo Vlade NRH*, 8, 1948–51.

[15] Ibid., *Izvještaj, Službeni Put po Primorju u Svrhu Pregleda i Ispravaka Nedostataka u Objektiva Namjenjenim Inostranom Turizam*, 1951.

[16] *Enciklopedija Jugoslavije, VI, "Petrovac"* (Zagreb: Leksikografski zavod FNRJ, 1955–1971), 483.

[17] "Budva i Njena Rivijera," *Turizam* 11–12 (1972): 25.

[18] "Receptivne Mogućnosti na Budvanskom Primorju," *Turizam* 6 (1972): 24.

[19] See Igor Duda, *U Potrazi za Odmorom i Blagostanjem. O Povijesti Dokolice i Potrošačkoga Društva u Hrvatskoj 1950-ih i 1960-ih* (Zagreb: Srednja Europa, 2005), 109–30.

[20] To what extent management "recommendations" or coercion played a role in such decisions in practice calls for more research. See: Wolfgang Soergel, *Arbeiterselbstverwaltung oder Managementsozialismus?* (Munich: R. Oldenbourg, 1979).

[21] "Receptivne Mogućnosti na Budvanskom Primorju," *Turizam* 6 (1972): 25.

[22] Undated documents in: HDA, fond *Glavna Uprava za Turizam i Ugostiteljstvo Vlade NRH*, 8, 1948–51. This neither meant that nationalized property was returned to former owners, nor that nationalization was stopped in 1953. A new nationalization law concerning "rented property and building land", for example, was issued in 1958 (*Službeni list 1958*, 52). In the Yugoslav constitution of 1963, state property was finally transformed into "social property" (Tomislav Borić, *Eigentum und Privatisierung in Kroatien und Ungarn. Wandel des Eigentumsrechtssystems und Entwicklung der Privatisierungsgesetzgebung.* (Vienna: Verlag Österreich, 1996)).

[23] "Rješava se Pitanje Izdavanja Privatnih Soba Turistima," *Glasnik* 13 (1953): 5.

[24] "Regres na Privatne Ležaje," *Glasnik* 5 (1953): 6.

[25] "O Kućnoj Radinosti u Turizmu," *Turistički pregled* 10–12 (1955): 15.

[26] "Značenje i Sadržaj Naših Novih Propisa o Turizmu," *Turizam* 5–6 (1956): 7.

[27] A 1960 list of *odmarališta* for the whole Biograd municipality (i.e. including nearby settlements) gives a figure of 21. *Popis Radničkih Odmarališta*, HDA, fond SSJ-VSSH 1286, box 484, 1960, 24.

[28] Fred B. Singleton, "Yugoslavia's Foreign Economic Relations," in *Südosteuropa-Handbuch, 1, Jugoslawien*, ed. Klaus D. Grothusen (Göttingen: Vandenhoeck & Ruprecht, 1975), 285.

[29] "Turistička Orijentacija Biogradske Komune," *Turizam* 1 (1964): 19. Other tourism accommodation recently operating or under construction in the municipality included the tourist "villages" in Pakoštane and Crvena luka, representing 12 percent of capacity in 1963.

[30] *Enciklopedija Jugoslavije, I, "Biograd (na moru)"* (Zagreb: Leksikografski zavod FNRJ, 1955–1971), 569.

[31] "Zakon o Ugostiteljskoj Djelatnosti Građana," *Narodne novine* 1965, 13.

[32] Borislav Uskokovič, *Turizam Crne Gore. Evolutivne i Perspektivne Promjene* (Nikšč: Univerzitetska Riječ, 1988), 87.

[33] The spread of *odmarališta* into private homes throws some doubt on the value of statistics indicating social tourism capacity. Do they include capacity leased from private households? This is not evident in the figures.

[34] *Službeni list 1963*, 12.

[35] *Narodne novine* 1974, 19 and *NN* 1974, 28.

[36] "Zakon o Ugostiteljskoj i Turističkoj Djelatnosti," *Turizam* 3 (1978): 27.

[37] *Turizam u Jugoslaviji. Statistički Podaci 1960–77* (Belgrade: Turistički Savez Jugoslavije, 1978).

[38] *Prostorni plan općine Biograd na moru do 2000.-te godine (revizija 1)* (Zadar: Zavod za urbanizam, 1985), 25.

[39] Stevan Stanković, ibid., 1990.

[40] Simo Elaković, ibid., 1989, 119.

Part V

Consumption, Fashion and Transgression

13

Shame, Desire and Longing for the West
A Case Study of Consumption[1]

Breda Luthar

Memory and the Study of "Normal Exceptions"[2]

Among the strongest individual memories of life under state socialism is the lack of desired goods, the "culture" of shortages, and the
"dictatorship" over needs. My aim is to examine at the micro level
the experience of the culture of shortages in a society of "really existing socialism": I will investigate the regular shopping trips by
Yugoslavs to the Italian border town of Trieste. This article analyzes
the formal properties of the cultural practice of "going shopping to
Trieste" between 1955 and the end of the 1960s, the period of hard-
line socialism, and draws on personal memories of those engaged
in such shopping expeditions. I will treat these shopping trips as
meaningful cultural practices and cultural phenomena that became
a quasi-institutionalized tradition in the late 1950s, when the border
between capitalist Italy and the Socialist Federal Republic of Yugoslavia began to open up gradually. Open borders strengthened the
status of Yugoslavia as an alternative to the "people's democracy"
of other Eastern European countries. Over time, seasonal shopping
trips to Italy became frequent and regular social events; they developed into a mass shopping frenzy in the 1970s, and continued until
the dissolution of Yugoslavia.[3]

A shopping expedition to Trieste was not only a social practice aimed at obtaining necessary and desired goods, but also a cultural phenomenon. The number of people who crossed the border
to do their seasonal shopping increased from year to year. Hours-
long waits at the border crossings with Italy, the authoritarian and

unpredictable behavior of Yugoslav border police and the silent disdain and aloofness of Italian border police did not discourage the shoppers. Between 1960 and 1969 the number of cross-border shoppers increased tenfold. According to official statistics, in 1959, for instance, 1,597,792 motor vehicles crossed the border; in 1963, the number had increased to 3,678,814, and by 1965 to more than 11,000,000.[4] By the mid-1970s, the journey to Trieste had become a monthly, or at least seasonal, event for the majority of the Yugoslav population. Seasonal shopping in Italy, especially in Trieste, became such an important part of the consumer and material culture in Yugoslavia that it should be understood as the cultural articulation of a specific moral economy where social relations are shaped by obtaining, using, exchanging and creating the social meaning of material artifacts.

On the one hand, I wish to outline the formal characteristics of the "shopping expedition to Trieste" that constitute the phenomenology of the practice: from the buying of hard currency and the reciprocal relations within the gray or second economy connected with shopping to the anticipation of the journey, the symbolic value and the public meaning of goods. On the other, I am also interested in the "hidden transcripts of power"[5] during the relatively hard times of socialism and the political regulation of needs: the black market, smuggling, communicative strategies and tactics of shoppers on crossing the border, and the gender divisions and ethnic and class differentiation involved in shopping practices.

By interviewing members of a generation that experienced the earliest Yugoslav shopping expeditions to Italy in the late 1950s and 1960s, I excavate memories of a special form of consumption under Yugoslav socialism. This article draws on 46 in-depth life-story interviews. Respondents, of whom two-thirds are women, were born between the early 1920s and the beginning of the 1940s and were at the time of interviewing between 65 and 85 years old. All respondents were from the western part of Slovenia, which had closer ties with Italy, or from the capital Ljubljana, characterized by a concentration of cultural and economic resources. The sampling was thus purposive and it embraced the then-emerging middle class. Since my survey inevitably addressed the topic of, at least officially, illegal smuggling, personal recommendations of acquaintances, family members and friends were invaluable in establishing initial contacts.[6] Focusing on cross-border shopping, smuggling brought back not only memories of desires, needs and scarcity, but also the related, often traumatic, experiences of the informants with political power and ideology. Memories of scarcity, desires, the symbolic meaning of goods, of a system of interaction between border officials and shoppers/smugglers, of the erratic and authoritarian behavior of the border police, and of powerlessness, resistance, and disobedience, mingle with recollections of foreignness and inadequacy when faced with the "West" in Trieste.

Drawing on these memories as a cultural narrative, we must take into account the fact that we are researching a past which is being organized with reference to the present. Remembering is always a reconstruction and representation of the past and not a recording of the past, and has more to do with invention, the present, the imagined and representation than with what actually happened. We should thus bear in mind that the interviews and stories of the respondents are not just data about the experience of socialist modernity, but also an active production of interpretations of shoppers in which the interviewees are involved in impression management and are taking on various identities. The testimony of the participants should thus be understood as the active production of meaning and as an interpretation of the events we are investigating. No matter how complex the relationship of these testimonies to history, the visual documents such as family photographs and verbal stories of the interviewees are an expression of historical events and circumstances. They represent a counterhistory or, rather, call into question the official history and at the same time show how memory of a relic of history can enable the integration of micro- and macro-level investigations and thereby an understanding of the total history. The investigation of the marginal institution of "shopping trips to Trieste" in the history of socialism is not just the analysis of a topic neglected in cultural, sociological or historical research, or a topic that is best grasped on a "micro" level and considered as an (un)necessary footnote to a structural analysis. On the contrary, micro-history or micro-sociology is also an analytical operation involving the narrowing of perspective to a microscopic scale of observation. The principle of qualitative research at the micro-level is the belief that microscopic observation will reveal aspects of the cultural form that were previously hidden and invisible to the analytic gaze, and, possibly, even reveal the essential structural dimensions of the society. Or, as argued by Levy:

> ... even the apparently minutest action of, say, somebody going to buy a loaf of bread actually encompassed the far wider system of the whole world's grain markets.And only a paradoxical and significant distortion of perspective would suggest that the commercial life of one village is of no interest beyond its meaning on a local scale.[7]

This investigation should thus give us the insight into the incoherencies, heterogeneities and conflicts within official socialist culture and explain the relation between official culture and its internalization by individuals. Oral history and the reconstruction of the life-stories of individuals give voice to aspects of the past that would otherwise remain silent. We consider the everyday and the ordinary not as footnotes to social or political history, but as being at the very center of relationships of economic, political, symbolic power.

Needs and Desires

Consumer culture is an inseparable part of the economic, political and cultural aspects of modernity. Each society formally and informally regulates the circulation of commodities. This means that it sets the rules with respect to the kinds of things that can be exchanged on the market, those that are excluded from the market and perhaps "sacralized"[8], and the conditions and means of exchange. In short, demand for products as an articulation of culturally constituted needs and desires is always culturally, legally, and economically regulated. The issue of needs and desires and of the meaning and definition of luxury is implicated in the broadly political question of the nature of social order and the definition of a good society. According to Berry, "the operant definition of luxury and need indicate a society's conception of itself ".[9] Thus the indirect control of demand, either by means of taboos, economic policy, fashion system, or by various promotional discourses such as advertising, is a universal characteristic of societies. Socialism, on the other hand, represents a political and social project and a form of economic organization characterized not only by cultural, legal, and economic constraints and control of demand, but also direct political forms of disciplining and limiting demand (i.e. the political and ideological "dictatorship over needs"). Feher et al. define "the dictatorship over needs" as the "determination of social production through the uncontrolled decision of a unified apparatus of power and through its underlying force".[10] It is, in short, the social formation that in principle organizes production from one administrative center and hence exercises political control over needs. However, political control over needs under socialism is not just the consequence of the power interests of a "unified apparatus of power", but is based on the ideology of socialist egalitarianism and through it on the essentialist view of human needs and the division of needs into "real" ones and "false" ones. This division legitimizes a specific moral economy and conceptualization of authentic life that can be used as a basis for classifying some needs as more, and others as less, authentic.

It is a sociological truism today that individual preferences, needs and consumption practices always take shape in a culture and within a certain way of life and cannot be defined universally outside the specific culture.[11] Even "basic needs" such as food or shelter are always empirically accessible only in the specific cultural forms they take and are at the same time discursive, that is, constitutive, for the "needed subject". According to Doyal and Gough, needs are embodied in the culturally variable "discursive position,"[12] which constitutes the individual subject. Culture thus shapes needs and practices of consumption; these practices and needs, as "technologies of self,"[13] on the other hand, constitute the historical subject. If we say that we need something, we are making a claim to a way of life that embodies our particular values. Or, as Harré put it, human beings have always lived in a double social order, the practical order and the expressive order, and the social significance of material things can be understood only if their roles in both these orders are identified.[14] A definition of real needs is, therefore, always an articulation of a definition of the good life, of the way we imagine how we should live. It comprises a reflection of how material and symbolic social resources are to be organized in relation to the definition of the good life and to values implied by it. Basic needs can therefore be defined not as those that sustain us as physical beings and satisfy our pre-existing biological needs, but as those needs that are necessary conditions for our cultural citizenship.[15] The need, thus, with which a socialist consumer responded to the idea of having a Vespa scooter, Italian shoes or nice underwear, is fundamentally social and political.

In socialist Yugoslavia – at least during the first 10 years after the Second World War – demand and consumption were regularly subjected to social definitions and control by direct political appeals, by law, or by an economic policy that translated political and economic controls into consumer demands. In the 1940s and 1950s, citizens of Yugoslavia were encouraged to defer consumption as a moral and political duty and political prerogatives framed the economic policy and individual consumption. But where there is power there is also resistance: the political control of demand in socialism was constantly threatened by oppositional behavior that challenged the official classification of needs and thereby also the dominant definition of the good life and official formulation of values and commitments. Shopping trips to the Italian city of Trieste may be understood as such a practice. For instance, our informants went shopping to Trieste to buy not only socks, nylon stockings, and Italian shoes, but also dolls, soft wool cardigans, bicycles, fabrics, blankets, washing machines, Vespas and fashionable underwear. These alleged luxury goods should not be regarded in contrast to necessities, but rather as "marking services", a notion used by Douglas and Isherwood as the opposite of "physical services" to emphasize the essentially social character of these goods – they are needed for mustering solidarity, exclusion, differentiation.[16] They are goods that enable cultural participation and "whose principal use is rhetorical and social, goods that are simply incarnated signs".[17] An Italian bicycle is just a physical object when observed independently of any system of social relations. But it is a luxury commodity and an object of aesthetic contemplation within a specific discursive configuration. The luxury status of a commodity, thus, is not the result of the intrinsic properties of the artifact, but the effect of its place within a determinate system of social relations, including the register of its consumption, which is defined by restricted access to luxury and its close connection with identity, subjectivity and the body. In this sense, these goods only responded to a fundamentally political necessity and, thus, represented an opposition to the order that operated on the official concept of needs. Beyond need and as a sign of personal autonomy, the experience of the consumption of goods acquired in Trieste may serve as a resource in the construction of individual and social identities, while on the other hand, border crossings represent the spaces of discipline and surveillance.

The Making of a Middle Class

Shopping expeditions to Trieste as a particular aspect of consumer culture that emerged at the end of the 1950s depended on political democratization and the open borders with Italy. However, they were as much a consequence, on the one hand, and a motor, on the other, of cultural and social transformations including a certain standard of living that redefined the value of needs and the notion of a "good life". We start with a brief examination of Yugoslav political, economic and social changes in the late 1950s and 1960s, the conditions of the modernization processes in socialism, and the making of the (socialist) middle class. Political changes, which led to partial democratization, were a result of the break with the Soviet Union and all other Eastern European countries in 1948, caused by persistent attempts by the Soviet Union to treat Yugoslavia as its satellite. The Soviet Union responded by reinforcing its economic blockade. By 1950, all trade between Yugoslavia and Eastern Europe was brought to a halt. Yugoslavia turned for military and economic aid to the West and began to moderate its previously extreme anti-western attitudes and to rethink the ideology and practice of Soviet-type socialism. As a pragmatic consequence of this opening towards the West, but also because of a genuine motivation to build an alternative model of socialism, the country transformed the Stalinist/etatist model of socialism and introduced certain political changes, as well as economic ones in the organization of "relations of production". Central planning was largely limited to the setting of long-term goals, while attributes of a market system and the concept of self-management were introduced in 1953. In practice, in the next 30 years, some aspects of industrial democracy were gradually established, and, from the mid-1950s onwards, the general political atmosphere allowed for a greater personal freedom, albeit without essentially affecting the Party's monopoly. Party control was, by and large, maintained, although it was decentralized and in the 1960s Party interference became less and less noticeable in everyday life.

Between 1953 and 1964, Yugoslavia had an extremely high rate of economic growth.[18] The rapidly growing Yugoslav economy was the result of a low starting point and of many structural changes influenced by industrialization, urbanization and modernization in general. The increased productivity brought a certain degree of prosperity which could not be overlooked, especially if compared with other Eastern European countries. Although the period from the late 1950s to the early 1960s onwards was also the period of social modernization and of relative political and cultural liberalization in other Eastern European countries,[19] consumption of consumer goods in Yugoslavia rose faster than in any other country of "really existing socialism".[20] In 1965, for instance, Yugoslavia had more motor vehicles per capita than some of the people's democracies where national income and per capita consumption were substantially higher. Savings deposits increased 25-fold between 1955 and 1965 and helped keep demand for consumer goods at a high level, thus making it less dependent on current incomes. Moreover, by 1965 the possession of durable goods represented a much more significant element of personal wealth than at any time since the Second World War. In Yugoslavia, the index of consumption per capita rose from 103.6 in 1954 to 130.1 in 1957.[21]

These political and economic processes were accompanied by social and cultural transformation, including a rearrangement of social groups: differentiation, urbanization, and industrialization necessarily brought with them new modes of community, new forms of social etiquette in the cities, and a distinctive new sociality or "structure of feeling"[22]. Moreover, new forms of self-understanding and self-cultivation – in short, new forms of individuality with distinctive ways of life – were emerging. The increased differentiation in earnings and occupational reclassification was only one aspect of the changes in the "social opportunity structure". The latter– as a social-structural process that opens up social space for class differentiation – is comprised of educational, income, lifestyle, and occupational elements. A class structure based on "quantity of competence", as Klaus Eder would put it, began to emerge, while education and lifestyle differentiation rather than income marked barriers between social classes.[23] The result of the changes in the "social opportunity structure" was an emerging middle class with a specific internal differentiation and enough available economic and cultural capital (qualifications, taste, and morals) to be spent on "marking services". For instance, the "Italianness" of products (fashionable clothes and shoes, Vespa scooters, home design and decoration) epitomized everything trendy, chic, modern, cosmopolitan, and international. These were the products to have, and they were part of an emerging tendency to use material goods as a means of representation, thus turning everyday existence into a symbolic display of taste and social affiliation and accepting everyday surroundings as the terrain for cultural distinction.[24]

Following our theoretical reasoning, the new middle class consisted of the first Yugoslav generation shaped by the socialist modernization process and marked by, among other things, free access to education and full-time employment for most women. The various groups of this generation were, by their position, bound to individualization. Individualization is understood here in two ways. First, as an objective individualization in the sense of detraditionalization, i.e. cutting off traditional ties and traditional social and cultural bonds, becoming an individual in an open space of options and, consequently, being condemned to constitute herself/himself as an individual. Second, individualization also stands for the chance to become a person with a highly individualized identity.[25]

Consequently, as Bourdieu would say, the ethos of necessity and morality of self-sacrifice and duty began to be replaced by the ethos of desire and a morality of fun.[26] The concern for the "seeming" is constitutive of the middle classes, and the phenomenon of cultural meaning and cultural production became an important factor in a vertical classification. Clearly, shopping expeditions to Trieste depended as much on the political changes and open border with Italy as on the transformation of the concept of the self and of the good life. This backstage and only semi-legal consumer culture was the result of a new structure of feeling characterized by changed identities and commitments. Essential to this structure of feeling was the privatization of the notion of "the good life". As noted previously, needs are discursive positions that articulate and constitute the collectivity and the individual subject. Therefore, shopping expeditions to Trieste were not only the result of an emerging middle class in Yugoslavia, but also a practice that constituted the middle class – thus a "technology of the constitution of the self" – through the practices of consumption.

Dreamworld of Consumption

Shadow Economy and Patriarchal Order

It is impossible to understand the nature of formal organizations without investigating the networks of informal relations and unofficial norms and describing how informal, unofficial rules govern the daily operation of organizations or local subcultures. What are

Boys from suburbia and their Italian Vespa scooters.

the distinctive characteristics of shopping expeditions that defined them as part of the networks of informal relations and unofficial norms in socialism? Shopping expeditions were not part of everyday routine shopping experiences but were planned, aspired to and imagined long before the actual journey. A result of a "dictatorship over needs" in socialism was the formation of a new, semi-legal space in which the consumer first had to create access to opportunities for exchanging goods. This informal or backstage sphere of cultural and economic exchange included a whole range of practices, social relations, interactions, forms of communication in micro-situations, new forms and new spaces for asserting power and new forms of hierarchies. In order to take place at all, the shopping expeditions had to be part of clientelistic ties, of an informal network of reciprocal personal relations, and of a second or shadow economy that enabled the "good life"[27] and were, thus, a significant part of sociability in socialism. The exchange of goods and services in personalized relations was characteristic of Eastern European socialism in general. According to Lonkila, the network of informal relations, where people used their relatives, friends, acquaintances and colleagues at work to obtain the desired or needed products and services (such as favors or important information), was a significant aspect of sociability in socialism.[28] These backstage networks grew into a second society where the mediated and personalized forms of social life transformed replaceable social relationships into the personal and unique (instead of a doctor you had an acquaintance who was a doctor; instead of going to a bank in order to exchange your money into Italian liras, German marks or any other hard currency, your friend's colleague who had relatives abroad exchanged your money for foreign currency to earn some extra money, etc.). The gray economy and informalization of the economy, accompanied by a reciprocal exchange of favors, information and goods unavailable on the market, instrumentalization of sociability, clientelistic and patron-client relations – all these resulted in particularism and in a culture of privatism that were constituent parts of social integration in socialism. Or, as one female respondent, an office clerk and engineer's wife responsible for the reproduction of the reciprocity networks, said, it enabled her family to have a "good life":

You had to have somebody who could do the sewing, somebody who did the knitting, crocheting, somebody to buy
smuggled things from, somebody to buy hard currency,
then someone in the shop who was prepared to give you an
imported item "under the counter".

The reciprocity networks were semi-public spaces, the extensions of the domestic sphere. It is thus not surprising that establishing, reproducing and maintaining the reciprocity of networks
remained women's work in spite of the practically full employment
of women in many parts of Yugoslavia, and their concomitant economic independence. Against the backdrop of the domestic revolution and of changes in organizing family economies, where a major
shift from housework as production to housework as consumption
took place, women remained responsible for the family economy,
and shopping became an important aspect of housework (consuming as "doing for others"), reflecting a specifically feminine cultural competence through which a patriarchal order was expressed,
while masculine domination remained unquestioned.

This, of course, shouldn't surprise us, as most of the research on
consumer practices establishes the gendered nature of "shopping"
and the association between shopping and femininity. The female
character of shopping is an articulation of the symbolic cleavage
between production and consumption and the equation of men
with production and women with consumption in western societies.
Shopping, together with window-shopping, with just-looking and
browsing, is here, thus, a recreational practice possessing value
in itself. Our interviews confirm that women were much more
engaged and competent shoppers than men. Female respondents
regularly shopped in the company of other women, looked forward
to shopping trips, combined shopping expeditions to Trieste with
socializing, establishing and confirming social relationships and, in
general, used shopping expeditions as a means to other ends, not just
acquiring goods. For women shoppers, strolling around, usually in
the company of other women, and the pleasure of looking at objects
that are styled to be looked at, was a constituent part of "female"
shopping practice and had a key role in the shopping experience.

Only in the process of strolling around and looking at things can the experience of "longing" occur, which generates "wanting", as Campbell argues.[29]

Purchases for others, bringing items to those who could not come along, expressed a relationship between the shopper and a particular other (children, partner, or family in general). Schudson argues, that "… an enormous portion of total consumption, for necessities as well as for luxury items, must be understood as preeminently social in nature, not individualistic or crudely materialistic or connected to trends towards narcissism".[30] Miller also argues against the thesis of consumption as individual and individualized practice. Rather, the act of buying goods is mainly directed at two forms of "otherness": the first expresses a relationship between the shopper and a particular other, the second a relationship to a more general goal – which takes the form of the values to which people wish to dedicate themselves.[31] Numerous female interviewees were talking of buying for others, for loved ones.[32] Shopping is thus the construction of the other as a subject who desires something.[33] The purpose of shopping is not so much to purchase things that a person wants, but to establish a relationship with those who want things. Similarly, Švab, who investigates a later period of "shopping tourism" in the 1970s and the 1980s, understands shopping trips as both a practice aimed at the satisfaction of personal needs, and as a family event, in a sense that it was extended to a broader social network of family and friends.[34] Consumption in its essence was thus an expression of social relationships, not a private and atomized act. Like the creation and maintenance of reciprocal relationships, the practice of shopping was not gender-neutral, but rather linked to the feminine role in the household as the unit of consumption. The reminiscences of female informants were much more likely than those of males to make reference to anticipating the needs and desires of significant others:

> … I used to buy things for my mum, and for my dad, slippers for mum, warm ones for the winter; whenever I went there I bought something for one or the other, or for my sister … always looked for something I could get for them.

By contrast, male discourse on shopping, together with the things that they bought in Italy and regarded themselves as responsible for (electrical goods, home tools and do-it-yourself shopping in general), confirm the notion of masculinity.[35] Male respondents were inclined to see shopping as a peripheral activity and interpreted shopping trips to Italy as instrumental and as purchase-driven activities related to the satisfaction of supposedly basic needs for goods unavailable at home. Their shopping expeditions were justified by their role in acquiring "important" commodities, or satisfying "basic" needs (such as bicycles, bicycle spare tires unavailable at home, Vespas; later, spare parts for the family car, car tires; and important family purchases in the early 1960s, such as washing machines, radios and gramophones), instead of buying clothes.[36] The interviews thus reconstructed the ideology of shopping, which served to maintain a continuity between shopping and traditional concepts of masculinity and femininity. While men are more inclined to see shopping as rational, instrumental and purchase-driven, women are more likely to view it as a pleasure-seeking activity, where "a fundamentally aesthetic and expressive gratification is involved".[37] In the words of a male shopper, men went to Trieste to buy urgently needed items. Women, on the other hand, went to buy desired goods:

> I used to buy technical stuff, things you needed but couldn't get here, or things that were cheaper there – like a radio, bike, later on tires, tools, car parts; and women, you know, they were buying clothes and bric-à-brac. There was lots of it in Trieste.

The masculine practice of shopping was thus placed in the framework of work and was based on the rhetoric of needs, while the feminine practice of shopping was placed (by men) in the framework of entertainment, free time, and satisfaction of desires. Accordingly, interviews with men resembled more an attempt to make a factual reconstruction of shopping expeditions: male respondents were elaborating on price differences, changing laws for importing goods, lack of specific goods in different periods, or were telling stories about smuggling successes, that is to say, about their deftness in duping customs authorities. Interviews with women, on the other hand, were closer to life-stories and the "ego-expanding experience".[38] While female respondents were telling "their stories", male respondents tried more to reconstruct "the history". Women nostalgically linked their recollections of the desire for various goods and their strategies for acquiring them with their memories of youth, and yearning for the community and extra time for sociability in socialism:

> We did not have much but we still enjoyed ourselves.
> I'd say that it was better in those days – we had hard lives, but things meant more to us.
> I was young and so pretty and with that jacket and Italian shoes.
> It was not important if you were hungry or not, it was important that you had company, could sing together.

Nostalgia expressed by our female interviewees is less about socialism itself and more about "the unrealized dreams of the past and visions of the future that became obsolete".[39] Furthermore, contrary to men, women often tended to recall the sensual and aesthetic aspects of goods, that is, how desired objects felt and looked and what pleasures they extracted from them. Interviews with women were replete with stories about longing for material artifacts, about sensual and aesthetic pleasures, and emotional attachment to goods. In short, involvement and commitment to goods, or the "internalization of goods",[40] was much more explicit in women respondents:

> ... I bought myself a coat, a nice one, and a leather purse, beige, and shoes, and when I walked around people looked at me as if I were an oddball. Once, when I went to Ljubljana, I had a plastic purse, blue with red lines, and everybody was asking me "where did you buy it?" and "where did you get it?" In Italy, I said.

However, in spite of the gendered nature of shopping, because of the specific situation (extraordinary circumstances and the unavoidable encounter with authority and the foreign), the gendering of shopping in Trieste was less than in ordinary, routine shopping. On the one hand, the male role was, because of the spectacular and extraordinary nature of shopping trips to Trieste, more important than in routine shopping trips: men were important as drivers, protectors, escorts, money-changers and mediators in relations with border authorities, and in this way participated in shopping while still maintaining their traditional role. The following is a recollection of one woman shopper of her husband's behavior in Trieste:

> He [the husband] ... simply sat in the car while I was running around to get goods for the whole family. He took a walk, and would not even buy his own shoes. Once the shoes I bought for him were a little small, but he kept them anyway ...

On the other hand, women were also compelled to remake the practice of shopping as a free-time activity, which implies not just the act of buying but includes, as stated above, also browsing, window-shopping, and daydreaming. That is, it was transformed from an expressive and aesthetic pleasure to a pragmatic activity: the purchase of everything unavailable back at home or buying until the money ran out. But clearly, women's responsibility for the family economy and shopping, despite changes, remained important. Despite the revolution in the private sphere, the dominant male position was unaffected: as with cooking and household chores, shopping also now took on the form of work "for others" and through this specifically female cultural competence the patriarchal order was expressed and reproduced.

Crossing the Border: Surveillance and Domination through Communication
Shopping trips were composed of a whole range of communicative interactions in which positions of superiority and subordination, power and powerlessness, class and ethnic differences, were established – the interactional order of reciprocal relations in the gray market of money and goods, communication at the border, interaction in Italian shops, the symbolic meaning of "western" artifacts, and so on. Crossing the border was one of the most

important micro-situations of the shopping trip. The power relations were not only expressed through interactional patterns at the border crossings, but communicatively produced by the subjects involved in communication at the border. In Foucault's terms, crossing the border was a disciplinary practice through which the reality of power relations was produced and not just exercised. Buying foreign currency on the black market, smuggling money to Italy, queueing for a few hours to cross the border, smuggling goods back home, communication with the border officer ... in short, the interactive order of the institution "crossing the border" was the most significant part of the entire expedition. Restrictions on exporting money and importing goods were extremely unrealistic, and customs regulations changed frequently enough for the majority of informants to emphasize their unpredictability. While smuggling money into Italy and goods back to Yugoslavia violated the law in both directions, it was, nevertheless, an important part of the expedition. On the other hand, however, "everything was allowed which was not explicitly prohibited".[41] In practice, official and formal rules were in such contradiction to the informal behavior that they did not operate at all. The roots of the informal system were therefore embedded in the formal organization itself and nurtured by the formality of its arrangements. The lack of predictability, the absence of positive rules or of the non-enforcement of formal rules and the arbitrariness of customs officials regarding law enforcement all contributed to the individualization of power (good vs. bad customs officials, informal conduct reserved for officers), to the feeling of uncertainty and risk taking, and to the internalization of restraint.[42] As citizens were treated as suspicious and guilty in advance, they were constantly under surveillance. The high degree of unpredictability meant that anybody could be defined as a criminal at any time and the arbitrariness of authority became the central principle of the exercise of power, as the stories of good and bad border officers or memories of "how lucky I was", "how I managed to outfox the authorities", or "how I got nabbed", testify:

At times customs officials were insolent, they wanted to see everything, and at other times they just let us go, it was a matter of luck. One woman was telling us that she bought God knows how many sweaters and put on all of them to

hide them from the customs official. He searched all her
bags and then asked her if she was too warm, and smiled.
A lady from our neighborhood bought a blanket with those
tassels, and she fixed it under her skirt but the tassels dan-
gled from underneath her skirt so the official told her that
she should cut them off. And that was all he told her.
Usually they asked if we had something to declare and we
said "nothing". Everybody said "nothing". I thought it was
so funny, how could you say "nothing" if you knew you
had things to declare. But if they didn't ask directly, like
"what is this?", we kept silent. Or, we said, yes, we have
bought some trifle, like souvenirs. If the custom official was
good, he said "OK", and we went through. And then we
laughed.

The narrative reconstructions of the communication between
the border officers and the informants/shoppers, who were always
also smugglers, are among the most emotional topics of the interviews. They are also the most interesting from the point of view
of how power was exercised through communication and performance in the process of border crossing. Memories of the respondents demonstrate that the arbitrariness of the customs officers
or policemen and their individualized power were central for the
shopping expedition. The antagonistic opposition between the official and unofficial sphere, and private and public language, as the
most important structural element of the societies of "really existing socialism", defined the interactional order/practices in public.
An important aspect of interaction was the lack of civility of customs officials and policemen to citizens/shoppers. The lack of civility refers to the absence of "civil indifference" that "treats others
as if they were strangers and creates social ties on the basis of this
social distance".[43] A well-traveled woman in her 60s is still haunted
by her memories of crossing the border and her feelings of powerlessness:

I still tremble when I cross the border even if I have nothing
to declare. I still feel like a criminal who has something to
hide.

Interviews hence lead to a conclusion that the experience of arbitrary power and the experience of one's own powerlessness when crossing the state borders can be interpreted as a minor collective trauma. However, these events are not inherently traumatic. According to Alexander, for traumas to emerge at the level of collectivity, individual memory has to be objectified through the representational process and thereby transformed into a collective one.[44] Among generations of Yugoslav shoppers, trauma remains in a latent stage as a personal memory and commonality of experience of "victims" and as a somatization/embodiment of relations of domination and of the experience of arbitrary power.

Strategy of the State and Tactics of the Citizens

The arbitrariness of the power of customs officials reported by our respondents was just an articulation of the absence of power among shoppers and resulted in the development of various informal tactics in the process of adjusting to the unpredictability of customs officials. These tactics included the way one should walk and talk to customs officials in order not to provoke them, how to talk and behave at the border in order to be let through without paying customs duties, where to hide money and goods, or how to pack or wear purchases. These tactics found their expression in an oral culture of gossiping about good and bad border crossings, good and bad customs officers, recommended tactics of smuggling, or proper behavior at border crossings. Oral culture was at the heart of the institution of shopping expeditions as seasonal potlatches. Many respondents, both female and male, happily recollected their many smuggling tactics and recounted how they deceived customs officials:

> In cigarette boxes, we opened them, then glued them back. Then in shoes, heels. We also ripped coats and stitched it inside. Then in shoe heels, I even took my shoes to the shoe maker to make a hole in the heel so I put money in it ... I have to admit that we smuggled as many things as we could ... And if we went by car we hid money in the back light.
> ... on the train we put clothes on and put things around and pretended they were not ours. And if they asked whose bag it was, we were silent.

All sorts of things, in the wallet, underneath the lining …
As I said, I was never searched like that. But you were always scared because you saw them searching others. If they
found money, they took all of it, they left nothing. They
even, there was this man from the south, he wore a belt
and stuffed money inside. Everybody used tricks. They had
those brushes with handles, hollow, and money inside. And
he came, pulled out that handle and took it out. They even
put money into bread.

De Certeau's distinction between "strategies" and "tactics"[45] is
useful for the conceptualization of the phenomenon of communicative construction of power when shoppers were crossing the state
border into Italy. According to de Certeau, strategy as the manipulation of power relationships becomes possible when a subject of
power (in our case a state power operating at border crossings) can
be isolated from the "environment" and has a place of its own and
can therefore determine the relationship with the outside Other
(citizens-shoppers). Strategy is thus a function of space, while tactic, by contrast, is determined by the absence of a place of its own:
"The space of a tactic is the space of the other" and "within the enemy's field of vision".[46] A panoptic practice is enabled by the division of space: foreign forces (shoppers) can be transformed into objects that can be observed and measured, and thus controlled. The
architectural construction of border crossings between Yugoslavia
and Italy enabled the panoptic practice: border crossings were built
to enable the visual surveillance of long lines of shoppers waiting
for hours to cross the border to Italy. The smuggling tactics of citizens-shoppers and the trickery concerning communication with
the border officials (from body posture to speech utterance) therefore operated on the imposed territory that belonged to the other
– to the state and border officials as its representatives. They were
determined by the absence of the power of the shoppers.

By operating within the framework defined by the state, the
expeditions to Italy and tactical practices of shoppers-smugglers
were actually contributing to the system rather than subverting it.
They were, as de Certeau would put it, "a certain game with the
system of defined space" […], "a maneuver within the enemy's

field of vision […] and within enemy territory".[47] Because the tactic does not have an autonomous place of its own, it depends on time – it always tries to turn the events into opportunities that must be seized. According to de Certeau, the tactic takes advantage of "opportunities and operates in isolated actions, blow by blow". As a consequence, the tactic can never keep what it wins. The shoppers simply made use of cracks opened by particular conjunctions in the surveillance of proprietary powers. Although the art of the weak, and determined by the absence of power, the tactics were practices which the strategy of the authorities had not been able to domesticate. They were, however, not in opposition to the system. The value of a tactic is symbolic: it demonstrates that strategic surveillance and power can never be complete.

In Trieste: Work and Pleasure

Although shopping trips share some common formal characteristics with tourism as an experience and as a cultural and social phenomenon (the anticipation that is constructed and sustained before the departure, the notion of "departure", and a scopic regime characteristic of tourism[48]), they are not to be interpreted as a tourist cultural practice.

Shoppers are hiding goods bought in Italy before crossing the border back into Yugoslavia.

Wessely defines the shopping tourism of former socialist Eastern European countries as "travel abroad with the explicit aim to buy goods, unavailable, difficult to find, or inordinately costly in one's home country, for personal use or reselling to compatriots".[49] But in the case of Yugoslav expeditions to Trieste, the term "shopping tourism" seems inappropriate, since the analysis of formal characteristics of the practice shows that they in fact had nothing to do with tourism as a distinct cultural form.[50] Shopping was not mainly a recreational practice as with tourist shoppers, who have a dual orientation, gazing both at the urban setting and at the goods on display in shops.[51] Typically, the Yugoslav shoppers in Trieste were under time pressure, and the shopping expedition was thus experienced as calculated work, which involved discipline and control to stroll past goods on display, not hedonistic strolling, browsing and shopping. There were very few flaneurs, city dwellers, browsers, or simply tourists among Yugoslav shoppers. When respondents were asked whether they ever went to Trieste as tourists or whether they ever visited tourist sites, only one respondent could recollect a visit to the Miramar Castle near Trieste, and even that was accidental – the family went to Trieste on the day of an Italian national holiday when all shops were closed, so shoppers could do nothing but become tourists. Moreover, shopping was as a rule integrated into business trips or even into tourist trips organized for workers by trade unions. Trieste was not perceived as a Mediterranean city worthy of a tourist's gaze, but rather a site of spectacular images of material artifacts in shop windows and well-dressed people in the streets. It was a series of images of "the good life" and a source of visual fascination, and the shoppers were the audience that was moving among spectacular images and establishing their own paths in the city, their own spatial narratives. The shopping, in fact, included visual pleasures and was, in this respect, closer to the viewing of pictures in a gallery than to buying. The mere act of buying should be understood in the context of the process of shopping, browsing, touching, window shopping, further, in the context of the experience of shopping as cultural practice and, lastly, within the broader context of the urban experience that includes the visual dimension of shopping. However, time limitations and the necessity of obtaining wanted or needed goods in Trieste required the capacity to manage swings between intense involvement and more

distanced, aesthetic detachment. Even when Italian shops closed
for lunch (between 1 pm and 4 pm) and shopping had to stop, Yugoslavs did not go for lunch and rarely went for a coffee, but engaged in window shopping to plan their afternoon purchases.

> Never in those 20 years did we eat there, or drink, never. It
> was a terrible waste of money. We had food with us [...] that
> was, for example, three pairs of stockings less.
> We always carried food with us, of course. Italians didn't
> like us much because of that, because we always ate there
> in secret.

Despite the fact that these expeditions included a ludic aspect,
a purchase had a central role for shoppers coming to Trieste. The
ludic, sensual aspect of the trip had to be integrated into the purchase-driven activity and within the instrumentalism of work. The
movement of shoppers was goal-directed. They were moving faster
than tourist-shoppers, and were, typically, almost running around
the town. Many informants remember that all available money had
to be spent prior to their return, which transformed the pleasure of
shopping and strolling around town into real work and/or into destructive consumption and excessive expenditure at the same time.
According to shoppers of both genders, many times it barely mat-
tered what was purchased as long as the money was spent:

> Sometimes we didn't know what to buy but we had to go
> – we had 5000 lira to spend but we rushed around the town
> for so long that we spent those liras without looking for
> something specific, because we didn't get a chance to decide
> what we actually needed, we just looked at things, at what
> they had, weighing what could be a good buy. Later on [...]
> I bought a ball.
> It was better to buy something, whatever, than nothing [...]
> because that was it for the next six months.
> I always took care to spend all the money. Sometimes, if we
> couldn't find things we wanted to have, we spent money on
> ice cream, chewing gums and matches that had flames in
> various colors.
> ... others finished their shopping, but I couldn't decide. Will
> you take the money back home?

As these recollections show, the expeditions to Trieste brought to extremes the contradictory relationship between the practice of spending and the experience of saving, on which consumption is based. According to Miller, even for the wealthy, the most important shopping experience is the experience of saving, where the value of commodity bought becomes not what it costs but what it saved. Thrift is, according to him, instrumental in creating a sense of future purpose that justifies present deferments.[52] The practice of shopping itself, thus, means spending, but shopping as experience means saving. The experience of saving has, of course, nothing to do with real saving. However, the shopping expeditions to Trieste were outside the boundaries of everyday social life and were the transgression of the ordinary, everyday, and routine shopping. Shopping became de-contextualized from social life, and the shopper engaged in self-indulgence, for only immediate gratification could have replaced the absence of the future purpose that justifies deferment and saving as an inherent part of the shopping experience.[53]

Clearly, shopping in Trieste was a highly contradictory practice: expeditions were generally labor-intensive activities executed

His first Fiat ("fičo").

under the constraint of necessity and social control. But although all kinds of constraints abounded (time constraints, lower status of Yugoslavs, small amount of money to spend), the expeditions were also part of a culture of semi-legal hedonism, indulgence, and temporary freedom from restraints of the identities and everyday life in socialism. Expeditions were therefore directed at the pragmatics of provisioning, but also at dreaming in a space where the objects of desire reminded consumers who they wished to be and how they wished to live, and enabled them to fantasize about themselves as someone else:

> There were Lambretta motorbikes, Vespa motorbikes, young men from rich families already had cars, and our young women in the first place found that alluring, but so did we, men, we were watching them, observing things.
>
> We put money aside all throughout the year, because you could not get anything in Ljubljana. I remember that you had to pay 5600 dinars for shoes, and my salary was 3000 dinars. So Trieste was like sunshine.
>
> They had nice textiles. [...] Shoes, everything was nicer down there.
>
> The first experience – we were highly curious, that was in the year '56 [...] Well, shops were packed with things while here you couldn't get anything; motor vehicles were all the rage at that time, you could see motorbikes of all sorts, nice motorbikes, so we felt like we arrived at some other place, different from here, like we were in a rich country, even though we were their first neighbors.
>
> Vespas came out in 1956 and came to Ljubljana around 1960. At that time the "hochstaplers" ("cool people") in Ljubljana already had Vespas. [...] and slippers, made of felt uppers and rubber soles, winter ones with a zipper. If you didn't have a pair, you weren't civilized, you had to have a pair of slippers like that.

Two "Hochstaplers" and their Vespa scooter smuggled from Italy in 1961.

Young woman posing on her Italian Vespa.

As a ludic social form, shopping is closely associated with modern urban subjectivity and with fantasizing about "being as someone else".[54] This inner world only constitutes shopping as daydreaming and the state "to be here for oneself" in an "as if" situation.[55] Sociability itself as offered by shopping thus contributes to the illusion that one can choose within the crowd any self that one wishes. Thus the feeling of well-being and the excitement which arises from the potential elimination of boundaries to the self are of fundamental importance, such that at the core of this ideal shopping experience is the feeling of freedom and erasing of limits that everyday life places on the self. The act of buying the necessities unavailable at home and to fulfill one's desires was just the tip of a much deeper experience of shopping as a cultural practice. Just observing the merchandise on display, being with things, the experience of a visually relatively glamorous city and its inhabitants compared to conditions under socialism, becoming familiar with the goods, the acquisition of the necessary cultural capital and skills of discrimination, planning, dreaming, imagining oneself as someone else, establishing an emotional relationship towards the merchandise and relationships with others through merchandise, the freedom of choice and from the restraints of the "dictatorship over needs" ... all this was part of the Trieste cultural practice of shopping.

Ethnicity, Shame and Cultural Hegemony of the West

The expeditions made visible what was normally hidden and officially repressed. According to our interviews, ethnic differentiation (Slovenes vs. "southerners") was a constitutive part of the cultural practice of shopping in Trieste. For instance, the close proximity of ethnicities (Slovenes, Serbians, Bosnians, Kosovo Albanians, etc.), otherwise rarely in contact with each other, made ethnic and/or class differences visible. Hierarchical categories regarding an understanding of self (Slovenes) and others ("southerners"), civilized and less civilized, were regularly expressed by Slovene informants. The question of ethnicity intruded into the interviews mainly indirectly, when respondents spoke of the arbitrary power of the centralized state represented by the border officers "from the south", or more directly, when they spoke of "those from the south who were buying for the black market" or those shoppers from the south "who were badly dressed and behaved improperly".

> I am surprised that I never caught it in the neck. I never did, every time I managed to convince them. You know, customs officials were from the south.
> We were scared because you never knew what was going to happen. There were many people from the south, but no Slovenes.
> Yes, customs officials from the south were stricter. Stricter, sometimes unfriendly, like they wanted to show you that they were the authority.
> We, Slovenes, we did not go there like they did, the Yugoslavs. The whole families [of Yugoslavs] went there, and they ... each with two to three bags, they went to buy, I don't know what, chewing gum. So you went to Trieste and you could see them, they were all around the town, especially in the center. These brothers of ours, who sat around with their bags.

Furthermore, many informants reported experiencing feelings of shame and embarrassment that arose from discrepancies in dress between Slovenes/Yugoslavs on the one hand, and Italians on the other. Indeed, the definitional threshold for what is old and worn out was inevitably higher in socialist Yugoslavia than in Italy. The shame was articulated partly through the ambition of Slovenes to set themselves apart from "southerners", who joined the shopping expeditions at the end of the 1960s and who looked even poorer than Slovene shoppers. The "more civilized" were ashamed of the "less civilized".

> We were ashamed because we looked so miserable. At that time, at the end of the 1950s, Italians were already wearing casual clothes, khaki pants and polo shirts, but we still dressed in heavy woolen tailor-made suits and wore ties. We put on our best clothes when we went there, but it was obvious straightaway that we were Yugoslavs.
> When you got to the other side you saw a different life, different people, a different language. People there were

well-groomed, their faces always looked so rested and happy, while we were glum and worn out by work ...
At that time we had enough to go to a coffee shop, there was a coffeehouse north of Ponte Rosso, so we could afford a coke or a cup of coffee. But those from the south sprawled on the grass and took out those ... and ate.

Characteristic of the experience of shame mentioned by many interviewees is that it had little to do with the nature of the situation, or even with the characteristics of the person feeling it, but rather arose from the socially dominant classification and was intensified, actualized and embodied in the individual situation and self-perception: shame is always present where difference is converted into hierarchy. Social shame comes from the acceptance of the criteria of the Other and the application of these criteria to oneself. In this sense, it is the result of the western orientalization of easterners. As adjustment to the norms of the Other (subjectification) and internalization of these norms (i.e. self-disciplining), shame emanates from

Tradition and modernity: From Vojvodina to Trieste in 1960's.

the cultural hegemony of the West, and is a source of symbolic surveillance and domination. The source of shame is therefore social,
the experience of shame, however, is subjective and embodied.[56]
The dependence on the evaluation of the Others is of constitutive
importance for the identity of the "easterners" and produces a specific subjectivity. Shopping in Italy became, thus, a permanent state
of bodily insecurity and symbolic dependence for many Slovene/
Yugoslav shoppers, who existed through western eyes. They anticipated an evaluation by the western Other and were condemned to
the judgmental gaze of the Other, which constituted them as poor
Slovenes/Yugoslavs.

Conclusion

The phenomenon of shopping expeditions to Trieste, which was
triggered by the shortage of goods under state socialism in the 1950s,
extended well beyond the satisfaction of needs. From a political perspective, shopping expeditions might be interpreted as containing
an element of control. In this sense, they served to strengthen and
legitimize the regime by offering freedom to travel and to consume
that was otherwise denied by the political project of state socialism
and its economic policy. Consumption was experienced as a domain of choice and as the evidence of personal autonomy also by
those who could not participate in seasonal shopping trips to Italy.
The politics of open borders can therefore be seen as a liberal tactic of localized subversion, or, in Barthes's words, "inoculation"[57]
against a small evil to protect the larger system from a more gen-
eralized subversion. Yet, the political perspective still says nothing
about the meaning of the shopping expeditions and their cultural
and social implications. Using "thick description"[58], the expedition
is explained as consisting of different micro-situations (interactions
at the border crossing, interactions in Italian shops, smuggling situations, etc.) that have meaning only in the context of the entire expedition and that are shaped by the basic institutional parameters
of the social system in which they were implicated.

Clearly, the principle of research at the micro level is the belief that microscopic observation will reveal aspects of the cultural
form that were previously hidden and invisible to the analytic gaze,

and, possibly, even reveal the essential structural dimensions of the society. Although we should not forget that a micro-phenomenon is never a simple microcosmic model for the national society and its ethnic, power, gender, and other relations and, vice-versa, that structural properties of society are not simple articulation of inter-action in micro contexts, we believe that shopping expeditions are more than simply comments on themselves. Therefore, the point of departure for this analysis was the question of what, if anything, these shopping expeditions were typical, i.e. the question of gener-alizability and the relation of this anomalous mundane culture of shopping to the social context. In brief, throughout our deconstruc-tion of the meaning of cross-border shopping, we sought to explain the macro-cultural location of the shopping trip.

There was a dual relationship between this specific shopping micro-situation and the social context. On the one hand, the macro-social context (i.e. the political, social and economic modernization of socialistYugoslavia in the 1950s), briefly explained in the first part of the article, imputes meaning to the anomalous and seem-ingly insignificant practice of shopping expeditions by revealing its significance and, consequently, showing how it was tied in with the system. On the other, the analysis of the meaning of shopping expeditions revealed the hidden incoherence of the social system, and the individual's negotiation and manipulation in the face of normative reality. On the most general level, the study of shop-ping expeditions as a cultural form can help us explore the close entanglement of materiality and sociality, and contribute to the un-derstanding of the politics of consumption under state socialism. The shopping expeditions in fact articulated a whole set of social relationships within which this periodic potlatch was taking place: the lack of civility, informalization of the economy and the result-ing instrumentalization of sociability in socialism, privatization of the notion of "the good life", the dichotomous antagonism between private and public spheres of life as a structural feature of a society, specificities of a symbolic framing of material objects and the mate-rial framing of social relations, etc. Last but not least, they revealed the institutionalized patterns of patriarchal gender relations, ethnic relations, and the hegemony of the West.

Acquiring consumer goods in socialism became politicized because it was a way of constituting selfhood against the dominant definitions of socialist subjectivity and collectivity and the corresponding definition of human needs. However, the acquisition of goods was politicized in yet another way: mass shopping trips across the border to Italy were indeed not against the law, but the regime at the border crossings did imply a moral condemnation of "capitalist materialism". The condemnation was manifest in unrealistic customs regulations, arbitrary treatment of shoppers by customs officials and their lack of civility, and in occasional but fairly regular politically driven tightening of border policies that were invariably unannounced and unpredictable. Another aspect of politicizing consumption was connected with the relation of the East to the West as expressed through shopping expeditions. As argued previously, basic needs can be defined not as those that sustain us as physical beings, but as those needs that are necessary conditions for our cultural participation. Eastern Europe or the European Orient was invented as an intellectual project of demi-orientalization.[59] Europe behind the Iron Curtain and beyond western civilization was Europe's periphery, excluded from the shared narrative of the capitalist "core", and, according to Wolff, occupying "an ambiguous space between inclusion and exclusion, both in economic affairs and cultural recognition".[60] Hence there was a lack of narratives through which the Yugoslavs could see and imagine themselves positively as Yugoslavs and Eastern Europeans. Being "outside" of the central narratives of European society and culture was a crucial dimension of inequality. We would like to suggest that shopping in capitalist Italy and acquiring western goods and knowledge about goods is to be understood as an attempt and a struggle to become part of western consumer culture and its practical and expressive order, from which Eastern Europe was excluded. The semi-oriental position of "those Eastern States of Europe" in relation to the civilized West was deeply implicated in even the most mundane and limited micro-situation of the shopping trip to Trieste.

Notes

[1] A version of this article was published in Journal of Consumer Culture Vol. 6, Nr. 2, 2006 under the title "Remembering Socialism. On desire, consumption and surveillance", 229–259. I am grateful to the Sage Publications for their permission to reprint the article.

[2] Actions that violate certain norms, but do so routinely. On the microhistorical study of "normal exceptions" see David A. Bell, "Total History and Microhistory: The French and Italian Paradigms," in *A Companion to Western Historical Thought*, ed. Lloyd Kramer and Sarah Maza (Oxford: Blackwell, 2002), 262–76.

[3] The border between Italy and Yugoslavia, hermetically sealed after the Second World War, was partially opened for crossings in 1955. The border opened more widely in 1967 when visas were abolished (Jože Pirjevec, *Jugoslavija 1918–1992 [Yugoslavia 1918–1992]* (Koper: Lipa, 1995), 255). More on crossing the border in Vida Zei and Breda Luthar, "Shopping across the Border" (paper presented at the "Everyday Socialism: States and Social Transformation in Eastern Europe 1945–1965" conference, The Open University Conference Centre, London, April 24–26, 2003).

[4] The number of Italian motor vehicles that crossed the border between Italy and Yugoslavia had also increased from 42,995 in 1959 to 138,700 in 1963 (see Statistical Office of the Socialist Republic of Slovenia, *Statistical Yearbook of the Socialist Republic of Slovenia* (Ljubljana: Statistični urad SR Slovenije, 1964), 260.

[5] James C. Scott, *Domination and the Arts of Resistance – Hidden Transcripts* (New Haven, CT: Yale University Press, 1990).

[6] Interviewing was carried out in two stages: 20 pilot interviews in 2001 were followed by the redefinition of the concepts and a further 26 interviews were conducted between 2003 and 2005. Somewhere at this point it also became obvious that the collection of new empirical data fitted into the existing conceptual framework and that new interviews were only variations on the existing themes that supported our conceptualizations. In analyzing the transcripts, we tried to move continuously from data to theory and back again. On the one hand, we were looking for material in the interview transcriptions that had a bearing on the concepts being initially developed. On the other, however, we tried to redefine the theoretical concepts by cross-checking the empirical material.

[7] Giovanni Levy, "On Microhistory," in *New Perspectives on Historical Writing*, ed. Peter Burke (Cambridge: Polity Press, 1991), 96.

[8] Igor Kopytoff, "The Cultural Biography of Things: Commoditization as Process," in *The Social Life of Things*, ed. Arjun Appadurai (Cambridge: Cambridge University Press, 1986), 64–91.

⁹ Christopher J. Berry, *The Idea of Luxury: A Conceptual and Historical Investigation* (Cambridge: Cambridge University Press, 1994), 199.

¹⁰ Ferenc Feher, Agnes Heller and Gyorgy Markus, *Dictatorship over Needs* (New York: St. Martin's Press, 1983), 89.

¹¹ See, for example, Mary Douglas and Baron Isherwood, *The World of Goods: Towards an Anthropology of Consumption* (London: Routledge, 1996[1979]); Daniel Miller, *Material Culture and Mass Consumption* (Oxford: Blackwell, 1987); Don Slater, *Consumer Culture and Modernity* (Cambridge: Polity Press, 1997a).

¹² Len Doyal and Ian Gough, *The Theory of Human Need* (London: Macmillian, 1991), 18.

¹³ See Foucault in Paul Rabinow, ed., *The Foucault Reader* (New York: Penguin, 1984), 369.

¹⁴ Rom Harré, "Material Objects in Social Worlds," *Theory, Culture & Society* 19 (5/6) (2002): 32.

¹⁵ Or, as Slater argues: "'Real needs' are rather the way in which particular real people and communities formulate their values, identities, commitments in terms of what they 'need' in order to live a kind of life they deem good." (Don Slater, "Consumer Culture and the Politics of Need," in *Buy This Book. Studies in Advertising and Consumption*, ed. Mica Nava et al. (London: Routledge, 1997b), 57.)

¹⁶ Mary Douglas and Baron Isherwood, ibid., 1996[1979].

¹⁷ Arjun Appadurai, ed., *The Social Life of Things* (Cambridge: Cambridge University Press, 1986), 38.

¹⁸ Economic growth between 1953 and 1964 was 12.7 percent (Michael C. Kaser, *The Economic History of Eastern Europe (1919–1975)* (Oxford: Clarendon Press, 1986), 38). The net personal income (wages) per worker rose 6.2 per cent per year (Harold Lydall, *Yugoslav Socialism. Theory and Practice* (Oxford: Clarendon Press, 1984), 74). The standard of living was lower in Yugoslavia during 1950–3 than anywhere else in Eastern Europe with the exception of Albania. The pre-war average level of consumption per capita was regained in 1954.

¹⁹ Susan E. Reid and David Crowley, eds., *Style and Socialism* (Oxford: Berg, 2000), 3.

²⁰ "Really existing socialism" is a term used by the so called Soviet-style societies themselves, in order to express the transitional reality of the existing system and distinguish it from the communism that was the ultimate goal.

²¹ See Michael C. Kaser, ibid., 1986, 46, Table 24.2. These are index numbers of per capita consumption. In general, consumption increased as a share of national income, and in absolute terms in all Eastern European countries at the time.

[22] Raymond Williams, *The Long Revolution* (London: The Hogarth Press, 1992).

[23] Klaus Eder, *The New Politics of Class* (London: Sage, 1993), 76. Consequently, as argued by Klaus Eder (ibid., 1993, 90), in order to modernize the concept of class we have to take into account the increasing relevance of culture for the objective as well as the subjective side of class. In state socialism, particularly, the discontinuity of the reproduction of economic elites and the radical reduction of the private sector economy led to the central importance of cultural and social capital in class differentiation.

[24] It should be noted, however, that Yugoslav middle-class youth's perception of Italy was just part of a more general mythology of good Italian taste and a shared predilection for Italian culture by the younger generation of Europe in the 1950s and 1960s. In Britain, Vespa scooters became an identity marker for the "Mods" subculture in 1958–9. On Italianicity of the British youth culture of the late 1950s, see Dick Hebdige, *Hiding in the Light: On Images and Things* (London: Routledge, 1988). Contrary to British Vespa owners or Mods, who were predominantly from working-class or lower middle-class backgrounds, in Yugoslavia, Vespa owners were older (according to eye-witness reports from 25 to 35 years of age) and well-educated urban youth.

[25] See Klaus Eder, ibid., 1993, 90.

[26] Pierre Bourdieu, *Distinction: A Social Critique of the Judgement of Taste* (London: Routledge, 2000), 367.

[27] Klaus Eder, ibid., 1993, 181.

[28] Markku Lonkila, "Informal Exchange Relations in Post-Soviet Russia: A Comparative Perspective," *Sociological Research Online* 2(2) (1997), http://www.socresonline.org.uk/socresonline/2/2/9.html (accessed January 2006).

[29] Colin Campbell, "Shopping, Pleasure and the Sex War," in *The Shopping Experience,* ed. Pasi Falk and Colin Campbell (London: Sage, 1997), 170.

[30] Michael Schudson, *Advertising, the Uneasy Persuasion* (London: Routledge, 1984), 141.

[31] Daniel Miller, ibid., 1987, 12.

[32] Miller convincingly links modern consumption and the ritual of sacrifice in traditional societies, and argues that the connection between shopping and capitalism is more indirect than suggested by the more simplistic theory of "the consumer society". See Daniel Miller, *A Theory of Shopping* (Cambridge: Polity Press, 1998).

[33] See Daniel Miller, ibid., 1998, 148.

[34] Alenka Švab, "Consuming Western Images of Well-Being – Shopping Tourism in Socialist Slovenia," *Cultural Studies* 16(1) (2002): 67.

[35] See Colin Campbell, ibid., 1997; Peter K. Lunt and Sonia M. Livingstone, *Mass Consumption and Personal Identity* (Buckingham: Open University Press, 1992).

[36] According to data from the federal customs administration, during the first 9 months of 1966, 22,500 washing machines, 13,000 cars, 8000 sewing machines, 1900 televisions and 2000 tape recorders were imported into Yugoslavia ("Redne Dajatve pri Zasebnem Uvozu Gospodinjskih Strojev [Regular Import Duties for Personal Household Appliences]," *Delo*, December 31, 1966, 14.) This of course refers only to goods on which customs were paid.

[37] Colin Campbell, ibid., 1997, 170.

[38] See Sharon Zukin, *Beyond Marx and Tito: Theory and Practice of Yugoslav Socialism* (London, New York: Cambridge University Press, 1975), 276.

[39] Svetlana Boym, *The Future of Nostalgia* (New York: Basic Books, 2001), xvi.

[40] Kaj Ilmonen, "The Use and Commitment to Goods," *Journal of Consumer Culture* 4(1) (2004): 27–50.

[41] Stark in Barbara Misztal, *Informality* (London: Routledge, 2000), 207.

[42] Žižek defines totalitarianism as a system without positive and universally valid rules; anything we do may be defined at any time as illegal or prohibited. The law exists, but it is completely arbitrary: we can at any moment become a criminal who violates the unknown law. See Slavoj Žižek, *Jezik, Ideologija, Slovenci [Language, Ideology, Slovenes]* (Ljubljana: Delavska enotnost, 1987), 218. More recently, he argued that "… the moment one accepts the notion of 'totalitarianism', one is firmly located within the liberal-democratic horizon" (Slavoj Žižek, *Did Somebody Say Totalitarianism?* (London: Verso, 2001), 3).

[43] Civility has in English etymological roots in city and civilization. According to Sennett, it has to do with protecting oneself against unknown others while maintaining the illusion of community and shared experience. See Richard Sennett, *Nestanak Javnog Čovjeka [The Fall of Public Man]* (Zagreb: Naprijed, 1989), 350. On the problem of sociability and social integration typical for socialism, see the excellent book by Barbara Misztal, ibid., 2000. On civil inattention and civil indifference see Erving Goffman, *Relations in Public: Micro Studies of the Public Order* (London: Penguin, 1971) and Anthony Giddens, *Modernity and Identity* (Stanford, CA: Stanford University Press, 1991), 46–7.

[44] Jeffrey C. Alexander, "Toward a Theory of Cultural Trauma," in *Cultural Trauma and Collective Identity*, ed. Jeffrey C. Alexander et al. (Berkeley, CA: University of California Press, 2004), 1–30.

[45] Michel de Certeau, *The Practice of Everyday Life* (Berkeley, CA: University of California Press, 1984), xix.

[46] Michel de Certeau, ibid., 1984, 37.

[47] Michel de Certeau, ibid., 1984, 36–7.

[48] See John Urry, *The Tourist Gaze* (London: Sage, 1990).

[49] Anna Wessely, "Travelling People, Travelling Objects," *Cultural Studies* 16(1) (2002): 3.

[50] Lehtonen and Mäenpää, who write on shopping trips to shopping malls, propose the term "trippism" rather than tourism. The latter is actually derived from the verb "to tour", which etymologically means traveling around from place to place or a long journey. Turo-Kimmo Lehtonen and Pasi Mäenpää, "Shopping in East Centre Mall," in *The Shopping Experience,* ed. Pasi Falk and Colin Campbell (London: Sage, 1997), 148.

[51] See John Urry, ibid., 1990.

[52] Daniel Miller, ibid., 1998, 104.

[53] See Daniel Miller, ibid., 1998.

[54] Turo-Kimmo Lehtonen and Pasi Mäenpää, ibid., 1997, 160.

[55] Colin Campbell, *The Romantic Ethic and the Spirit of Modern Consumerism* (Oxford: Blackwell, 1987), 198.

[56] See Sighard Neckel, *Status und Scham: Zur Symbolischen Reproduktion Sozialer Ungleichheit [Status and Shame: Toward a Symbolic Reproduction of Social Inequality]* (Frankfurt: Campus Verlag, 1991).

[57] Roland Barthes, *Mythologies* (London: Paladin, 1983), 150.

[58] Clifford Geertz, *The Interpretation of Cultures* (New York: Basic Books, 1973), 3–30.

[59] See Larry Wolff, *Inventing Eastern Europe* (Stanford, CA: Stanford University Press, 1994).

[60] Larry Wolff, ibid., 1994, 9.

14

Cooking in Socialist Slovenia
Housewives on the Road from a Bright Future to an Idyllic Past

Blanka Tivadar and Andreja Vezovnik

Milk and Bread Don't Go Together

Food is imbued with numerous symbolic meanings and plays a number of social functions in everyday life. It can be used to express social differentiation – food practices can distinguish between social classes, some foods may carry a distinctively masculine or feminine charge, marking boundaries between ethnicities, or life-cycle stages.[1,2] While food has the power to separate people, it can also bind them together. The most frequently reported social function of food is the construction and reproduction of personal relationships through commeness: "one major emotion that is constantly linked with food is that of love, particularly maternal love, romantic love and wifely concern for the well-being of one's husband."[3] Also, food practices communicate one's political and ethical beliefs, for instance, freeganism, the boycotting of food companies, and the selection of various fair-trade and eco-labeled foods. However, although food may be used to *express* social differentiation or political opinion, it also *reflects* underlying economic disadvantages and the "materialities" of a particular economic and political regime.[4] This also means that "suggested" food practices (in popular cookbooks and on recipe pages in leading magazines of the time) may mirror social, cultural, economic and political characteristics of a particular period.

This article considers several texts on cooking published during the period of socialism in Slovenia. The findings are based on a qualitative analysis of texts from the Slovenian women's and family monthly, *Naša žena* ("Our Woman"). The magazine was chosen for its longevity and reputation. Originating in January, 1941, as the first legal socialist women's magazine and being the oldest women's magazine still published today, *Naša žena* allowed us to follow changes throughout the period of socialism in Yugoslavia, right after the Cominform in 1949 – when Jugoslavia strove for independent industrialization and socialist democracy – to 1990, just before Slovenia's secession from Yugoslavia. For each decade, we analyzed two volumes: 1949/1950, 1959/1960, 1969/1970, 1979/1980, and 1989/1990. The selected texts were mainly recipes, food columns and practical suggestions for housekeeping and cooking; the rest include articles on food topics, as well as advertisements for food and kitchen technologies.

The aim of the analysis is to show how *Naša žena's* suggestions and advice for cooking and housekeeping followed, supported and perpetuated the main socialist ideas and values, like industrial progress, hard work, sacrifice for the benefit of the state, solidarity, social equality, and duty. Textual analysis allowed us to track and locate the main discourses in a broader socio-cultural context to show the main ideological mechanisms working behind the apparently innocent texts such as cooking advice.

In the period of Slovenian socialism we identified two main trends in *Naša žena's* view of everyday life. From the late 1940s until the late 1970s *Naša žena* tried to spread and legitimate the socialist program for rapid modernization. Fast growing industries and technological development were two main socialist symbols of a successful and economically independent society. At the micro level of this analysis, milk emerged as a powerful symbol, promoted especially in the period, when the main political aim was to build a new, coherent system. The connection between building a new state and building a strong bone structure becomes evident in promoting milk as an absolutely necessary source of gaining physical power and building an organic structure. Along with drinking milk to recover strength after labor, convenience also seemed to be an influential idea. Promoting the idea of saving time and broadly introducing products of the food industry supported the myth of a politically active and economically self-sufficient woman, who was, above all, still a housewife caring for the family.

The second trend occurred in the 1980s, when, due to an economic and political crisis the utopian vision of "self-managing socialism" started to melt. When the myth of modernization suddenly had to be replaced with a powerful alternative, *Naša žena* started to follow the model of a Western democratic society. The introduction of post-modern fashions in food preparation – e.g., organic food and macrobiotics – was necessary to familiarize the reader with approaching social changes and to assume a critical position vis-à-vis the negative aspects of the modernization process.

However, this is also the time when the Yugoslavian identity had to be replaced with an equivalent, if not more powerful idea of a new Slovenian identity. Answers were sought in the real essence of Slovenism and in forgotten traditions. For instance, at that time home made brown bread emerges as the most powerful symbol, connoting homeliness, rootedness in peasant life, and the return to nature.

The analysis of symbols and/or discourses emerging from *Naša Žena's* articles and advertisements may work as a valid explanation of how the complex, ideologically driven mechanisms penetrate in each and every level of the social environment.

Striving Hard for Modernization

At the end of the 1940s the standard of living was low, and in several aspects even lower than before World War II. There are two main reasons: Yugoslavia's exceptional investment in heavy industry – one third of the country's gross national product – at the expense of consumer goods, and Yugoslavia's conflict with the Cominform (1948), resulting in an economic blockade by the Soviet Union and her allies. Another consequence was the threat of a military engagement with the Cominform states; thus, Yugoslavia was spending a large portion of her national product on armament. In addition, the drought of 1950 further complicated the country's difficulty with supplies. A distinguishing feature of this period were ration coupons for staple food and for manufactured goods, such as footwear, clothes, matches and kerosene. Open-market purchases were possible, but at significantly higher prices.[5] The supply of food and of consumer goods in stores was insufficient, and the products were of a low quality. In 1949, particular shortages included flour, milk, apples, vegetables, footwear and heating fuel. Also, monthly increases in the cost of living exceeded the growth of incomes, with food prices rising the fastest. Consequently, people would engage in additional part-time jobs or moonlight, but still failed to make ends meet.[6]

The recipes and dietary guidelines of 1949 and 1950 reflected these unfavorable post-war economic circumstances: above all they sought to answer the question of how to manage. Judging by a recurrent, explicit emphasis on the use of seasonal foods, supplies must have been largely determined by the respective seasons, and cooking by the need to economize. Thus, the general meat shortage must have been a reason why most recipes called for vegetable stews and soups. *Naša žena* suggested choice meat only for holiday dishes (e.g. filet mignon, rabbit in a sauce), and inferior cuts, at best, for everyday dishes (e.g., meatballs). This puts *Naša žena*'s "mock broths," such as mock beef broth or mock brain broth in perspective; they were meatless imitation soups whose stock was made with a small quantity of vegetables, covered with plenty of water and thickened with *cowboy roux* (a pale mixture of flour and water). Tomatoes were used to provide meat-like coloring.

However, the recipes, particularly those for deserts, also called for ingredients in short supply, like eggs, milk, cream, flour, and apples. As a rule, these *Naša žena* recipes would add the phrase "if you have any," for instance, to the required "zest of lemon," a frequent ingredient. Proposing hard-to-get ingredients seems to clash with the magazine's otherwise down-to-earth philosophy. The paradox may be explained, on one hand, by yearning for prosperity, a good life and better fare, including *Naša žena*'s desire to broaden the culinary horizons of its readers. On the other hand, there may have been a material reason. The rationing system was rather differentiated; the consumers were entitled to different amounts of provisions depending on age, education, physical strain imposed by their work, and on the importance of their occupation for the nation, and the like.[7] This meant that some were able to receive more (better) food allowances than others.

The standard of living began to rise in the mid-1950s, when the period of rapid industrialization ended. Until 1960 Yugoslavia was among countries with the fastest growing national income.[8] The higher standard of living at the end of the 1950s, and particularly in the late 1960s, the progress of the country's food processing industry, and shopping tourism in neighboring Italy and Austria, where Slovenes would go to buy food items in short supply in Slovenia – sugar, coffee, rice, lemons[9] – modernized the recipes of *Naša žena*. By the end of the 1950s they contained much more meat and better cuts than before (offal and bacon as well as steaks, chops and roasts). Also rice appeared, one of the basic components of today's Slovenian diet. Culinary herbs and spices, marjoram, rosemary, thyme, and bay leaf, ingredients of festive dishes after the war, with the exception of parsley and pepper, began to be recommended for everyday cuisine. Oil increasingly replaced lard, while frying became popular, and recipes for shortcrust pastry suggested a more important role for butter in the diet. An extraordinary number of recipes involved eggs (e.g. various savory omelets, spinach with eggs, lamb's-lettuce with eggs). Eggs were recommended in *Naša žena* for being allegedly healthy, "containing practically everything that a living being needs to develop and prosper", and for being practical, "A working wife will often find eggs to be a lifesaver."[10]

A rising standard of living in the 1960s, influenced by low unemployment, resulted in an increase in real purchasing power. In most families, particularly in towns, both partners in marriage were breadwinners, the rate of employed women was as high as 40 percent,[11] and the average size of private households stood at 3.5 members.[12] Therefore, the living standard of Slovenians was relatively high. In addition, the pricing of staple food items, such as bread, sugar, cooking oil, beef, milk and eggs, became more accessible.[13] The upward trend of the standard of living continued in the 1970s. Favorable economic conditions, largely the result of foreign loans and open borders, allowed citizens to travel abroad freely and positively affected the consumer mentality of the masses. For instance, shopping in Trieste for food (especially coffee), footwear, gold jewelry, denims, toys, automobile spare parts etc., became very popular among Slovenians and other Yugoslavs. Stores now offered more choices, particularly in the 1970s, although improvement had been noticed since the late 1960s. Supermarkets and department stores were springing up in Ljubljana and Maribor. The then largest department store in Slovenia, *Maximarket* in Ljubljana, was visited by 84,000 people during the first four days of its opening[14] – a turnout that amounted to almost 40 percent of the capital's population.

In the late 1960s *Naša žena* started to issue advice on the use of new cooking techniques. The first one was about how to broil meat over charcoal on an open grill. This method was, according to the recipes, associated with the contemporary vogue of spending one's leisure time or vacation picnicking or camping. The second new technique, previously restricted to making pastry, was about how to bake main dishes in an oven, emphasizing gratinating, while the third important one could be traced to the late 1950s, we may call it "warming up." The columnists were much enthused over manufactured convenience foods and often recommended them, whether as an entrée, such as canned pea soup, or as an alimentary article, for example mayonnaise or tomato paste in a tube or ready-made layers of sponge cake.

Lesson One: How to Become a Modern Housewife

Educating housewives was *Naša žena*'s main concern during the socialist period. The housewife was the nation's second self, reconstructing it by caring for the family and working in a factory. Her task was to carry out the building of a whole new society, a socialist idea that was reflected in *Naša žena*'s collectivist discourse. At the end of the 1940s and in the early 1950s *Naša žena* presupposed an ignorant housewife, who was also unskilled in preparing food and keeping house. With World War II over, *Naša žena* saw its mission in educating the housewife in economic and intelligent uses of egg powder and dried milk. *Naša žena* constantly denied the housewife's having proper knowledge and tried to return her to the right track with phrases like, "A large number of our housewives think that only a soup made from meat is any good, but this is not so",[15] or, "Many housewives erroneously believe that ..."[16] Registering their ignorance and imparting the correct understanding was very common. With such strong forms of the educational discourse, *Naša žena* used second or third person plural forms of address (like *you should, they should*) to refer to the crowd of the yet uneducated housewives, thereby distancing itself from them and positioning itself as a relevant authority. The educational function focused primarily on familiarizing housewives with the convenient use of new food products and kitchen equipment. For instance, *Naša žena* instructed housewives about obvious activities such as dishwashing. "Washing dishes is the least popular domestic job ... However, with the right working procedure you can considerably shorten the work process and the effort ...You have to provide a proper drying surface, a proper sink or bowl, and a vast surface with a strainer. And it is worth remembering: the longer the food rests stay in the dishes, the more difficult will be to remove them."[17]

In the 1960s *Naša žena* tried to educate the housewife about more essential issues of food preparation, for example, how to use canned food, a pressure cooker or an electric oven. Since the 1970s *Naša žena* introduced her to what was modern, good-looking and tasty. The role of a housewife was no longer considered antiquated. Educating housewives about modern housekeeping was in the interest of socialism in order to be able to modernize unhygienic and underdeveloped houses and farms. Several practical courses in cooking, child-care, housekeeping, and dressmaking were organized and advertised by the socialist party. *Naša žena* took on the task of encouraging and inviting housewives to accept the cultural and political ideas of collectivism and modernization behind educational organizations. Making women skilled meant making them accessible to everyone and, therefore, serving the public interests. A particularly strong spirit of collectivism pervaded into some of *Naša žena*'s special sections. There readers published practical advice to help their peers with their own ideas and knowledge. "How many times do we want to make our family or at least our children happy, but we think we can't, because we don't have white flour, eggs or any other ingredients. But it is not like food ration coupons can prevent us from preparing something sweet and tasty. From my own experience I can provide a few examples of recipes that you should try, too. I always succeed."[18]

This kind of advice may be explained by a strong collectivist spirit, which was especially present during the earliest period when intelligent and practical solutions to everyday problems were more than welcome. However, assuming the success of education in the 1980s, tips for cooking were no longer just explanations of essential and pragmatic procedures, but also included recipes for "non-essential" cooking techniques, such as gratinating, using a grill or *Römertopf* (a covered, unglazed clay pot), and decorating with a pastry bag. In the 1980s only the first personal plural address was used (void of an *us*-versus-*them/you* attitude), which is considered to be the most neutral way of addressing readers.

Introducing Novelty

The late 1950s and early 1960s were a period not only of political and cultural liberalization but of economic and social modernization in Eastern Europe and the Soviet Union. A fundamental characteristic of socialist societies was their desire for rapid and efficient modernization, which had to be expressed in material culture and infuse all fields of every-day life. The strongest symbols of modernization were various manifestations of the country's technological progress. Among Eastern socialist regimes these symbols of progress were visible in such forms of technology as nuclear power, space crafts and washing machines.[19] Yugoslavia, too, increasingly placed emphasis on a technologically driven conception of modernity. Socialism arose as a radically modernist social movement emphasizing industrialization and presenting itself as an industrial society.[20]

Yet, modernization demanded novelty, a fast tempo of life and labor efficiency. The rapid changes induced by the socialist modernization process affected ordinary people the most. Several new appliances, such as pressure cookers, mixers, gas cookers, electrical kitchen ranges, freezers, and washing machines, had been widely introduced into most of the Slovenian homes by the mid-1970s. In 1960 a worker with an average personal income had to work 526 hours and 31 minutes to buy an electrical kitchen range; in 1970 the number of working hours had been reduced by 2.5 times.[21] The quality of a wide range of kitchen equipment and other aids for the housewife was comparable to that of neighboring Italy.[22]

The modern kitchen was to be an extension of the modern workplace and the discipline of office or factory work was to be transferred to domestic tasks. Labor and fatigue, historically associated with cooking, would be things of the past. Modern cooking would be clean, organized and easy.[23] It was, therefore, consistent to propagate the use of technologically advanced equipment that promised better living conditions. The most frequent arguments were time savers and convenience. For instance, the difference between time spent in the kitchen then and in the period of modernization, was expressed like this, "If I had to do it like grandma, I'd first have to clear out the ashes, bring in the firewood … kindle a fire and keep building it up. Now I just turn on the gas and light it. Then I'd have to go into the hen house to catch the live chicken I'd bought at the market, I'd have to slaughter it, to scald it, to pluck it, to gut it. Now I just pull a plastic bag out of an oven dressed chicken, and all the giblets are neatly packed in there, the liver without the gallbladder and the gizzard is clean."[24]

Naša žena was presupposing a conservative and skeptic house-wife who needed a slow and careful introduction to novelty. Acquainting the readership with novelties had been common since the end of the 1950's, after postwar reconstruction of the nation, and eating was not just a struggle to survive. Recipes kindly and carefully encouraged the housewives to try new combinations of ingredients, foreign dishes, new cooking techniques and industrial food products, "Let's try to change the customary taste of our salads as well,"[25] was followed by recipes that included the use of oil, lemon juice, sweet Hungarian paprika and horseradish. Headlines like "Rice in a slightly different way"[26] probably implied a lack of diversity of food ingredients and a routinized cooking process. In order to promote novelty, liberalization and openness, adjectives such as "new" (e.g., "new recipes", "new marinades") and "modern" (e.g., "Pop-art cake: For this modern cake three fillings are stirred in …")[27] and those associating a dish with a foreign country (e.g., "Dutch" apple sweet, "French" stew, "Italian" spinach) were common, especially during holidays, meaning that foreign dishes were considered exclusive.

By the end of the 1970s, exotic combinations of ingredients became increasingly frequent. Housewives were encouraged to combine meat with fruits, or strawberries with cheese, and to prepare exotic dishes, for example, from Ghana. Warde notes similar developments in British monthlies a decade earlier, where several magazines applied the adjectives like "gourmet" or "stylish" to recipes for foreign dishes, appealing to innovation and internationalism, as food columnists' attempted to cultivate the culinary sophistication of their readers.[28] However, *Naša žena* neither explicitly nor implicitly linked foreign cuisines to distinctiveness, cosmopolitanism or sophistication. Foreign dishes were to bring variety into one's daily life and, at most, a diversion to break the monotony of work.[29]

In order to familiarize readers with new and exotic dishes and ingredients, the spelling of every foreign words or labels was Slovenized, e.g., *kečap* instead of *ketchup*, or the meaning of a name was explained. Along with exotic combinations and ingredients cooking started to include explicit elements of pleasure. From 1980 onward the housewives were encouraged to experiment and use their imagination by *Naša žena* to stimulate their interest in novelty and create the phantasm of experiencing pleasure in food preparation.

Until the end of the 1960s introducing novelty was self-evident, while in the 1970s saving time became the major argument for innovation. However, by the 1980s a curious technique of persuasion emerged in *Naša žena*. Beginning with the opening to the West and the slow decomposition of Yugoslavia, introducing novelty became a means of turning toward Western European habits and life-style. Because major political changes were expected with the approaching end of the utopian system, an introduction of novelty had to be more persuasive. Thus, it started being introduced through the already known food or tastes, e.g., "… a few less well-known fruit and vegetable preserves, as well as those we do know well but which have been prepared a little differently or with a spicy or with the addition of condiments …;"[30] or, "Many will find the taste of these dishes strange, perhaps even disagreeable. But do sample them, because they contain nothing you haven't met in a different composition and in the company of other spices."[31] A novelty was legitimized on the pretence that it is timeless – it is, according to Hobsbawm,[32] "the invention of tradition." In these cases, new food becomes a symbol of the new political situation: we must slowly get used to it, but to help us we should keep in mind that it is only a slight recombination of the already known, therefore, nothing is to be feared.

Warming Up to Fuel Economy

Another manifestation of technological developments was the rapidly growing number of products of the food industry – especially canned meat and vegetables, bouillon cubes, instant soups and dishes, different types of frozen food, and pudding powders – that had become popular since the late 1950s and that were widely used a decade later. In 1965 a major economic reform affected the industrial sector, in general, and food processing emerges as one of the most developed industries in Yugoslavia. The main goal of the economic reform was to build a model socialist economy that would be able to compete with developed countries.[33] Although the resulting products certainly reduced time in the kitchen, *Naša žena* uncritically took on the task of introducing the novelties to Slovenian housewives and, thus, add to prosperity in the wake of the rapid industrialization of the country. "Frozen foodstuffs retain their nutritional value; sometimes the quantity of certain vitamins in them even rises, for the reason that provitamins have been converted into free vitamins ..."[34]

For the same purpose the food industry started an aggressive commercial campaign mainly promoting manufactured convenience foods. Saving time was the main argument in persuading the housewife to buy such products. "Frozen dishes and foodstuffs will save a working wife a great deal of time as well as drudgery."[35] The connection between saving time and the food industry had become explicit by the end of the 1960s. An article on instant soups concluded with the following claim, "Nope, these days there really is no longer any need for us to stand at the kitchen range for hours on end."[36] However, convenience was promoted also by suggesting simple dishes, such as stews, "... our age of universal haste and hurry is also becoming the age of one-pot stews;"[37] or by recommending simplicity in food preparation – especially in sweets recipes, even though frequently a rather complex recipe was recommended. In addition, advice for simplifying or shortening kitchen work never included the involvement of male members of the household.

It is rather obvious that *Naša žena* spread the ideology of time-saving convenience to assist the growing food industry. In 1960, *Naša žena* widely introduced the use of canned food into everyday cooking practices. Gainfully employed women were particularly encouraged to use canned food. If the time spent in the kitchen was shortened, the housewife would have more time to spend at work, "It is true that canned food is more expensive. Having said that, we should bear in mind the circumstances under which our work, too, has its own value."[38] Hence, housewives should be grateful to the food industry for such products. "Food manufacturers have done a lot of the cooking the consumer would have had to do."[39] At the same time, though, *Naša žena* reflected on the quality of canned food. "If, however, someone uses canned food on a daily basis, they must take great care to meticulously supplement their diet with vitamins ..."[40] Still, reflections on the quality of manufactured food totally disappeared in the late 1960s, when the food industry had reached its height. *Naša žena*, still presupposing a skeptic and suspicious housewife, decided to stand surety for food industry products. This implicit skepticism of the housewife is demonstrated in a rhetorical question, "... one can put together an entire dinner using exclusively *Podravka* products. Twenty minutes, and it's on the table, lacking nothing at all. Don't believe me? I have tried it out."[41]

Saving time seems to connect with the socialist work ideology, which dictated that the majority of the female population should be employed.[42] Subsequently, Slovenia had a high rate of gainfully employed women. But they were doubly burdened. One part of their engagements was bound to their private lives and included mothering, caring for the family members and being a housewife. Their second role was related to public matters and demanded an employed and politically active woman. However, the role of the mother was the most important one; therefore, socialism's recognition of the equality of women was limited to working mothers.[43] The ideal socialist woman conscientiously had to complete her working tasks in order to contribute to the economic plan while, and at the same time, giving birth to and raising as many new citizens as she could. Especially during the postwar years, the public function of women was strongly promoted. Even motherhood was not just a private matter; in the Yugoslavian socialism it was considered also a social function. Women did not care only for their own children; due to strong collectivist ideas, they had to take care of all the orphans and the diseased and be there for those needing care and help.[44] At the beginning of 1949, Tito proclaimed motherhood a so-cial duty, equally important as work in factories or institutions.[45]

Family care, housework and employment dictated a fast "pace of life." Women were therefore encouraged to expedite their house-work; in cooking this frequently meant lowering the level of food quality. "Working women are often pressed for time, because we need to do a lot of domestic work on top of our jobs ... We can now get a variety of ready-cooked and instant articles of food in our stores as well as tools for rapid food preparation."[46]

However, in the late 1980s a switch from the socialist values of work to post-modern values of leisure time appeared in the ar-guments economizing food preparation. The idea of saving time due to full time work was slowly replaced by the idea due to the enjoyment of leisure time. Articles about evening entertainment for special occasions contain the following claims: "This is why in most instances laying out a cold buffet is the most convenient form of en-tertaining. We prepare all the food and drink in advance, and then we can take a rest and tidy up in peace ..."[47]

Healthy Eating as a Civic Duty

A conviction that diet and health are interrelated was noticeable in each of the analyzed time spans, but the perspective altered at least every ten years. Opinions about what constituted healthy nutrition shifted from diversified and quantitatively sufficient nourishment in the 1940's to a pressing insistence on proteins and vitamins in the 1950's and 1960's, and to demonizing sugar and fats and glorifying fruit and vegetables in the 1970's.

During the decade after World War II the synonym for a healthy diet was a diversified diet; in *Naša žena*'s understanding this meant being nourished on a combination of "proteins, fats, starch, sugar, salt, water and vitamins."[48] However, the quantity of the consumed nutrients was an important condition too, "... and we must take care that a sufficient amount of food comes on our table."[49] In a time of scarcity, repleteness was a legitimate goal for a housewife. Among the strategies was serving a soup as a first course ("a soupless din-ner is hardly a full meal")[50] and thickening a soup with a mixture of flour and water ("cowboy roux") or by boiling it with noodles or other types of soup pasta.

In the late 1950s the meaning of a healthy diet changed slightly as balance gave space to proteins, vitamins and minerals. In this context, *Naša žena* exalted milk, "Recent dietetic findings show that milk is a vital, irreplaceable aliment …"[51] It also often encouraged the consumption of eggs and milk, and fruit and vegetables. No food or its components were truly painted evil yet. But it is worthy to note one article, which mentions in passing that raw vegetables were salty enough and should not be salted, because "in this way we reduce the daily intake, and this will only benefit our body."[52] Another example appears in the April 1959 issue in a summary of an article from a German magazine, *Gleicheit*. It is entitled, "What do doctors say about sugar?" and warns that too much sugar brings on rheumatism and, in children, caries. Aside from these exceptions, articles providing nutritional instruction mostly attended to the problem of how to "enrich" and "supplement" one's daily diet.

The titles of *Naša žena*'s recipes often contained the adjective, *izdaten*, without any contemporary negative connotation of rich (food) or ample (meal), emphasizing its denotative meaning "appeasing hunger for a protracted period, very satisfying, substantial, hearty" (e.g. *izdatna skutina sladica* "a sustaining curd-cheese cake;" cf., German, *ausgiebig*). Certain frequently occurring phrases – such as *better the flavor, enrich the dish, perfect it by adding* e.g. *cheese, parsley, cream* – showed a fascination with proteins and vitamins and possibly also a fervent and no longer (as well as not yet, again) morally reprehensible Western-like desire for indulgence and abundance. Even manufactured convenience foods contained not a word on additives, hidden fats or high-energy value. The one serious warning, repeatedly occurring in connection with tinned food, was about vitamin insufficiency, but the housewife was expected to make up for it easily by serving a green salad and fruit as a side dish.

In the 1969 issues of *Naša žena* two views of the food/health relationship began to coexist. The earlier and still quite frequent one, saw (varied enough) food as a source of wellness and only linked a particular food with a disease, if a diet lacked certain nutrients, or advised cutting down on some foods in cases of preexistent diseases (e.g., on eggs to patients with gastric dysfunction or cholecystitis), "Those who can appreciate their good health take good care of what they eat. That is why everyone who wants to preserve their health should be aware of the fact that the cause of a number of illnesses lies exactly in improper nourishment, insufficient in substances (especially proteins, vitamins and minerals) which are necessary for the human organism to function properly."[53] According to this view a person was healthy on the condition that his/her menu was of an adequate variety, and if getting ill (but not on account of eating too much of anything) an individual had to watch their diet.

The second, less frequent but already explicit view was, unlike the first one, very similar to the contemporary one of dissuading people from the use of certain ingredients. Thus, the late 1960s articles already connected an excessive fat and sugar intake with being overweight, which, in turn, was regarded as contributing to cardiovascular diseases, diabetes and a shorter life expectancy.

The late 1960's introduced a new topic: being overweight. A far cry from today's anxious concerns, *Naša žena* used the term *debelušnost* (roughly: "being on the fat side, chubbiness, plumpness") rather than, *debelost* ("fatness, obesity"). Articles dealing exclusively with slimming were few, about two per year, and being slim was not associated with good health, while being overweight was implicitly treated as a hereditary predisposition: *Naša žena* recommended raw fresh fruit and vegetables to those, who are *nagnjeni* (i.e. "inclined, susceptible, predisposed") to be corpulent. The clichés, which introduced advice on slimming, were, "if you would like to stay slender," or "if we want to lose weight." But by the end of the 1970s *Naša žena* had already adopted a dogmatic style of writing, "those who need to lose weight have to eat …" In the late 1960s, a woman's preoccupation with her weight was seen as an exception rather than as one of the chief determinants of her nutrition, according to the weekly menus for dieting women. The latter guided them from Monday to Sunday from breakfast to supper, and warned women to consult their physicians before going on any diet, no matter how mild.

By 1979 demonizing food rich in fat and sugar and glorifying vegetables and fruit had become the prevailing approach to writing about healthy eating, and weight control was gradually incorporated into an ethical obligation. Articles describing particular foods (e.g., cabbages, cottage cheese, chestnuts) invariably specified their

energy values in calories, and *Naša žena*'s recipes would more frequently follow suit with statements, e.g. "instead of real cream, we
can whip up some store-bought cream from a package, which has
fewer calories"[54] or, "this dainty will be even better – but also a bigger sin against slimness – if we substitute milk with cream."[55]

How did arguments for healthy eating change in the course
of time? In the late 1940s *Naša žena* clearly expounded the connection between proper nourishment, physical fitness, and energy to
work and produce a new society. There was only one purpose of
healthy eating: to give a person energy to work. Likewise, the only
purpose of work was the development of the newborn state. The
responsibility for healthy eating was placed on the woman-work-
er-mother, whose cooking had to be her active contribution to the
establishment of the new social order. "To take care of every family member's health means, to a large extent, to take care of what
and how they eat. Only if properly fed can people be healthy, and
only healthy people can work well and be creative. Therefore every
housewife shoulders a large responsibility, the responsibility for
the health, strength and progression of the nation."[56]

Naša žena consistently and relentlessly urged its reader to assist
in the rebuilding of her homeland and the building of socialism.
The perfect woman was, simultaneously, housewife, mother, worker and volunteer social worker, cooking daily and with pleasure,
cleaning the apartment, creating a cheerful atmosphere at the table,
preserving and pickling since early spring to lay in a good store of
provisions for the winter, making her own cleansers and soaps (lye
from wood ash, chestnut scald and potato bucking for washing woven fabrics, nettle infusion for washing greasy dishes) and tending
to the sick and poor.

By the end of the 1950s, *Naša žena* had stopped explicitly connecting healthy eating and civic duty. It had – or seemed to have
– desisted from its nation-building mission of guiding the woman,
at any cost, in her kitchen by the exigencies of the socialist social order. The magazine began to invoke a new authority, science, in sen-
tences like these, "more recent scientific discoveries about nutrition
are indicating ...," "... scientists have established...," or "... modern experts recommend." Henceforth, healthy eating apparently
became more and more a question of individual choice. A woman

who cared little about healthy eating was no longer an enemy of the state, but increasingly an enemy of herself and as such even more susceptible to ideologies and expert advice of all kinds.

Reviving Bread for a Better Future

Broadly speaking, there were two spells of re-traditionalization in *Naša žena* during the reign of socialism with two very different meanings. The first one emerged as a response to the economic crisis in the late 1970s, while the second one gathered momentum in the late 1980s, when diversification from socialism and Yugoslavia seemed necessary in order to lay the foundations for a new democratic society. A nationalist discourse promoting Slovenian identity by glorifying traditional food seemed a handy approach to setting the boundary between new democratic Slovenia and old autocratic Yugoslavia.

In the late 1970s the rate of inflation hovered around 20 percent, Yugoslavia had difficulties repaying her external debt; there was also a beginning shortage of gasoline.[57] A breakdown in the supply of electricity resulted in deliberate power cuts by the government for at least a few hours per day. Aggravating the situation was a shortage of such staples as cooking oil, sugar, coffee, bananas, washing powder, toilet paper, sanitary napkins, and numerous other daily necessities taken for granted by people. Consequently, Slovenes in large numbers would go shopping in neighboring Italy and Austria, and smuggling merchandise became very widespread.[58]

Recipes and food articles at the end of the 1970s were witness to the economic crisis. Columnists would offer advice on how to use food economically (only eat as much as needed and buy only as much food as can be used immediately, so that no food will be thrown away); how to substitute cheaper ingredients for expensive ones (vinegar instead of wine for flavor, more modest cuts of pork for Széged goulash); how to replace scarce fresh red meat (goulash with canned meat); and how not to let leftovers go to waste (revive stale mustard with vinegar, bread may be turned into breadcrumbs, bread dumplings or pastry so that "the very last crumb is put to good use").

There were two kinds of instructions on how to be a thrifty cook. One kind openly addressed the on-going dearth. The other kind, however, sought to avoid dwelling too much upon high price tags and food scarcity, because the country's bad economic situation implied a bad economic policy. Articles in *Naša žena*, therefore, preferred to deal with the daily plight of the Slovene homemaker by promoting simple folk dishes and "granny's style of cooking." It was a period in which *Naša žena* teemed with allegedly traditional recipes from non-Slovene parts of Yugoslavia, with recipes for meatless stews whose main ingredient was seasonal vegetables, and with recipes for conventional domestic dishes, likewise containing potatoes and other inexpensive vegetables, but little meat. The December issue (1970) volume ran a succession of recipes for fondue, punch, layer cakes, and cookies, whereas the central topic in 1980 volume was "national dishes in day-to-day cooking", featuring mostly dishes of organ meats, beans, potatoes, and cabbages. Everyday life was getting less and less sweet as evidenced by the presence of only two desert recipes in this issue, both for traditional Slovene pastry.

A more complex drift toward a radicalized version of traditionalism gathered momentum in the late 1980s, also evident in *Naša žena*, which celebrated traditional customs and feasts; and revived traditional home-made dishes. Until the 1980s, feasts were rarely mentioned explicitly in *Naša žena*, although more recipes for sweets would be offered in the December, February and April issues in accordance with celebrations of Christmas, New Year's Eve, Shrovetide and Easter, though only implicitly. Christmas and Easter were not publicly celebrated, although not forbidden, and people celebrated them in the privacy of their homes. In 1987, Jože Smole, president of the Slovenian Socialist Association, was the first Slovenian politician who televised a Christmas address to Slovenian citizens.

At the end of the 1980's (when traditional festivities were mentioned explicitly) *Naša žena* presented sumptuous recipes with choice meats and typically festive pastries. In addition to this revival of feasts, there was a large number of recipes for traditional Slovenian dishes. Rather than young beauties in their latest fashion, who had crowded the culinary pages at the end of the 1960s, articles in *Naša žena* now featured white-aproned elderly farmwives, letting the female reader in on their recipes for home-made bread and traditional country-style wedding cakes, baked in a farmstead stove. "Then the urban housewife will ... turn on her oven, and I'll go and heat up my up-country stove."[59] The adjective, "home-made," was present in a significant number of these recipes.

However, the most indicative example of re-traditionalization was the homemade bread revival in 1990. It was suggested that almost every dish be eaten with a slice of homemade brown bread that recaptured a sense of homeliness and tradition. "Today home made bread is almost a specialty. Therefore, our reader Anja would like to try out different recipes for homemade bread. However, not only she, but probably any housewife wants to lavish her family with goods from the homely oven."[60]

This was just one year before Slovenia's secession from Yugoslavia. Bread is one of the most powerful and frequent symbols in Slovenian literature. A shortage of bread stands for social misery and, therefore, longing for bread means hoping for better times. Bread is also a symbol of the Slovenian nation and native land, home and homeliness. A nation without its "bread" cannot survive; therefore, bread represents a nation's existence.[61] Shedding light on the symbolism of bread means understanding the meaning of the bread revival at a time of political instability and a retrieval of one's true national identity.

Post-Modern Fashions

Tradition is complementary to nature. "Tradition as nature, nature as tradition: this equivalence is not as extreme as it may sound. What is 'natural' is what remains outside the scope of human intervention. 'Nature' in the modern era has become contrasted with the city; it is equivalent to 'countryside' and quite often has the connotation of a rural idyll."[62] Some of the post-modern fashions in food consumption are oriented toward nature and became popular at the end of the 1980s, with people turning toward macrobiotics, organic food and cooking from scratch with fresh and natural foodstuffs.

In 1989 and 1990 *Naša žena* quite propagandistically advocated organically grown food: it published information on the activity of societies for "biodynamic" agriculture, their very punctilious advice on farming and gardening, and advertisements for their products.

In several of its issues, *Naša žena* publicized ideas and rules of macrobiotic dietetics. Its information on organically grown food was not, however, a mere technical directive on plant cultivation: instead it was interlaced with appeals for self-realization and personal growth. In *Naša žena*'s presentation the cultivation of one's own organic garden was also a way to self-fulfillment, supposedly developing one's creativity, enabling one to unwind after a hard day, helping one to learn from nature and offering an oasis, in which to think beyond the mindless haste of modern life. However, growing vegetables has always been a widespread activity in Slovenia. As late as in 2000, not less than 68 percent of all Slovenian households cultivated their own kitchen gardens, with 19 percent of them living in towns.[63] In today's urban districts, an old-line housewife and a post-modern Sunday olericulturist may be found digging in their respective allotments next to each other. Defined figuratively, the former is a factory worker, who keeps a garden to save money, because land ought not to be left untilled, and she at least knows what her family eats; the latter is a schoolteacher and working the soil means a chance to regain contact with nature, return to her roots, enjoy a spiritual experience, counterbalance her intellectual toil and learn about growing plants environmentally friendly.

Advocating "poisonless food" the magazine became increasingly critical of the food processing industry, which, until recently, it had glorified. "The common cause of these civilizational diseases, entailed by an incorrect diet, … is the deficiency of vital, natural substances in our diet, which predominantly consists of industrially processed foodstuffs."[64] The political activism of the 1950s, thus, was transformed into an ecological one in the 1980s. The better future, promised by *Naša žena* to the postwar housewife – if she would help attain the sociopolitical goals – was moved into a distant past, "when people grew their food without mineral fertilizers and pesticides, and when fields were not furrowed by tractors but turned with plows that beasts of draught pulled."[65]

Alongside the agitation for organic eating, much of *Naša žena*'s space in that period was devoted to articles about the salubrity of fresh fruits and vegetables and recipes pertaining to them. The magazine tended to connect fruit and vegetable eating somewhat with the findings of the scientific medicine about "civilizational diseases", somewhat with sensual pleasure, "in April just seeing the earliest crisp vegetables is enough to make our mouths water,"[66] and somewhat with its new outlook on the human body. It no longer described the body as a machine needing to be adequately and regularly fueled, but as a thinking organism possessing its own wisdom and will and communicating to the individual when it had been fed correctly or incorrectly and about which nutrients it was lacking, "... once the winter months are over, our body literally starts hankering after fresh produce, as if it knew that it needed a new stock of vitamins and minerals. And it may well be that it does know, that the instinctive craving for what it needs is a remnant from a long ago, when humankind lived more instinctively and less rationally."[67]

The exceptionally acute concern over an alleged omnipresence of poisons in food and a growing incidence of "diseases of our modern age" may be explained perhaps by means of the theoretical accounts offered by Anthony Giddens[68] and Ulrich Beck.[69] Although their analyses of the postmodern turn to body and health concerns omit post-socialist societies, we may nevertheless draw a few parallels between their exposition and the Slovenian situation in the late 1980s.

Firstly is the conviction, already widespread in post-industrial societies (Slovenia hardly belonged to them at the time), that the wider social environment has become fraught with different global risks, such as nuclear, chemical, genetic and ecological mega-hazards.[70] *The Slovene Public Opinion* survey[71] shows that in 1990 that 55 percent of the population thought that "water pollution, industrial waste and chemicals" were causing damage to their health, and 62 percent were convinced that damage to their health was being done by "the use of chemicals in food products."

Secondly, Giddens and Beck ascertain that simultaneously people face the erosion of modern institutions such as the welfare state, patriarchal nuclear families and full employment.[72] Because their future is uncertain and because they find it practically impossible to influence the global social conditions, they actively construct their life style through focusing on themselves, on their bodies, diet, health, or spirituality.[73]

Slovenia was entering the 1990's suffering from a huge economic crisis, marked by a runaway inflation and mass unemployment. Inflation spiraled upward in the 1980s and grew into a hyperinflation by the end of the decade. Real personal income decreased by more than one fifth between 1981 and 1990, while prices for basic necessities increased by almost 50 percent between 1981 and 1985 and by almost 320 percent between 1986 and 1990.[74] More than three quarters of the population claimed that they were doing worse than five years earlier, that it was more difficult to get employment and to bear the expense of raising their children.[75] It was also the time of sharp political conflict with Serbia and the Yugoslav army, both fearing that Slovenia might sooner or later try to break away from Yugoslavia. In light of these developments one may conclude that *Naša žena's* obsession with health, most visible in its vexation at poisoned food and modern-age diseases, was an appeal to its female audience to engage with the wider social environment, fraught with the interplay of ecological and political dangers and an economic crisis.

Conclusion

What does the analysis of recipes suggest about the status of women in socialism? *Naša žena* was a kind of The Good Citizen's Handbook. Cooking tips and recipes were, in fact, directions and instructions to women for adjusting their home-management activities to the needs of a particular social order. Until the end of the 1970s, the magazine was giving advice to women-wife-mothers-housewives on "how to cook socialism," while in the 1980s it was suggesting how to build a nation state and get ready to live in a risk society. "Tips and tricks" were authoritarian, rigid and explicit at the beginning, and increasingly kind, playful and implicit toward the 1990s. Paradoxically, they both left little room for freedom. Even though, it is easier to resist explicit rather than implicit instruction, because it is clear and open. At the time of the party's obsession with state enemies, it was very risky to resist openly to "well meant" advice. A more modern technique of persuasion – an offer without coercion[76] – is even more effective: women are instructed in a way that gives them a feeling of making a free decision regarding their behavior. Moreover, a woman believes that taking advice works for herself and her interests, therefore, fighting against "sensible" advice would mean fighting against her "true inner self."

Socialism saw the woman as an indispensable caretaker of the nation. Therefore, women were asked to be mothers, housewives and factory workers and were also expected to be educated and politically active. In exchange for all these functions, they acquired formal and legal equality, although they were still loaded down with feminized social tasks, mainly involving the ethics of care. Their expected political activity was confined to similar tasks carried out in the private sphere – taking care of orphans, helping other women with child-care, or educating their counterparts in housekeeping etc. Women's political activities were, therefore, seen as a transfer of a moral life from home into the public arena. This meant that women could not really influence important policy making of the government. In addition, women working in the industrial sector were still paid less than their male colleagues, while domestic work remained their sole duty and responsibility. Although formally equal, the private sphere was left untouched by socialist equality politics, and socialism did not manage to change the division of domestic labor.

In the early stages of socialist modernization, the amount of housework was expected to be dramatically reduced due to both the creation of public diners and public laundries, and to technological advancements in the home. However, it never happened. Therefore, society still had to legitimize the traditional roles of women, and *Naša žena* was one of the vehicles to achieve this purpose. Through apparently innocent practices, such as recipe columns and cooking advice, *Naša žena* indoctrinated "modern socialist women" to embrace "traditional," "bourgeois" gender roles. They were precisely the ones, which socialism had declared to be abolishing, but which were necessary for the reproduction of the socialist economy. Invisible domestic work expected from and done by women, included tidying, cooking, raising children, caring for their husband, nursing of family members, alleviating external frustrations (school, workplace), and creating a pleasant atmosphere within the family home.[77] Together these activities ensured the material survival of a socialist labor force. However, the 1970's witnessed a decline of the women's role in nation-building ideologies, and women were chained to the stove by the idea of experiencing pleasure in preparing food. Therefore, cooking suddenly became every woman's desire and a means to gain the illusion of freedom from experimentation while discovering new flavors and exotic countries.

However, the housewife was never allowed to cook her way into an ideal society. Once *Naša žena* would be sending her into the modern future, into an epoch of "full-scale development," but before reaching it, *Naša žena* directed her into a pre-modern one. The Slovenian housewife is always on the road, even though she spends most of her time on less than a square perch of her kitchen.

Notes

[1] Alan Beardsworth and Teresa Keil, *Sociology on the Menu. An Invitation to the Study of Food and Society* (London: Routledge, 1997), 52–3.

[2] Deborah Lupton, *Food, the Body and the Self* (London, Thousand Oaks, New Delhi: Sage, 1996), 1.

[3] Deborah Lupton, ibid., 1996, 37.

[4] Alan Beardsworth and Teresa Keil, ibid., 1997, 53.

[5] Zdenko Čepič, "Preskrba Prebivalstva in Obvezni Odkupi," in *Slovenska Novejša Zgodovina: Od Programa Zedinjena Slovenija do Mednarodnega Priznanja Republike Slovenije 1848–1992*, ed. Jasna Fischer (Ljubljana: Mladinska knjiga, 2005), 895.

[6] Zdenko Čepič, "Urbanizacija in Življenjska Raven," in *Slovenska Novejša Zgodovina: Od Programa Zedinjena Slovenija do Mednarodnega Priznanja Republike Slovenije 1848–1992*, ed. Jasna Fischer (Ljubljana: Mladinska knjiga, 2005), 1013.

[7] Mateja Jeraj, *Slovenski Sindikati in Socialna Politika 1945–1950* (Ljubljana: Arhiv Republike Slovenije, 1995), 122.

[8] Zdenko Čepič, "Zvišanje Življenjske Ravni," in *Slovenska Novejša Zgodovina: Od Programa Zedinjena Slovenija do Mednarodnega Priznanja Republike Slovenije 1848–1992*, ed. Jasna Fischer (Ljubljana: Mladinska knjiga, 2005), 1087.

[9] Zdenko Čepič, "Urbanizacija in Življenjska Raven," in ibid., 2005, 1015.

[10] *Naša žena*, February, 1959, 59.

[11] Statistical office of the Republic of Slovenia, "Dejstva o Ženskah in Moškix v Sloveniji," http://www.stat.si/doc/pub/dejstva_zenske_moski.pdf.

[12] Statistical office of the Republic of Slovenia, "Area, Households and Population, 1921–2002 Censuses," http://www.stat.si/letopis/2005/04_05/04-02-05.htm.

[13] Zdenko Čepič, "Zvišanje Življenjske Ravni," in ibid., 2005, 1087–8.

[14] Zdenko Čepič, "Demografske in Socialne Spremembe," in *Slovenska Novejša Zgodovina: Od Programa Zedinjena Slovenija do Mednarodnega Priznanja Republike Slovenije 1848–1992*, ed. Jasna Fischer (Ljubljana: Mladinska knjiga, 2005), 1135.

[15] *Naša žena*, December, 1949, 88.

[16] *Naša žena*, November, 1949, 80.

[17] *Naša žena*, April, 1969, 59.

[18] *Naša žena*, supplement *Naš dom*, January, 1949, 8.

[19] David Crowley and Susan E. Reid, "Style and Socialism: Modernity and Material Culture in Post-War Eastern Europe," in *Style and Socialism: Modernity and Material Culture in Post-War Eastern Europe*, ed. David Crowley and Susan E. Reid (Oxford, New York: Berg, 2000), 3, 9.

[20] Mirjana Ule, "Kriza Industrijske Moderne in Novi Individualizem," *Družboslovne razprave* 6, no. 7 (1998): 71, 72.

[21] Zdenko Čepič, "Demografske in Socialne Spremembe," in ibid., 2005, 1127–38.

[22] F. Krishna Moorthy, *After Tito What?* (Atlantic Highlands: Humanities Press, 1980), 143.

[23] Cecilia Novero, "Stories of Food: Recipes of Modernity, Recipes of Tradition in Weimar Germany," *Journal of Popular Culture* 34, no. 3 (2000): 166.

[24] *Naša žena*, April, 1969, 51.

[25] *Naša žena*, April, 1959, 126.

[26] *Naša žena*, December, 1960, 376.

[27] *Naša žena*, September, 1970, 61.

[28] Alan Warde, *Consumption, Food and Taste* (London, Thousand Oaks and New Delhi: Sage, 1997), 59–60.

[29] Cecilia Novero, ibid., 2000, 178.

[30] *Naša žena*, September, 1980, 58.

[31] *Naša žena*, September, 1980, 61.

[32] Eric Hobsbawm, "Introduction: Inventing Traditions," in *The Invention of Tradition*, ed. Eric Hobsbawm and Terence Ranger (Cambridge: Cambridge University Press, 2002), 5–6.

[33] Primož Hainz, "Obdobje Krepitve Samoupravnega Družbenega Razvoja 1963–1971," in *Zgodovina Slovencev*, ed. Zdenko Čepič (Ljubljana: Cankarjeva založba, 1979), 912–3, 916.

[34] *Naša žena*, December, 1959, 399.

[35] *Naša žena*, January, 1970, 56.

[36] *Naša žena*, July/Avgust, 1969, 57.

[37] *Naša žena*, February, 1969, 54.

[38] *Naša žena*, February, 1960, 58.

[39] *Naša žena*, February, 1960, 58.

[40] *Naša žena*, February, 1960, 58.

[41] *Naša žena*, February, 1960, 57.

[42] Mateja Jeraj, *Slovenke na Prehodu v Socializem: Vloga in Položaj Ženske v Sloveniji 1945–1953* (Ljubljana: Arhiv Republike Slovenije, 2005), 123, 259–60.

[43] Barbara Einhorn, *Cinderella Goes to Market: Citizenship, Gender and Women's Movements in East Central Europe* (London: Verso, 1993), 40.

[44] Mateja Jeraj, *Slovenke na Prehodu v Socializem: Vloga in Položaj Ženske v Sloveniji 1945–1953* (Ljubljana: Arhiv Republike Slovenije, 2005), 125, 175.

[45] *Naša žena*, October, 1949, 221.

[46] *Naša žena*, March, 1970, 59.

[47] *Naša žena*, December, 1990, 68.

[48] *Naša žena*, January, 1949, 8.

[49] *Naša žena*, February/March, 1950, 12.

[50] *Naša žena*, December, 1949, 88.

[51] *Naša žena*, July/August, 1960, 233.

[52] *Naša žena*, July/August, 1960, 232.

[53] *Naša žena*, April, 1969, 55.

[54] *Naša žena*, July/August, 1979, 49.

[55] *Naša žena*, March, 1979, 59.

[56] *Naša žena*, January, 1949, 8.

[57] Aleš Gabrič, "Politična Kriza," in *Slovenska Novejša Zgodovina: Od Programa Zedinjena Slovenija do Mednarodnega Priznanja Republike Slovenije 1848–1992*, ed. Jasna Fischer (Ljubljana: Mladinska knjiga, 2005), 1149.

[58] Zdenko Čepič, "Gospodarska Kriza," in *Slovenska Novejša Zgodovina: Od Programa Zedinjena Slovenija do Mednarodnega Priznanja Republike Slovenije 1848–1992*, ed. Jasna Fischer (Ljubljana: Mladinska knjiga, 2005), 1151–2.

[59] *Naša žena*, October, 1990, 53.

[60] *Naša žena*, February, 1990, 54.

[61] Witness Slovenian prose writers Ivan Cankar, Boris Pahor and Prežihov Voranc.

[62] Anthony Giddens, "Living in a Post-Traditional Society" in *Reflexive Modernisation: Politics, Tradition and Aesthetics in the Modern Social Order*, ed. Ulrich Beck, Anthony Giddens and Scott Lash (Cambridge: Polity Press, 1994), 76.

[63] Blanka Tivadar, "Družbeno Strukturiranje Prehranjevalnih Vzorcev" (PhD diss., Fakulteta za družbene vede, 2001), 196.

[64] *Naša žena*, May, 1990, 26.

[65] *Naša žena*, April, 1990, 18.

[66] *Naša žena*, April, 1990, 76.

[67] *Naša žena*, April, 1990, 76.

[68] Anthony Giddens, *Modernity and Self-Identity: Self and Society in the Late Modern Age* (Stanford: Stanford University Press, 1991).

[69] Ulrich Beck, *World Risk Society* (Cambridge: Polity Press, 1999).

[70] Ulrich Beck, ibid., 1999.

[71] Niko Toš, ed., *Vrednote v Prehodu I. Slovensko Javno Mnenje 1968–1990* (Ljubljana: Fakulteta za družbene vede, 1997), 45.

[72] Ulrich Beck, ibid., 1999.

[73] Anthony Giddens, ibid., 1991, 5, 178.

[74] Neven Borak and Zdenko Čepič, "Gospodarska Struktura Slovenije," in *Slovenska Novejša Zgodovina: Od Programa Zedinjena Slovenija do Mednarodnega Priznanja Republike Slovenije 1848–1992*, ed. Jasna Fischer (Ljubljana: Mladinska knjiga, 2005), 1212–5.

[75] Niko Toš, ibid., 1997, 2, 86.

[76] Tanja Kamin, "Mediatization of Health and 'Citizenship-Consumership' (Con)Fusion," in *Ideological Horizons in Media and Citizen Discourses. Theoretical and Methodological Approaches,* ed. Birgitta Höijer (Göteborg: Göteborg University/Nordicom, 2007), 127.

[77] Majda Hrženjak, *Invisible Work* (Ljubljana: Mirovni inštitut, 2007), 24.

15
Žuži Jelinek
The Incredible Adventures of a Socialist Chanel

Djurdja Bartlett

The relationship between smart dress and the conceptual order had a different dynamic in each of the socialist countries. In Yugoslavia, the ideological role of smart dress was to distance the Yugoslav socialist system from the Soviet type of socialism. This was an important element in the ideological dispute between Yugoslavia and Soviet Union, which appeared on the pages of women's magazine *Svijet (World)*[1] in the early 1950s. However, private fashion salons were the only enterprises that could really design and produce such a dress. Žuži Jelinek was the most important of those post-war fashion designers. Before opening one of the first private fashion salons in socialist Yugoslavia, she had been a fashion designer with her own salon in Zagreb in the years before World War Two. Coming from a poor Jewish family, Jelinek worked her way up the professional and social ladder during the inter-war period.[2] When war broke out, she left her business to become the member of the partisan resistance movement. In 1945, Jelinek returned to liberated Zagreb to open *The First Partisan Fashion Salon*, located at the best address, the city's main square.[3] Her political loyalty and connections facilitated her relationship with the socialist regime which allowed her to restart her career and from the mid-1950s actively promoted her activities in the state-owned media in exchange for her pre-war knowledge and experience. Jelinek delivered smart clothes for her individual clients, many of whom belonged to the new socialist elite, but the regime especially appreciated her willingness to cooperate with the newly established textile industry, which struggled with a lack of both technological and cultural capital.

Following the introduction of communist rule, it seemed that Yugoslav textile industry would conform to the Soviet pattern. Textile and clothing companies were nationalized, and re-organized in order to suit the new socialist system. The first Croatian fashion magazine *Naša moda (Our Fashion)* praised the Soviet model of fashion production at that time.[4] Such a propagandistic approach demonstrated that socialist Yugoslavia had started to adjust to the Soviet organizational and representational patterns in the textile and clothing industries.[5] The Soviet Union had the most important role at the first post-war *Zagreb Fair* held in spring 1947. However, the political break with Stalin in 1948 and the following Soviet siege liberated, as well as constrained, Yugoslav socialism. It was forced to move closer to the West economically and away from the Soviet Union ideologically. Those movements happened simultaneously, and had a significant impact on both the real and symbolical role of dress in Yugoslavia. Both private fashion salons such as Žuži Jelinek's, and the budding textile industry were supposed to produce and promote the required smart dress.

In 1947 textile production exceeded the 1939 output level by 14 per cent, and was 46 per cent higher in 1949, even though the number of textile plants had stayed the same through the whole period.[6] In the early 1950s new textile mills were put into operation, and textile production doubled during the 1950s compared with the pre-war level.[7] Those accomplishments not only justified the socialist system in comparison to the previous capitalist society, but even more so the Yugoslav version of socialism. Post-war textile rations were abolished at the beginning of 1948, and the domestic media tried hard to demonstrate that Yugoslav socialism was going to be completely different from the austere and restrictive Stalinist version. The daily *Narodni list (People's Newspaper)* reported in 1953 that the *Spring Zagreb Fair* made domestic visitors proud by offering many novelties in different fields, from heavy industry to cosmetics and textiles.[8] The first fashion show with outfits produced by domestic industry took place in the same year at the *Zagreb Fair*.

Naša moda and its successor, women's magazine *Svijet (World)*, fulfilled an ideological function in promoting the phenomenon of fashion. *Svijet* covered women's issues, literature, and the arts, with an emphasis on various luxurious life-style topics and latest fashions, which were copied directly from the western fashion press. The topics were decided politically, as the editor-in-chief was always a loyal Communist Party member. The presence of sophisticated dresses was related neither to the real conditions within the textile industry nor to everyday reality, as in the late 1940s and early 1950s the newly established domestic textile and clothing factories were not capable of delivering the smart and fashionable outfits that had been published in *Naša moda* and *Svijet*. The main problem of the Yugoslav textile industry was not centralization, even though an ambitious level of production had been imposed by the First Five-Year Plan. Rather, the activities of the new factories were negatively affected by a lack of professional knowledge and organizational skills of the new politically appointed managers and the technically uneducated workers.

However, the domestic textile and clothing industries succeeded in delivering merchandise to the shops even though its quality and style did not match the dream. *Naša moda* reported in 1946 that the textile company *Tivar* had begun to produce ready-to-wear clothes.[9] In 1952, the *Zagreb Business Directory* listed a large number of state-owned shops retailing textiles, clothes and fashion details.[10] The population of Zagreb grew rapidly in the immediate post-war period. While the city had 280,000 inhabitants prior to the war,[11] its population grew to 404,000 by the late 1950s.[12] During that period Zagreb went through a process of rapid urbanization through which its new citizens acquired formal education and, influenced by an established urban culture, adopted new urban life-styles. It was the first time in Croatia's history that such a process of massive and rapid urbanization had taken place.[13] Those civilizing processes included knowledge about proper grooming, from basic cleanliness to the use of cosmetics. In that context, new sartorial rituals were also learned and negotiated. While the adoption of different types of dress and appropriate urban ways of wearing them was encouraged, it was not supposed to clash with the socialist ideals that permitted smartness but banned any excess. Highly urbanized retail practices were also promoted. The most important retailer, the pre-war Austrian-owned department store *Kastner & Öhler*, located on Zagreb's main square, was nationalized after the war. It was renamed *NaMa* and immediately began to dedicate its shop windows to carefully arranged displays of dresses and textiles.[14] Mirko Sagrak, in his book *Shop and Shop Window* published in 1952, promoted the early official approval of embellishment in everyday life. The book was both a basic manual for inexperienced socialist shop managers and an etiquette guide on sophisticated shopping rituals.[15] Opposed to the deprivations of the Soviet and East European type of socialism, Yugoslav socialism in the early 1950s attempted to develop in the direction of everyday cosiness.

In 1956, *Svijet* reported that the state-owned companies *Varteks*, *Vesna* and *DTR* presented decent, reasonably priced clothes at a fashion show, produced from domestic fabrics.[16] However, the encouraging media reports often pointed to underlying problems from unfashionable styles to the failure of the industry to deliver the outfits that had been seen on the catwalks to the shops. The weekly *Globus* stated that only 20 percent of Yugoslav dress fabric production was used by the ready-made clothing industry, compared to 70 percent in the West.[17] The fact that all other textile production was used by seamstresses, private fashion salons and home dressmakers, pointed to the inadequate supply of ready-to-wear clothes in the shops, as well as to their unappealing shapes. In fact, the journals reported that even the textile supplies suffered terrible delays, and that the fabrics, samples of which had been presented at the fairs, would arrive at the shops only at the end of the season.[18]

The new socialist industry proved unable to mass-produce smart, good-quality dress. While it struggled, the private fashion salons succeeded in preserving their fashion rituals. They retained their pre-war cultural capital as well as the expertise to produce good quality dress for individual customers. In their socially ephemeral field, private fashion salons preserved both the physical existence of smart dress and its symbolical role. The first fashion show under socialism, organized by the magazine *Naša moda*, took place in Zagreb as early as 1946, and exclusively presented the clothes designed and produced by the private fashion salons. The Croatian association of private tailors, established in the late 1940s, was active in organizing seasonal fashion shows in the following decades. The private salons' fashion shows preceded those organized by the state clothing companies by a couple of years, and took place with the full approval of the regime in the solemn headquarters of the Crafts Association in the centre of Zagreb. The event would last for ten consecutive days every September, and was attended both by members of the pre-war elite and the new privileged socialist groups. Mila Mirković, one of the first professional Croatian models recalled:

> The private fashion salons' seasonal fashion shows were important social gatherings throughout the 1950s. They rivalled the prominent theatre premieres, and I was usually presented with flowers by the leading Croatian actress Bela Krleža at the end of the show.[19]

Lacking in such lustre, the seasonal fashion shows of the state clothing companies, which started in the early 1950s, did not attract such a dedicated following. The modelling profession was not yet properly established, so the same group of models also presented clothes at the state clothing companies' fashion shows. However, their dresses were not considered exciting, not only because they were industrially produced and presented at the unattractive premises of the Zagreb Fair pavilion, but also because they did not have the direct connection to fashion's past that the private fashion salons provided. The media also paid much more attention to the private salons' fashion shows than to those organized by the state clothing companies. *Svijet* praised the private salons' fashion show in 1956, but prudently warned that a couple of the ninety outfits were extravagant and inappropriate, and claimed that no woman would choose them[20]. But the public craved those long evening outfits, velvet bows on lace dancing dresses, romantic billowing skirts, and carefully cut suits that emphasized an hourglass figure, because they were evocative of the splendid traditions of the pre-war fashion. Fashion accessories, such as stoles, hats, long white gloves, high heels and jewellery only contributed to the allure of the dresses presented by the private salons.

Private fashion enterprises were generally divided in two groups. While the number of people they employed and the size of their premises were measurable factors, the elements that decided on their social status, such as their location, their clientele and their aspirations, were more fluid. Most of the members of the Croatian Crafts Association were small dressmakers or fashion accessories makers, employing only their owner, who quietly continued their pre-war practice within the new but favourable legislation. Many of them took part in the Crafts Association seasonal fashion shows, some of them presenting a small collection of dresses, while others contributed hats, shoes and other fashion accessories to their colleagues' catwalk presentations. On the other hand, some private fashion enterprises employed up to five people, which was a legal maximum, held their own seasonal fashion shows, kept their premises at the prestigious addresses and provided custom-made clothes for the upper echelons of the new society. They ambitiously attempted to present themselves as proper fashion salons, emulating the traditions of pre-war Zagreb, when the city indulged in various urban social rituals, from balls, theatre premiers, luxurious fashion shops and specialized women's and illustrated magazines that informed on the latest Paris fashions.

In the inter-war years, Zagreb, as a fashion capital of pre-war Yugoslavia, already had its International Fair, a strong professional association of crafts, and sophisticated craftsmen who travelled the world, from Paris to Leipzig, Prague, Vienna and Budapest, in order to bring home the latest fashion information and adapt it to their designs. A series of fashion shows of Vienna's fashion institution Wiener Modellgeselschaft began in Zagreb in 1937, presenting the latest Viennese fashions to an audience of professionals. At the same time, the leading Zagreb fashion salons held their fashion shows at the hotel Esplanade or at the National Theatre, while the textile companies showed their new collections at the Zagreb Fair.[21] The owners of the most appreciated post-war private fashion salons – such as Žuži Jelinek, Tilda Stepinska and Terka Tončić – came from a similar pre-war professional and social background. With the tacit approval of the regime and its laws that limited but did not prevent private ownership, they renewed their activities and re-opened their fashion salons at the end of the war. The phenomenon of fashion did not disturb the system, as a fully developed bourgeois society did not exist in pre-war Yugoslavia. After the war, the regime did not feel threatened by the disempowered bourgeois minority and its previous urban traditions and rituals.

Highly urbanized and elegant Western dresses were granted a precise ideological function in the domestic fashion press. They were Yugoslavia's own escapist shortcut from post-war poverty, from the inherited technological backwardness, and the prevailing rurality into an aspiration for a highly developed and urbanized socialist society.

Thus, smart dress performed two significant symbolical roles. In addition to opposing Stalinism, it was also officially perceived as a dream ticket to the much-craved modernity, both in its printed version in the media, and its physical version. Private fashion salons were the only enterprises that could really design and produce it. Žuži Jelinek's fashion salon was the most ambitious among them. While her colleagues were happy to serve their elite clientele, Jelinek simultaneously catered for her individual customers and actively pursued and secured public attention and praise in her various dealings with the regime and its need for an urban and smart dress. In that role, Jelinek cooperated with the large state-owned textile factories, advised on proper dress in newspaper columns, and wrote a book on good taste. While the examples of her direct public engagement gained a lot of media attention, supplying appropriate dresses for individual clients also had an important role in the new society and its ways of establishing new rituals.

Following the Communist take over of power, the urban middle class was reduced to one-fifth of its size in the interwar period, and was seen as a kind of class relic by 1947.[22] A new, politically powerful class began to take shape, which was different in every respect from both the middle class and elite of the pre-war period. In most parts of Yugoslavia, the members of the new communist elite were on average in their early thirties, without formal secondary education, and of rural origin.[23] The gatherings at the seasonal fashion shows organised by the private fashion salons brought together members of the disempowered urban elite with representatives of the new, powerful but unsophisticated elites of rural origin. New civilizing rituals and new rules of propriety were also polished in private fashion salons through the medium of smart dress. Žuži Jelinek was aware of a subtle symbolic transaction between a new socialist middle class customer and a socialist couturière. In 1961, she dedicated an entire chapter in her book *The Secrets of a Well-Dressed*

Woman: The Rules of Attractiveness and Good Taste to the relationship between a seamstress and her client:

> The relationship between the seamstress and her customer should not be only commercial. The seamstress has to become a friend and confidante of her client, and should be able, relying on her style and knowledge, to help her to become attractive and well-dressed woman.[24]

While delicately advising on proper etiquette, Jelinek also emphasized the role of the cultural agent for the representatives of her profession. She argued that the dressmaker had to speak French and Italian in order to learn first hand, and certainly before her client, about the latest trends from the leading fashion magazines.[25] The long standing fashion editor of *Svijet*, Magda Weltrusky was Jelinek's client in the late 1950s:

> I dressed at Žuži Jelinek before I got married. It did cost a lot of money, but my father was paying for it, while afterwards money mostly went to acquire a house, and refurbish it. It was a period of grand fashion salons, but for me Žuži was the best, as she owned the latest western fashion magazines, such as *Vogue*. You would flick through magazines, and choose a model and fabric as well, as Žuži offered to her clientele fabrics that she procured from the West. Žuži was not really a fashion designer, but she was definitely an excellent seamstress. She knew how to re-produce the cut of a dress from the picture, as those journals did not have paper-patterns. However, Žuži was not supposed to be left on her own; you had to be active as a client. On the occasion when I relied on her to choose the fabric and the style of dress, I finished owning an outfit that I never put on.[26]

A Croatian business woman Maja Kosić remembers that her mother was also a regular Jelinek client from the late 1940s, and that the designer would make her mother's dresses from the precious fabrics that her father would bring from his business trips to the West. From today's perspective, Kosić observed that Jelinek's dresses in the 1950s and 1960s demonstrated perfect craftsmanship but that their style conformed to the rules of conventional elegance. Outfits mainly consisted of a dress with a jacket, shirt-waist dresses or cocktail dresses. They were highly priced, but acquiring custom-made dresses in private fashion salons was the only way to dress smartly in Croatia at that time, remembered Kosić.[27] The new elite ordered their outfits at Žuži Jelinek's fashion salon because of her close connections with the regime, although some were customers of other, competing private fashion salons. Tilda Stepinska also made clothes for the most important members of the Croatian Nomenklatura, including Marija Bakarić, wife of president of Croatian government Vladimir Bakarić, who herself was president of the Croatian Women's Anti-Fascist Organization, and for Anka Berus, a prominent member of the Croatian Resistance movement, later a highly placed political figure. Stepinska however kept her pre-war clients including Čuča Smokvina, a prominent socialite from the inter-war years.[28]

While her main competitors, such as Stepinska, were also very successful in acquiring important clients and dressing them up in smart, perfectly executed dresses, Žuži Jelinek excelled in her numerous public engagements. In the mid-1950s, she entered into collaboration with *Varteks*, which was both a textile and a ready-to-wear clothing factory. While in 1956 Jelinek's special collection from *Varteks'* fabrics was exhibited in her salon, the newspaper reported that the originality of her outfits accentuated the patterns and quality of *Varteks'* fabrics.[29] The political approval of collaboration between state industry and the private fashion salon demonstrated the vulnerability of the Croatian state clothing industry, which had to rely on private designers as they could provide both experience and style. The Zagreb daily *Vjesnik* acknowledged that the cooperation between Varteks and Jelinek, "known for her excellent outfits only to a narrow group of her private clients, could bring freshness to the state-produced ready-to-wear".[30] In her work, Jelinek continually insisted on collaboration with the textile industry, which proved her loyalty to the regime, and consequently attracted a lot of media attention. In 1958, the official Women's association sponsored Jelinek's fashion show in which she collaborated with the *Zagrebačka tvornica svile (Zagreb Silk Factory)* and the wool cloth company *Zora (Dawn)*. A newspaper that covered economic issues reported that the state-owned companies were encouraged to buy designs by the private designers and put them into mass-production.[31]

The aesthetics of Jelinek's dresses was not a problem. Although her style was polished and informed about the latest fashion trends, her innate minimalism matched the ideal of socialist moderation, adding it a much-craved dose of glamour. In my interview with her, Jelinek emphasized that she had learnt her trade in pre-war Paris, working, among others, at the Nina Ricci fashion house, and being especially inspired by Coco Chanel.[32] In her post-war period, back in her Zagreb salon, Jelinek stayed true to the aesthetic conventions of Paris chic, which continued to rule the traditional French fashion throughout the 1950s. The weekly *Globus* announced in 1960:

> Concerning her design style, Žuži Jelinek is our Coco Chanel. She says: "I hate over-dressed women. Therefore, I suggest simple fashion to our women. Simple fashion is always elegant, and thus a woman that dresses simply but tastefully is always elegant".[33]

Globus had already praised Coco Chanel's functional and comfortable fashion a year earlier, in 1959. In that article, the magazine reminded its readers that Chanel had already caused a couple of fashion revolutions in the past, but stressed that she understood that there was no need for a new revolution in dress, as contemporary fashion already fulfilled all women's needs and "allowed a woman to dress aesthetically and practically, but still look beautiful, be free in her movements, elegant, and even to attract attention".[34] At that time, Chanel was already considered conservative by the Western fashion media, because her seasonal collections did not present any significant changes in her well-established style.[35] Chanel was also challenged by the newcomers such as Pierre Cardin and Andre Courrèges who brought radical novelty into Paris fashion imagery.

Roland Barthes analyzed the big change that happened in the Paris 1960 fashion world by opposing its two main antagonists. Barthes stated that Chanel chic could not stand "the look of newness," and that a change in a "discreet detail" was the only distinction in dress it allowed for, while a revolutionary new-comer Andre Cour-règes advocated violent change in his radically new and youth-ful shapes of dress.[36] He emphasized: "So, it is the notion of time, which is a style for one and a fashion for the other, that separates Chanel from Courrèges."[37] Jelinek's style matched that of a "clas-sicist" Chanel and her eternal chic, and that was, conveniently, the aesthetics that socialism also embraced from the mid-1950s on. Re-porting on a fashion show that *Svijet* organized with Žuži Jelinek, the magazine announced that changes had been avoided in devis-ing the fashion trends for the new season:

> As fashion for the coming spring and summer season is overwhelmed with enormous changes, the outfits at our fashion show were cleverly designed. The middle ground was applied between this year's and last year's fashion. All outfits are adjusted to our women and to our circumstances; if our ready to wear industry accepts them, we can claim in advance that our women will be dressed very nicely and tastefully.[38]

To develop socialist good taste in the 1950s, the official dis-course borrowed aesthetic categories from petit-bourgeois "good taste". Those categories were needed to dilute the asceticism of proletarian style, which socialism never officially renounced. So-cialist good taste was the result of the merger of proletarian style with petit bourgeois "good taste". It was produced through the hybridization of their mutual characteristics, like modesty, bland-ness, appropriateness and comfort. At the same time, prettiness and elegance were two crucial categories appropriated from petit bourgeois good taste, and added to its socialist version. As Roland Barthes argued, such petit-bourgeois norms are bourgeois truths, which have become degraded, impoverished, commercialized, slightly archaic and out of date.[39] Due to poverty, lack of tradition in smart dress rituals, and its insufficiently educated practitioners, socialism picked from the residue of bourgeois culture while im-posing its dress practices and its aesthetics rules. A sense of mea-sure was a key concept in the new stylistic synthesis of modesty and elegance. There were clear boundaries between the categories of appropriateness and inappropriateness, within which socialist fashion operated, and the socialist women's magazines, etiquette books, and manuals on fashion preached against any transgression.[40] In her book on the rules of attractiveness and good taste, Jelinek advocated that a woman should not feel obliged to wear the latest fashion. The fashionable woman:

> … is in danger of becoming a fashion doll, and nobody appreciates that. Fashion fads change so fast that it is very difficult to keep up with their pace. The most fashionable dress will be out of fashion before you had even chance to put it on three times.[41]

Socialist good taste and its Western counterpart also shared the concept of time. Both versions of "good taste", petit bourgeois and socialist, were almost immutable, and equally scared of unpredictability and individuality.[42] Socialist good taste was an ideal medium to filter, neutralize and slow down fashion changes, and to offer safe sartorial choices to those who were new to sophisticated rituals of dressing up. Thus, Coco Chanel, who season after season merely perfected the smart woman's work suit that she had designed in the mid-1950s, was an ideal role model for a socialist fashion designer. Similar to her French counterpart, Jelinek offered smart dress choices that could take a serious woman from work to play, and still precisely defined her dignified role in the society:

> The opinion that the politically engaged woman-worker does not need to take care of her dress-style is wrong. On the contrary, her appearance will be more appropriate if she is dressed tastefully but simply. A lot of people take an interest in her looks, many women have her as a role model and she has to give an example by the way she dresses.[43]

So, what was the most appropriate style for her? It was a simple but elegant jacket and skirt made out of a good quality fabric in colder months, or a cotton *chemise dress* in the summer, or an ensemble consisting of a little blouse with three-quarter sleeves combined with a pleated skirt. A little feminine hat, short white gloves, a string of pearls or a brooch could be added in socially more demanding situations, such as at official party meetings, formal parties, cocktails, important anniversaries and The First of May Parades.[44] Other newspapers, such as a daily *Narodni list*, praised Jelinek's ability to acknowledge the latest trends but adjust them to the rules of socialist moderate aesthetics:

> This fashion show ... succeeded to present the latest world fashion trends, adjusted to the requirements of our taste. The outfits paraded on the catwalk neither resembled the fashions of the last seasons nor unacceptable, too original ideas shown in the foreign fashion journals. These outfits presented an abundance of novelty, yet, they do not require sudden change of habits and concepts of beautiful clothing.[45]

Jelinek was relentless in her advisory role, granting interviews to the media and writing columns for a weekly *Vjesnik u srijedu*, promoting the aesthetics of socialist good taste equally to members of newly urbanized middle class, female workers and farm-women. A whole chapter of her book on good taste was dedicated to the latter, as no category of socialist citizens could be left out of appropriate dress codes. Jelinek summed her extensive advice to a farmwoman in ten rules:

> 1) Stop wearing folk costume in everyday life; 2) Dress in the style of city ladies; 3) Wear skirt and blouse while working; 4) Do not wear too long skirts; 5) Attend a course on the proper care of your skin and the proper style of clothing; 6) Cut off your long hair and save the braids; 7) Do not wear distasteful colours; 8) Take good care of your folk costume and wear it on Sunday or holidays; 9) Do not pair folk costume with modern shoes or short hair; 10) Take the scarf off your head and wear it only while working.[46]

While Jelinek enthusiastically embraced a ruling socialist aesthetics, and tirelessly tried to promote it, she nevertheless would usually mention her up-to-date knowledge on the latest Paris fashion trends in her dealings with the domestic media. Her regular trips to Paris and the latest copies of *Vogue* that she casually kept on the coffee table in her salon had their specific role in establishing her as a much praised socialist fashion designer. Jelinek's loyalty to the concept of conventional elegance throughout the 1960s, long after Paris fashion left it, suited the slow socialist narrative and its fear of sudden change. She was celebrated because her dresses were not threatening but smart and elegant in a way, which was appreciated by the socialist regime. Her private fashion salon was based in Zagreb, but Jelinek was well-known throughout the country. In 1960, her first independent fashion show in Belgrade was held in the prestigious space of *Dom sindikata*, usually reserved for important state events, and attended by two thousand people. *Globus* reported that many of those who did not succeed in obtaining a ticket on time were paying 1,000 dinars for one on the black market.[47]

Žuži Jelinek sought and received not only domestic but also international attention. In 1959, *Globus* presented Jelinek's attempt to establish her fashion house in New York. Her American adventure was recoded into a rags-to-riches story in order to suit socialist ideals.[48] In *Globus'* story, the socialist Cinderella lived on yoghurt and bread-rolls, and secretly sliced the sausage she had brought with her from home in her luxurious hotel suite, while at the same time adjusting dresses for the slim American models who presented her fashion show. Upon her arrival in New York she discovered that the American models had considerably slender figures, and subsequently spent two days and nights on dress repairs, without any rest. Through sheer hard work and wits, continued *Globus*, she was eventually rewarded with an interview in the *New York Times*, which resulted with the invitation for a dinner at David Rockefeller's home. The useful social connections she made there assisted her recognition by the American media and leading department stores such as *Lord&Taylor*. Jelinek's trip was covered in detail in *Globus*, which displayed pictures of her waving from the aeroplane stairs dressed in fur and partying with high society on the *Queen Mary* on her way to America.[49]

When Jelinek presented her new collection in Bergdorf Goodman and other leading New York department stores in 1959, she employed a professional P.R. Martha G. Palmer who ensured high profile media attention, including her interview with the *New York Times*.[50] In that interview, Žuži Jelinek confirmed her talent in dealing with the media abroad, by playing with the image of the socialist fashion designer. When asked if there was any common denominator between her and her American counterparts, she answered: "It's Paris, of course. What happens to fashions every season depends directly on what the French couture does. But, of course, I copy them".[51] However, Jelinek's American project failed. Although she enjoyed enthusiastic and professional support in America, she could not produce her clothes in sufficient quantities for the American market.

Following a series of fashion shows in New York, Palmer wrote a desperate letter to her in Zagreb in December 1959.[52] She reminded Jelinek of the media attention she had secured for her and the department stores' orders that had followed, and demanded that the orders should be delivered. Understanding that Jelinek's small private salon could not manufacture the considerable pre-ordered quantities, Palmer appealed to the Yugoslav side in general to live up to their business obligations. The Croatian media failed to report on Jelinek's production and delivery problems, which got in the way of her success in America, and presented her subsequent business trips to the USA as a series of successes.[53] The regime invested Žuži Jelinek's dresses with an ideological task: to present Yugoslavia as a liberal and civilized country, and the media attention of American and Croatian magazines served that purpose to perfection.

Even the most prestigious among Yugoslav private fashion salons could not develop into proper fashion houses, as they were legally allowed to employ only up to five people. However, Jelinek, a business woman with an obviously strong entrepreneurial spirit, continued to pursue the international recognition. In 1961, the Croatian media reported on the large, hundred-outfit collection that Jelinek first showed at the most prestigious Zagreb hotel *Esplanade* only to take it a week later to an Asian tour, presenting her clothes in Iran, India, Burma, Ceylon and Israel.[54] She presented a fashion show in Japan as well, and came back to New York on a couple of occasions. Jelinek's 1961 autumn and winter collection was, however, presented at the Yugoslav Embassy at United Nations. The invitation cited the prestigious Fifth Avenue address, but that fashion show only had a representational purpose. A year later, under the political pressure, Žuži Jelinek left Croatia for Switzerland, her only crime being her individualistic attitude and business shrewdness.[55]

Jelinek's entrepreneurial attitude was punished. The owners of the private fashion salons were not expected to be serious business people in their own right. They were supposed to grant some sophistication and glitter to the image of socialist fashion at a time when the regime wanted to re-connect socialist sartorial codes with western fashion. *Globus* readily compared Jelinek to Coco Chanel, and introduced a new weekly feature "Diors Among Us", dedicated to the owners-designers of private fashion salons, promoting them as celebrities.[56] Although the private fashion salons perceived themselves as bastions of proper bourgeois values, and kept up appearances with seasonal fashion shows, their dresses gradually became dated in an environment that was neither creatively nor economically encouraging. The official discourse recognized the existing private fashion salons as a useful medium to present fashion practices that suited the socialist slow flow of time: classical, elegant, timeless, and possessing a tradition that Yugoslav socialism suddenly desired. The pre-war cultural capital that only private fashion salons could provide was needed to ideologically re-affirm smart dress.

Private fashion salons existed throughout socialist times, but their symbolic role diminished after the 1960s with the arrival of youth culture and improved access to the latest western fashions. By that time, their craftsmanship and insistence on the rules of conventional elegance appeared to be old-fashioned. A new type of private fashion shop called a boutique brought about the demise in importance of the private fashion salon. The success of the boutique was due to the owner's flexibility to react fast to the latest fashion trends. It meant that the entrepreneurial owner would travel to Italy, obtain the most fashionable item, cut it into pieces at home to master the cut, and re-produce a couple of thousand cheap copies for the masses interested in fashion fads. The diminutive size of the boutiques, which, nevertheless, usually occupied the best locations in the city centres, and the levels of trade that the owners declared to the tax authorities disguised the truth about their huge business activities and big profits. The owners were also served by a cheap work force in the shadow economy, which contributed to their sudden wealth. While the authorities imposed a limit of five employees on the owners of private fashion salons, and controlled their activities in the 1950s and 1960s, the relaxed attitude towards the owners of boutiques during the 1970s demonstrated that the regime valued the capability of the boutiques to deliver fashion to the increasingly fashion-aware masses more than the strict application of the laws which would curb their business activities. Žuži Jelinek's private fashion salon survived throughout the socialist period, but it became more and more marginalized, due both to her outdated aesthetics of conventional smartness and her customers' increasing ease of access to fashionable Western clothes.

Notes

[1] *Svijet [World]* was started in 1953 in Zagreb, and published by the state-owned publishing house *Vjesnik*.

[2] I am grateful to Mrs Žuži Jelinek for granting me an interview and giving me access to her well organized and well-kept private archive (Interview, Zagreb, February 26, 2001).

[3] In an interview, a respected Croatian journalist Đorđe Zelmanović reminisced that Jelinek triumphantly returned to Zagreb, on the top of a partisan tank (Interview, Zagreb, February 24, 2001).

[4] *Naša moda [Our Fashion]* was started by the state-owned publishing house *Vjesnik* in February 1946, and it closed down at the end of 1948. *Naša moda* favourably reported on the fashion show in the *Moscow House of Fashion* ("U Moskovskom Domu Modela [In the Moscow House of Fashion]," *Naša moda*, N 4, 1946), while a highly approving article on the one of the Moscow state-owned fashion ateliers was published in October ("Moskovski Modni Atelje [Moscow Fashion Atelier]," *Naša moda*, N 9, 1946).

[5] In 1946, the first Yugoslav *Five-Year Plan* prioritised the rapid development of heavy industry and the collectivization of agriculture, similar to the Five-Year Plans in other new East European socialist countries in the late 1940s.

[6] "Yugoslav Textile Industry," *Revue des Exportateurs et Importateurs*, N 3, 1958.

[7] Ibid.

[8] *Narodni list [People's Newspaper]*, May 17, 1953.

[9] "From Wool to Ready-Made Clothes [Od vune do gotovih odijela]," *Naša moda*, N 2, March, 1946. The magazine described in detail how 750 workers were employed in a new department to cut, sew, finalize and iron ready-made clothes using new electronic machines *Tivar* was a pre-war textile company, but it was eventually renamed into *Varteks* and grew into one of the biggest textile and clothing companies in Yugoslavia following the war.

[10] *Poslovni Adresar Grada Zagreba [Zagreb Business Directory]* (Zagreb: Savremena tehnika, 1952). There were sixty-two shops selling textiles, twenty-seven shops selling shoes, thirteen shops selling fashion accessories such as hats, socks, underwear and leather goods, and one shop selling fur coats. Thirteen of the shops retailing ready-to-wear clothes mainly belonged to the clothing factories themselves, such as *Varteks* and *Naprijed*.

[11] Lelja Dobronić, *Zagreb* (Zagreb: Spektar, 1985), xi.

[12] Jack C. Fischer, "Urban Analysis: A Case Study of Zagreb, Yugoslavia," *Annals of the Association of American Geographers* vol 53, N 3 (1963): 278.

[13] In the subsequent forty years the agricultural population in Croatia dropped from around two thirds of the total population to just under one third. For an overview, see Vesna Pusić, "A Country by Any Other Name: Transition and Stability in Croatia and Yugoslavia," *East European Politics and Societies* 6 (3) (1992): 242–59.

[14] *NaMa* is shortened version of *Narodni Magazin*, which means the *People's Department Store*.

[15] Mirko Sagrak, *Prodavaonica i Izlog [Shop and Shop Window]* (Zagreb: Progres, 1952), 76–80.

[16] "Modna Revija [Fashion Show]," *Svijet*, N 5, 1956.

[17] "Proljetne Laste Lete na Istok (Spring Swallows Fly to the East)," *Globus*, N 32, February 7, 1960, 38–40.

[18] "Sajam Mode 1958 [The Fashion Fair 1958]," *Svijet*, N 6, 1958.

[19] Bela Krleža was the wife of the most important Croatian writer Miroslav Krleža. Bela Krleža and Mila Mirković were friends through their husbands, who were respectively the director and deputy director of the *Yugoslav Lexicographic Institute*. The fact that the wife of the highly positioned intellectual was a model demonstrates that fashion was symbolically granted a high social position (My interview with Mrs Mirković, Zagreb, May 22, 2001).

[20] "Modna Revija [Fashion Show]," *Svijet*, N 5, 1956. Although the review was related to the presentations by both the clothing industry and private salons, the accompanying images showed only the salons' outfits.

[21] Magda Weltrusky, "Zagrebačka Moda [Zagreb Fashion]," in *Zagreb Modni Vodič [Zagreb Fashion Guide]*, ed. D. Helebrant (Zagreb: Zadružna štampa, 1988), 31–43.

[22] The upper and middle classes, who enjoyed fashion rituals and sophisticated urban life-styles, were a minority even in the prevalently rural country before the war. In 1938, the society of pre-war Yugoslavia was prevalently rural, consisting of 87 percent peasants and poor workers, 11 percent urban middle class and 2 percent high bourgeoisie (Lenard J. Cohen, *The Socialist Pyramid: Elites and Power in Yugoslavia* (London: Tri-Service Press, 1989).)

[23] For an overview of the educational, class, geographical, generational and ethnic background of Yugoslav post-war elite, see Lenard J. Cohen, ibid., 1989, 106–24.

[24] Žuži Jelinek, *Tajna Dobro Odjevene Žene: Pravila Privlačnosti i Dobrog Ukusa [The Secret of the Well-dressed Woman: The Rules of Attractiveness and Good Taste]* (Zagreb: NIP, 1961), 160.

[25] Žuži Jelinek, ibid., 1961, 159.

[26] My interview, Zagreb, July 2005.

[27] My interview, Zagreb, July 2005.

[28] I obtained the information on Tilda Stepinska activities and her clientele from the Croatian P.R. Tomica Javorčić, whose mother worked as a seamstress in Stepinska's salon from the 1950s till 1970s (Interview, Zagreb, November 2005). As a boy, Javorčić would deliver dresses to Stepinska's clients for his pocket money. He also stated that Stepinska's luxurious fabrics arrived as parcels from Switzerland to different Zagreb private addresses, including the homes of her seamstresses. In such a way, customs duties could be avoided.

[29] "Varteks Priredio u Zagrebu Modnu Reviju [Varteks Presented a Fashion Show in Zagreb]," *Borba*, November 6, 1956.

[30] "New Ready-to-Wear Varteks' Outfits," *Vjesnik*, April 24, 1957.

[31] *Privredni Vjesnik*, March 7, 1958.

[32] Interview, February 2001.

[33] "Ambasador Mode [Ambasador of Fashion]," *Globus*, June 6, 1960, pp 28–29, p 28.

[34] "Chanel 1959. Pariz: Jesenja Moda za Normalne Žene [Chanel 1959. From Paris: The Autumn Fashion for Normal Women]," *Globus*, August 22, 1959.

[35] Valerie Steele commented that, contrary to the French and English, only the American magazines, which themselves feared fashion changes, praised Chanel after her comeback in 1954. (Valerie Steele, "Chanel in Context," in *Chic Thrills*, ed. Juliet Ash and Elizabeth Wilson (Berkeley: University of California Press, 1993), 118–26.) On the other hand, observ-

426   *Djurdja Bartlett*

ing similarities to her styles from the 1920s and 1930s, the West European media pronounced Chanel's 1950s collections conservative and old-fashioned (Amy de la Haye and Shelley Tobin, *Chanel: The Couturiere at Work* (London: Victoria and Albert Museum, 1994).)

³⁶ Roland Barthes, "The Contest between Chanel and Courrèges. Referred by a Philosopher," in *Roland Barthes: Language of Fashion* (London: Berg, 2006), 106–7. (Originally published in *Marie Claire*, September, 1967, 42–4.)

³⁷ Ibid.

³⁸ "Modna Revija [Fashion Show]," *Svijet*, April 1, 1958.

³⁹ Roland Barthes, *Mythologies* (London: Granada Publishing Limited, 1976), 140–1.

⁴⁰ See, for example, advice on a proper dress in Đorđe Zelmanović, *Ilustrirani Bonton: Pravila Lijepog Ponašanja u Kući, izvan Kuće, na Putu* (Zagreb: Stvarnost, 1963).

⁴¹ Žuži Jelinek, ibid., 1961, 91.

⁴² Ted Polhemus and Lynn Procter argued that any "good taste" in Western clothes, ranging from the upper class to the middle class or the petit-bourgeois version, is an anti-fashion statement. See Ted Polhemus and Lynn Procter, *Fashion and Anti-Fashion* (London: Thames and Hudson, 1978).

⁴³ Žuži Jelinek, ibid., 1961, 115.

⁴⁴ Žuži Jelinek, ibid., 1961, 116.

⁴⁵ *Narodni list*, March 7, 1958.

⁴⁶ Žuži Jelinek, ibid., 1961, 141.

⁴⁷ "Ambasador Mode [Ambasador of Fashion]," *Globus*, June 6, 1960, pp 28–29, p 29.

⁴⁸ "Žuži of Yugoslavia," *Globus*, N 2, 1959, 40–1.

⁴⁹ Ibid, 40. *Globus* also stated that Jelinek met a professional photographer at that dinner, and that he advised her to use an American model in the presentation of her collection to the American media. That model happened to be famous Suzy Parker, *Globus* proudly announced, adding that both the photographer and Suzy Parker did a fashion shoot for free.

⁵⁰ Thanks to Palmer's P.R. connections, Jelinek was presented not only in the *New York Times*, but also in the *Herald Tribune, Women's Wear Daily*, the hotel's magazine *Host* and the National Broadcasting System.

⁵¹ G. Emerson, "Yugoslavs Also Copy Paris Style," *New York Times*, May 4, 1959.

⁵² Martha G. Palmer's letter is in Jelinek's private archive.

⁵³ See, for example: "Ambasador Mode [Ambasador of Fashion]," *Globus*, June 6, 1960, pp 28–29, p 29; "Bruxelleska Vjenčanica Žuži Jelinek [Žuži Jelinek's Brussels' Wedding Gown]," *Svijet*, November 6, 1968, 35.

[54] Interview, February 2001.

[55] In the interview she gave to me (February 2001), Mrs Jelinek claimed that President Tito proclaimed her an enemy of the people in public speech on February 23, 1962. I did not find evidence for that claim in the contemporary media. On the occasion of our interview, she also stated that prior to that Tito invited her for a visit and told her that she could not travel around the world to present fashion collections under her personal name anymore. Instead, she was supposed to officially become the designer of the Macedonian clothing company *Tetex*. In her words, she rejected the offer, only to leave for Switzerland and eventually become, in the more entrepreneurial-friendly atmosphere, a successful and rich businesswoman. Nevertheless, her motivation for her abrupt departure could have been, at least partially, caused by the break-up of her first marriage that happened at that time. She returned to Croatia in 1964 to run her private fashion salon. After making peace with Tito, she even designed clothes for his wife Jovanka in the 1960s and 1970s.

[56] In one feature, Jelinek's counterpart, Tilda Stepinska emphasized that, while she was always inspired by French haute couture, she only chose ideas suitable for "our conditions". Stepinska highlighted that she dressed "women who held high political office in the country, or represented it abroad, and therefore needed elegant and functional clothes" (B. Stošić, "Diori Su Među Nama [Diors Are Among Us]," *Globus*, N 15, October 11, 1959, 40–1).

16

A Face in the Market
Photography, Memory, and Nostalgia

Hanno Hardt

Markets are places of exchange for goods and services as well as words and gestures, reflecting the world of human enterprise in the colorful gestalt of a communal discourse. Indeed, they are the mirrors of their community, capturing moments of barter and social communion, and they constitute the site where expectations meet and struggle over the meaning of a bargain is a well rehearsed spectacle. But above all, markets remain a visible expression of cultural and economic structures of social energy.

At the time of Yugoslavia the Ljubljana marketplace was a daily declaration of a belief in a common humanity revealed by the routines of vendors from many parts of the federation and the lively response of a discerning clientele. Together these individuals filled the generous space of the market with expectations, whose vigor created a milieu of small talk and friendly banter. In such an atmosphere of mutual dependence, suspicion and belief, the exchange of goods and money seemed merely a necessary byproduct of an anticipated social event for those gathered to do business and for others who came from the city. Especially on weekends, the traditional walk through the old town included a stopover at the market for coffee, chats, and visits to the favorite vegetable or flower stands, beyond arts and crafts displays, past spices, meats, and cheeses and around stands with wicker baskets, woolen goods or shoes.

Patrons and flâneurs alike were greeted by expectant faces, heedful glances, or inviting smiles, which offered confidence in the encounter and satisfaction with a purchase. There was constant commotion in an atmosphere of nervous anticipation, considered pacing, pricing, and close inspections of stalls loaded with non-industrial merchandize. It was mostly the contemplation of food, however, in its many varieties, which defined the common interests in local produce, fresh off the fields of Bosnia or Macedonia, with kajmak from Serbia and green salad from Dalmatia adding variety to the selection of homegrown products.

As such, the market became a realistic and sensible encounter with the multicultural and multi-ethnic nature of Yugoslavia and a reminder of its possibilities grounded in the promises of socialism. Day-in, day-out, individuals from far-away places added temperament and style to the routines of commerce, their faces indelibly marked by traces of life in its many guises with scars of survival and defeat. They constituted the vanguard of an alternative vision of an industrious life, demonstrating perseverance and patience in their desire for commercial success, while dedicating time and effort throughout the seasons to their modest enterprise. Their presence helped build confidence in the availability of food products, and the market became a first and last resort for those looking to augment their daily diet.

But photographs are never just statements of a final truth, or ultimate historical evidence of times past. Their meaning and significance change in the course of their existence. Thus, over time they are objects of a never-ending challenge of memory as contemporary conditions or ideological perspectives help render yet another interpretation of the past. Indeed, photography has acquired the power to displace memory and remembering becomes but an act of remembering photographs. Ever since their invention, the photographic idea rules the day, when having been there means having snapped the picture to be stowed away for later proof or verification. Thus looking at these images of the Ljubljana market suggests a complicity of photography and memory in the process of reconstructing the past as a better world. Photography has become the arsenal of memory, if not the modern form of memory, from which we draw information, solicit emotions, and develop a sense of nostalgia.

Moreover, photographs respond to a yearning for that-which-no-longer-is with their concreteness, which heightens the sense of loss and fans the flames of nostalgia. Thus, viewing photographs also is always an act of mourning the irretrievable, the mythical homeland, Heimat or fatherland. Nostalgia as a historical emotion recovers the idea of Yugoslavia as a cultural experience, which celebrates the values of diversity, peace and collaboration. Once removed from its original intent, the photograph becomes a culturally determined text, open to appropriation, interpretation and use by the forces of memory. Nostalgia builds on these forces, which embrace the photograph as reality to revisit a historical moment.

Indeed, photographs are freeze-frames of history, whose extension into the present lends visibility to the course of time. Nostalgia exploits memory (and therefore photography) for romantic bouts of longing without responsibility, re-constructing times and places with feverish desire.

Thus, the meaning of a documentary photograph changes to yet another fiction with every gaze of the reader, whose knowledge, coupled with curiosity, exploits the ambiguity of the image. Accordingly, its meaning is limited only by the limits of the imagination, from which nostalgia rises to help reinvent the past, while its physical presence confirms not only its material quality, but also authenticates its use in reproducing a nostalgic version of reality.

Twenty-odd years later, these photographs may well exceed their documentary claims to reinforce a fashionable Yugo-nostalgia that has swept over the contemporary Balkan states of ex-Yugoslavia in their various social, political, and economic conditions, from Euro-centered Slovenia to Euro-skeptic Serbia. Nostalgia becomes an effective antidote to politics as these photographs enter into the discourse of economic despair, political defeat or cultural voyeurism as icons of a "better" time. They are evidence of a lost era, but at the same time, an invitation to utopian visions of life under Tito's socialism. Thus, these faces may trigger nostalgic recollections of the diversity of cultures, the sound of Macedonian songs, the pleasure of guaranteed vacations under the Dalmatian summer sun, and the sights of fertile valleys on journeys across Bosnia, all colored by a longing for the good times, when life seemed uncomplicated. Nostalgia deflects from current crises as wishful thinking clouds memory, reconstituting that which has never been.

Under these circumstances, the market with its vendors as an image of the past becomes isolated from the prevailing economic and political conditions of its time, when collective interests rather than individual enterprise ruled the commercial life of the country.

Consequently, these photographs turn into a nostalgic instance of a recovered past, when the hardship of daily routines with nighttime journeys into the city, weeks of braving inclement weather, and meager profits at the end of the day give way to fantasies of a simple and secure existence, an honest day's work, and a peaceful reality of political conformity and cultural diversity.

These are the faces of individuals, whose labor produced the atmosphere of the market. They are the signature images of a specific time. Although their capture in these photographs reveals as much as it hides, their presence speaks not only to the vitality of the occasion, but also to the passage of time and the presence of previous commercial routines. Collectively these portraits constitute the enigmatic face of Yugoslavia, reflecting individuality, character, cunning, doubt and inner strength among the stalls of the Ljubljana market, furnishing Yugo-nostalgia with a symbolic image of brotherhood and unity in action.

At the same time, portraits are a product of collaboration between photographer and subject, when the act of posing becomes an act of self-construction. The realized expression is not only a response to the camera eye but also an affirmation of being in the world. It is the documented existence of the self at a specific historical moment.

Consequently, each of these photographs constitutes an autobiographical disclosure and becomes an individualized representation of the self looking beyond the frame while confronting an unrealized future. Surrounded by an aura of nostalgia these gazes meet where past and present are joined for a reunion, however incomplete, among the uncertainties of yet another day.

Still and all, emerging from the course of time, these photographs reveal the instant, in which mutual consent and spontaneity created a collaborative moment of trust long enough to commit each face to memory by way of making a photograph.

Note: The photographs were taken between 1984 and 1989 at the Ljublja-na market; they are part of a ten-year documentary project by the author, which began in 1984.

About the Authors

Djurdja Bartlett gained her PhD on *Ideology and Clothes: the Rise and Decline of Socialist Official Fashion* at the London College of Fashion, University of the Arts London (2006), where she now works as a Research Fellow. Her book *FashionEast: the Spectre that Haunted Socialism* is published by MIT Press (2010). She is editor of a volume on Russia, East Europe and the Caucasus in the *Berg Encyclopedia of World Dress and Fashion* (2010). [email: d.b.bartlett@fashion.arts.ac.uk]

Igor Duda is a teaching assistant in Croatian contemporary history at the Department of Humanities, Juraj Dobrila University of Pula, Croatia. He received the M.A. (2004) and Ph.D. (2009) degrees in history from the University of Zagreb. He published the book *U Potrazi za Blagostanjem. O Povijesti Dokolice i Potrošačkog Društva u Hrvatskoj 1950-ih i 1960-ih* (2005) and his book on everyday life and consumer culture in Croatia in the 1970s and 1980s is forthcoming. [email: igor.duda@unipu.hr]

Hanno Hardt is professor of communication and media studies at the Faculty of Social Sciences, University of Ljubljana, Slovenia and a professor emeritus of mass communication and communication studies at the University of Iowa, USA, whose current research and teaching interests focus on ideas of history and photographic evidence. His most recent book is entitled, *Des Murs Éloquents. Une Rhétorique Visuelle du Politique* (Klincksieck, Paris). [email: hanno.hardt@fdv.uni-lj.si]

Breda Luthar is professor of media studies at the Faculty of Social Sciences, University of Ljubljana, Slovenia. She teaches undergraduate and graduate courses on media and communication, popular culture, media audiences and consumer culture. Her research focus is on politics and popular culture, class and cultural distinctions and consumer culture. [email: breda.luthar@fdv.uni-lj.si]

Danka Ninković Slavnić is a graduate student at the Department for journalism and communication studies, Faculty of Political Science in Belgrade, Serbia. Areas of her interest are visual culture, photography above all, and media and identities. She was working for more than six years as a photojournalist for numerous Serbian daily newspapers and magazines. [email: dninkovic@yahoo.com]

Tanja Petrović is research fellow at the Scientific Research Center in Ljubljana, Slovenia and at the Institute for Balkan Studies in Belgrade, Serbia and assistant professor at the University of Nova Gorica, Slovenia. Her main academic interests lie in the field of intersection of linguistic, social and cultural phenomena in the Balkans and Central Europe, with emphasis on ideologies and remembering. [email: tanja.petrovic@zrc-sazu.si]

Martin Pogačar is a doctoral researcher at the University of Nova Gorica / SRC SASA joint program Interdisciplinary Studies of Ideas and Cultures and a member of the SRC SASA's Section for Interdisciplinary Research in Humanities. His interests are relations between new media and history, online ethnography, and popular culture as complementary historical source, focusing on former Yugoslav popular culture in particular. [email: martin.pogacar@siol.net]

Maruša Pušnik is assistant professor at the Department of Media and Communication Studies at the Faculty of Social Sciences, University of Ljubljana, Slovenia. Her research interests include media, popular culture and practices of everyday life, cultural history of media, collective memory and nationalism. She has published several articles on media construction of national identity, on communication and the cultural construction of borders, and on the relationship of media, history and culture. [email: marusa.pusnik@fdv.uni-lj.si]

Gregor Starc is assistant professor at the Department of Sport Management at the Faculty of Sport, University of Ljubljana, Slovenia.

His areas of research include anthropological aspects of sport and play, sport history, nationalism, cultural studies of leisure and institutional dimensions of everyday life. He coedits the *Anthropological Notebooks* and *Kinesiologica Slovenica* journals, he is the author of *Disciplining the Body through Sport* (Ljubljana, 2003), and has published several articles on sport and leisure studies. [email: gregor. starc@fsp.uni-lj.si]

Karin Taylor worked as researcher at Graz University, Austria, from 2001 to 2008 where she focused on the history of everyday life and popular culture in the socialist countries of Southeast Europe (1945-1989). She is the co-editor of a volume on tourism and leisure in Yugoslavia due to be published in 2010: *Yugoslavia's Sunny Side – A History of Tourism in Socialism (1950s-1980s)*. The book includes two chapters based on her own research. Previously, she published the book, *Let's Twist Again – Youth and Leisure in Socialist Bulgaria* (Münster: LIT, 2006). She is now based in Zagreb, Croatia. [email: karin.taylor@zvucniplanet.hr]

Blanka Tivadar is a researcher at the Centre for Social Psychology, an assistant professor of sociology and a head of Analytical Sociology Unit at the Faculty of Social Sciences, University of Ljubljana, Slovenia. Her area of expertise is sociology of health, sociology of food and eating and sociology of consumption. [email: blanka. tivadar@guest.arnes.si]

Gregor Tomc is associate professor at the Faculty of social sciences, University of Ljubljana, where he teaches sociology of youth and sociology of creativity. His research interests span from cultural science (contemporary culture, above all music), cultural policy (above all democratization of access to cultural production for all citizens) and cognitive social science (incorporation of social science into cognitive science research). He publishes at home and abroad. Recently, he was a co-editor of two cultural science readers – *Urban Tribes* (2000) and *Coolture* (2002) and is the author of two books of cognitive social science – *Sixth Sense: Social World in Cognitive Science* (2000) and *Mental Machine: Brains as an Organ Motor on Mental Drive* (2005). [email: gregor.tomc@fdv.uni-lj.si]

Andreja Vezovnik, PhD is a postdoctoral fellow at the Faculty of Social Sciences, University of Ljubljana, Slovenia. Her area of expertise concerns discourse theory and critical discourse analysis. She has been mostly doing researches on Slovenian cultural and political identity, the phenomena of new fatherhood, on food consumption practices, and on the construction of socialist and post-socialist discourse in media. [email: andreja.vezovnik@fdv.uni-lj.si]

Bojana Videkanić is an art historian wokring towards her doctoral degree at the Departement of Social and Political Thought at York University, Toronto, Canada. Her research deals with art and visual culture of the Socialist Yugoslavia. She teaches art history and theory at Ontario College of Art and Design and York University. [email: boyanav@rogers.com]

Radina Vučetić, M.A, is a teaching assistant at the General Moden History, Department of History, Faculty of Philosophy, University of Belgrade. At the moment, she works on PhD thesis *Americanization of Yugoslavia in the '60-ies*. She has published a book *Evropa na Kalemegdanu: "Cvijeta Zuzorić" i Kulturni Život Beograda 1918-1941* and numerous articles relating to Yugoslav social history in the 20th century. Her area of research interest includes Western influences on Belgrade and Yugoslavia, Yugoslav-American relations, Americanization in Yugoslavia, Yugoslav modernization in the 20th century, gender history, history of everydaylife. Since 2003 she is a member of the editorial board of *The Annual for Social History*. [email: radina@sbb.rs]

Dean Vuletic received his PhD in modern European history at Columbia University in 2009 with his dissertation *Yugoslav Communism and the Power of Popular Music*. He completed his Bachelor's degree in European Studies at the Australian National University, and he was awarded its University Medal for his thesis on Croatian-Israeli relations. As a Fulbright scholar he pursued a Master's degree in East European Studies at Yale University, where he wrote his thesis on the gay and lesbian history of Croatia. He has published several book chapters and journal articles on his topics of research, and he currently teaches courses in modern European history at Columbia University and the Cooper Union. [email: dv2107@columbia.edu]

Index

CPSIA information can be obtained at www.ICGtesting.com
Printed in the USA
LVOW060106191012

303470LV00001B/130/P